THE GOOD
FIGHT

THE GOOD FIGHT

Why Liberals—and Only Liberals—

Can Win the War on Terror and

Make America Great Again

PETER BEINART

HarperCollins*Publishers*

HarperCollins books may be purchased for educational, business, or sales promotional use. For information, please write: Special Markets Department, HarperCollins Publishers, 10 East 53rd Street, New York, NY 10022.

FIRST EDITION

Designed by Nancy Field

Printed on acid-free paper

Library of Congress Cataloging-in-Publication Data.

Beinart, Peter.
    The good fight : why liberals—and only liberals—can win the War on Terror and make America great again / Peter Beinart.—1st ed.
        p.   cm.
    Includes bibliographical references.
    ISBN-10: 0-06-084161-3
    ISBN-13: 978-0-06-084161-4
    1. United States—Foreign relations—2001– 2. War on Terrorism, 2001–3. United States—Politics and government—2001– 4. Liberalism—United States. 5. Progressivism (United States politics). 6. Liberalism—United States—History—20th century. 7. United States—Politics and government—20th century. 8. United States—Foreign relations—20th century. I. Title.

    E902.B44   2006
    973.93—dc22   2006041198

06 07 08 09 10 NMSG/RRD 10 9 8 7 6 5 4 3 2 1

To Diana

Contents

Introduction

THIS IS A book about American liberalism, a political tradition so reviled that its adherents dare not speak its name. Sometime in the 1960s, conservatives began using "liberal" as an epithet, and after a while, liberals gave up trying to defend its honor. When pressed for a self-description today, many prominent liberals choose "progressive." And then they explain that they don't like labels.

There's no shame in ideological change. In its modern American context, liberalism—the belief that government should intervene in society to solve problems that individuals cannot solve alone—began with Franklin Roosevelt. Progressivism has older roots and different emphases. But yesterday's liberals haven't become today's progressives to evoke a different intellectual tradition; they have become progressives to escape intellectual tradition. With the flip of a label, they have cast off decades of disappointment and failure. Unburdened by the past, they can now define themselves on their own terms.

Except that they cannot define themselves, precisely *because* they are unburdened by the past. Progressives want to tell a story about what they believe—something large and unifying, something that explains their creed to the nation and to themselves. But such stories are not born in test tubes; they are less invented than inherited. Before today's progressives can conquer their ideological weakness, they must first conquer their ideological amnesia.

What they need to remember, above all, is the cold war. Bill Clinton—by defusing racially saturated issues like welfare and crime, and wisely managing the economy—restored public faith in government action. But he did so at a time when the United States had turned in on itself, when international threats no longer shaped national identity. Today's political environment is more like the one that stretched from the late 1940s through the late 1980s, when debates about America were interwoven with debates about America's role in the world. And in this environment, conservatives have a crucial advantage: they have a usable past. Ask any junior-level conservative activist about the cold war, and she can recite the catechism: how liberals lost their nerve in Vietnam and America sank into self-doubt until Ronald Reagan restored America's confidence and overthrew the evil empire. Since September 11, conservatives have turned that storyline into a grand analogy: the Middle East is Eastern Europe, George W. Bush is Ronald Reagan, Tony Blair is Margaret Thatcher, the appeasing French are the appeasing French. And running through this updated narrative is the same core principle that animated conservative foreign policy throughout the cold war: other countries are cynical and selfish, but the United States is inherently good. The more Americans believe in their own virtue, the stronger they will be.

Liberals have mocked the simplicity of this vision. They have derided the Bush administration's foreign policy by analogy, and its often tenuous grasp—and promiscuous rearranging—of the facts at hand. But while liberals pride themselves on their empiricism, that empiricism is no match for a narrative of the present based upon a memory of the past. When liberals finally got their shot at George W. Bush in 2004, it turned out that Americans didn't much care which candidate could recite his six-point plan for safeguarding loose nuclear material. They gravitated to the man with a vision of national greatness in a threatening world, something liberals have not had in a very long time.

THE ARGUMENT OF this book is that there is such a liberal vision, and today's progressives can find it in the heritage they have tried to escape. Its roots lie in an antique landscape, at the dawn of America's struggle against a totalitarian foe. And it begins not with America's need to believe in its own virtue, but with its need to make itself worthy of such belief. Around the world, the United States does that by accepting international constraints on its power. For conservatives—from John Foster Dulles to Dick Cheney—American exceptionalism means that we do not need such constraints. Our heart is pure. In the liberal vision, it is precisely our recognition that we are not angels that makes us exceptional. Because we recognize that we can be corrupted by unlimited power, we accept the restraints that empires refuse. That is why the Truman administration self-consciously shared power with America's democratic allies, although we comprised one-half of the world's GDP and they were on their knees. Moral humility breeds international restraint. That restraint ensures that weaker countries welcome our preeminence, and thus, that our preeminence endures. It makes us a great nation, not a predatory one.

At home, because America realizes that it does not embody goodness, it does not grow complacent. Rather than viewing American democracy as a settled accomplishment to which others aspire, we see ourselves as engaged in our own democratic struggle, which parallels the one we support abroad. It was not the celebration of American democracy that inspired the world in the 1950s and 1960s, but America's wrenching efforts—against McCarthyism and segregation—to give our democracy new meaning. Then, as now, the threat to national greatness stems not from self-doubt, but from self-satisfaction.

And at home and abroad, the struggle for democracy is also a struggle for equal opportunity. For many conservatives, liberty alone is the goal, and government action to promote social justice imperils it. But for modern liberals, championing freedom around the world requires championing development, because as the architects of the Marshall Plan understood, liberty is unlikely to survive in the midst of economic despair. And liberty also relies on equal opportunity at home. Vast economic inequality and deep economic insecurity alienate Americans from their government and leave it easy prey for the forces of private interest and concentrated wealth. That undermines American democracy, and with it, American security, because it is democracy's galvanizing power that gives America its critical advantage in long standoffs against dictatorial foes.

This vision has sometimes divided liberals themselves. Recognizing American fallibility means recognizing that the United States cannot wield power while remaining pure. From Henry Wallace in the late 1940s to Michael Moore after September 11, some liberals have preferred inaction to the tragic reality that America must shed its moral innocence to act meaningfully in the world. If the cold war liberal tradition parts company with the right in insisting that American power cannot be good unless we recognize that it can also be evil, it parts company with the purist left in insisting that if we demand that American power be perfect, it cannot be good.

APPLYING THAT TRADITION today is not easy. Cold war liberals developed their narrative of national greatness in the shadow of a totalitarian superpower. Today, the United States faces no such unified threat. Rather, it faces a web of dangers—from disease to environmental degradation to weapons of mass destruction—all fueled by globalization, which leaves America increasingly vulnerable to pathologies bred in distant corners of the world. And at the center of this nexis sits jihadist terrorism, a new totalitarian movement that lacks state power but harnesses the power of globalization instead.

Recognizing that the United States again faces a totalitarian foe does not provide simple policy prescriptions, because today's totalitarianism takes such radically different form. But it reminds us of something more basic, that liberalism does not find its enemies only on the right—a lesson sometimes forgotten in the age of George W. Bush.

Indeed, it is because liberals so despise this president that they increasingly reject his trademark phrase, the "war on terror." Were this just a semantic dispute, it would hardly matter; better alternatives to war on terror abound. But the rejection signifies something deeper: a turn away from the very idea that antitotalitarianism should sit at the heart of the liberal project. For too many liberals today, George W. Bush's war on terror is the only one they can imagine. This alienation may be understandable, but that does not make it any less disastrous, for it is liberalism's principles—even more than George W. Bush's—that jihadism threatens. If today's liberals cannot rouse as much passion for fighting a movement that flings acid at unveiled women as they do for taking back the Senate in 2006, they have strayed far from liberalism's best traditions. And if they believe it is only George W. Bush who threatens America's freedoms, they should ponder what will happen if the United States is hit with a nuclear or contagious biological attack. No matter who is president, Republican or Democrat, the reaction will make John Ashcroft look like the head of the ACLU.

OF COURSE, LIBERAL alienation from the anti-jihadist struggle does not spring merely from alienation from George W. Bush. It also springs from deep anger over the war in Iraq.

I supported the war because I considered it the only remaining way to prevent Saddam Hussein from obtaining a nuclear bomb. I also believed it could produce a decent, pluralistic Iraqi regime, which might help open a democratic third way in the Middle East between secular autocrats and their theocratic opponents—a third way that offered the best long-term hope for protecting the United States.

On both counts, I was wrong. Partly, I was wrong on the facts. I could not imagine that Saddam Hussein, given his record, had abandoned his nuclear program, even as the evidence trickled out in the months before the war. And I could not imagine that the Bush administration would so utterly fail to plan for the war's aftermath, given that they had so much riding on its success. But even more important than the facts, I was wrong on the theory. I was too quick to give up on containment, too quick to think time was on Saddam's side. And I did not grasp the critical link between the invasion's credibility in the world and its credibility in Iraq. I not only overestimated America's capacities, I overestimated America's legitimacy. As someone who had seen U.S. might deployed effectively, and on the whole benignly, in the Gulf War, the Balkans, and Afghanistan, I could not see that the morality of American power relies on the limits to American power. It is a grim irony that this book's central argument is one I myself ignored when it was needed most. If at times in these pages I judge others for having failed to appreciate certain aspects of the liberal spirit, I do so with the keen awareness that I have not always been its most faithful custodian myself.

IRAQ WILL HAUNT American politics for years to come. But the war on terror will likely last even longer than that. How the United States fights it will help shape the kind of country it becomes in this young century. And how liberals fight it will help determine whether liberal again becomes a label Americans wear with pride. Winning the war on terror and reviving liberalism, in other words, are two sides of the same fight. The premise of this book is that the liberal tradition provides the intellectual and moral resources necessary for victory. By rediscovering it, a new generation of American liberals can also discover ourselves.

THE GOOD
FIGHT

1

A New Liberalism

THE TRIP BEGAN badly. Within minutes of former vice president Henry Wallace's arrival at the Minneapolis airport, the crowd waiting to greet him had already begun to squabble. Wallace's aunt and uncle, who were Minnesota residents, wanted to drive their famous nephew to his hotel. But the leaders of Minnesota's Democratic-Farmer-Labor (DFL) Party insisted that he travel in their car instead, in a show of solidarity. Communists were like that. In the transportation sweepstakes, Hubert Humphrey, the 35-year-old mayor of Minneapolis, came in a distant third. Not only was he denied the honor of ferrying the country's leading liberal politician in his car, but the Communists didn't even give him a seat in theirs. So he had to wait to speak to his political idol until later that night.

Despite their differences, Humphrey revered Wallace. The younger man was jovial, corny, everybody's best pal; the older man was mystical and introverted, a lover of humanity but rarely of those around him. But they were both Midwesterners, and they both worshipped the New Deal, seeing it not merely as a template for America, but for the entire world. At the 1944 Democratic Convention, Humphrey had unsuccessfully fought to renominate Wallace as vice president, rather than the hackish Harry Truman. On the day Franklin Roosevelt died, Humphrey poured out his soul to the man he hoped would one day be president. "I simply can't conceal my emotions," he wrote to Wallace. "How I wish you were at the helm."

Now, more than a year later, Humphrey needed Wallace's help. Nineteen forty-six had been difficult for the young mayor. During the war, when the Minnesota left had united in a popular front, Humphrey had gotten along fine with the Communists. But now they were moving against him. In June, Communists and their allies had packed the state DFL convention in Saint Paul, choosing their own slate to run the party, and passing resolutions excoriating Truman's new hard line toward Moscow. When Humphrey rose to speak, the crowd greeted him with cries of "fascist" and "warmonger." He persevered, until a security guard growled, "Sit down, you son of a bitch, or I'll knock you down." And so, without finishing his remarks, Humphrey did.

If things were turning ugly in Minnesota, they weren't much better on the international stage. In February, Stalin warned that American capitalism and Soviet Communism were on a collision course. In March, Winston Churchill journeyed to Fulton, Missouri, and after an introduction by Truman, declared that "an iron curtain has descended across the Continent," dividing Western Europe from the "police governments" to the east. Humphrey wasn't eager for the cold war—he had hoped World War II would leave a new era of international cooperation and development in its wake. But he couldn't ignore events in the world, and in his backyard. By the end of summer, he was condemning Soviet despotism and declaring Minnesota's popular front dead.

Wallace was headed the other way. In September, in a rally at Madison Square Garden, he attacked the "numerous reactionary elements" seeking to undermine "peace based on mutual trust" between the United States and the USSR. He was still in government, serving as Truman's secretary of commerce. Yet he was contradicting Truman's foreign policy. Eight days later, he was out of a job.

Despite all this, Humphrey—the inveterate optimist—still believed that when he sat down with Wallace, they would see eye to eye. When they finally did, at Wallace's hotel that night, he explained what was happening in Minnesota and pleaded for Wallace's help in taking the party back. Wallace seemed puzzled by the talk of Communist treachery. After all, he explained, he knew only one Communist himself. Humphrey was stunned: Several open Communists had driven Wallace from the airport. Liberalism was headed for civil war and the man he once idolized would be on the other side.

BUT IN THE fall of 1946, that civil war was still months away and Wallace was still a liberal icon. Shortly after his firing, the American left gathered in Chicago to defend their hero, denounce the growing cold war, and mobilize for November's midterm elections. All the biggest liberal groups were there—the National Citizens Political Action Committee, the Independent Citizens Committee, the NAACP, and the Congress of Industrial Organizations (CIO)—for what historian Alonzo Hamby has called "one of the widest and most representative assemblies of liberals ever brought together." The conference demanded that Truman "exert every effort" to repair the deteriorating relations between Washington and Moscow. To Wallace, it sent a special message: "Carry on with confidence that you have the support of . . . millions upon millions of Americans."

Liberals left Chicago giddy at their show of strength and confident about the fall campaign. In mid-October, CIO president Philip Murray, the left's most influential labor leader, predicted that "we expect this movement to become in due course the most powerful liberal and progressive organization brought together in the history of the country." The liberal newspaper *PM* exulted that "the great wave of conservatism that was supposed to sweep the country after the war is a delusion."

Richard Nixon knew better. In September 1945, the 32-year-old Navy lieutenant commander received a letter from a prominent banker back home in Whittier, California. The letter asked if he would like to be a candidate for Congress on the Republican ticket in 1946. Nixon quickly agreed.

The district, California's twelfth, was represented by a five-term liberal Democrat named Jerry Voorhis. Voorhis was hardly a Soviet apologist. In fact, he had angered Los Angeles–area Communists by criticizing Russian repression in Eastern Europe. But he did have ties to the National Citizens Political Action Committee and the CIO, and for Nixon, that was enough. Fusing the two organizations under the sinister rubric "the PAC," he made their supposed support of Voorhis the centerpiece of his campaign. "I welcome the opposition of the PAC with its Communist principles and its huge slush fund," proclaimed Nixon in late August. In October, a Nixon ad accused Voorhis of having voted with the "Communist-dominated PAC" forty-three out of forty-six times. In the campaign's final days, voters across the district received the same ominous call: "This is a friend of yours. . . . But I can't tell you who I am. Did you know that Jerry Voorhis is a Communist?"

Nixon wasn't unique. Across the country, conservative Republicans attacked liberal Democrats as soft on inflation, labor militancy, and perhaps most damaging of all, Communism. Charging that "a group of alien-minded radicals" had seized the Democratic Party, Tennessee congressman B. Carroll Reece called the election a "fight basically between communism and Republicanism." The Chamber of Commerce distributed 400,000 copies of a pamphlet entitled *Communist Infiltration in the United States*, which painted the labor movement as a vehicle for Soviet subversion. Wallace campaigned across the country, drawing large crowds, but Democrats who accepted his support often found themselves under relentless conservative attack. Truman, his approval rating at a pitiful 32 percent by November, didn't campaign at all. Instead, an exhausted Democratic Party tried to bolster its candidates by broadcasting Roosevelt's old speeches.

Two months before the election, *New York Herald Tribune* columnists Joseph and Stewart Alsop saw the disaster about to unfold. Liberals, they charged, "had consistently avoided the great political reality of the present: the Soviet challenge to the West." As a result, "in the spasm of terror which will seize this country . . . it is the right—the very extreme right— which is most likely to gain victory." A 37-year-old circuit court judge named Joseph McCarthy, on his way to a Senate seat from Wisconsin, could not have put it better himself.

The election was a massacre. Republicans gained an astonishing thirteen seats in the Senate and fifty-five in the House, taking control of both chambers for the first time in sixteen years. Nixon cruised to victory. "Bow your heads," wrote TRB, *The New Republic*'s political columnist, "conservatism has hit America."

ONLY ONE LIBERAL faction was not implicated in the 1946 disaster, and it was barely a faction at all. America's four largest liberal organizations may have admitted Communists, but a fifth, the Union for Democratic Action (UDA), did not. Founded in 1941 by former socialists who favored America's entry into World War II, the UDA was small, perpetually broke, and widely reviled for its refusal to admit Communists. With few active chapters and a mere 5,000 members, it was, admitted national director James Loeb, "the pariah of the liberal movement."

The UDA had already been planning a conference for early 1947, but the conservative landslide gave it new urgency and new appeal. And so on Saturday, January 4, 1947, an unexpectedly large crowd showed up at Washington's stately Willard Hotel. Many arrived fresh from the skirmishes that heralded the coming liberal civil war. Humphrey was there. So was Michigan's Walter Reuther, the ascetic, hard-driving 39-year-old who had seized control of the United Auto Workers the previous spring—defeating a Communist-backed faction in a race marked by barroom brawls and near-riots. From the International Ladies Garment Workers Union came David Dubinsky, who had learned his anti-Communism in a Soviet jail after organizing a bakery strike in his native Poland. From Harvard came Arthur Schlesinger Jr., not yet 30 and already in possession of a Pulitzer Prize for his history of Jacksonian America. Eleanor Roosevelt, who had grown to loathe the Soviets during her human rights work at the UN, gave the conference its New Deal bona fides. And Reinhold Niebuhr, the tall, unaffected Midwesterner widely acknowledged to be America's leading Protestant theologian, provided the theoretical heft.

In the famed hotel where Abraham Lincoln spent the night before his first inaugural, they altered American history. Renaming their organization Americans for Democratic Action (ADA), the men and women of the Willard committed themselves to a new liberalism. On domestic policy, as Steven Gillon notes in his history of the organization, *Politics and Vision*, its principles were familiar: the defense of civil liberties and the expansion of the New Deal. But on foreign policy, the ADA broke ranks, declaring its opposition to Communism overseas and its refusal to cooperate with Communists at home. It was, Loeb wrote, "a declaration of liberal independence from the stifling and paralyzing influence of Communists and their apologists in America" based upon the conviction that "no movement that maintains a double standard on the issue of human liberty can lay claim to the American liberal tradition."

At the heart of the ADA's new liberalism was a term that had only recently entered the American lexicon: *totalitarianism*. Most liberals loathed fascism, an ideology against which the United States had just fought a world war. But many saw Communism as something different—a noble dream, if flawed in practice, and a powerful ally in the fight against imperialism abroad and for economic justice at home. For the ADA, however, fascism and Communism were both totalitarian ideologies. They both sought, as Schlesinger put it in his 1949 manifesto, *The Vital Center*, to utterly control society, smashing all independent sources of authority in pursuit of "the unlimited domination and degradation and eventual obliteration of the individual." They both threatened the principles liberalism held most dear.

Many on the left greeted the ADA's founding with scorn. The CIO "deplor[ed] the division in the liberal movement." The *New York Times* urged the ADA to merge with the recently formed Progressive Citizens of America (PCA), which encompassed many of the groups that had lauded

Wallace in Chicago the previous September. Wallace, who since leaving the Truman administration had become editor of *The New Republic*, penned a column titled "The Enemy Is Not Each Other."

But they were missing the ADA's essential point. For the new liberals, the enemy *was* each other. Critics accused the new organization of undermining liberal unity against the right, and the ADA replied that Communists actually hindered that effort by discrediting liberals. But more fundamentally, they argued that liberalism had an enemy that was not on the right. Liberalism, in Schlesinger's phrase, stood in the "vital center" between the two great totalitarian poles of Communism and fascism. To define it merely as conservatism's antithesis was to deny liberalism's full moral identity.

Over the next decade and a half, this antitotalitarian liberalism would become the dominant ideology in American public life. It would spend its first years engulfed in a civil war on the left, only to be thrown on the defensive for much of the 1950s by an emerging cold war right. But it would survive these challenges. And as a new decade began, and a new spirit took hold, it finally began to realize the vision of national greatness born at the Willard Hotel.

AS LIBERALISM WAS being reborn, so, it seemed, was the world itself. On February 21, 1947, a British embassy official drove to the State Department, where he informed Undersecretary of State Dean Acheson that His Majesty's government, itself under desperate economic strain, could no longer continue aiding the besieged governments of Greece and Turkey. For more than a century, Britain had been the greatest power on earth. Now, as one State Department official put it, "Great Britain had within the hour handed the job of world leadership with all its burdens and all its glory to the United States."

The Greek monarchy was hardly an ideal supplicant. Under assault from Communist rebels backed by the new Soviet bloc, it was not merely authoritarian, but chaotic as well. Next door, the Turkish government was three years away from its first free election. But for Truman, "imperfect democracies" were vastly superior to "totalitarianism." And at 1:00 P.M. on March 12, in a speech carried live on radio, he called on Congress to provide economic and military aid. "At the present moment in world history," he declared, "nearly every nation must choose between alternative ways of life. . . . One way of life is based upon the will of the majority, and is distinguished by free institutions. . . . The second way of life is based upon the will of a minority forcibly imposed upon the majority . . . it must be the policy of the United States to support free peoples who are resisting attempted subjugation by armed minorities or by outside pressures." It was the right policy, clothed in a doctrine that was both stirring, and dangerously broad.

The left was largely hostile. The pro-Wallace PCA called the aid proposal "American imperialism." Florida senator Claude Pepper, the country's preeminent Southern liberal, warned that the Greek insurrection had popular roots. Wallace himself said he would support the aid only if it went through the United Nations. And in the House, left-leaning California congresswoman Helen Gahagan Douglas introduced a bill to do just that.

The ADA was torn. Some in its ranks found the prospect of arming nondemocratic governments appalling. Others agreed with Gahagan Douglas that any aid should go through the UN. But after an impassioned debate in late March, the ADA decided to support a policy that it considered flawed but necessary. And this moral realism became a hallmark of the new liberalism. Liberals like Pepper and Gahagan Douglas did not want Greece and Turkey to fall to Soviet aggression. Yet they could not bear to see the United States back faulty governments. So they urged President Truman to refer the matter to the United Nations, even though the Soviet Union's presence on the Security Council rendered it incapable of decisive action. Schlesinger dubbed this kind of reasoning "doughface-ism." The original doughfaces were "northern men with southern principles"—Northerners who opposed slavery but could not bring themselves to support the Civil War. Schlesinger called the Wallace liberals "democratic men with totalitarian principles." They opposed Communism, but would not endorse practical steps to combat it, so as not to implicate themselves in a morally imperfect action. In the "doughface fantasy," Schlesinger wrote, "one can denounce a decision without accepting the consequences of the alternative." It is a fantasy to which liberals fall prey to this day.

IF THE TRUMAN doctrine forced the new liberals to check their gut, the Marshall Plan spoke to their heart. In early 1947, Europe was desperate. In much of the continent, food production had still not recovered from the war. There were grave shortages of coal, and inflation was raging out of control. In April, Secretary of State George Marshall returned from a foreign ministers meeting in Moscow in a near panic. Private conversations with Stalin had left him convinced that the Russians believed several postwar West European governments would fall. Already, Communists held four ministries in France's Fourth Republic, including defense. The "patient," Marshall warned, "is sinking while the doctors deliberate."

On June 5, 1947, in a speech at Harvard's commencement, Marshall presented America's response: a vast aid program to help save European democracy. Marshall and Truman required the Europeans to draw up the program themselves so it would not bear the taint of U.S. imperialism. And they resisted efforts to use it as a lever to force European countries to remake their economies in America's image. The Marshall Plan clearly served U.S. interests: America needed Europe to recover so it could once again provide a market for American goods. But the Truman administration pursued that self-interest with generosity and restraint. Above all, the Marshall Plan reflected the core liberal idea that preserving freedom requires combating economic despair. It was based, in the words of economist and ADA member John Kenneth Galbraith, "on the shrewd notion that people who are insecure, hungry, and without hope are not ardent defenders of liberal institutions or discriminating in the political systems they embrace."

This time it wasn't the men and women of the Willard who stood alone; it was Wallace. The ADA championed the Marshall Plan, sponsoring a speaking tour on its behalf by Dean Acheson, briefly in private legal practice before returning to the Truman administration as secretary of state. The CIO was also sympathetic, and cheered Marshall at its annual convention. Even the Wallace-friendly magazine *The Nation* gave its support. Wallace himself, however, hesitated. He seemed open to the idea at first, when it appeared that the USSR and its East European clients might qualify for the aid. But when they spurned it, rejecting the requirement that recipients open their economic records, Wallace grew critical. By October, he was calling the Marshall Plan an effort to impose "reactionary governments and influence the economic system of Western Europe to the benefit of Wall Street." "We are not loved in Europe," he warned, "and the more we use economic pressures to intervene in European affairs, the worse we are hated."

Eventually, Wallace's opposition to the Marshall Plan would be seen as the beginning of the end of his hold over American liberals. But in the spring and summer of 1947, his appeal on the left still dwarfed Truman's. In May and June, Wallace drew 27,000 people to a PCA-sponsored rally in Los Angeles, and 20,000 to another in Chicago. His supporters not only dominated the Democratic parties in Minnesota and Oregon, but threatened to seize control in Wisconsin, California, and Washington State as well. In June, Gael Sullivan, executive director of the Democratic National Committee, informed a worried Truman administration that "There is no question that Wallace has captured the imagination of a strong segment of the American public." Some party insiders feared the only way to head off the Wallace threat would be to put him on the ticket in 1948.

But it was soon too late for that. In mid-December, the PCA called on Wallace to mount a third-party challenge. And in a national radio address on December 29, he answered the call. Accusing Truman of pursuing a "reactionary war policy which is dividing the world into two armed camps and making inevitable the day when American soldiers will be lying in their Arctic suits in the Russian snow," he announced his candidacy for president in 1948.

FOR A THIRD-PARTY candidate, Wallace looked frighteningly strong. In January 1948, a Gallup survey showed him winning between 13 and 18 percent of the vote in New York, enough to throw the state to likely Republican nominee Thomas Dewey. In mid-February, a Wallace supporter trounced a pro-administration Democrat in a special congressional election in the Bronx. A *New York Times* poll taken shortly afterward showed Wallace's support rising in Michigan, Pennsylvania, Illinois, and California, potentially putting those states out of reach for Truman as well. Experts predicted his insurgent campaign might win 4 million votes.

Truman, by contrast, looked like a political dead man. A spring *Newsweek* poll of forty-five Democratic senators found only six publicly in favor of his nomination as the party's presidential candidate, and thirteen against. In March, *Time* wrote that "only a political miracle or extraordinary stupidity on the part of the Republicans can save the Democratic Party, after 16 years in power, from a debacle in November."

Even the antitotalitarian liberals considered Truman an embarrassment. After Roosevelt's magnetic energy, they found it painful to watch this small party man, who flapped his arms as he served up banality after banality. "President Truman," wrote Schlesinger, "appears to have little instinct for liberalism; he knows the words rather than the tune."

But that would change. In November 1947, Clark Clifford, Truman's chief political strategist, sent him a forty-three-page memo on the upcoming campaign. Clifford considered the South safely Democratic. But he feared that Wallace's strength among blacks, union members, western progressives, and Jews might throw the election to Dewey. He urged an alliance with the ADA. And on Clifford's advice, Truman put a young ADA member named William Batt in charge of formulating policies to lure liberals back.

The new strategy exploded into public view on January 7, when Truman kicked off the 1948 campaign with a State of the Union address that liberal *New York Post* editor T. O. Thackrey called "little short of inspiring." It almost perfectly mirrored the platform of the ADA: national health insurance, an increased minimum wage, higher Social Security benefits, and tax reform that cut rates for low-wage workers while raising them for corporations. Perhaps most dramatically of all, Truman vowed that he would soon come back to Congress to offer legislation based upon the recommendations of the Presidential Committee on Civil Rights, which had presented its report that fall.

A month later, Truman returned, bearing legislation to abolish the poll tax, integrate the military, outlaw segregation in interstate commerce, and make lynching a federal crime. Explaining his new agenda, the president made a moral equation that would become central to the new liberalism: He linked the struggle against Communism to the struggle against racial injustice. Actually, he linked them in two different ways. First, he said the denial of democracy at home undermined America's moral authority abroad. "If we wish to inspire the people of the world whose freedom is in jeopardy," declared Truman, "if we wish to restore hope to those who have already lost their civil liberties, if we wish to fulfill the promise that is ours, we must correct the remaining imperfections in our practice of democracy." But there was a second link, buried in Truman's penultimate phrase: "If we wish to fulfill the promise that is ours." Expanding democracy at home wasn't just a matter of global public relations. It was the key to unlocking the nation's full power. For the Truman administration, America's great advantage over the Soviet Union was its cohesion, its ability to meet domestic challenges without coercion, and the resulting threat of revolution or social collapse. And no challenge was greater than

America's legalized racism. As George Kennan, head of policy planning in the Truman State Department, put it, in the cold war struggle, "It may be the strength and health of our respective [political] systems which is decisive." Then, as now, defeating enemies abroad required renewing democracy at home.

BUT NOT EVERYONE in the Democratic Party was prepared to embrace civil rights in anti-Communism's name. In fact, as delegates arrived in Philadelphia for the 1948 Democratic National Convention, *Time* observed that "Not since the South rebelled against Stephen Douglas in 1860 had the party seemed so hopelessly torn and divided." Segregationist leaders, led by Mississippi's Fielding Wright and South Carolina's Strom Thurmond, warned that if Truman's new commitment to civil rights became party dogma, they would bolt. And Clifford, fearing he had taken the South too much for granted, was prepared to accept a one-paragraph platform statement on civil rights that committed the party to none of the initiatives Truman had proposed in February.

The ADA, however, would accept no such retreat. From a rented fraternity house on the University of Pennsylvania campus, its leaders plotted strategy. The battle began in the Resolution Committee, which, after ten hours of bitter debate, passed a vague, weak statement that satisfied virtually no one. The segregationists and the ADA both appealed to the Platform Committee, which after twelve more fruitless hours passed the controversy onto the convention floor. Convention chairman Sam Rayburn announced that on the following day, Wednesday, July 14, both sides could bring their civil rights planks to a full vote.

Terrified of a Southern walkout, Truman was furious at the ADA. Humphrey, the ADA's vice chairman and leading officeholder, was skittish himself, fearful that appearing hostile to the South and to the White House could cost him his bid for the Senate that fall. Finally, at five o'clock on Wednesday morning, the young mayor, still only 37 years old, agreed to lead the fight on the convention floor. Later generations, who came to know Humphrey on television, where he usually looked uncomfortable, never appreciated his oratorical power, the quality that led Minnesotans to pass around bootleg audiotapes of his speeches like samizdat. But it was blindingly clear in the Municipal Auditorium that morning. "There can be no hedging . . . no watering down," Humphrey told the assembled delegates, in perhaps the greatest speech of his career. "To those who say that we are rushing this issue of civil rights—I say to them, we are 172 years late. To those who say this bill is an infringement on states' rights, I say . . . the time has arrived for the Democratic Party to get out of the shadow of states' rights and walk forthrightly into the bright sunshine of human rights." As Humphrey spoke, ADA members carrying civil rights banners rose from their seats and began marching down the convention aisles. With the support of big-city bosses hoping to energize the black vote that fall, the ADA's resolution passed. Thurmond and the other segregationists marched out of the convention hall, and out of the national Democratic Party.

Later that day, Truman took the podium to accept his party's nomination. He attacked the Republican Congress, and announced he would call it back for a special session on July 26, "Turnip Day" in his home state of Missouri, to demand that it enact his State of the Union agenda. It would be a very different campaign, and a very different Democratic Party, than anyone had foreseen a year before.

A FEW WEEKS later, Wallace also came to Philadelphia, to accept the nomination of the newly formed Progressive Party. But his candidacy was already running into trouble. In late February, the government of Czechoslovakia, the last in Eastern Europe not under the Soviet boot, had fallen to a Communist coup. A few days later, Jan Masaryk, the country's pro-Western foreign minister, fell to his death in circumstances widely considered suspicious. While many liberals recoiled in horror, Wallace blamed America. The United States, he suggested, had prompted the coup by calling on the Czechs to defy the USSR and participate in the Marshall Plan. He claimed that Masaryk had committed suicide as the result of depression or cancer.

The Progressive Party convention made it even clearer that Wallace would never condemn Soviet oppression. Delegates from Vermont, worried that the new party's platform contained no criticism of the USSR, offered an amendment reading, "Although we are critical of the present foreign policy of the United States, it is not our intention to give blanket endorsement to the foreign policy of any nation." It was voted down.

By summer, liberals were moving away from Wallace. In July, he resigned as *New Republic* editor, and by October, Loeb would be calling the magazine an ADA house organ. Literary journals like *Commentary* and *Partisan Review*, populated by anti-Stalinist socialists, blasted writers and artists who refused to see the nightmare that real-world Communism had become. The NAACP fired W. E. B. Dubois, its adviser on colonial affairs, for opposing Truman's foreign policy and the organization's growing opposition to Communism. In Minnesota, Humphrey wrested back control of the Democratic-Farmer-Labor Party, just in time to keep it from endorsing Wallace.

But most important was the change in the labor movement. Much of labor's rank and file was Catholic, and at church they heard impassioned sermons denouncing Soviet repression of their coreligionists in Eastern Europe. In June, CIO general counsel Lee Pressman, the one Communist Wallace had told Humphrey he knew, announced he would run as a Progressive candidate for Congress. Backed by Walter Reuther, CIO president Philip Murray replaced him with anti-Communist labor lawyer and future Supreme Court Justice Arthur Goldberg. The CIO affiliated itself with the ADA and endorsed Truman. The following year it expelled eleven Communist- and fellow traveler–controlled unions from its ranks. It was a momentous shift. For the next two decades, an alliance between intellectuals and the labor movement would undergird antitotalitarian liberalism. And for Harry Truman, it came just in time. Had labor not turned, he never would have stood a chance.

No longer just a small group of intellectuals, the ADA was now the vanguard of an anti-Communist, pro-Truman network with deep influence among the Democratic base. And it used that newfound power to go after Wallace. In three widely publicized pamphlets, the ADA called Wallace a Communist dupe who had apologized for the Czech coup. In newspaper advertisements, it drew attention to the Communist ties of prominent Wallace supporters. And in October, Niebuhr drafted a passionate "Appeal to Liberals," which called Wallace's foreign policy views a "betrayal of free people throughout the world." By the final weeks of the campaign, Progressive Party candidates were withdrawing from races against local Democrats, and Wallace's crowds were dwindling.

As Wallace weakened, Truman gained strength. He unilaterally desegregated the military and created the Fair Employment Board to spur integration of the federal civil service. The special Turnip Day congressional session refused to pass his domestic agenda, but that just gave him more ammunition. In September, he set out across the country by train. From Reading, Pennsylvania, to Dexter, Iowa, to Fresno, California, he attacked the "do-nothing, good for nothing 80th congress" for opposing Social Security, aid to farmers, labor rights, and progressive taxation. While still far from eloquent, he was starting to connect. "All over the country," he told a cheering crowd in Ardmore, Oklahoma, "they call me Harry. I like it . . . because I'm trying my best to serve you with everything I have." Three days before the election, he traveled to Harlem, where he spoke before a crowd of 65,000. All in all during his cross-country tour, he gave 351 campaign speeches to roughly 12 million people.

Dewey, by contrast, campaigned like a man who had already won. He refused to debate, avoided specifics, and plotted his cabinet. He linked the Democrats, the Communists, and the CIO, but with Wallace and his supporters now out of the party, the charge carried far less weight than it had in 1946. He accused Truman of having abandoned Poland to Stalin, and for doing too little to aid the Nationalists in China. But he failed to raise serious public doubts about the Democrats' commitment to fighting the cold war. Partly, that was because Dewey, who high-mindedly supported Truman's response to the USSR's June blockade of West Berlin, was a more genteel politician than Nixon or McCarthy. But it was also because in the intervening two years, the liberal wing of the Democratic Party had transformed itself, and that transformation had altered the terms of partisan debate.

On election eve, experts remained sure Dewey would win. The final Gallup poll showed him ahead by 5 points. Fifty Washington correspondents unanimously predicted that Truman would go down to defeat. *Life* published a photo of Dewey above the caption "The Next President."

They were all wrong: Truman won by just over 2 million votes. Had Wallace garnered the 4 million commentators expected when he launched his campaign, he would have thrown the election to Dewey. But he received only 1.2 million. Democrats took back both houses of Congress, and Humphrey won his race for the Senate. It was, noted the *New York Times*, "A miracle of electioneering for which there are few if any parallels."

The Communist Party would never again be a significant force on the American left, and the ADA, wrote *The New Republic*, could "now speak with . . . authority for the country's liberals." In *The Vital Center*, published the following year, Schlesinger looked back at the struggle just completed. "When the challenge of Communism finally forced American liberals to take inventory of their moral resources," he wrote, "the inventory resulted in the clear decision that freedom had values which could not be compromised in deals with totalitarianism." "The failure of nerve," he concluded, "is over."

THE BATTLE WITHIN liberalism had ended, and it would be a generation before it erupted again. But an even more grueling struggle with the right was just getting under way. That new struggle began on a bitterly cold day in January 1949, when Truman delivered an inaugural address that offered his fullest account yet of the new liberal foreign policy. Essentially, it rested on three interlocking planks. The first was containment: military efforts to prevent Soviet aggression. The USSR, in Schlesinger's metaphor, was like an intruder trying to enter a house. If it found the door open, it would enter. But if it found it locked, it would give up. Containment meant locking the doors—convincing the Soviets that aggression would be difficult and costly. In his first term, Truman had done so by sending arms to Greece and Turkey, making the Navy a conspicuous presence in the Mediterranean, and even suggesting universal military training to show U.S. resolve. In his inaugural, Truman proposed giving containment institutional form: NATO. The new organization not only publicly committed the United States to Western Europe's protection, but came with more than $1 billion in military aid to help America's allies strengthen their own defenses as well.

These efforts, Truman officials insisted, were not designed to provoke war; they were meant to avoid it. By persuading Moscow that aggression was futile, the United States hoped to gradually modify its behavior. "The shape of Soviet power," Kennan explained, "is like that of a tree which has been bent in infancy and twisted into a certain pattern. It can be caused to grow back into another form; but not by any sudden or violent application of force. The effect can be produced only by the exertion of steady pressure over a period of years in the right direction." Containment required patience. It was a doctrine predicated, above all, on confidence that America had the stamina for a long fight.

The second element in liberal foreign policy was development, or what Schlesinger called "reconstruction." In the house metaphor, it meant making sure the inhabitants weren't so desperate that they unlocked the door from the inside. If democracy couldn't provide economic opportunity it would lose people's faith. This was the principle behind the Marshall Plan.

And in his inaugural, Truman proposed extending it to countries emerging from colonial rule, in a "bold new program for making the benefits of our scientific advances and industrial programs available for the improvement and growth of underdeveloped areas." It was called Point Four, and Truman clearly loved it—devoting more of his inaugural address to the proposal than to anything else. In fact, he and his advisers repeatedly insisted, especially early in his presidency, that economic development was more important than military containment to defending freedom.

Thirdly, liberal foreign policy involved restraint. Rather than wield its enormous power alone, the United States would share it with other countries. NATO was the expression of this idea. So was Truman's support for the UN, the International Monetary Fund, and the World Bank, all founded near the end of World War II. Partly, this reflected the Truman administration's recognition that in an interdependent world, the United States could guarantee neither its security nor its prosperity alone. But it reflected another recognition as well. Niebuhr, who Kennan called "the father of us all," had attended State Department planning meetings after the 1948 election. And the theologian's overriding message was that for all of their accomplishments, Americans should not fall in love with their own virtue, and should not expect non-Americans to take that virtue on faith. The implication, which the administration built into its policies, was that by limiting its power, the United States could make that power more accepted in the world. "We all have to recognize—no matter how great our strength," Truman declared, "that we must deny ourselves the license to do always as we please." Within NATO, to be sure, the United States was first among equals. But as with the Marshall Plan, Europeans wielded real influence over how NATO was born and how it worked. And American policy makers in the early cold war, unlike their contemporaries today, didn't try to force America's allies into lockstep with U.S. policy. Rather, they assumed that assertive, nationalist governments—even if they sometimes proved unruly—would resist Communism better than American vassals. As one State Department official put it, the goal was to foster allies "strong enough to say 'no' both to the Soviet Union and the United States, if our actions should seem so to require."

AS TRUMAN AND Niebuhr were defining cold war liberalism, cold war conservatism was slowly being born. Its version of the meeting at the Willard Hotel did not occur until 1955, with the founding of *National Re-*

view. And even then, it would take another decade before a Republican nominee for president espoused the journal's views. The principles underlying conservative anti-Communism were hard to discern in the postwar years. They were obscured first by lingering right-wing isolationism, embodied by Ohio senator Robert Taft. And then by the nonideological, business conservatism of Dwight Eisenhower, whose presidency gave the 1950s a patina of ideological consensus. Still, spasms of the conservatism that exists today kept erupting in the 1950s, in the anti-Communist crusades of Joseph McCarthy and Richard Nixon, in the rhetoric of Eisenhower's more ideological secretary of state, John Foster Dulles, and, of course, in the pages of William F. Buckley's contentious new magazine.

Cold war conservatives took a dim view of Truman's enthusiasm for international economic development. Partly, it was a matter of cost. So anxious were many on the right for tax cuts and a balanced budget that they resisted even higher defense spending. But foreign aid raised particular hackles, since many conservatives saw it as part of a liberal effort to rationalize Communism by suggesting that America's real foe was not the ideology itself, but the forces that produced it. "The universities of India and the Arab world, and also of Europe and America, have bred more communists than have the backward villages," declared James Burnham, a *National Review* senior editor and the most important foreign policy thinker on the emerging cold war right. In 1956, *National Review* praised the governor of Utah for refusing to pay income tax because part of the money went to foreign aid.

For the right, nothing was more important to the cold war struggle than ideological clarity. Because it wanted non-Communist governments to enjoy local legitimacy, the Truman administration tolerated large ideological deviations among its allies, as long as they resisted Soviet influence. Dulles, however, who painted the cold war as a quasi-religious struggle between good and evil, had less patience for governments that would not wholly commit to America's side. "Because the [Eisenhower-Dulles] administration had so little faith in the ability of non-communist nationalism to sustain itself," writes the historian John Lewis Gaddis, "it resorted to frantic and overbearing attempts to shore it up, in the process appearing to violate the very principles of sovereignty and self-reliance it was trying to preserve." Burnham went even further, arguing that the only way to stop Communism's advance was to cease relying on other countries at all, and build "an American empire which will be, if not literally world-wide in formal boundaries, capable of exercising decisive world control."

If the new conservatives' greatest desire was moral certainty, their greatest fear was that after decades of liberal government, Americans no longer possessed it. Americans, they worried, lacked the faith of their fanatically self-confident Communist foes, and this made them dangerously weak. On the right, Truman's policy of containment seemed like both an expression of this moral relativism, since it tolerated Soviet evil, and a disastrous miscalculation, since the United States lacked the will to endure such a long standoff. Dulles attacked the Democrats for "treadmill policies which, at best, might keep us in the same place until we drop exhausted." In 1960, rising conservative star Barry Goldwater warned that "No nation at war, employing an exclusively defensive strategy, can hope to survive for long." Once he became secretary of state, Dulles quickly abandoned his calls for militarily "rolling back" Soviet power, since doing so risked nuclear war. But among conservative intellectuals, it remained an article of faith that if the United States continued to merely "contain" the Soviet Union, it was doomed.

IF THE RIGHT'S hunger for moral clarity fueled its opposition to Truman's foreign policy, it animated its resistance to his domestic agenda as well. For liberals, containment required a stronger home front. And a stronger home front required expanding the New Deal—tempering capitalism's instability and inequality so Americans would not turn against it, as many had during the depression. The challenge, in Niebuhr's words, was to "make our political and economic life more worthy of our faith and therefore more impregnable." In his 1949 State of the Union address, Truman proposed a more progressive tax system, a 75-cent-per-hour minimum wage, national health insurance, expanded Social Security, and the repeal of the antiunion Taft-Hartley Act. And once again, he demanded laws banning lynching, the poll tax, and segregation in interstate commerce. The goal, he said, was that "every American has a chance to obtain his fair share of our increasing abundance." It was the same principle that animated his economic development efforts abroad: by fostering equality of opportunity the United States could ensure that liberty survived.

But for conservatives, the liberal push for equality did not strengthen America in its cold war struggle; it undermined the very ideological distinctions upon which that struggle relied. Viewed from the right, the New Deal had already moved America perilously far along what Austrian émigré economist Friedrich Von Hayek famously called "the road to serfdom." And the more the United States aped Communism, the less it would prove able to resist it. "The liberal's arm cannot strike with consistent firmness against communism," wrote Burnham, "because the liberal dimly feels that in doing so he would be somehow wounding himself."

Determined to prevent America from slipping further down the totalitarian slope, a congressional alliance between Republicans and Southern Democrats stopped Truman's domestic agenda in its tracks. The American Medical Association dubbed his health care plan a "monstrosity of Bolshevik bureaucracy." The conservative writer Russell Kirk called the federal school lunch program a "vehicle for totalitarianism." And on civil rights, the attack was much the same. When Strom Thurmond's 1948 Dixiecrat platform condemned "totalitarian government," it wasn't talking about Moscow; it was talking about a federal government in Washington that crushed states' rights. And the new conservative intellectuals also overwhelmingly opposed civil rights, largely because they saw it as a vehicle for enhanced government power. As *National Review* titled one article on the subject, "Integration is communization."

But the right's greatest effort to restore moral clarity was its campaign to root out Communists in American life. Richard Nixon kicked off that effort in 1947, when the newly elected congressman helped author a particularly nasty and duplicitous piece of legislation that both required Communist organizations to register with the government and, in flagrant violation of the Fifth Amendment's right against self-incrimination, essentially made such membership a crime. The question of Communist subversion gained national attention the following year, when a disheveled, affectless former Communist named Whittaker Chambers informed the House Un-American Activities Committee that Alger Hiss—top official in the State Department, member of the American delegation that met with Stalin at Yalta, secretary-general of the inaugural meeting of the United Nations, president of the Carnegie Endowment for International Peace, and all-around liberal golden boy—had been a Soviet spy. And two weeks after Hiss was sentenced for perjury, Joseph McCarthy appeared before the Republican Women's Club in Wheeling, West Virginia, and sent the red scare to new levels of frenzy, declaring that "I have here in my hand a list of 205 . . . names that were made known to the Secretary of State as being members of the Communist Party and who nevertheless are still working and shaping policy in the State Department."

For the right, the question lurking behind all these cases was whether America believed in its creed strongly enough to expel those who did not. As *National Review* founder William F. Buckley and his brother-in-law, L. Brent Bozell, wrote in their 1954 book, *McCarthy and His Enemies*, "Not only is it *characteristic* of society to create institutions and to defend them with sanctions. Society *must* do so—or else they cease to exist." Conservatives were dubious that an America seduced by liberalism retained the strength to do that. Chambers, the Communist-turned-conservative whose 1952 conversion tale, *Witness*, powerfully shaped the cold war right, argued that modernity—and particularly the decline in faith in God—had left Americans too mentally and spiritually weak for a drawn-out struggle against their implacable Communist foe. Like his ideological progeny today, he hoped a religious revival might resuscitate "this sick society, which we call Western civilization." But he wasn't optimistic. After leaving the Communist Party, he told his wife, "We are leaving the winning world for the losing world."

In fact, however, conservatives were pleasantly surprised by the public response to their crusade against Communist subversion. Many Catholics, believing that Franklin Roosevelt had abandoned their Eastern European coreligionists to Stalin at Yalta, were predisposed to look for nefarious motives. And McCarthy played on their suspicion of the East Coast foreign policy elite, newly embodied by Hiss. "The bright young men who are born with silver spoons in their mouths," he declared in Wheeling, "are the ones who have been the most traitorous." For conservatives, long alienated from a country they feared was moving inexorably to the left, McCarthyism represented an unexpected reconciliation. And it provided a lesson in how to mix anti-Communism and class resentment, a brew that would only grow more potent in the decades to come.

IF CONSERVATIVES SAW the red scare as a sign of domestic health, antitotalitarian liberals struggled to make the opposite case: that McCarthy and his allies undermined the anti-Communist cause. As with civil rights, that argument had two parts. First, liberals said, McCarthyism damaged America's reputation. While conservatives applauded America's new faith in its moral superiority, liberals worried that McCarthyism undermined that superiority in the eyes of the world. "It will be difficult," wrote Niebuhr, "to appreciate the extent of the damage done to our prestige by this phenomenon." Secondly, liberals argued that granting Communists the right to speak and assemble freely was a sign not of moral relativism but of moral confidence—confidence that American principles could win an open clash of ideas. NSC 68, the Truman administration's famed statement of grand strategy, declared that the United States must "tolerate those within it who would use their freedom to destroy it. . . . The free society does not fear, it welcomes, diversity." As Kennan had argued, America's lack of domestic coercion was its critical advantage in the cold war fight.

That was what anti-Communist liberals *said*. What they actually did, in the heat of the red scare, was not always as admirable. Shaken by the right's victory in 1946, Truman, in March 1947, established a grossly unfair loyalty program for government employees, which denied alleged Communists the right to confront their accusers or see the evidence against them. The ADA at first supported the effort, then criticized its implementation, giving the impression of an organization trying to have it both ways.

Truman partially redeemed himself in 1950 when he vetoed the Mc-Carran Act, a descendant of Nixon's earlier effort to virtually criminalize membership in the Communist Party, declaring that "In a free country, we punish men for the crimes they commit, but never for the opinions they have." But in 1954, Humphrey proposed doing exactly that. Trying to head off Republican legislation that used the red scare to undermine labor rights—and fearful that Republicans would red-bait Democratic senators up for reelection in 1954 (himself included)—Humphrey introduced the Communist Control Act, which made membership in the Communist Party a crime meriting up to five years in prison. It was, argued socialist editor Michael Harrington, "an abject capitulation by liberalism to illiberalism." This time, the ADA, despite its closeness to Humphrey, dissented. But it still limited its critique to some of the bill's obnoxious side provisions. On the central question of whether the federal government should ban the Communist Party, the ADA didn't take a clear stand. It was not exactly a profile in courage.

But if the new liberals were at times complicit in the red scare, their impassioned anti-Communism also helped liberalism survive it. Again and again, they called McCarthyism a diversion concocted by conservatives who cared more about cutting taxes than fighting the Soviets. "The over-riding issue before the American people today," declared the ADA in 1953, "is whether the national defense is to be determined by the demands of the world situation or sacrificed to the worship of tax reductions and a balanced budget." Asked Democratic senator Clinton Anderson, "Who is fighting the Communists anyhow? Can it be the people who talk about spy rings in the State Department and then vote against appropriations for military aid?"

These rejoinders didn't entirely inoculate liberals from the conservative assault of the early 1950s. But neither did that assault succeed in rescinding the New Deal revolution. By agreeing to small increases in the minimum wage, unemployment insurance, public housing, and Social Security, Eisenhower ratified the welfare state that so many on the right loathed. And while the GOP recaptured the House and Senate in 1952, it lost them again in 1954, and Democrats controlled both chambers for the rest of the decade.

The Democratic Congress, of course, was far from uniformly liberal. But as Buckley himself conceded, liberals largely set the terms of national debate. The reasons were many, including the enduring prestige of the New Deal and the fact that the business community had not yet established an intellectual counterestablishment to disseminate the right's ideas. But even with these advantages, had liberalism not reinvented itself at the Willard Hotel, the escalating anti-Communism of the early cold war might have buried it. To imagine history's different course, the new liberals had only to watch what happened to their old adversaries on the left. In his reelection campaign in 1950, Florida senator Claude Pepper, who had warmed up for Wallace at Madison Square Garden four years earlier, was accused of treason, and didn't even survive the Democratic primary. That same year in California, Helen Gahagan Douglas, who had demanded that aid to Greece and Turkey go through the UN, was denounced as "pink right down to her underwear," and lost by the largest margin of any Senate candidate in the country. Her tormenter? The indefatigable Richard Nixon.

McCARTHYISM HAD TAKEN its toll, but cold war liberalism survived. And then, on October 4, 1957, liberals found the wind suddenly at their back. The reason was *Sputnik*, a silver aluminum orb the size of a beach ball that made the USSR the first country in space. The *New York Times* announced the launch in a highly unusual three-row headline. A Gallup poll found that 50 percent of Americans considered it a blow to national prestige. It was a crushing symbolic defeat, and prompted a wave of alarm no less intense than the one sparked by Whittaker Chambers and Joseph McCarthy—but with very different ideological overtones. It wasn't just that *Sputnik* undermined the GOP's anti-Communist bona fides, much as the red scare had undermined the Democratic Party's. It wasn't even that *Sputnik* produced a wave of calls for new spending on defense, science, and education. Above all, *Sputnik* laid the groundwork for a different vision of national greatness. If conservatives had seen in McCarthyism a new spirit, in which Americans summoned the self-confidence to cast out the Communists in their midst, liberals saw in the response to *Sputnik* a new spirit in which Americans turned away from private concerns and committed themselves to building a country strong enough at home to compete abroad.

For antitotalitarian liberals, no one encapsulated America's cultural malaise better than Nixon, who while leading Nikita Khrushchev through the American exhibit in Moscow in 1959, pointed to a model kitchen and explained that this is "what freedom means to us." "Under the spell of materialism," wrote Schlesinger, "our nation has allocated its abundance to private satisfaction rather than to public need, with the result that the wealthiest nation in the world suddenly seems to be falling behind in education, falling behind in science, falling behind in technology, falling behind in weapons, falling behind in our capacity to stir the minds and hearts of men." Eisenhower's business conservatism, he argued, had asked little of the country, and committed it to nothing grander than the gratifications of suburban life. As a result, Americans risked becoming, in Niebuhr's words, "soft and effete," unable to compete with a ruthless and fanatical foe.

Schlesinger called for "the reorganization of American values." But unlike Whittaker Chambers or today's Christian right, he didn't propose a religious revival; he proposed a nationalist one, in which citizens put aside personal indulgence and came to the aid of their embattled country. Instead of merely proclaiming their country's greatness, as they had in the complacent Eisenhower years, Americans would have to prove it. After years on the defensive, liberals were again finding their voice.

THE SOMEWHAT UNLIKELY vehicle for this liberal resurgence was John F. Kennedy, a man many liberals viewed with suspicion. If Truman had been too rough for the ADA's sensibilities, Kennedy was too smooth. "He seems to me," commented Loeb, "to have ice-water in his veins and something very mechanical where his heart ought to be." And it wasn't just Kennedy's style. While the junior senator from Massachusetts wasn't a Nixon-style red-baiter, he wasn't exactly an opponent of red-baiting either. He had voted for the loathsome McCarran Act and managed to miss the Senate vote condemning McCarthy—which was hardly surprising given that McCarthy had employed his brother Robert.

The ADA's candidate in 1960 was Hubert Humphrey. And when Humphrey stumbled in West Virginia, and pulled out of the race, some liberals wanted to haul out Adlai Stevenson—whom Eisenhower had defeated in 1952 and 1956—for yet another try. But like Truman twelve years earlier, Kennedy brought the liberals on board by letting them shape the party's message. He named former Connecticut governor and ADA stalwart Chester Bowles to head the convention's platform committee, which after tepid statements in 1952 and 1956 firmly committed the Democrats to civil rights. And just before the Democratic convention, Schlesinger signed a "message of intent to all liberals" assuring them that Kennedy was ideologically acceptable.

If Kennedy's alliance with the liberals seemed at times like a marriage of convenience, he did have something in common with the men and women of the Willard. In the fall of 1946, when the Alsops were warning of liberalism's blindness to the Soviet threat, Kennedy was one of the few liberal Democrats who understood. Just 29 years old, and seeking a congressional seat outside Boston, he had made the cold war a centerpiece of his campaign, declaring that "the time has come when we must speak plainly on the great issue facing the world today. The issue is Soviet Russia . . . a slave state . . . embarked upon a program of world aggression."

It was an instinct he would need in 1960, running against that other Navy veteran elected to Congress in 1946, Richard Nixon. Conventional wisdom held that Kennedy's strength would be domestic policy, where he could exploit Nixon's record as vice president in an administration that had suffered three recessions in eight years. Nixon, by contrast, planned to run on national security, which the public rated its number one concern, and where polls favored the GOP.

Nixon, by now an old hand at painting Democrats as soft, if not pink, tried to do the same to Kennedy. He asked Eisenhower's attorney general,

William Rogers, to dig up material showing that Kennedy was "dangerous to the cause of peace and dangerous from the standpoint of surrender." James Buckley, William F.'s brother, penned "An Open Letter to American Catholics," urging them to oppose their coreligionist because "Kennedy has chosen to identify himself with that segment of American society which is either unwilling or unable to regard Communism as more than a childish bugaboo."

But as an early cold warrior, and a World War II hero to boot, Kennedy's record did not offer much fodder. Nixon's best chance came in early October, when Kennedy said the United States should not pledge to defend Quemoy and Matsu, islands the Chinese Communists were trying to recapture from the Nationalists in Taiwan. "It is shocking for a candidate for the presidency of the United States," Nixon declared, "to say that he is willing to hand over a part of the Free World to the Communist World."

Kennedy tried to turn the discussion to Fidel Castro's recent takeover in Cuba, admonishing Nixon that "The people of the United States would like to hear him discuss his views on an island not four miles off the coast of China but ninety miles off the coast of the United States." He blamed Nixon for America's supposed missile gap with the Soviet Union, a charge that Eisenhower knew from U.S. spy planes was trumped up, and which Kennedy may have known was false as well. And he repeatedly called for higher defense spending, alleging—as the ADA had throughout the 1950s—that Eisenhower and Nixon had "tailored our strategy and military requirements to fit our budget" rather than the other way around. All in all, each candidate tried to prove himself more hawkish than the other. And each largely failed.

But Kennedy's central theme was the one born at the Willard and revived by *Sputnik*: renewal at home in the service of freedom abroad. The first debate between the two candidates was supposed to center on domestic policy. Nixon had wanted it that way so he could pivot to his strength—international affairs—in the more important debates later on. When the two men met in Chicago on September 26, however, Kennedy confounded expectations by making the cold war the framework for his opening statement. "We discuss tonight domestic issues," he declared, "but I would not want . . . any implication to be given that this does not involve directly our struggle with Mr. Khrushchev for survival." From there he ranged widely: from America's unused steel mill capacity to West Virginia children so poor they had to bring home their school lunches to feed their families to the fact that "a Negro baby . . . has about one-half as much chance to get through high school as a white baby." How exactly these injustices imperiled national security was left vague. But Kennedy insisted that, somehow, rectifying them was essential to confronting the Soviet threat. "Can freedom be maintained under the most severe . . . attack it has ever known?" he concluded. "I think it can be. And I think in the final analysis it depends upon what we do here."

In the second debate, held October 7 in Washington, Kennedy echoed Schlesinger and Niebuhr even more explicitly—arguing that fighting Communism required not merely a shift in domestic policies but a shift in domestic values, from private gain to public sacrifice. "I'm talking about a national mood," he said. "I'm talking about our willingness to bear any burdens in order to maintain our freedom and in order to meet our freedom around the globe. . . . I would not want people to elect me because I promise them the easy, soft life." In every debate, and virtually every speech, Kennedy invoked the cold war to explain why America must reject complacency at home. And two days before the election, addressing 30,000 people at 3:00 A.M. in Waterbury, Connecticut, the exhausted candidate walked onto a hotel balcony and made his case one more time: "We defend freedom. If we succeed here, then the cause of freedom is strengthened. If we fail here, if we drift, if we lie at anchor, if we don't provide an example of what freedom can do in the 1960s, then we have betrayed not only ourselves and our destiny, but all those who desire to be free."

WHEN KENNEDY TALKED about providing "an example of what freedom can do," it wasn't hard to see the implications for civil rights. His choice of Lyndon Johnson, a Texan, as his running mate had bothered some liberals. But because Johnson strengthened Kennedy's position in the South, he actually freed him to talk more progressively about race. In the second debate, Kennedy criticized the Eisenhower administration for tolerating private discrimination and the denial of voting rights, saying, "There is a very strong moral basis for this concept of equality of opportunity. . . . We have to practice what we preach. We set a very high standard for ourselves. The Communists do not." As it had for Truman, the cold war offered Kennedy a way to depict civil rights as something that benefited the country as a whole, not just blacks.

But the most important test of Kennedy's commitment to civil rights came behind closed doors, and completely out of the blue. On Wednesday, October 19, Martin Luther King Jr. and fifty-two other civil rights activists were arrested for trying to eat at the Magnolia Room restaurant in Atlanta's Rich's Department Store. Five days later, the others were released, but King was sentenced to four months in the notoriously brutal Reidsville State Prison, deep in rural Georgia. Coretta Scott King, six months pregnant, feared he would be lynched.

Nixon, though personally sympathetic to civil rights, feared jeopardizing his chances in the South and declined to intervene, despite a plea from baseball pioneer Jackie Robinson. For his part, Kennedy had already been warned by three Southern governors to keep his distance from King. But on the morning of October 26, Kennedy's brother-in-law, Sargent Shriver, who oversaw civil rights for the campaign, reached him at Chicago's O'Hare Airport, where he was about to leave for a campaign swing through Michigan. Shriver urged Kennedy to contact Mrs. King and express his concern. And without consulting his advisers, Kennedy impulsively made the call. The following day, Robert Kennedy prevailed on a Georgia judge to release King on bail.

In the white media, almost no one noticed. But the incident made headlines in the black press. The Reverend Martin Luther King Sr., who as a fellow Protestant had supported Nixon, changed his mind, announcing that "Because this man . . . was willing to wipe the tears from my daughter[-in-law's] eyes, I've got a suitcase of votes, and I'm going to take them to Mr. Kennedy and dump them in his lap." The Sunday before the election, Democrats distributed 2 million pamphlets entitled " 'No Comment' Nixon versus a Candidate with a Heart, Senator Kennedy" to black churches across the country.

The night before the election, the race was widely considered even, with the momentum on Nixon's side. But when the returns came in, they showed Kennedy the victor, by a mere 118,000 votes. He received 80 percent of the black vote, up from Stevenson's 60 percent, and in states like Illinois, Michigan, and South Carolina, which Kennedy won by tiny margins, black support helped put him over the top. As in 1948, a Democratic candidate had done the right thing on race, and it had helped him win the presidency. Kennedy had shown that, despite Loeb's assessment, he did indeed have a heart, at least at that one key moment. And it had made all the difference.

IF THE TRUMAN administration had developed liberal anti-Communism largely with an eye to Europe, Kennedy tried to adapt it to the new arena of cold war struggle: the third world. The new president had long been fascinated by what he called "the lands of the rising people." In 1951, as a 34-year-old congressman, he traveled with his brother Robert and sister Pat through Israel, Iran, Pakistan, Thailand, French Indochina, Singapore, Korea, and Japan. And he came back convinced that defeating Communism required, above all, economic and political development. "If one thing was bored into me as a result of my experience in the Middle as well as the Far East," he declared in a radio address upon his return, "it is that Communism cannot be met effectively by merely the force of arms. The central core of our Middle Eastern policy" should be "not the export of arms or the show of armed might but the export of ideas, of techniques, and the rebirth of our traditional sympathy for and understanding of the desires of men to be free."

That desire to be free, Kennedy noted, manifested itself in anticolonial movements across the developing world. And he urged America to support them. Just as Truman had tried to align America with nationalist sentiment in Western Europe and Japan, Kennedy suggested doing the same in countries rushing toward independence, even if it meant welcoming governments over which the United States had little control. In a 1957 *Foreign Affairs* article, he attacked Eisenhower and Dulles for their "failure to appreciate how the forces of nationalism are rewriting the geopolitical map of the world." In a Senate speech that same year, he said, "the single most important test of American foreign policy today is how we meet the challenge of imperialism." And he called for self-determination in Algeria, a suggestion that earned him an angry visit from the French ambassador.

As president, Kennedy implemented a version of containment more like Truman's than Eisenhower's: higher defense spending, a bigger army, and less reliance on the threat of nuclear retaliation. But in keeping with his past views, he also tried to emulate Truman's economic assistance efforts and his sympathy for foreign nationalism. In March 1961, Kennedy invited congressional leaders and Latin American ambassadors to the East Room of the White House, where he unveiled the Alliance for Progress, "a vast cooperative effort, unparalleled in magnitude and nobility of purpose, to satisfy the basic needs of the American people for homes, work and land, health and schools." The United States pledged $20 billion over ten years to Latin American countries that committed themselves to land reform, progressive taxation, and free elections. It was an enlightened answer to Castro's revolution, which Kennedy feared could spread elsewhere in the continent. And it mirrored the efforts of liberalism's great ally: the labor movement. In 1961, Walter Reuther helped establish the American Institute for Free Labor Development, which trained Latin American labor unionists "with particular emphasis on the theme of democracy versus totalitarianism." And by decade's end, the AFL-CIO was devoting 20 percent of its budget to supporting democratic labor movements across the world. The spirit of Point Four was back.

In Latin America, the Alliance for Progress evoked an enthusiastic popular response. But the continent's leaders, many of them wealthy oligarchs, largely resisted reform. And even within the State Department's Latin America division, the initiative met opposition, rendering its ultimate impact modest at best. More successful was the Peace Corps. As early as 1952, Connecticut senator Brien McMahon, addressing a meeting of the ADA, had proposed an "army" of young Americans who would scatter throughout the developing world as "missionaries of democracy." Later, Humphrey took up the idea, and in 1961, Kennedy signed an executive order creating the program. Like the Alliance for Progress, the goal was to stop Communism by addressing the economic conditions that facilitated its spread. "Widespread poverty and chaos," Kennedy said, "lead to a collapse of existing political and social structures, which would inevitably invite the advance of totalitarianism." By the spring of 1964, there were 10,000 Peace Corps volunteers spread across the globe.

In his dealings with developing nations, Kennedy also tried to move away from Dulles's "us versus them" tunnel vision. "The independence of nations is a bar to the Communists' 'grand design,'" he said, "[but] it is the basis of our own." And facing a potential crisis in Laos, he put theory into practice, negotiating an agreement that preserved its cold war neutrality rather than sending in arms and troops to capture it for America's side.

But there was a fundamental problem. The principle Kennedy was trying to implement—American support for non-Communist nationalism—took as its premise that genuine nationalist movements could never be Communist. Communism, Acheson had argued in 1947, "was not a doctrine which people picked up and looked over and either adopted or rejected." It was brought about "either by an internal organization financed by other countries, or by external pressure to adopt a system of government which had the inescapable consequence of inclusion in the system of Russian power." That had worked well enough for Truman.

But in the developing world, where Communism's anti-colonial stance gave it particular prestige, things were more complicated. In British Guiana, for instance, a tiny imperial holding on its way toward independence, Kennedy flagrantly contradicted his eloquent anticolonialism and urged London to scrap free elections because he feared an alleged Communist would win. Luckily, the British refused. In Vietnam, however, he and his successors were not so fortunate. Kennedy's foreign policy team assumed that Ho Chi Minh—because he was a Communist—could not be the authentic voice of Vietnamese nationalism. Fortified by this assumption, the Kennedy and Johnson administrations set out to contain Communism in Indochina. Except that they were also trying to contain nationalism, which Kennedy had all but admitted the United States could not do. The more feverishly Kennedy's whiz-kid advisers tried to square that circle, the deeper they sank—until antitotalitarian liberalism itself began to crack, and the struggle that ended in 1948 began anew.

But in the early 1960s, those dark days seemed an eternity away. And if Kennedy's short presidency did not replicate Truman's foreign policy glory, it did bring liberalism's greatest domestic dream to the brink of fruition. Despite his election eve call to Coretta Scott King, there were widespread doubts about Kennedy's commitment to civil rights. And in his first two and half years in office, he did little to dispel them. He appointed more African Americans to government posts and frequently invited blacks to the White House, but that was about it. In April 1962, the ADA's Joseph Rauh called the president's record on the issue a "bitter disappointment."

Two forces, however, were pushing Kennedy toward action. The first was the nonviolent freedom movement gathering force throughout the South. And the second was the liberal interpretation of the cold war—the Kennedy administration's desire to cast off what Secretary of State Dean Rusk called "the biggest single burden that we carry on our backs in foreign relations." By the summer of 1963, Kennedy could no longer evade the issue. In April, when civil rights protesters tried to integrate Birmingham's department stores and lunch counters, Sheriff Eugene "Bull" Connor ordered his men to attack them with fire hoses, clubs, and dogs. Two months later, Governor George Wallace defied a court order to integrate the University of Alabama, thumbing his nose at the federal government.

Finally, Kennedy acted. On June 11, with the cameras rolling, his deputy attorney general confronted Wallace on the campus steps. And at eight o'clock that night, he addressed the nation, calling segregation a moral issue that could no longer be ignored. "When Americans are sent to Vietnam or West Berlin," he said, linking civil rights and anti-Communism yet again, "we do not ask for whites only." The following week, he sent civil rights legislation to Congress. In August, Martin Luther King addressed 250,000 people at the March on Washington. And in November, Kennedy flew to Dallas, where he was murdered.

But the momentum for freedom was now too strong. In June 1964, with majority whip Hubert Humphrey as floor leader, the Senate broke its first civil rights filibuster in history and passed legislation guaranteeing equal access to employment and public accommodations. That fall, Lyndon Johnson won the biggest election victory in presidential history, and the Democratic Party built its largest congressional majorities since the 1930s. The vision born at the Willard Hotel—that by opposing totalitarianism the right way, America could become a better country—seemed to finally be coming true.

The culmination came the following spring. In March 1965, civil rights protesters prepared to march from Selma, Alabama—a city whose population was more than 50 percent black and whose registration rolls were 99 percent white—to the state capital in Montgomery to dramatize the struggle for voting rights. As 600 peaceful demonstrators crossed the Edmund Pettus Bridge on the outskirts of the city, they were attacked by state troopers and sheriff's deputies, in a beating so vicious it sent fifty people to the hospital.

Eight days later, Lyndon Johnson addressed a joint session of Congress. Echoing Humphrey's speech seventeen years earlier, he declared, "We have already waited a hundred years and more, and the time for waiting is gone." He demanded immediate passage of a voting rights bill. And as he reached his speech's conclusion, he paused, before uttering the words: "We shall overcome." For a moment, the audience sat in shocked silence. One Southern congressman muttered, "Goddamn." Then the chamber broke into a thunderous standing ovation. Watching on television from Selma, Martin Luther King did something his aides had never seen before. He began to cry.

2

Losing America

ON A JUNE day in 1962, a high school student named Jim Hawley arrived at the United Auto Workers camp in Port Huron, Michigan. The fifty-nine men and women gathered there for the inaugural convention of Students for a Democratic Society (SDS) didn't know what to make of the taciturn 17-year-old. For one thing, he hadn't been invited. For another, he wanted "observer" status—a bizarrely formal request given the surroundings. But Communists were like that.

The college students of SDS had little memory of liberalism's 1948 civil war. And many considered Communists something of a joke, the bogeymen of an earlier generation. "Do you mean to say there was a Communist here?" exclaimed one young activist upon hearing of Hawley's presence. "I've never seen one." But if Communism was largely alien, anti-Communism was not. It helped define American culture—the conformist, unjust, complacent culture SDS was gathering to denounce. If anti-Communism required that Hawley be spurned, Hawley would be welcomed. And in this trivial, almost comic, way, the assault on antitotalitarian liberalism began.

SDS was born as the student arm of the League for Industrial Democracy (LID), an anti-Communist labor organization backed by Walter Reuther's United Auto Workers (hence the Port Huron locale) and David Dubinsky's International Ladies Garment Workers Union—two of the unions that had helped found the ADA. But generational conflict erupted almost immediately. SDS's inaugural manifesto, as initially drafted by a recent University of Michigan graduate named Tom Hayden, attacked anti-Communist liberals for having "abstracted Russians to demonic proportions" to "mask . . . their own timidity" in promoting social change.

The Soviet Union, it claimed, was "a conservative status quo . . . harassed and weakened nation" and its American admirers posed a far smaller threat to democratic values than the "paranoid quest for [anti-Communist] decontamination."

To the LID, it sounded like Henry Wallace all over again. The League hauled Hayden and his colleagues before its board, lectured them on totalitarianism ("Would you give seats to Nazis too?" asked one LID official), and cut off their funds. At a subsequent meeting, an LID veteran opened his shirt to reveal the scars from a brawl with Communists in the 1930s. To the activists of SDS, the battle lines seemed clear: an older generation was imposing its tired, stultifying ideology on the idealistic young.

But if the fight was about age, it was also—more subtly—about class. In *The Sixties*, his memoir-cum-history of the period, former SDS president Todd Gitlin notes that the Port Huron Statement sparked a confrontation not merely with the old bulls of the LID, but with one of SDS's own. Tom Kahn, the son of a Brooklyn transport worker, was only 23, but already a dedicated anti-Communist and a fierce partisan of labor. And from the beginning, he seethed with anger at the arrogant "Ivy League-type[s]" around him. After reading Hayden's manifesto, he warned him that SDS risked being labeled Communist. "People are going to attack us," he predicted. "Yeah," Hayden replied, staring Kahn in the face, "and you're going to be one of them. . . . You will try to destroy us." As it turned out, he was absolutely right.

FOR A GENERATION, liberalism had defined itself by its twin, indivisible commitments to freedom: civil rights at home and antitotalitarianism abroad. But in the decade following Port Huron, both came under attack from a new movement of the left, which turned antitotalitarianism on its head. As that movement gained force, the liberalism born at the Willard Hotel began to buckle. Its foreign and domestic visions were severed. And a new liberal creed emerged that denied America's moral potential and, in the process, forfeited its own.

Hayden had drawn his vision for SDS in part from his experience the previous year working with the Student Nonviolent Coordinating Committee (SNCC). And in the coming years, these two signature organizations of the New Left would launch parallel attacks on liberalism's ideological foundations. Like SDS, SNCC was an organization of young people—mostly black Southerners who had left college to work for civil rights. Like SDS, it rejected anti-Communism. Like SDS, it was suspicious of the political process and the compromises it required. And even more than their SDS allies, the young men and women of SNCC had put their bodies on the line—enduring beatings, bombings, shootings, and the daily terror that came with defying Jim Crow.

By 1963, SNCC was struggling. It had thrown itself into voter registration in Mississippi, the most backward, brutal state in the South. But local white authorities resisted fiercely, the Kennedy administration offered little help, and after two years, less than 6 percent of the state's black population was registered. So Bob Moses, director of SNCC's Mississippi project, along with other civil rights leaders, came up with an idea to galvanize national attention: Freedom Vote. The premise was simple: If Mississippi would not let blacks register for the state's gubernatorial election that fall, they would hold a mock election of their own—in the safety of their own communities—and thus demolish the myth that African Americans didn't want the franchise.

Freedom Vote would prove a high point of unity in the civil rights movement, bringing together young and old, black and white, moderate and militant. But just as Port Huron sowed the seeds of conflict between cold war liberals and the New Left over anti-Communism, Freedom Vote set in motion events that would spark a second great rupture—over race. To help with Freedom Vote, SNCC called upon two seasoned activists. The first was Bayard Rustin, an African American Quaker, an ADA board member, the organizational genius behind the 1963 March on Washington, and a man the civil rights movement badly needed but feared embracing because he was gay. The second was Allard Lowenstein, the charismatic, hyperactive pied piper of campus liberalism. What they shared were beliefs in anti-Communism, racial integration, and America's capacity for redemption—beliefs that would eventually make them pariahs in the protest movements they once called home.

Moses frequently consulted Rustin on strategy. And he dispatched Lowenstein to campuses like Stanford and Yale, where he gathered money and publicity for Freedom Vote, inspiring close to a hundred mostly white college students to make the dangerous trip south. Freedom Vote proved a massive success, bringing roughly 85,000 black Mississippians to the "polls" to vote for the candidates of the multiracial Mississippi Freedom Democratic Party (MFDP), and splashing SNCC's work across the pages of *Newsweek* and the *New York Times*.

Emboldened by its success, SNCC hatched something even bigger for 1964. The new effort, dubbed Freedom Summer, would bring not hundreds but thousands of college students to Mississippi to register black voters, teach in Freedom Schools, build the Mississippi Freedom Democratic Party, and more generally, attack segregation in every corner of the state. And that effort would culminate in a dramatic challenge to the national Democratic Party—a slate of Mississippi Freedom delegates demanding to be seated at the party's 1964 convention in Atlantic City.

But by December 1963, tensions were already starting to show. SNCC received aid from two organizations with Communist ties: the National Lawyers Guild and the Southern Conference Educational Fund. Most SNCC activists, like their ideological soulmates in SDS, could not have cared less. Their only litmus test was commitment to civil rights. For Lowenstein, however, Communism was never irrelevant. It was unacceptable, he told one Mississippi activist, for a freedom movement to be "using people who don't really believe in freedom."

Over the following months, Lowenstein quietly pulled away, but Freedom Summer rolled on. Over 800 white activists, mostly students from the North, came to Mississippi. In June, two of them, Andrew Goodman and Michael Schwerner, gave their lives for the movement when, along with a local activist named James Chaney, they were dragged from their car and shot to death on a remote Mississippi highway.

Despite such acts of terror, SNCC and the other civil rights groups stuck to their plan. They developed a parallel nominating structure, holding precinct, county, and statewide elections, which chose sixty-eight delegates to the Democratic convention, sixty-four of them black. Rustin remained a critical eminence grise, linking the Mississippi activists to supporters throughout the nation. At one point, Moses and his allies even asked him to oversee the entire convention challenge. But Rustin, fearing SNCC's militant instincts were ill suited to the political realities it would confront in Atlantic City, demanded complete control. His request was denied, the first hint of a rift that would blow open in the months to come.

ON FRIDAY, AUGUST 21, 1964, the delegates of the Mississippi Freedom Democratic Party, mostly poor farmers, arrived in Atlantic City. In a graphic testimonial, they included in their caravan the burned-out car in which Schwerner, Chaney, and Goodman had been riding the day they were murdered.

On Saturday, the delegates addressed the Credentials Committee. Live on national television, MFDP vice chairman Fannie Lou Hamer described being tortured—on orders from Mississippi state police—for trying to register to vote. Her testimony was so explosive that President Johnson called an impromptu press conference to divert the cameras' gaze. But on the news that night, viewers heard Hamer's testimony in full, including her haunting closing words: "All of this is on account [of] we want to register, to become first-class citizens, and if the Freedom Democratic Party is not seated now, I question America."

The controversy over the MFDP suddenly threatened to swallow the convention. Five Southern delegations announced that if the black delegates were seated, they would walk out. For the first time since 1948, race threatened to rip the Democratic Party apart. And Johnson, determined to avoid a rupture, called upon the patron saint of 1948, Hubert Humphrey, for help.

Humphrey's desire for the vice presidency was no secret. And Johnson decided to make him earn it. The White House floated a compromise: two MFDP delegates would get at-large seats; the others would be the convention's "honored guests," and in 1968, Mississippi would send an integrated slate. Humphrey was dispatched to convince the black delegates to take the deal, thus avoiding a battle on the convention floor. To make the case, Humphrey tried to enlist his old civil rights ally and ADA colleague Joseph Rauh, who was serving as the MFDP's legal counsel. But Humphrey and Rauh—representatives of an older, less confrontational, liberalism—were unprepared for the MFDP's blunt, unwavering moral force. Hamer, a sharecropper's wife, would later recount her showdown with the future vice president of the United States. "All that we had been hearing about . . . Hubert Humphrey and his stand for civil rights, I was delighted to even have a chance to talk with this man," she explained. But when Rauh told her that Humphrey's chances for the vice presidential nomination rested on an MFDP compromise, "I was amazed, and I said, 'Well, Mr. Humphrey, do you mean to tell me that your position is more important to you than four hundred thousand black people's lives [the African American population of Mississippi]?' . . . and I left out of there full of tears."

Humphrey wasn't the only liberal hero bloodied by the fight over the MFDP. Over the following days, the pillars of the civil rights establishment tried to convince Hamer and her Mississippi allies to accept a compromise, and each in turn discredited himself in SNCC's increasingly radical eyes. Rauh tried valiantly—under fierce administration pressure—to serve his clients, and ultimately opposed Johnson's offer. But he fell out with SNCC nonetheless, and Moses refused to speak to him for fifteen years. Lowenstein—still close to the MFDP's more moderate NAACP wing—lobbied Northern liberals on the delegates' behalf, but was also denounced by SNCC activists for allegedly backing a deal. And in a last-ditch effort, Rustin, Martin Luther King, and other African American leaders spoke to the delegates in the local church that served as their makeshift headquarters. Rustin told them they had changed the Democratic Party forever. But as the civil rights movement entered the political process, he insisted, it would have to learn to compromise, and would need allies like Humphrey in the work ahead. As he spoke, a SNCC activist shouted out from the back: "You're a traitor, Bayard, a traitor!"

In the end, the delegates rejected the compromise. And for those involved in the MFDP fight, it colored everything that happened afterward. For the cold war liberals, Atlantic City was proof that America was finally achieving its moral potential. "They don't know the victory they got," Johnson told Walter Reuther. "Next time no one can discriminate against Negroes." Rauh said, "We made great progress," and called the 1968 convention, where Mississippi fielded an integrated delegation, "one of the high points of my lifetime."

For SNCC and its supporters on the New Left, by contrast, Atlantic City exposed liberalism as a fraud. "This proves," said SNCC's Stokely Carmichael, "that the liberal Democrats are just as racist as Goldwater." Staughton Lynd, the white radical who had run SNCC's Freedom Schools, called the "bitterness at those national civil rights personalities who urged acceptance of the compromise on grounds of political expediency . . . indescribable."

And for Lowenstein and Rustin, who believed in antitotalitarian liberalism, but knew it had to evolve to survive, Atlantic City was an unmistakable sign that even greater battles lay ahead.

RUSTIN, IN PARTICULAR, watched developments in 1964 and 1965 with mounting alarm. To most observers, liberalism had never looked stronger. That fall, Johnson and Humphrey trounced Republican Barry Goldwater at the polls. Congress passed the Civil Rights and Voting Rights Acts. And Johnson announced the Great Society, an ambitious effort to expand

economic opportunity and security, building on the work Roosevelt and
Truman had begun more than two decades before. Addressing the ADA's
convention, Arthur Schlesinger said 1965 offered "the greatest opportunity for constructive liberalism in a generation."

But Rustin sensed ominous rumblings below the political surface. A
month before the showdown in Atlantic City, an off-duty police officer
had shot a black 15-year-old on New York's Upper East Side. Two days
later, Harlem erupted, as thousands smashed cars, broke windows, and
fought pitched battles with police. The following night, speaking at a Harlem church, Rustin appealed for nonviolence, and was taunted and booed.
When he and other civil rights leaders tried to lead a peaceful march,
residents spat on them.

Malcolm X had recently declared that "the day of turning the other
cheek to those brute beasts is over." And nonviolence was falling out of
favor in SNCC as well. Knowing the rage that years of official abuse and
neglect had produced in slums across the country, Rustin foresaw a terrible chain reaction: black violence, inflamed by militant black leadership,
producing a white backlash that would destroy liberalism just when it was
poised to produce real change.

Rustin drafted a telegram, sent by the NAACP's Roy Wilkins to the
other major civil rights leaders, warning that "the Civil Rights Act of 1964
could well be diminished or nullified and a decade of increasingly violent
and futile disorder ushered in if we do not play our hand coolly and intelligently." The leaders called for a moratorium on civil disobedience until
after the election, and the rest of the year passed relatively quietly.

But Rustin wasn't wrong—just premature. Segregationist Alabama
governor George Wallace's 1964 primary challenge to President Johnson
had shown surprising strength in white working-class pockets of Indiana, Maryland, and Wisconsin. And although crushed overall, Goldwater had won five states in the Deep South—previously unthinkable for a
Republican.

For Rustin, there was only one way to cool the black fury he had
seen in Harlem, and the white resentment that had garnered Wallace
45 percent of the vote in the Maryland primary. The civil rights movement, he argued, must move beyond a narrow racial agenda and present
an economic program that benefited poor blacks and poor whites alike. In
an extraordinary 1965 article in *Commentary*, Rustin urged liberals to focus
less on racism per se than on education, because "we are in the midst of

a technological revolution which is altering the fundamental structure of the labor force, destroying unskilled and semi-skilled jobs—jobs in which Negroes are disproportionately concentrated." More than twenty years later, the African American sociologist William Julius Wilson would base an influential theory of the American underclass on exactly this insight.

Rustin's great hope was the labor movement, the political incubator of the white working class. In 1964, he addressed the Teamsters, a union that would become synonymous with white backlash—and received rave reviews. Everywhere, his message was the same: that liberals must make "the program for racial equality . . . so intertwined with progressive economic and social policies as to make it impossible to choose one without the other." And in early 1965, he created the A. Phillip Randolph Institute to bring blacks into the labor movement and commit unions to a broad agenda of economic change.

But Rustin was increasingly isolated. In 1965, SNCC began expelling whites from the organization. The following year, its new president, Stokely Carmichael, coined the term *Black Power* to describe the group's turn from integration to separatism. Another major civil rights group, the Congress of Racial Equality (CORE), also embraced Black Power, and its new president called nonviolence "a dying philosophy." Rustin warned that Black Power "threatens to ravage the entire civil rights movement." But the movement was quickly leaving him behind. As former CORE leader James Farmer would later tell the *New York Times Magazine*, "Bayard has no credibility in the black community. . . . Bayard's commitment is to labor, not to the black man."

Black separatism, the first element in Rustin's chain reaction, was gaining strength. And on August 11, 1965, the second ingredient exploded into view, when Watts went up in flames. Sparked by the arrest of a black man for drunk driving, riots raged in African American neighborhoods of Los Angeles for six days, leaving more than 4,000 arrested, almost 1,000 injured, and 34 dead. The following year, riots broke out in Cleveland and Chicago as well. And between 1964 and 1967, armed assaults rose 77 percent.

The result was exactly what Rustin had feared. From April 1965 to September 1966, the percentage of Northern whites who said the government was pushing civil rights "too fast" almost doubled, to over 50 percent. On September 20, 1966, Republican congressional leader Gerald Ford demanded to know "how long are we going to abdicate law and order—the backbone of any civilization—in favor of a soft social theory that the man who heaves a brick through your window or tosses a fire-bomb into your car is simply the misunderstood and underprivileged product of a broken home?" That November, Republicans picked up forty-seven seats in the House, and a former Democrat and ADA member named Ronald Reagan rode law and order into the California governor's mansion.

Ford called the midterms "a repudiation of the President's domestic policies," and in 1967, a more conservative Congress slashed antipoverty spending. Less than two years after his address to the ADA, Schlesinger pronounced "the Great Society . . . except for token gestures, dead."

IF WHITE BACKLASH was shattering liberalism's domestic hopes, Vietnam was doing the same to its vision of America's role in the world. The New Left's attack on liberal anti-Communism had preceded the war. In the academy, its first major statement came in 1959, when William Appleman Williams published *The Tragedy of American Diplomacy*, which described the USSR as essentially defensive, and blamed the cold war on American capitalism's relentless search for new markets. Even three years later, the Port Huron Statement contained only one passing reference to Vietnam. But after 1965, when the first major antiwar protests broke out, the New Left's arguments found a wider audience. If rising African American anger fueled the black left's assault on racial integration, rising anger over Vietnam fueled the white left's assault on anti-Communism.

The New Left's contention—that the principles which drew America into Vietnam were born at the Willard Hotel—was both true and false. As John F. Kennedy had learned, liberal anti-Communism rested on several axioms, and sometimes they clashed. George Kennan, the strategist behind Truman's early policies toward the USSR, believed nationalism and Communism could coexist. Partly for that reason, he urged the United States to contain only Soviet Communism, not indigenous Communist movements, and even then only when circumstances were favorable. In his 1947 speech urging aid to Greece and Turkey, however, Truman had ignored that distinction, pledging the United States to oppose virtually any Communist movement. Behind that perilously expansive vision was the growing assumption that Communism and nationalism were incompatible. And with Kennan's distinction gone, containment suddenly meant preventing Communism's spread in every corner of the globe.

For Kennedy and Johnson, that assumption became a blindfold, preventing them from seeing the enemy in Vietnam for what it was: not an agent of Moscow or Beijing, but a nationalist movement led by a Communist Party. Instead, the United States earnestly, valiantly, and brutally tried to build an artificial nationalism, based on the "nation" of South Vietnam. Policy makers spent the 1960s anguishing about why, despite their best efforts, their allies in Saigon would not fight for their country. But that "country" had been artificially created in 1954, not because the Vietnamese desired partition, but to deny Ho Chi Minh's Vietminh guerrillas the full victory over French colonialism they seemed likely to win on the battlefield. Even then, North and South Vietnam were meant to be reunified in national elections two years later, but Saigon—with Washington's support—reneged. As David Halberstam wrote, "no one really believed there was such a thing as South Vietnam. But . . . [l]ike water turning into ice, the illusion crystallized and became a reality, not because that which existed in South Vietnam was real, but because it became real in powerful men's minds."

To be fair, distinguishing between Communist movements with broad nationalist support, and those largely controlled from the outside, was not easy. The Communist rebels in Greece, for instance, had enjoyed some domestic backing, while Hanoi received more than $2 billion in aid from China and the USSR between 1965 and 1968. Anti-Communism was a noble principle, but turning it into wise foreign policy required informed, nuanced judgments. The tragedy of American policy toward Vietnam was that the officials best able to make those judgments were almost never in the room when key decisions were made. After China's fall to the Communists in 1949, which McCarthy and his allies deemed a stab in the back by a treasonous State Department, the Far Eastern Affairs division had been gutted, its most gifted analysts farmed out to other bureaus or hounded out of government altogether. As a result, Halberstam writes, the Kennedy and Johnson administrations "made the most critical of decisions [about Vietnam] with virtually no input from anyone who had any experience on the recent history of that part of the world."

So in one sense, antitotalitarian liberalism did lead to Vietnam: it provided the intellectual building blocks that arrogant, blinkered men—who had forgotten their creed's emphasis on restraint—assembled in disastrous fashion. But other antitotalitarian liberals—including Niebuhr and, after 1965, Schlesinger as well—drew on the same tradition to critique America's Vietnam disaster. It was possible to consider liberal democracy fundamentally superior to Communism, to see the Soviet Union as a potential aggressor that the United States must contain, to believe American power essential to a better world—and still oppose the war. All it required was recognizing that since Vietnamese Communism was the product of Vietnamese nationalism, not Soviet or Chinese power, it could not be militarily contained—and its triumph did not threaten American security.

For the New Left, however, Vietnam was merely a symptom of the real disease: anti-Communism. It was the anti-Communist consensus, argued the radicals like Hayden, which defined the limits of acceptable opinion, marginalizing those who felt there was something wrong at America's core. And the true enforcers of that consensus were not conservatives, but anti-Communist liberals. They were the ones running the universities where the New Left was born, and running the government it wanted to bring down. They were the ones putting a humane, reformist face on capitalism at home and imperialism abroad. And so for the New Left, it became a point of pride to attack not the Neanderthal right, but the true guardians of establishment power. Addressing a November 1965 antiwar march in Washington, SDS president Carl Oglesby declared: "The original commitment in Vietnam was made by President Truman, a mainstream liberal. It was seconded by President Eisenhower, a moderate liberal. It was intensified by the late President Kennedy, a flaming liberal. Think of all the men who now engineer that war—those who study the maps, give the commands, push the buttons, and tally the dead: Bundy, McNamara, Rusk, Lodge, Goldberg, the President himself. They are not moral monsters. They are all honorable men. They are all liberals."

The word *honorable* was important. Unlike some of Wallace's supporters in the late 1940s, the New Left did not romanticize Moscow. But consorting with Communists provided a way to transgress "honorable" liberalism's boundaries. And in this way, SDS revived the very axiom the ADA had been founded to oppose: no enemies on the left. In December 1963, when Alger Hiss turned up at an SDS National Council meeting, he received a raucous welcome. The following April, SDS supported the right of two Communist-front groups to join a major antiwar march. "We refuse to be anti-Communist," wrote Hayden and Staughton Lynd. "It serves as the key category of abstract thought which Americans use to justify a foreign policy that is often no more sophisticated than rape."

AT ITS JUNE 1965 convention, SDS removed the word *totalitarian* from its description of the form of government it opposed, a final break with the liberal tradition. But the New Left didn't quite abandon the concept of totalitarianism. Instead, it inverted it. In 1964, Herbert Marcuse, the New Left's leading political theorist, condemned the "totalitarian tendencies of the one-dimensional society"—societies like the United States. Lynd wrote that Kennedy's assassination proved that the correct "perspective for the coming period is fascism." And *Studies on the Left*, a University of Wisconsin Marxist journal that influenced SDS, wrote in 1964 that "there are, indeed, many similarities between American society today and that of Germany in the years before and during Nazi rule."

America's Nazi-like crimes, of course, were most obvious in Vietnam. But the point of the analogy was that America was totalitarian not only there, but in Watts and Mississippi as well. And if America was totalitarian everywhere, the methods for fighting it must be similar everywhere. Here the liberal vision was turned on its head. For cold war liberals, America's fight against Soviet totalitarianism abroad had served as the impetus for reform at home. But for the New Left, it was the fight against *American* totalitarianism abroad that served as the impetus for *revolution* at home. In Latin America and Vietnam, groups like SDS saw models for their struggle inside the United States. "The Vietnamese revolutionaries," in Todd Gitlin's words, "were a more victimized and better organized version of ourselves."

With Che Guevera as their inspiration and the Vietcong as their model, SDS and its allies turned in the late 1960s from the language of persuasion to the language of conflict. Conflict, argued the New Left, would strip the establishment of its enlightened, liberal façade, laying bare society's true choice: between fascism and revolution. The challenge, Hayden explained, was to "arouse the sleeping dogs on the Right."

But in America, unlike in Cuba or Vietnam, polarization left the masses on the other side of the barricades. Marcuse recognized this, acknowledging that "the majority of people in the affluent society are on the side of that which is . . . not that which can and ought to be." He saw students, not workers, as the likely agents of radical change. And the more revolutionary New Left students became, the more blue-collar Americans showed how antirevolutionary they really were. In September 1967, SDS began using a new term to describe the police: pigs. And almost five years after Port Huron, a disgusted Tom Kahn fulfilled Hayden's prophesy of betrayal. The New Left, he wrote in *Commentary*, "contains strands of middle class prejudice—a lack of appreciation for, or identification with, the historic and *continuing* role of labor in the day-to-day lives of literally millions of working people." In the coming years, wherever anti-Communist liberals fought the New Left, Tom Kahn was there.

The rising disaffection of the white working class offered the right an enormous opportunity: its best chance since the days of Joseph Mc-Carthy to fuse anti-Communism and class resentment. In 1968, George Wallace ran for president again, this time not merely against civil rights, but against the antiwar movement as well. He appealed to the "average man in the street, this man in the textile mill, this man in the steel mill, this barber, this beautician, the policeman on the beat." And he delighted his blue-collar crowds by taunting the student left. "If any demonstrator lies down in front of my car when I'm President," he vowed, "that'll be the last car he lays down in front of."

Richard Nixon seized the opening too. Counted out by everyone after losing to Kennedy, and then losing again in the California governor's race in 1962, Nixon had clawed back. He campaigned ferociously for Republican candidates in 1966, and in one of the great political comebacks in American history, captured the GOP nomination in 1968. His campaign theme was "law and order"—a phrase broad enough to capture the backlash against black rioters and white radicals alike. "Working Americans," he declared in his acceptance speech, "have become the forgotten Americans. In a time when the national rostrums and forums are given over to shouters and protesters and demonstrators, they have become the silent Americans." The New Left was polarizing the country. And a resurgent right was reaping the rewards.

IN 1965, AMIDST black fury and white backlash, Rustin had hoped a singular focus on economic justice could keep the liberal coalition from tearing itself apart over race. Two years later, with the antiwar movement gathering gale force, Lowenstein threw himself into a parallel crusade: to prevent liberalism from tearing itself apart over Vietnam. Disheveled, chronically late, and perpetually in motion—never sleeping in the same place twice, forever huddled in conversation deep into the night—he roamed the country searching for a candidate to challenge Johnson for the Democratic nomination. A passionate opponent of the war, Lowenstein wanted someone to run against Vietnam. But he also wanted someone to wrest the antiwar movement away from groups like SDS. He attacked the New Left's "politics of alienation." And he praised the soldiers fighting in Vietnam, saying that "people have no conception . . . of the degree to which American troops do the most difficult things with courage." He told the organizers of a large antiwar march to denounce the Vietcong's crimes as well as America's, and to hold their rally on July 4, proceeding from Arlington National Cemetery to the Washington Memorial, led by an honor guard, and flanked by American flags.

At Princeton, Lowenstein was booed by members of SDS. When he spoke at Grinnell College, left-wing hecklers threw garbage on the stage. Partly, they loathed his anti-Communism, a faith he had acquired in the 1950s, while battling Communist youth groups in the National Students Association. But the antipathy went beyond that. The New Left could not abide Lowenstein's fervent, brazen patriotism, his insistence that America had a moral purpose at home and in the world. Unlike the older liberals who had convened at the Willard, Lowenstein was intimately, gut-wrenchingly familiar with the furies the 1960s had spawned. But those furies made him appreciate Niebuhr's core insight even more keenly than had the optimistic liberals of the Kennedy years. Lowenstein knew that American greatness was not fated, that his country was capable of brutal injustice. Yet he believed America could be redeemed through struggle. The right leader, he insisted, could show even the angriest of radicals that America was not "inherently sick." Lowenstein was, in journalist Jack Newfield's words, "the last and best liberal . . . one who always goes into revolutionary situations, yet always stays a liberal."

On November 30, Minnesota senator Eugene McCarthy answered Lowenstein's call. McCarthy also wanted to give the antiwar young—in-cluding two of his own children, who were student peace activists—an al-ternative to the New Left. "There is deep anxiety and alienation among a large number of people," he later explained. "So we have demonstrations and draft card burning and all the rest. Someone must give these groups entrance back into the political process."

Students flocked to McCarthy's campaign. And on March 12, 1968, he won a stunning 42 percent of the vote in the New Hampshire pri-mary—leading Johnson to abandon his quest for reelection. But the very qualities that helped McCarthy co-opt the New Left alienated the white working class. The only published poet in the Senate, Eugene McCarthy was more ironic than impassioned. Politically and culturally, he resembled Adlai Stevenson, another man whose cerebral, detached style proved more popular with intellectuals than ordinary voters. Students admired McCar-thy's apparent distaste for political compromise. To working-class Democrats, however, he often appeared elitist and remote. "The better-educated people vote for us," McCarthy boasted, unwisely. And he mocked labor leaders as "old buffaloes"—a slur they remembered by wearing buffalo pins on their lapels at the Democratic National Convention in Chicago.

Nowhere was McCarthy's failure to bridge the class divide more evident than within the ADA. In the 1940s and 1950s, the organization's influence had rested on its ability to unite intellectuals and labor, to bring together Schlesinger from Harvard and Reuther from the UAW. But by the 1960s, places like Harvard were producing fewer people who thought like Schlesinger. In 1962, ADA members sponsored a resolution denouncing Kennedy's "wasteful, useless and extremely dangerous" military buildup—a sharp departure from the group's traditional support for a large defense budget. As one member explained, "many young people" considered the organization "old-hat, stale, and somewhat conservative."

Trying to connect to a new generation, in 1966 the ADA put Lowenstein—then 37 years old—on its board. The following year, it made him vice president. But Lowenstein and his student allies were on a mission to defeat Lyndon Johnson, a mission many ADA labor leaders—who loathed the antiwar movement—adamantly opposed. The organization faced a stark dilemma. Unless it supported McCarthy, it would consign itself to irrelevance among the activist young. But backing him, as Joseph Rauh warned, would split "the liberal-labor-Negro coalition that had elected every liberal president and made possible every liberal advance since the 1930s." On February 10, 1968, in the most important ADA meeting since the Willard Hotel, the National Board voted 65 to 47 to endorse McCarthy's presidential bid. Within weeks, more than a thousand new members, many of them young, joined the organization. But representatives of the steel workers, the garment workers, and the communication workers all resigned. "The coalition," one labor leader declared, "is finished."

AS WINTER TURNED to spring, Schlesinger and other prominent liberals began insisting that only one man could hold cold war liberalism together: Robert Kennedy, the president's younger brother and the junior senator from New York. When Lowenstein went searching for a candidate against Johnson, Kennedy had been his first choice. But Kennedy had resisted, joining the race only after New Hampshire showed how vulnerable Johnson really was.

The differences between Kennedy and McCarthy echoed the differences between John Kennedy and Adlai Stevenson a decade before. Unlike McCarthy and Stevenson, Robert Kennedy made some liberals uneasy. He didn't seem above politics; to the contrary, he had a reputation as a ruthless street fighter. And on civil liberties and civil rights, he had a checkered past: he had worked for Joseph McCarthy in the 1950s, and as his brother's attorney general, had let the FBI bug top black leaders' phones.

But Kennedy had come around on civil rights, and by 1968 he was talking about poverty with unusual fervor. While McCarthy's support base—like the antiwar movement itself—was overwhelmingly white, Kennedy enjoyed such intense backing from African Americans and other minorities that his wife, Ethel, while watching election returns one evening, exclaimed, "Don't you just wish that everyone was black?" When King was murdered, McCarthy made no statement at all, but Kennedy went into the Indianapolis ghetto and broke the news to a largely black crowd, giving one of the most eloquent speeches of his career.

In an intriguing twist, Kennedy also spoke far more forcefully than McCarthy about stopping crime, and explicitly opposed school busing. Whether his views sprang from commitment or calculation—whether he was fulfilling Rustin's dream of a vision that could hold together blacks and blue-collar whites or just cynically telling different audiences what they wanted to hear—remains a topic of heated debate. In fact, Kennedy biographers can't even agree on how much working-class white support he actually enjoyed. But it was clearly enough to outpace McCarthy. In a poll conducted before the Indiana primary, for instance, McCarthy won college-educated voters by more than two to one—yet Kennedy, powered by blue-collar Irish, Polish, and black votes, beat him overall.

The two men also had different conceptions of America's role in the world. Their positions on Vietnam itself were virtually indistinguishable: Both called for an end to bombing and a coalition government in South Vietnam. But McCarthy's critique went far beyond the war itself. "Vietnam," he said at a rally in Cambridge, Massachusetts, "is part of a much larger question, which is, is America going to police the planet?" In another speech, he blamed the war on "a moral mission"—dating from the 1950s—"in which we took it upon ourselves to judge the political systems of other nations."

"I am not entirely convinced," said McCarthy, "that Senator Kennedy has entirely renounced that misconception." And he was right not to be convinced. McCarthy was foreshadowing the new liberalism that would emerge after 1968—which questioned whether America had much to offer the world. Kennedy, by contrast, pledged in his announcement speech that his campaign would be about "our right to moral leadership of this planet." That right, he was suggesting, was no longer self-evident. But it could still be earned. On June 4, after beating McCarthy in the California primary, Kennedy took the stage at Los Angeles's Ambassador Hotel, and told 1,500 manic, deafening supporters that "We are a great country, an unselfish country, and a compassionate country"—defiant words coming from a liberal in 1968. After finishing his speech, he turned, and exited through the hotel's kitchen, where he was shot three times. Twenty-five hours later, he was dead.

KENNEDY'S DEATH HAD a strange effect on McCarthy. The Minnesota senator, a reluctant, surly candidate to begin with, grew increasingly hostile to the voters he was ostensibly courting, and to his own staff. As his campaign unraveled, the nomination fell to Hubert Humphrey, who used his pull with party leaders to secure a majority of convention delegates without competing in a single primary. It should have been the culmination of Humphrey's glittering career, the capstone of everything he had achieved in the two decades since the Willard Hotel. Instead, he spent the campaign in an ideological straitjacket, reviled by both sides in a country he no longer really understood.

As vice president, Humphrey had endured the special torture Lyndon Johnson reserved for weaker men. The public humiliation had begun even before Humphrey took office. In November 1964, he had publicly suggested that he might help set the administration's education policy. Johnson berated him, then told reporters, "I've just reminded Hubert that I've got his balls in my pocket." When Johnson saw Humphrey cruising the Potomac on a presidential yacht, he announced that in future, his vice president would have to request such privileges from White House aides, in writing.

Once, Humphrey had dared to voice his disagreement—arguing against the administration's fateful 1965 decision to begin bombing North Vietnam. And the consequences were brutal. For more than a year, he was excluded from every aspect of Vietnam policy—every meeting, every delegation, every memo. So great did the stigma grow that other administration officials began avoiding him for fear of being tainted. Humphrey tried to rehabilitate himself by doing what he had done in Atlantic City:

helping Johnson with liberals. But by 1967, the divisions had grown too wide. When Humphrey tried to justify the administration's Vietnam policy in a private meeting with his old ADA colleagues, Schlesinger screamed at him.

On the campaign trail, Humphrey was desperate to distance himself from the war. Twice he requested Johnson's permission to announce his own, more dovish, Vietnam policy. Twice Johnson refused. In September, when Humphrey suggested that the United States might soon bring some troops home, Johnson publicly rebuked him, saying that "no man can predict when that day will come."

All the while, Humphrey was shadowed by antiwar protesters. At a rally in Seattle, a man with a bullhorn yelled, "We have come not to talk with you, Mr. Humphrey. We have come to arrest you." The Democratic convention descended into chaos as thousands of antiwar protesters battled police in the Chicago streets. But if the New Left considered Humphrey a war criminal, Nixon was telling blue-collar whites that Humphrey was the New Left's spineless enabler—a man with "a personal attitude of indulgence and permissiveness toward the lawless." With the country divided against itself, contempt for Hubert Humphrey was the one thing on which left and right could agree.

Finally, on September 30, Humphrey finally broke with Johnson on the war, calling for an unconditional halt to bombing. The next day in Nashville, a sign in the crowd read, "If you mean it, we're with you." With some antiwar liberals returning to the Democratic fold, Humphrey appealed to working-class whites. In speeches and leaflets written by Tom Kahn, he countered Nixon and Wallace's cultural appeals with an economic one—blasting them for supporting policies that hurt the workers they supposedly championed. And labor, Humphrey's old ally, rallied to his cause. By late October, Humphrey had cut Nixon's lead in half. And as the campaign drew to a close, he seemed to gain ground with each passing day. Despite everything, it looked like the liberal coalition might hang together after all.

But in the end, Nixon won by 500,000 votes, less than a single percentage point. Fifteen million Democrats had defected to either Nixon or Wallace. Throughout the 1960s, the left and right had waged a ferocious assault on cold war liberalism—and in 1968, it fell.

THE NEW LIBERALISM that followed retained many of the same domestic principles. But crucially, it no longer connected them to the struggle for freedom around the world. Led by Niebuhr, the cold war liberals had been painfully aware of America's capacity for injustice—it was the critical dividing line between them and the emerging cold war right. But they claimed it was this very recognition, and the restraints it fostered, that made American democracy fundamentally superior to its Communist adversaries. The New Left also saw a clear divide between totalitarianism and freedom. It just flipped it—calling America the totalitarian state and leftist rebels the forces of freedom.

But for many post-Vietnam liberals, the distinctions had lost their meaning. In the wake of Vietnam, it was no longer clear that people in the third world wanted, or needed, "freedom." If anything, they seemed to want revolution, something very different from the American-style democracy John F. Kennedy had pledged to fight for around the world. Totalitarianism, too, seemed to mean less and less. With Stalin gone, the Soviet Union—while still a brutal dictatorship—had drifted further from the totalitarian ideal of absolute state control. And the split between Moscow and Beijing convinced many liberals that it was national interest, not ideology, that motivated U.S. adversaries. As early as 1965, Arkansas senator William Fulbright, perhaps the most influential congressional advocate for the new liberal foreign policy, wrote that the "communism of Eastern Europe and the Soviet Union is slowly being humanized. . . . As it becomes clear to each side [in the cold war] that it is safe and profitable to do so, ideological barriers can be expected gradually to erode away." In 1970, when political scientist Graham Allison interviewed more than 100 elite 25- to 34-year-olds—the best and brightest of their generation—they overwhelmingly agreed that "the distinction between the Communist bloc and the Free World obfuscates more than it illuminates."

Partly, the turn away from anti-Communism reflected a new focus on transnational problems that seemed to transcend the ideological divide. Instability in the newly decolonized third world, argued some liberals, was a problem the superpowers needed to manage together. So was the environment, an emerging focus of liberal concern. And then, of course, there was the threat of nuclear war—a problem that could be mitigated only through superpower negotiation.

But beyond that, liberals abandoned the language of totalitarianism and freedom because they simply no longer believed the United States was a beacon to the world. Here the country's misdeeds in Vietnam fused with its misdeeds at home—its chronic racism, violence, and inequality. Allison would find that his elite young respondents believed "the U.S. government is no more moral—in any simple sense of individual morality—than other governments." In 1967, Fulbright declared that America—rather than the Great Society Johnson had proclaimed—was, in fact, a "sick society." Two years later, Schlesinger would say the country "is undergoing a crisis of self-confidence."

But the country wasn't undergoing a crisis of self-confidence—at least, not to the degree liberals were. Even as they grew disillusioned with Vietnam, most Americans saw the war as a tragic mistake, not as evidence that the United States had little worth teaching the world. The new liberals retained high hopes for government action at home, particularly against racism and poverty. But under Truman, Kennedy, and Johnson, those hopes had been intimately linked to a faith in government action abroad. And once the two were decoupled, liberals no longer seemed to believe in America's potential for greatness. In 1969, social theorist Christopher Lasch applauded the New Left for turning many liberals "from admirers of American democracy into harsh critics." But most Americans remained admirers. And to them, liberals became complicit in the New Left's campaign to demean and destabilize institutions and traditions they still revered.

AS THE 1972 presidential campaign began, cold war liberals still dominated the Democratic field. But they were competing for the same shrinking political terrain. Humphrey ran again, but by this time seemed like the ghost of a more innocent age. Party heavyweights flocked to Maine senator Edmund Muskie, who was identified with neither the antiwar movement nor with the war itself. But Muskie's initial appeal—that he could be all things to all Democrats—ultimately produced a candidacy with no message and no core.

The candidate who most aggressively defended cold war liberalism was Washington senator Henry "Scoop" Jackson, a frugal, morally upright Norwegian American whose personal style seemed as old-fashioned as his politics. Dubbed the "senator from Boeing" for his dogged support of the Seattle-based defense contractor, Jackson was an unapologetic hawk. But he was also a New Deal liberal who had voted for every civil rights bill, helped create Medicare, supported greater antipoverty spending, and introduced landmark legislation protecting the environment.

Jackson turned his campaign into a crusade against what he deemed

liberalism's loss of faith in America. The country, he declared in his announcement speech, was "fed up with people running down America.
This society is not a guilty, imperialistic, and oppressive society. This is not
a sick society. This is a great country . . . that is conscious of its wrongs
and is capable of correcting them." And he excoriated the new liberals
for seeing concern about rising crime as "a code word for racism and
repression." "Until we are prepared to acknowledge that law and order is
a real problem," Jackson declared, "we just won't solve it." Helping craft
this defiant message was his speechwriter, the disillusioned former SDSer
Tom Kahn.

Nixon reportedly saw Jackson as his greatest potential threat. But Jackson had to share his natural base of support, the disaffected white working
class, with George Wallace, who competed in the Florida and Maryland
primaries before being shot and paralyzed on May 15. So once again, cold
war liberalism was undermined from both sides. The left called Jackson a
warmonger and a racist. But his steadfast support for civil rights hurt him
among angry blue-collar Democrats, who flocked to Wallace instead.

With his opponents suffocating each other to his right, South Dakota
senator George McGovern orchestrated the new liberalism's takeover of
the Democratic Party. Like McCarthy's candidacy in 1968, McGovern's
was powered by the antiwar movement. But four years later, that movement had burrowed more deeply into the party apparatus. In 1970,
antiwar liberals had beaten cold war Democrats in primaries across the
country. In Michigan, Washington State, and elsewhere, antiwar activists
had taken over their state parties. By 1969, even the ADA was calling not
merely for negotiations in Vietnam, or a coalition government with the
Communists, but immediate, unconditional withdrawal.

Some of McGovern's top aides came from the antiwar movement,
and they set out, as one explained, "to consolidate the left-wing." The
activists were a little older now, and more politically savvy. As McGovern's
Wisconsin organizer put it, if the foundation of the McCarthy campaign
was students, the foundation of the McGovern campaign was teachers.
And those teachers didn't only protest; they gave money. The antiwar
movement produced a new pool of small donors, who provided McGovern with much of his campaign funds.

McGovern himself was the perfect vehicle for this new liberalism. He
was a rural minister's son and a decorated World War II pilot. Quiet and

reflective, his temperament was anything but radical. Robert Kennedy had called him "the most decent man in the Senate." But from the beginning, he had opposed cold war liberalism. In the audience at the 1948 Progressive Party convention, he would write in his autobiography that "both the domestic health of the nation and the peace of the world would have been better served by the hopeful and compassionate views of [Henry] Wallace than by the 'Get Tough' policy of the Truman administration." He cast grave doubt on America's moral authority in the world, calling Nixon's bombing of Vietnam "the most barbaric action that any country has committed since Hitler's effort to exterminate [the] Jews." And he rejected the ideological categories that had defined liberalism since the Willard Hotel. "The war against Communism is over," he told author Theodore White. "We're entering a new era and the Kennedy challenge of 1960 is pretty hollow now. Somehow we have to settle down and live with them."

WHEN THE DEMOCRATIC Party convened to nominate McGovern in Miami Beach, it looked dramatically different than it had four years before. In the aftermath of 1968, a reform commission—initially chaired by McGovern himself—had passed new rules that prevented local politicians from controlling state delegations, and required that delegations be as diverse as the states they represented.

In principle, greater openness and greater diversity were laudable. But in practice, the reforms disempowered the very people who were deserting the Democratic Party already: working-class whites. Between 1968 and 1972, the percentage of black and female delegates tripled; the percentage of delegates under 30 quadrupled. And as McGovernites replaced blue-collar party regulars in many states, upper-middle-class reformers grew in number as well.

The result was a convention far to the left of the party's voters. The reforms had made the primary process more democratic, but ironically, they had largely cut out elected officials—who understood their constituents far better than the activists who replaced them. Chicago mayor Richard Daley's Cook County slate was rejected as insufficiently diverse, and replaced by one that matched the party's new requirements. But as *Chicago Sun-Times* columnist Mike Royko observed, among the city's fifty-nine "reform" delegates, there was only one Italian and three Poles—and barely

anyone who had won an election. "Anybody who would reform Chicago's
Democratic Party by dropping the white ethnic," Royko quipped, "would
probably begin a diet by shooting himself in the stomach."

In the end, the convention proved a festival of balkanization. The
platform included separate sections on the rights of the poor, Native
Americans, the handicapped, the mentally retarded, the elderly, veterans,
women, and children. A separate plank supported "the right to be different, to maintain a cultural or ethnic heritage or lifestyle, without being forced into a compelled homogeneity." The day after his nomination,
McGovern held a press conference to announce the new chairman of the
Democratic Party, a white woman, and the new vice chairman, a white
man. A black delegate raised his hand and suggested that if a woman was
leading the party, it was only fair that an African American should be vice
chairman. And McGovern quickly agreed.

WHAT BAYARD RUSTIN had understood, and the McGovernites did not,
was that identity politics was a double-edged sword. Once blue-collar whites
perceived that blacks were gaining power on the basis of group rights,
they began making such claims themselves. In a bizarre homage to Black
Power, policemen began wearing "Pigs is Beautiful" shirts. In the words
of historian Stephen Aiello, white ethnics grew bitter that in the "them-
against-us philosophy, defined in the 1960s on a racial basis . . . the blacks
seem to get everything." So they decided: "If black is beautiful, olive is
gorgeous."

Nixon exploited this identity politics backlash masterfully. In 1969,
when the Senate rejected his two Southern nominees to the Supreme
Court, partly because of their past segregationist views, he denounced
"the act of regional discrimination that took place in the Senate yesterday."
With Northern whites, Nixon's efforts to deepen the "black-blue" divide
were assisted by a series of court decisions that ordered white and black
children bused outside their neighborhoods to integrate regional public
schools. And in a particularly devilish twist, the Nixon administration in
1969 announced the "Philadelphia Plan"—a quota system for minorities
in white-dominated, heavily unionized jobs like plumbing and pipe fitting.
Rustin denounced the plan, saying blacks needed job training, not quotas,
which would only "exacerbate the differences between blacks and other
racial and ethnic groups." But exacerbating those differences was exactly
what Nixon had in mind. Years later, former Nixon aide John Ehrlichman

would write that the president took great pleasure "in constructing a political dilemma for the labor union leaders and the civil rights groups."

But if Nixon was shrewdly dividing the Democratic coalition, he also appealed to a common national pride. "It has become fashionable in recent years to point up what is wrong with our . . . American system," he declared, echoing Scoop Jackson. "I totally disagree. I believe in the American system." McGovern, by contrast, sounded to many voters like he saw little in America worth admiring. His central argument—indeed, the central argument of the new liberalism born in 1968—was that to repair itself, the United States needed to retreat from the cold war. As McGovern's campaign slogan put it, the country must "come home." And by 1972, most Americans *did* want to leave Vietnam. But they didn't want to abandon anti-Communism, and U.S. leadership in the world. It wasn't just that anti-Communism connoted national strength. It also connoted national faith, a faith that America stood for something worthy of pride.

That yearning for national greatness linked domestic and foreign affairs. The antitotalitarian liberals had said racial justice would help America defend freedom around the world. But as McGovern turned away from a unifying mission abroad, he also lost the capacity to frame a unifying mission at home. Civil rights, sold by Truman and Kennedy as a way to empower the country as a whole, became in the early 1970s merely a way to empower one group. That group, African Americans, voted for McGovern in 1972. But barely anyone else did. And Nixon was reelected in one of the largest landslides in American history.

IF NIXON BURIED liberalism in 1972, however, he resuscitated it a mere two years later. Most obviously, he boosted liberal fortunes by immolating himself in the Watergate scandal. But just as significantly, he ended the war in Vietnam, established diplomatic ties with China, and ushered in détente with the Soviet Union, alienating himself from the cold war right in the process. These policies, by making the world appear less threatening, helped liberals return from the political dead. Unfortunately, after a tranquil interlude, the cold war would return with a vengeance. And when it did, liberalism's failure to define a unifying mission in the world helped bury it once again.

The 1974 midterm elections, held just three months after Nixon resigned, brought more than fifty new Democrats to Congress. With an average age of only 40, the new generation was dubbed "neoliberals." In many ways, they represented the antiwar movement's further assimilation into the political mainstream. Like the McGovernites, neoliberals were good-government reformers—a useful identity in the wake of Watergate. Like the McGovernites, they drew their strength more from the middle and upper middle class than from working-class whites. And like the Mc-Governites, they kept a wary distance from labor. The tectonic plates that had undergirded American politics since the New Deal were shifting. If civil rights and Vietnam had pushed hawkish, culturally conservative Democrats toward the GOP, they were driving upscale, culturally liberal Republicans in the other direction. And in this strange new landscape, the neoliberals pursued policies, and constructed coalitions, strikingly differ-ent from those that had sustained Democrats in the past. As one member of the 1974 class, Colorado senator and former McGovern campaign man-ager Gary Hart, put it, "We are not a bunch of little Hubert Humphreys."

That was particularly true on foreign policy, where most neoliberals were closer to McGovern than Humphrey. But their new political synthe-sis worked because in the mid-1970s—for the first time since the cold war began—foreign policy was politically secondary. As pollster Burns Roper put it in 1975, the public is "almost oblivious to foreign problems and foreign issues."

It was this same turn inward that led, in 1976, to Georgia governor Jimmy Carter's election as president. Although he didn't come out of the antiwar movement, Carter had much in common with the neoliberals elected two years before. Like them, Carter was high-minded. Personal integrity, encapsulated in his pledge "I will never lie to you," was a critical part of his post-Watergate appeal. And like the neoliberals, Carter be-lieved that dogma—including the traditional liberal faith in larger govern-ment—impeded problem solving, which he saw as an essentially technical exercise. Carter's personal attributes made him particularly attractive. His evangelical faith gave his high-minded reformism a populist tint. His lack of Washington experience—potentially crippling when foreign policy was the primary test for an aspiring president—proved an asset after Water-gate. And both Northerners and many Southerners liked the idea of a pro–civil rights Georgian in the White House, embodying a newly moder-ate, respectable South.

Carter marginalized Arizona congressman Morris Udall and a series of other candidates running to his left. And he had even less trouble on his right, where Scoop Jackson doggedly campaigned on a liberalism that was rapidly ceasing to exist. Jackson attacked Carter for proposing cuts in the defense budget. He trumpeted his opposition to busing. And he proposed more domestic spending—promoting national health care and suggesting that Carter wasn't sufficiently pro-labor. But in every area, the party had moved in the opposite direction: becoming more dovish, more culturally liberal, and more skeptical of big government. Humphrey ran again, which kept Jackson from consolidating labor support. And so did Wallace, who siphoned off votes among the white working class. Once again, a Republican president deemed Jackson his toughest potential opponent. And once again, the Democrats wouldn't give Jackson their nomination.

But this time, a Democrat won anyway. Carter had the good fortune to run against an incumbent saddled by recession. And he tied Ford to the crimes of his disgraced predecessor, referring repeatedly to the "Nixon-Ford" administration. Foreign policy, which had helped sink Humphrey and McGovern, barely figured in the general election campaign. And in a mid-decade lull in the cold war storm, Jimmy Carter narrowly won the presidency.

For liberalism, it would prove a false dawn. Carter's lack of familiarity with Washington, which had helped him in the campaign, left him unable to effectively wield power there. And his technocratic approach to governing never captured the public imagination or identified him with a larger national goal. "He thinks he 'leads' by choosing the correct policy," wrote James Fallows, one of his former speechwriters, "but he fails to project a vision larger than the problem he is tackling at the moment." In some ways, Carter's presidency exposed the hollowness at neoliberalism's core. As the political scientist William Schneider noted in an article about the class of 1974, "instead of ideology, neoliberals have concepts," yet the "higher the office, the more ideology matters."

Nowhere did it matter more than in foreign policy. To the extent Carter tried to define an international vision, it was human rights. Nixon and Henry Kissinger's cold-blooded realpolitik had sanctioned brutal abuses by U.S. allies, including Augusto Pinochet's 1973 coup against a democratic, left-leaning government in Chile. And the United States seemed equally amoral in its dealings with the USSR—an amorality epitomized by Gerald Ford's refusal to meet with acclaimed Soviet writer and dissident Alexander Solzhenitsyn in 1975. Carter capitalized on the growing calls for a more ethical stance. He established a Bureau of Human Rights in the State Department, met with Soviet dissidents, and cut off aid to

Chile and other autocratic governments, particularly in Latin America. "Human rights," Carter declared, "is the soul of our foreign policy."

Human rights collided with anti-Communism—since some of America's strongest cold war allies were harshly repressive. To some degree, however, effective anti-Communism also *required* human rights—since democracies proved better long-term bulwarks against Communism's spread than dictatorships. But whatever chance Carter may have had to construct a new, more human rights–centered anti-Communism was undercut by liberalism's ambivalence about the very concept of anti-Communism. After Vietnam, any American president would have shown new caution in confronting nationalist, anti-American movements in the third world. But it was one thing to recognize the limits of American power and another to celebrate antidemocratic third-world revolutions as a positive good. "There's nothing wrong with their deciding to live under a socialist system," said Andrew Young, Carter's ambassador to the United Nations, about the people of Angola—although they had never elected their Marxist dictatorship, which had taken power with the help of Cuban troops. And in February 1979, he predicted that the Ayatollah Khomeini would be seen as "some kind of saint when we finally get over the panic of what is happening" in Iran—a claim undermined that very month, when Tehran began executing hundreds of political opponents.

If anti-Communism and human rights were difficult enough to reconcile on their own, the task was made even harder by the new liberal focus on nuclear disarmament. Carter extended Nixon's arms control talks, eventually negotiating a second Strategic Arms Limitation Treaty, SALT II. But the Soviets were hardly prepared to bargain over nuclear missiles while Washington hectored them for jailing dissidents. Trying to solve this conundrum, Carter at times implied that human rights was simply another nonideological issue of mutual concern. In his first speech to the UN, he said the United States would "work with potential adversaries as well as our allies to advance the cause of human rights." But human rights *wasn't* an issue of mutual concern. It was fundamentally antithetical to Soviet ideology. Carter couldn't stress this ideological conflict because he needed the Kremlin's help in pursuing the cooperative agenda that had become so important to liberals since Vietnam. As a result, he ended up stressing human rights less in the Soviet bloc than in pro-American autocracies. By 1978, Solzhenitsyn was denouncing Carter officials for showing "anger and inflexibility . . . when dealing with weak government[s]" while being "tongue-tied and paralyzed when they deal with powerful governments" like the USSR.

Finally, Carter didn't realize that whatever moral impact he wanted to have around the world depended on American strength. Secretary of State Cyrus Vance suggested that the United States offer Moscow "positive incentives" for good behavior. And on his first day in office, Carter announced the withdrawal of U.S. nuclear weapons from South Korea, a goodwill gesture he expected would produce reciprocal concessions.

It didn't. Instead, the Soviets accelerated their military buildup, aggressively courted client states across Africa, and deployed fighter planes to Cuba. By December 1979, Carter had reversed course, proposing a 5 percent defense increase and declaring, "we must understand that not every instance of the firm application of power is a potential Vietnam." That same month, the Soviets made their most provocative move yet, sending 85,000 troops into Afghanistan to protect a pro-Kremlin government threatened by Islamic rebels. For the first time, the USSR had sent troops into a country outside the Eastern bloc, and Carter responded by abandoning SALT II, limiting U.S.-Soviet trade, and boycotting the 1980 Olympics in Moscow.

The Afghan invasion proved even more unnerving because less than two months earlier, Iranian militants had taken more than one hundred Americans hostage in retaliation for Carter's decision to let Iran's ousted shah enter the United States for cancer treatment. Together, Afghanistan and the hostage crisis forced national security back onto political center stage. The percentage of Americans saying the government should spend more on defense, which stood at 11 percent in 1973, rose to 56 percent by 1980. And the percentage saying the United States should defend a European ally under Soviet attack jumped from 48 percent in 1975 to 70 percent five years later. The cold war was back, and the mood was ripe for Ronald Reagan.

AT FIRST, THE new focus on national security helped Carter. Polls in November 1979 showed him trailing Ted Kennedy—who would soon challenge him in the Democratic primaries—more than two to one. But when the hostages were seized, Americans rallied around their president. And Kennedy found it hard to attack the commander in chief during a national emergency. Carter defeated him handily in Iowa and went on to reclaim the Democratic nomination.

Carter's advisers thought foreign policy would help him in the general election too. In Reagan, he faced the most right-wing nominee since Goldwater, the culmination of the conservative movement's takeover of the Republican Party. And like Johnson in 1964, Carter tried to paint Reagan as a man too extreme to trust with the nuclear button. The choice in November, Carter said, would "help to decide whether we have war or peace." Facing Reagan in their one debate, Carter mentioned that his young daughter, Amy, considered the threat of nuclear war the greatest challenge confronting the country—a reference that evoked Johnson's legendary 1964 "daisy" ad, which portrayed a young girl counting down to a mushroom cloud.

Reagan's easygoing, avuncular persona made him far harder to demonize than Goldwater. The biggest difference between 1964 and 1980, however, wasn't the personality of the conservative candidate; it was the character of American liberalism. From the beginning, Niebuhr's vision, with its emphasis on American fallibility, had left liberals vulnerable to the charge that they didn't truly believe in their country. But Truman, Kennedy, Johnson, and even Allard Lowenstein had responded by invoking America's potential greatness, if it resisted complacency. By 1980, however, Carter had no more great missions to propose. He had taken office promising personal virtue and the right answers. But many of his answers appeared to have failed. Inflation was even higher than when he took office. America was being threatened and humiliated around the world. And once stripped of its reputation for competence, neoliberalism had nothing left.

Carter had made one bold effort to move beyond wonkery, to define the kind of unifying national purpose that antitotalitarian liberalism once provided. But his infamous July 1979 "malaise" speech hadn't defined such a purpose so much as highlighted its absence. The speech employed that signature post-Vietnam liberal phrase "crisis of confidence." Carter was speaking about the country, but to many Americans, he was speaking about himself and his creed.

Reagan promised what conservatives had been promising since the cold war's dawn: the end of self-doubt. "Pride in our country," he thundered, "seems to be out of fashion." He accused Democrats of having "lost faith in their own country's past and tradition." Even his age, initially considered a liability, evoked an earlier, more confident era. Reagan's most important promise was a return to prosperity. But he also promised a return to the old certainties about America's role in the world. When a reporter asked if he wanted to "bring back the Cold War," Reagan replied, "When did it ever go away?"

Carter also strained to connect to an earlier time. "I'm proud to be a Democrat," he declared in his last rally of the campaign. "I believe in the heritage and mission of Franklin D. Roosevelt. I believe in the heritage and mission of Harry Truman. I believe in the heritage and mission of John Fitzgerald Kennedy. I believe in the heritage and mission of Lyndon Baines Johnson. I believe in the heritage and mission of Hubert Humphrey." But it was just a list of names. No vision linked the liberal present to the liberal past. Carter spent the campaign's final days crisscrossing the country, asking Democrats to "come home." But he could never really explain to what.

IT WAS A massive defeat: A loss of 489 electoral votes, 12 seats in the Senate, and 33 in the House. *Newsweek* called it a "counter-revolution." Utah senator Orrin Hatch said Reagan's victory marked the end of "fifty years of liberal government." *National Review*'s William Rusher declared, "Our old enemy liberalism has died."

For Scoop Jackson, it was a final blow. Reagan, he said, "struck at the very heart of our party—the tradition . . . of a strong and resolute America, leader of the Free World, proud of its greatness." Many of his supporters, dubbed neoconservatives, joined Reagan's administration. But when Reagan aides offered Jackson a cabinet post in return for his presidential endorsement, the old man refused, saying, "I still believe in the New Deal." Three years later, he was dead.

The ADA was now little more than a shell. It "was formed in the forties, as I recall by Mrs. Roosevelt and Hubert Humphrey, in order to prevent the radical left from taking over the Democratic Party," mused New York mayor Ed Koch in 1981. "Now . . . the ADA has *become* the radical left in the Democratic Party. . . . Who cares about ADA? I don't." By the mid-1980s, Schlesinger and Rauh were urging the organization to disband.

Lowenstein had descended into paranoia, obsessed with conspiracy theories about Robert Kennedy's murder, certain that the death that destroyed liberalism must have had deeper, darker roots. Then, in March

1980, Lowenstein himself was assassinated by a deranged former protégé. His ashes were buried at Arlington National Cemetery, halfway between JFK and RFK's graves.

Rustin, who had foreseen the collapse earliest, lived the longest. Depressed, exhausted, and nearly dead from a heart attack in 1971, he had moved away from the civil rights movement, finding solace working with refugees and in the open, loving relationship with another man that America finally allowed. In 1987, at the age of 75, another heart attack killed him.

Rustin's legacy, said former Urban League president Vernon Jordan at his funeral, "not even death can take from us." But it would be many years before a new generation of liberals recaptured that legacy. And even then, it would take a fight.

3

After the Fall

AT FIRST, REAGAN brought liberals together. In his dark shadow, they found unity, and the ideological fissures of the Vietnam years finally began to heal. That was the good news. The bad news was that the new liberal consensus proved intellectually stifling and politically disastrous. The left had reunited in a graveyard. It was only later, when the consensus began to fray, and old divisions took new form, that liberalism's rebirth began.

The standard bearer for this graveyard unity was Carter's vice president, Walter Mondale. Mondale's cold war roots stretched back to the very beginning. As a sophomore at Macalester College in 1947, he had joined the student wing of the ADA and distributed leaflets for Hubert Humphrey's campaign to wrest Minnesota's Democratic-Farmer-Labor Party from the supporters of Henry Wallace. But because he was a generation younger than Humphrey, and less implicated in the policies that led to Vietnam, Mondale adapted to liberalism's changing fashions in a way his mentor never could. In 1968, as Humphrey's emissary to the McCarthy insurgents, Mondale engineered a compromise Vietnam plank that won the support of both camps. Four years later, McGovern's aides sounded out the young senator about a spot on the ticket, which Mondale refused before going home to Minnesota and making sure the McGovernites and their establishment foes didn't rip his beloved DFL apart. Through such efforts, this small-town minister's son proved himself a master conciliator, a man singularly adept at soothing the fractious constituencies that comprised the post-Vietnam Democratic Party.

By the time Mondale ran for president in 1984, conciliating had grown easier because the Democratic Party had grown smaller. Scoop

Jackson's neoconservative offspring, unburdened by his New Deal domestic views, had ensconced themselves in Reagan's coalition. Much of the white South had also joined the GOP. And the labor movement had made peace with the feminists, civil rights activists, and middle-class reformers it battled in 1972, in part because women and minorities constituted a growing share of its shrinking membership. When the AFL-CIO and the now ultra-dovish ADA both endorsed Mondale's candidacy in the primaries, Massachusetts congressman Barney Frank declared: "It's a sign that Democrats have healed the breach of the Vietnam War." And he was right. Unfortunately, they had only deepened their breach with the rest of the country.

If Mondale was the politician who best embodied the new liberal consensus, the foreign policy issue that best embodied it was the nuclear freeze. Few political movements have moved so rapidly from the margins to the center of American public life. In August 1980, when peace groups proposed that a mutual, verifiable halt to the testing, production, and deployment of nuclear weapons be incorporated into the Democratic platform, the proposal was quickly rejected, since it contradicted Jimmy Carter's plan to deploy 572 intermediate-range missiles in Western Europe. But when Reagan took office, the freeze became a liberal crusade. The reason was simple: terror of nuclear war. By 1981, the arms control negotiations that had soothed liberal nerves throughout the 1970s had come to a dead halt with the demise of SALT II. And Reagan quickly made it clear that détente would not be revived anytime soon. Instead, he launched a massive military buildup, plunging superpower relations to their lowest depths since the Cuban missile crisis. As Reagan pushed forward with the missile deployments in Europe, hundreds of thousands marched for peace in London, Amsterdam, and Bonn. The unfortunate tendency of some on the right to suggest that a nuclear war could be fought and won added to the swelling panic. In 1982, Jonathan Schell's *The Fate of the Earth*, which depicted life in a post-nuclear dystopia, reached number three on the *New York Times* best-seller list. The following year, 100 million Americans watched *The Day After*, a network TV movie that brought the same nightmarish vision into their living rooms. In 1983, the nuclear freeze passed the House of Representatives. *Time* declared, "An idea whose moment may have arrived is sweeping the United States."

While the freeze enjoyed broad popular support, at least in theory, it was very much a movement of the left. Vietnam had alienated many liberals from the old cold war categories, prompting a search for new ways of seeing the world. In the 1970s, third-world underdevelopment, human rights, and the environment had all laid their claim. But in the threat of nuclear war, liberals finally found an issue large enough to fill the ideological void. And since the Democratic Party contained fewer Scoop Jacksons and Hubert Humphreys, there was barely anyone left to defend the older view. When the freeze reached the House floor, more than four-fifths of Democrats voted yes. By 1984, it had won the endorsement of seven of the eight Democrats seeking the White House. If the Democratic primaries of 1972 and 1976 had been, in part, struggles over whether anti-Communism remained liberalism's prism for seeing the world, by 1984 that struggle was over. And it was this new consensus that permitted liberals to come together in support of the nuclear freeze.

The problem was that the military threat posed by nuclear weapons was inseparable from the political threat posed by the Soviet Union. And in their understandable fixation with the former, the Mondale liberals missed the connection. As Carter had recognized, the freeze would have prevented the United States from deploying intermediate-range missiles in Western Europe to counter the new Soviet deployments in the Eastern bloc. And in so doing, it would have thrown America's commitment to the defense of its European allies into doubt. When Western European governments asked America to deploy nuclear missiles on their soil, what they were really seeking was a tangible guarantee that the United States would go to war against the Soviet Union to protect London and West Berlin, even at the price of Chicago and New York. Imperiling that guarantee would have imperiled NATO, which was exactly what the Soviets wanted.

If the arms race was your sole focus—and for many liberals in the early 1980s, it was—this was beside the point. U.S. missile deployments seemed to lower the threshold for nuclear war, and given Reagan's apparently cavalier views on the subject, that represented an appalling danger. But from the largely discarded perspective of anti-Communism, the health of NATO mattered enormously. And in retaining this prism, Reagan—for all his sins—was vindicated by history. The "euromissile" struggle represented Moscow's last great political offensive against the West. When NATO held firm, and Reagan launched his military buildup, it strengthened those elements within the Soviet elite who recognized that their dysfunctional social system could no longer compete. The political pressure generated by the freeze movement may have pushed Reagan, by 1984, toward a new appreciation of the virtues of arms control, a shift that left him surprisingly responsive to Mikhail Gorbachev's overtures (far too responsive, in the eyes of much of the right). Still, it was ideological change in the East, not antinuclear sentiment in the West, that played the larger role in easing the nuclear terror of the early 1980s. And because he saw the world through a cold war lens, Reagan glimpsed the potential for that change and took steps to hasten it, while the liberals united against him did not. By Reagan's second term, some liberals had themselves recognized that, and begun to challenge the failed consensus of the Mondale years. But in 1984—when the freeze elicited more applause than virtually any other line in Mondale's presidential announcement speech—that reconsideration was still several years away.

THE LIBERAL CONSENSUS of the early 1980s was not entirely free of friction, but that friction was primarily racial and generational, not ideological. Jesse Jackson's historic 1984 presidential bid sparked exhilaration among African Americans, and taxed the patience of even a master mediator like Mondale, who did not secure Jackson's support until well after the Democratic convention. Equally significant was the generational challenge from Gary Hart, who, in 1984, came to embody that strange new breed called neoliberals who had entered Democratic politics a decade before.

Like many other neoliberals, Hart's political career began as a rebellion against the cold war liberal establishment. At the age of 35, he had run McGovern's guerrilla campaign. Upon winning a Senate seat in the Democratic landslide of 1974, he had famously declared that he and his newly elected comrades "are not a bunch of little Hubert Humphreys." But by 1984, not even Walter Mondale was a little Hubert Humphrey; the cold war liberal establishment was gone. The holdovers from that earlier age—men like Mondale, Ted Kennedy, and House Speaker Tip O'Neill—had long ago internalized the cultural liberalism and foreign policy dovishness that once set McGovern's children apart. The largest remaining ideological difference was on economics, where the neoliberals—in keeping with their white-collar roots—spoke the language of fiscal restraint and capital formation, not economic security and Great Society largesse. But even here, the differences were shrinking. Mondale, the great adapter, sensed the pro-business currents coursing into the party. By the early 1980s, he too was vowing to cut taxes on business, lift onerous government regulations, and provide "free market incentives." And it was he, in his acceptance speech at the 1984 convention, who stuck a fork in tax-and-spend liberalism by proposing a tax hike not to fund social programs but to trim Reagan's deficits.

None of this stopped Hart from savaging Mondale at every turn, accusing him of representing "the old arrangements and special-interest agenda that have locked up our party and this nation for too long." But for all his talk of "new ideas," Hart wasn't proposing an ideological break. Rather than challenge the liberal consensus, he merely rephrased it in technocratic terms. On the arms race, for instance, where Hart had made himself something of an expert, he endorsed the nuclear freeze and denounced Reagan's buildup, just like Mondale—then delved into mind-numbing detail about alternative weapons systems and procurement policies that could improve military efficiency. With Hart gaining momentum after upset victories in New Hampshire, Maine, and Vermont, Mondale defenestrated him during a debate by paraphrasing a popular hamburger commercial. "You know," said the cagey veteran, "when I hear your ideas, I'm reminded of that ad, 'Where's the beef?' " The line haunted Hart, but it was unfair. Like Carter before him, and like many other neoliberals, Hart was a serious student of public policy. He had plenty of worthy proposals for improving government efficiency and management. What he lacked was a vision tying them together.

Mondale didn't have one either. After trying to draft his presidential announcement speech, one of his speechwriters admitted that "we had a hell of a time putting down on paper what this campaign was going to be all about." It was the same problem that had plagued every Democratic presidential nominee since 1968: liberals no longer had a narrative of national greatness that linked America's mission at home and abroad. The traditional domestic vision—government intervention to expand equal opportunity—was now so freighted down with racial baggage that for many whites the very terms *opportunity* and *fairness* had become code for racial redistribution. In foreign policy, the closest thing liberals had to a message was the prevention of nuclear war and another Vietnam. But while Americans clearly wanted neither, the narrative itself didn't convey confidence or national purpose.

Reagan, by contrast, simply updated the classic conservative storyline he had employed four years earlier. Then, he accused Carter of undermining America's faith in itself. Now, he celebrated an America that believed again. With Lee Greenwood's "I'm Proud to Be an American" as his campaign theme song, Reagan declared that the nation had regained its confidence—and from that, peace, prosperity, and morality all flowed. "The era of self-doubt," he proclaimed, "is over." And America seemed to agree.

SOON AFTER REAGAN'S reelection landslide, the Democratic National Committee commissioned an extensive study, consisting of forty-three focus-group sessions in six cities, and a 5,500-person nationwide poll. But when the results came back showing that white voters saw Democrats as craven toward blacks, party chairman Paul Kirk ordered every copy of the study destroyed. It wasn't that Democratic leaders didn't know what ailed them; it was that they didn't want to know.

But the fact that Kirk had to suppress the study showed how fragile the liberal consensus really was. And in January 1985, it finally began to fray. That month, a congressional aide named Al From distributed a memo entitled "Saving the Democratic Party," which attacked the strategy of "making blatant appeals to liberal and minority interest groups in hopes of building a winning coalition where a majority under normal circumstances simply does not exist." In February, ten governors, fourteen senators, and seventeen members of the House announced the formation of the Democratic Leadership Council (DLC), with From and his colleague Will Marshall as its first staffers. The attack on interest groups was not new: neoliberals like Hart had said much the same thing. But while the neoliberals generally ducked contentious cultural and international issues, taking refuge in wonkery, the New Democrats, as they became known, were more willing to wade in troubled waters. To some degree, they had no choice. The neoliberals had a strong following among upscale liberals, the very people who were becoming the party's new base. Many New Democrats, by contrast, hailed from parts of the West, and especially the South, where the party was in free fall. They had to win hawkish, culturally conservative whites; it was a matter of political survival.

Almost immediately, the DLC became a racial lightning rod. Critics dubbed it the "Southern white boys' caucus." Jesse Jackson said the organization was composed of Democrats who "didn't march in the sixties and won't stand up in the eighties." Douglas Wilder, the African American lieutenant governor of Virginia, said the group was making a "demeaning appeal to white Southern males." The DLC's elected officials were disturbed. They fancied themselves representatives of the New South, and they relied on African American support to win. Head-on confrontation, it became clear, was too costly. The DLC softened its rhetoric, dodged divisive racial issues, and recruited African American and female officeholders into its ranks. It kept challenging long-held party orthodoxy, especially on economic policy, where its free-market views clashed with labor. But it also pursued a more indirect approach. Powerful Southern Democrats—angry that their party kept selecting presidential candidates who could not compete in their states—were agitating for a mammoth regional primary, a "Super Tuesday" in which virtually all the Southern states would vote, and thus reassert their influence over the choice of a nominee. This change in process nicely dovetailed with the DLC's desired change in ideology, and the group aggressively pushed it. Instead of serving as the voice of the white South, with all the racial and ideological discomfort that entailed, the DLC would let the South speak for itself. It would be up to aspiring presidential candidates to respond.

WHILE THE DLC tried to entice future presidential contenders to break with the Mondale consensus, a parallel break was emerging on foreign policy. By 1985, Reagan's embrace of arms control had brought the freeze movement to an end. But that merely diverted liberal attention to an equally charged cold war debate—over Central America.

In the 1980s, liberal activists had a slogan: El Salvador is Spanish for Vietnam. The tiny Central American country boasted a reactionary, often brutal government, which was fighting a Marxist, but nationalist, insurgency. And as in Vietnam, the United States seemed to be getting sucked in. Less than two months after taking office, Reagan boosted military aid to the Salvadoran regime and sent in Green Berets to help train government troops. For many liberals, it was a first step toward quagmire. As they had with the Vietcong, the American far left showed sympathy for the Farabundo Marti National Liberation (FMLN) rebels. Most liberals didn't share that sympathy, but they felt the government in San Salvador was no better, and that as in other parts of the third world, Marxist revolution—if not welcome—was neither preventable nor particularly dangerous. The often ugly history of the United States in Latin America gave the debate an even darker cast. Since Vietnam, liberal foreign policy had been defined more by fear of imperialism than fear of totalitarianism. And in El

Salvador, imperialism's shadow seemed all too real. Some congressional Democrats urged cutting off military aid and letting El Salvador sort out its own problems.

Reagan, of course, saw things differently. He described the conflict as a battle between good and evil, ignoring the government-aligned death squads that murdered civilians by the thousands, and even replacing Carter's ambassador to El Salvador for too aggressively promoting human rights. Administration officials dwelled on the insurgency's ties to Cuba and the Soviet bloc, downplaying its local roots. Secretary of State Alexander Haig called the insurgency "a textbook case of indirect armed aggression by Communist powers."

At first glance, it was a classic post-Vietnam debate: liberal anti-imperialism versus conservative antitotalitarianism. But inside Congress, a third stance—liberal *and* antitotalitarian—began to form. A group of Democrats began arguing that while the United States must help avert a Communist takeover in El Salvador, the only way to do so was by fundamentally changing the character of the regime. They proposed conditioning U.S. aid on human rights, land reform, negotiations with the rebels, and free elections. El Salvador, they were suggesting, was more like Greece in the late 1940s than South Vietnam: The rebels did not have a monopoly on nationalist support, and the country was not a colonial fiction. Supporting a flawed government might cost the United States its purity, but if done correctly, it could serve democratic principles in the end.

After initially rejecting the congressional conditions, the White House was eventually forced to swallow a weakened version. And although the Reagan administration manipulated the facts to make sure military aid continued to flow, the criteria accomplished two things. First, they strengthened administration moderates who recognized that the Salvadoran regime needed dramatic reform. Second, they scared the regime into thinking the United States might really cut off aid, leaving it to face the insurgents alone. In December 1983, Vice President George Bush traveled to San Salvador and wielded the congressional criteria like a club. In a speech toasting the country's president, he warned icily that "if these death squad murders continue, you will lose the support of the American people." The following year, El Salvador held a free election, and a centrist, Jose Napoleon Duarte, won on a platform of land reform, reconciliation with the guerrillas, and an end to the violations of human rights. Duarte had trouble asserting control, government abuses continued, and so did the civil war. But another free election followed, and by the early 1990s, aided by the end of the cold war, El Salvador finally achieved stable democracy and peace.

If El Salvador marked a small departure from liberal orthodoxy, a few congressional Democrats went further and applied the same logic in nearby Nicaragua. For many liberals, Jimmy Carter's Nicaragua policy had been the model of an enlightened, post-Vietnam approach to the developing world. Rather than spurning the leftist Sandinista rebels who had overthrown the dictatorship of Anastasio Somoza, Carter had welcomed them to the White House and offered them economic aid, in an effort to strengthen their moderate, democratic elements. Reagan, however, quickly reversed course, ending U.S. assistance on the grounds that the Sandinistas were supporting violent unrest in El Salvador and sending the CIA to help train a group of anti-Communist counterrevolutionaries, the contras, some of whom hailed from Somoza's old regime.

Immediately, liberals and conservatives divided into opposing camps. As in El Salvador, Reagan waxed Manichean about his dubious, right-wing allies, infamously calling the contras the "moral equal of our Founding Fathers." And as in El Salvador, his dreams of military victory left him skeptical about efforts at negotiation. For many liberals, by contrast, the reigning mantra was "U.S. out of Central America." The Sandinistas, in their view, were certainly no worse than the contras. And in any case, they were a homegrown revolution like the Vietcong, which would only grow stronger, more repressive, and more anti-American if Washington played its old imperial role.

The anti-imperialist position didn't require believing that the Sandinistas were benign. But it helped. And among liberals in the mid-1980s, that question provoked heated debate. In 1986, the magazine *Mother Jones* sent a left-leaning journalist named Paul Berman to Nicaragua to investigate the true nature of the Sandinista regime. Berman's article called the Sandinistas Leninists and condemned their human rights abuses and disastrous economic policies. But *Mother Jones*'s new editor, a little-known former alternative weekly editor from Flint, Michigan, named Michael Moore, tried to kill the story, saying it would play into the Reagan administration's hands. It was an old argument. Berman was saying liberals should oppose any denial of freedom. For Moore, liberalism's only struggle was against the right.

Berman was not alone. In early 1985, a young, aggressive DLC member from Oklahoma, Congressman Dave McCurdy, also traveled to Nicaragua. And he too came back "disturbed . . . by evidence of growing Sandinista repression." Like Berman, McCurdy had opposed contra aid. But he began to argue, in contrast to many of his Democratic colleagues, that the United States had the right, even the obligation, to try to prevent the Sandinistas from consolidating their dictatorship. McCurdy, along with DLC Senate heavyweight Sam Nunn, coalesced around what became known as the El Salvador model. They would back nonmilitary aid to the contras, not to help them escalate their guerrilla war, as Reagan wanted, but merely to keep them alive, and thus pressure the Sandinistas to negotiate a path to democracy. Those negotiations, the New Democrats hoped, would be led by Nicaragua's neighbors, with the United States ceding some control in order to foster a process considered legitimate in the region. And they pushed for a regional economic development effort, to show that the United States didn't see Central America as merely a military battleground. Finally, McCurdy and his allies demanded that, as in El Salvador, the United States condition future contra aid on respect for human rights, forcing the rebels to purge former Somoza loyalists from leadership roles.

The strategy bore fruit. The contras stayed alive, and when Costa Rican president Oscar Arias began hammering out a peace plan with the Sandinistas in 1987, he found them a useful bargaining chip. The Nicaraguan regime, in desperate economic straits as the result of U.S. sanctions, abandonment by Moscow, and their own mismanagement, was desperate for the United States to shut off contra aid. Reagan, with his fervent commitment to the rebels, proved an obstacle to negotiations, since Arias's strategy required convincing the Sandinistas that if they held democratic elections, Washington would cut the contras loose. In 1989, however, the more pragmatic George H. W. Bush took office, and when Gorbachev assured his former clients that the United States would abandon the contras in return for a free, internationally supervised election, the Sandinistas agreed. It was a gamble they expected to win. But like autocratic governments before them, they overestimated their public support. And when the results came in, Nicaragua's new president was Violetta de Chamorro, the leader of the nonviolent opposition. Both the Sandinistas and the contras had lost, and a genuine democrat had won.

McCurdy and his allies were only bit players in the Central America dramas of the 1980s. The hopeful turns in El Salvador and Nicaragua were the product of various forces, many of them beyond America's control. But for the evolution of liberal foreign policy, their efforts mattered. Whether they realized it or not, the New Democrats were stumbling toward the synthesis that had eluded Jimmy Carter: a liberal antitotalitarianism for the post-Vietnam world, which prized human rights without taking refuge in morally pure isolationism, promoted liberty without pretending that the threats to liberty came only from the other side, and ceded some U.S. control to gain legitimacy abroad. It was a synthesis that would reappear years later, once the cold war was gone.

ONE SUPPORTER OF nonmilitary aid to the contras hoped to ride this new strain in liberal foreign policy all the way to the White House. As 1988 drew near, the DLC's Super Tuesday strategy seemed to be falling into place. Fourteen Southern states, every one except South Carolina, lined up their presidential primaries or caucuses for the same day, creating an 1,100-delegate bonanza for whichever Democrat could win over Dixie. Initially, Nunn or Virginia governor Charles Robb seemed most likely to reap this harvest. But both declined to run, opening a path for one of the DLC's youngest founders, the 39-year-old senator from Tennessee, Albert Gore Jr.

Gore did his best to execute the game plan. He hewed firmly to the political center, warning that "our nominating process has pushed everyone way over to one side, everyone being afraid of being outflanked on the left." And the centerpiece of that effort was his hawkish line on foreign policy. Gore boasted of his support for the missile deployments in Europe, and his campaign manager denounced the "neo-isolationism that has gripped some parts of the Democratic Party." All this was designed to produce a landslide victory in the South, where Gore had concentrated his resources. But while Gore did well on Super Tuesday, he did not do well enough. And his mediocre finish revealed a flaw in the DLC's plan. Gore was certainly the favored candidate among the culturally traditional, hawkish whites who largely determined the outcome of general elections in the South. But by 1988, so many of those voters had joined the GOP that the Democratic primary electorate was no longer remotely representative of the region as a whole. Gore won five Southern states, but a large African American turnout garnered Jesse Jackson the same number. And

the governor of Massachusetts, Michael Dukakis, won Texas by appealing
to Hispanics (in part with his Spanish-speaking skills) and Florida by woo-
ing transplanted Northern retirees.

In the rest of the country, Gore found even less support. Among Democratic primary voters, most of whom considered Reagan a dangerous
warmonger, Gore's hawkish line held little appeal. If it had caught on
anywhere, it would have been among the blue-collar whites who in years
past had cast primary ballots for Scoop Jackson, Hubert Humphrey, or
even George Wallace. But winning them would have required a populism
that Gore could never muster. An awkward speaker most at home with
the minutiae of arms control and environmental policy, Gore never addressed their racially loaded anxieties about welfare and crime, and he
never spoke to their visceral fears about economic survival. As one critic
put it, "he's been more concerned with elitist issues like population growth
in the next century than . . . gut economic issues." Outside the South,
Gore lost working-class votes to Richard Gephardt, who sparked less light
but more heat with a fiercely protectionist campaign centered on the economic threat from East Asia. And by winning the well-educated, culturally
liberal, dovish voters who had become the Democratic Party's mainstay,
Dukakis cruised to victory. The DLC's strategy had failed.

FIRST ELECTED GOVERNOR in 1974, Dukakis was the ultimate neoliberal, embodying all that was best and worst about the breed. His "Massachusetts miracle," which had turned dying mill towns into high-tech
centers, was a shining testament to the marriage of liberal principles and
market methods. His intellectual home was Harvard's Kennedy School of
Government, where ideology was suspect and quantification was king. His
favored rhetorical technique was the list. Unlike Hart, who had strained
to find a larger theme, and failed, Dukakis barely even tried. He ran as a
manager. "This election," as he famously put it, "is not about ideology,
it's about competence." ABC News anchor Peter Jennings called him "the
smartest clerk in the world."

The Economist likened Dukakis to Jimmy Carter, and the comparison was instructive. Neoliberals often seemed bloodless and aloof, which
left them vulnerable to populist attacks. Carter had escaped that danger
because although he lacked a populist temperament, his small-town,
Southern, evangelical roots gave him a populist veneer. Dukakis, with his
vaguely exotic Greek American heritage and suburban Massachusetts

pedigree, had to generate his populism himself. He needed to forcefully show working-class whites, alienated from the Democratic Party by divisions of culture and race, that he was on their side. And he failed dismally. "Crime," read an early draft of his convention acceptance speech, "is when a seventy-year-old man is attacked and beaten. . . . Crime is *real*. I know, because that seventy-year-old man was my father . . . don't let anyone tell you that the chief executive you're looking at right now is soft on crime." Good lines, but Dukakis never delivered them. In the second presidential debate, when CNN's Bernard Shaw asked Dukakis whether he would support the death penalty for someone who raped and murdered his wife, and Dukakis responded by citing statistics about the Massachusetts crime rate, one journalist in the audience turned to another and announced that the race was over.

Crime bled into foreign policy, raising parallel questions about toughness and moral clarity. In 1976, Carter had had the good fortune to run in the first campaign of the cold war in which national security barely mattered. But in 1988, Dukakis had the misfortune to run in the last one where it still did. Polls showed that with the Soviet threat waning, economic competition had become the public's primary foreign policy concern. For the Dukakis campaign, this was welcome news, and the Massachusetts governor did little to modify his dovish views, which combined liberal anti-interventionism and an idiosyncratic focus on international law. In his acceptance speech, Dukakis devoted only a few sentences to defense.

But the governor's advisers had missed something. While Americans told pollsters they felt more threatened by Japanese cars than Soviet missiles, many also said they could not support a candidate who seemed weak on defense. As one public opinion expert explained, national security retained "a sort of veto power." Late in the campaign, Dukakis's opponent, Vice President George H. W. Bush, ran a flurry of ads attacking him as soft on foreign policy, crime, and patriotism. Bush could not match the positive narrative that Reagan had presented four years earlier. But by weaving together a series of emotionally laden images—Dukakis looking goofy in a tank, Dukakis furloughing convicted murderers, Dukakis vetoing a bill mandating the pledge of allegiance—his campaign brilliantly evoked the right's old line of attack: that liberals would not defend America from its enemies, at home or abroad, because they did not truly *believe* in America. Republicans spread rumors that Dukakis's wife had burned a flag. New Jersey governor Tom Kean accused the Democrats of altering the shades of red, white, and blue on their convention podium so they no longer matched Old Glory. Secretary of Education William Bennett said people in Dukakis's "Brookline-Cambridge world . . . have disdain for the simple and basic patriotism of most Americans." To win a presidential election when Americans still felt scared, liberals needed more than a narrative of national strength; they needed a narrative of national faith. And that was far more than the decent, capable, technocrat from Massachusetts could provide.

IF MONDALE'S LOSS had strained the liberal consensus, Dukakis's tore it apart. Ideological problems, the DLC had learned, could not be solved by changes in process. And so it turned to a more frontal approach. At its annual conference in March 1989, a political theorist and Democratic operative named William Galston gave a speech that would later become the essay "The Politics of Evasion." Galston endorsed the neoliberal turn in Democratic Party economics, but warned that it was not nearly enough. The "American people," Galston and coauthor Elaine Kamarck argued, "do not respond to a progressive economic message, even when Democrats try to offer it, because the party's presidential candidates fail to win their confidence in other key areas such as defense, foreign policy, and social values." Galston and Kamarck avoided policy details, but on crime, welfare, and military force they were proposing the very heresies that the liberal consensus was designed to suppress.

Unsurprisingly, the speech provoked a furor. The panel convened to discuss its findings turned nasty, with Charles Robb and Jesse Jackson screaming at one another as the cameras rolled. But this time, the DLC didn't duck the fight. Instead, it formed a think tank, the Progressive Policy Institute (PPI), to build on Galston and Kamarck's work. Over the next two years, PPI laid the groundwork for the most important shift in liberal thinking since the McGovern campaign. It continued the neoliberal project of using market mechanisms, rather than new bureaucracies, to achieve traditional liberal goals. But the New Democrats also looked for ways to bridge the cultural divide separating liberals from the white working and middle class. To show that the party could be trusted to protect against crime, PPI proposed more police, waiting periods for the sale of handguns, and boot camps for young offenders. To show that Democrats wanted to strengthen the traditional family, not undermine it, PPI called for government-mandated family leave, a larger tax exemption for children, and the requirement that welfare recipients find work. And to show that Democrats believed in national unity, not separatism, PPI criticized racial quotas and proposed a program of national service. Most importantly, the proposals reflected a larger vision, which the DLC called "a new politics of reciprocal responsibility." Government would offer citizens greater opportunity, not guarantees of any particular outcome. And to receive government's help, citizens would have to take responsibility themselves. Unlike the neoliberals, the New Democrats were not merely arguing that government action could be efficient. They were arguing that it could be moral.

It was a powerful message, but it was a message about government's relationship to society, not America's relationship to the world. In the mid-1980s, the New Democrats had been more aggressively anti-Communist than other liberals, and more supportive of military spending. But by 1989, when the DLC made its ideological break, anti-Communism was becoming irrelevant and even Republicans were cutting defense. What the Dukakis campaign had sensed prematurely—that the debate over geopolitics was giving way to a debate over geoeconomics—was now indisputable. As a result, much of the DLC's foreign policy work focused on globalization: how America could achieve economic growth and social justice in an increasingly interdependent world. How America should respond to the security challenges of a post–cold war world, by contrast, remained unclear.

Nothing highlighted this confusion more graphically than Saddam Hussein's August 1990 invasion of Kuwait. As President Bush began massing American forces in the Saudi desert, Vietnam once again framed the public debate. For the left, which made its slogan "No Blood for Oil," U.S. economic motives in the Gulf gave the conflict a blatantly imperialistic cast. For mainstream liberals, the problem was less American imperialism than American casualties. Few rejected the administrations right to intervene: after all, Saddam had swallowed a sovereign nation, and given his quasi-fascist tendencies, he was a highly unsympathetic spokesman for the third world. But justified or not, most liberals still thought war would prove too costly, so they urged the Bush administration to rely on sanctions instead.

A few liberals broke ranks and argued that military action was not only justified but wise—that both politically and militarily, the Gulf bore little resemblance to Southeast Asia. "If Democrats are not prepared to support the use of force in a situation like this," wrote New York congressman Stephen Solarz, "when the aggression is so unambiguous, the international community so cohesive, and the stakes so great, how can anyone ever expect the Democratic Party to support the use of force in defense of vital American interests." New Democrats, however, could not unite behind Solarz's position. The DLC's most influential foreign policy thinker was Sam Nunn, who enjoyed enormous prestige in part because of his close ties to the military. But the military feared another Vietnam as well, and following its lead, Nunn came out in opposition. In so doing, he gave other Democrats hawkish cover for a dovish vote.

As it turned out, the fears were misplaced and the war proved a resounding success. For liberals, it taught three critical lessons. The first was that the U.S. military was capable of destroying its enemies while sustaining few casualties. The second was that voting against a popular war could be political suicide. In the eyes of many observers, Nunn's opposition cost him his chance at the White House, while Al Gore and Joe Lieberman, two of the ten Senate Democrats who voted yes, were each later named to national tickets. Finally, for many liberals, the Gulf War—with its broad international coalition and UN mandate—reaffirmed the virtues of multilateralism. It became the standard against which future coalitions were judged. The only problem with learning from the Gulf War was that it was such an unusual case. As the 1990s progressed, it grew increasingly clear that cross-border aggression was not a harbinger of the future but a relic of the past. Liberals still lacked a clear foreign policy vision, and it was difficult to extrapolate one from a set of circumstances so unlikely to reoccur.

IF FOREIGN POLICY had been America's criterion for choosing a president in 1992, it would not have chosen Bill Clinton, a man with no national security experience who had avoided service in Vietnam. His opponent, by contrast, was a war hero president who had presided over the Soviet Union's collapse and led the United States to its greatest military victory in a half-century. When Clinton's alleged draft-dodging hit the press, Nebraska senator Bob Kerrey, perhaps remembering what George Bush had done to Michael Dukakis, said, "Bill Clinton should not be the nominee of our party because he will not win in November." He would "be opened up like a soft peanut" on the question of national security.

But Bob Kerrey was wrong, because in 1992, for the first time since 1976, national security barely mattered. In 1988, almost 25 percent of the public had told pollsters that foreign policy was the most important problem facing the country. Four years later, with the Gulf War finished and the cold war gone, the percentage was almost zero. In 1988, according to Democratic pollster John Martilla, the Soviet threat remained "the gateway through which all aspiring national American politicians must pass." By the early 1990s, Americans were telling pollsters that the country's greatest foreign threat was illegal drugs.

In 1988, Al Gore had planned an entire primary campaign around national security. In the 1992 primary, by contrast, national security hardly came up. Instead, it became a referendum on neoliberal economics. In April 1989, Al From had traveled to Little Rock, Arkansas, to offer then-Governor Clinton a deal. If he assumed the chairmanship of the DLC, the organization would provide him with staff, funding, and ideas that he could use in a presidential bid. After some delay, Clinton accepted and began touring the country, developing New Democratic themes. Chunks of his October 1991 presidential announcement speech, in which he promised to "provide more opportunity, insist on more responsibility, and create a greater sense of community," closely echoed DLC literature—which was not surprising given that the organization's Bruce Reed had helped author it.

But the 1992 race didn't develop as Clinton and the DLC had planned. They had expected to run against New York governor Mario Cuomo, a fiercely eloquent tax-and-spend liberal and a man who had attacked the DLC for its "implicit position that we have something we have to apologize for." Instead, Cuomo decided not to run, and Clinton found that his most formidable opponent was yet another neoliberal—and a Greek American from Massachusetts to boot—Senator Paul Tsongas. Tsongas was perhaps the most fiscally conservative candidate to seriously contest a Democratic presidential nomination in the late twentieth century. He had written a book urging Democrats to be more pro-business and declared, "I think government has a deadening impact." He proposed a tax credit for business investment and Medicare cuts to reduce the budget deficit. It was a testament to the party's changing class structure that he garnered any significant support at all.

On economics, of course, New Democrats and neoliberals had much in common. But running against Tsongas, Clinton offered a very different economic critique than he would have against Cuomo. He called Tsongas a "soulless economic mechanic" whose proposals "smack of trickle-down economics." He implied that Tsongas was anti–Social Security and attacked him as antilabor, even though the DLC itself was not terribly fond of labor unions. And he contrasted his call for a middle-class tax cut with Tsongas's proposal to reduce taxes on business, saying "we cannot put off fairness under the guise of promoting growth."

It was a shrewd strategy. Clinton's economic populism helped him win the working-class voters who had spurned Gore four years earlier. But he also won them because, unlike Gore, he aggressively pursued the DLC's cultural agenda, taking dramatic steps to inoculate himself on the toxic, interconnected, issues of race, welfare, and crime. Like no presidential contender since Robert Kennedy in 1968, Clinton stepped self-consciously into the breach separating blacks and the white working class. Like Kennedy, he was blessed with a deep, natural rapport with African Americans, the product of his Arkansas Baptist upbringing and his genuine commitment to civil rights. Like Kennedy, he could be ruthless, flying through the night to Little Rock weeks before the New Hampshire primary to sign the death warrant for a mentally impaired murderer. And like Kennedy at his best, he delivered the same message on both sides of the racial divide. In an echo of Kennedy's famed campaign in Gary, Indiana, Clinton traveled to Macomb County, Michigan, the quintessential backlash suburb, where Democratic pollster Stanley Greenberg had found that "virtually all progressive symbols and themes have been redefined in racial and pejorative terms." Addressing a virtually all-white crowd, he declared, "I do not believe we have any hope of doing what we have to do in America unless we come together across racial lines." The next morning, he went to Pleasant Grove Baptist Church in Detroit and asked its black congregants to "tell the people of Macomb County, 'If you'll give up your race feelings, we'll say we want empowerment, not entitlement, we want opportunity, but we accept responsibility.' " Both audiences erupted in cheers.

BY JUNE, WHEN Clinton accepted his party's nomination, he had altered the domestic face of American liberalism. "The party platform," commented the New York Times, "has whole sections that would have been hooted down not too many years ago." Rather than choosing a representative of the old consensus, Clinton chose Gore, another Southerner with roots in the DLC. "They're a new generation of Democrats, Bill Clinton and Al Gore," announced a campaign commercial. "And they don't think the way the old Democratic Party did. They've called for an end to welfare as we know it, so welfare can be a second chance, not a way of life.

They've sent a strong signal to criminals by supporting the death penalty. And they've rejected the old tax-and-spend politics."

As he had with Tsongas, Clinton slammed Bush for his supposed indifference to the economic struggles of average Americans. And Bush did his best to validate the charge, becoming defensive and incoherent when a questioner in the second debate asked how the budget deficit personally affected him, and stumbling when asked the cost of a gallon of milk. By taking race off the table and convincing voters that government would not provide something for nothing, Clinton had made possible a return to that most classic of Democratic themes: Republicans don't care about working people. It was the great irony of the New Democrat project: by committing heresy against the liberal faith, they had given that faith new life.

But critically, this revival was taking place at a moment when Americans had turned away from the world beyond their shores. In 1988, Dukakis had acted as if the cold war was over, but in 1992, Bush didn't grasp that it really was. One of his ads showed fighter planes taking off while he said, "To win the peace, we must be a military superpower." Another asked, "In a world where we're just one unknown dictator away from the next major crisis, who do you trust?" A third went after Clinton's lack of service in Vietnam, declaring, "The question then was avoiding the draft. Now, for Bill Clinton, it's a question of avoiding the truth."

This was exactly what Bob Kerrey had feared. But Bush's national security attacks fell flat, and that changed the entire dynamic of the campaign. For decades, Republicans had linked threats at home and threats abroad to convince blue-collar whites that Democrats didn't love America enough to defend it. In 1992, however, with one-half of the equation gone, the entire formula collapsed. Assisted by Ross Perot's third-party candidacy, which siphoned off downscale Republican voters, Clinton beat Bush two to one among Reagan Democrats; he won a plurality of the white working class; he even won veterans. After the election, a Bush strategist recounted his effort to whip up members of a focus group by telling them that while evading the draft, Clinton had said he "loath[ed] the military." The focus group disapproved, he remembered. "But in the end that didn't matter much to them. We couldn't make it as salient as the economy. That's what it came down to."

IN HIS FIRST two years in office, Clinton governed as he had campaigned: on domestic issues. "Foreign policy is not what I came here to do," complained the new president in April 1993. "Don't take too much of his time," his chief of staff warned his national security adviser. The major exception was globalization. Clinton pressured Japan to lower its trade barriers. He pushed the North American Free Trade Agreement through Congress over the objections of Ralph Nader, some environmental groups, and the AFL-CIO. And he convinced Congress to ratify a global accord reducing tariffs and creating the World Trade Organization. In so doing, Clinton fostered an angry new debate among liberals about the merits of a more economically interconnected world. But it was a debate he shaped and even relished—since it was deeply interwoven with the domestic economic themes on which he had run for president.

Issues of war and peace, by contrast, were an unwelcome intrusion. During the campaign, Clinton had argued that, with the cold war over, America's mission was to spread democracy, a doctrine his national security adviser later called "democratic enlargement." But the methods for this enlargement were vague, and at times, Clinton officials seemed to imply that democracy would spread naturally, powered by economic integration and technological change.

This offered little guidance for dealing with the messy third-world crises that Clinton confronted almost immediately. And the new president dealt with them belatedly, and usually not well. In his final days in office, George Bush had sent American troops into Somalia, where they saved countless lives by securing the Mogadishu port so humanitarian groups could distribute food. But the mission gradually expanded, and in October 1993, an ill-conceived raid on a Somali warlord left eighteen Army Rangers dead. Cameras recorded an American pilot's naked body being dragged through the streets. With no good options, Clinton pulled out. But he had sent a dangerously weak message. The same month the Rangers were killed, the United States and Canada sent 200 lightly armed peacekeepers to Haiti to help restore order in the wake of a coup that had deposed elected president Jean-Bertrand Aristide. As they approached shore, they encountered a mob wielding machetes and shouting, "We are going to make this another Somalia!" The American warship turned around and returned home. Clinton's secretaries of defense and state offered to resign. The press began murmuring about the second coming of Jimmy Carter.

The nadir came in the spring of 1994, when the Clintonites—still spooked by Somalia—sat on their hands and watched genocide unfold in Rwanda. At first, they seemed prepared to tolerate it in the Balkans as well. During the 1992 campaign, Clinton had pledged military action to stop the slaughter in Bosnia, the tiny country that had broken away from Yugoslavia, only to be dismembered by its larger Serbian neighbor, while an international arms embargo denied it the means to fight back. And less than four months after taking office, he dispatched Secretary of State Warren Christopher to convince the Europeans to lift the embargo and launch air strikes against the Serbs, thus giving Bosnia a chance at life. But Clinton was barely convinced himself, and when the Europeans rejected the plan, he seemed almost relieved. As months turned to years, the Clintonites squabbled and dithered. Aides began telling the press that the president was chronically indecisive. French president Jacques Chirac returned from a trip to Washington declaring that the job of leader of the free world was vacant.

Finally in 1995, the fog began to lift. The Clinton administration averted its eyes as Croatia flouted the arms embargo and assaulted Serb forces. In July, the Serbs committed their greatest atrocity yet, massacring almost 8,000 boys and men in the town of Srebrenica. The next month, NATO finally launched the air strikes that Clinton had promised three years earlier. With the balance of power shifting on the ground, the United States muscled the parties into accepting a partition plan, which NATO enforced with 60,000 troops.

When Clinton ran for reelection the following year, none of this much mattered; foreign policy was still politically irrelevant. At Clinton's second debate with Republican Robert Dole, moderator Jim Lehrer had to practically beg the audience to ask a foreign policy question. But to many liberal intellectuals and politicians, Bosnia did matter. In fact, it was a revelation. On Central America, a few congressional Democrats had decided that not every third-world intervention was Vietnam. In the Gulf War, the party had learned the awesome power of the American military, and the political risk of betting against it. On Bosnia, however, the shift became visceral. Serbian nationalism—racist, bloodthirsty, and white—was one variety for which liberals felt no sympathy. America's motives were also different: This time, it wasn't securing oil—it was preventing genocide. Finally, there was little immediate danger to American troops, since the war was being fought from the air. Paul Berman, the writer who had clashed with Michael Moore on Nicaragua, spoke for an entire category of liberals: "We who used to be the party of anti-intervention (because we were anti-imperialists)," he declared, "should now become, in the case of various dictators and genocidal situations, the party of intervention (because we are democrats)." It wasn't exactly liberal antitotalitarianism, since America's Balkan foes didn't merit the name. But the spirit was similar and the change was real.

IN HIS SECOND term, Clinton's foreign policy grew more decisive and more hawkish—with one of the loudest proponents of military action in Bosnia, Madeleine Albright, replacing Christopher as secretary of state. With Bosnia finally quiet, Serbia's murderous leader, Slobodan Milosevic, turned his attention to the independence-minded province of Kosovo, whose autonomy he had revoked several years earlier. In early 1999, with the province on the verge of ethnic war, Albright convened the two parties in the French city of Rambouillet. The Kosovars agreed to a peace deal, to be enforced by NATO. But Milosevic refused, and moved 40,000 troops to the Kosovo border. This time, the Clintonites did not delay. For seventy-eight days, while the Serbs cleansed Kosovo of ethnic Albanians, NATO bombed; until the Serbs finally gave up, and the Kosovar Albanians began returning home.

As the bombs fell, a new liberal foreign policy vision finally began to take shape. In April, Clinton's ally, British prime minister Tony Blair, traveled to Chicago to outline what he called "a new doctrine of international community." Blair, whose New Labour Party worked closely with the DLC, began with a familiar New Democrat theme: globalization. Just a year before, the East Asian financial crisis had exposed the frightening fragility of a world economic system in which capital was so mobile that it could bankrupt whole nations virtually overnight. Blair proposed a new financial architecture to stabilize the global economy, just as the Allied powers did at Bretton Woods in the final days of World War II. He urged a new push for free trade and for the relief of third-world debt, to promote global economic development. And arguing that environmental problems had also grown too large for any one government to manage, he called for dramatic new efforts to combat global warming.

But the most striking part of Blair's speech was its discussion of military force. "The principles of international community apply also to international security," he argued. "When oppression produces massive flows of refugees which unsettle neighboring countries, then they can properly be described as 'threats to international peace and security.' " Kosovo, in other words, was just the beginning. The world's advanced democracies would intervene—and violate national sovereignty—to stop a government's domestic brutality from destabilizing other countries. But just as in the economic and environmental spheres, they would do so together, through powerful new international institutions. "Any new rules," for military intervention, Blair argued, "will only work if we have reformed international institutions with which to apply them." Bill Clinton echoed the argument. "What are the consequences to our security of letting conflicts fester and spread?" he asked at a speech that year in San Francisco. The "real challenge of foreign policy is to deal with problems before they harm our national interests."

Clinton and Blair were reconciling themselves to military force. But like the antitotalitarian liberals of the early cold war, they were also trying to marry force to international legitimacy. The post–cold war world, it turned out, harbored a basic contradiction. Since one country's pathologies spread ever more rapidly beyond its borders, a globalized world required greater violations of national sovereignty. Yet given the extraordinary power disparity between the United States and every other nation, if America assigned itself the right to intervene in countries that posed no immediate threat, it would breed deep fear and resentment, no matter how high-minded its stated motives. Ironically, then, the more proactive the United States wanted to be, the stronger international institutions had to become. "The best way to advance our interests without provoking anti-American coalitions," wrote Progressive Policy Institute president Will Marshall in 2000, "is to work through thickening networks of alliances, international institutions, and rule-based regimes that promote global cooperation. It's time to drop breast-beating rhetoric about being the world's 'sole superpower' and instead think of ourselves as 'first among equals,' willing to play by the same rules we hold others to." Through their interest in globalization, the Clintonites were rediscovering Niebuhr's core insight: that America should not fall in love with the supposed purity of its intentions. Rather than blaming other countries for fearing that America might be corrupted by its overwhelming power, America should fear that corruption itself. And it should guard against it by giving other democracies a voice in its decisions, as it did at the dawn of the cold war. In that way, by restraining American power, and thus preserving American legitimacy, the United States could wield more influence than if it made freedom of action its overriding concern.

As the Clinton administration wound to a close, this post-Kosovo vision looked like it might endure. To be sure, Clinton and Blair stood by meekly in the fall of 1999 as Russia's Boris Yeltsin launched a brutal second war in Chechnya—underscoring the blunt reality that for large, powerful states, sovereignty was as inviolate as ever. Yet in September, after the Indonesian military responded to East Timor's vote for independence with a massive slaughter, the United States pressured Jakarta to accept an Australian-led peacekeeping force. Clinton even sent American troops to help with transportation and logistics. And the following year, UN Secretary-General Kofi Annan endorsed a report challenging the international body's long-standing defense of near-absolute state sovereignty. Instead, paralleling Blair's speech in Chicago, the report argued that when a state failed its minimum obligations to protect its people, the international community could step in. And it urged the UN Security Council to reform itself to make such action easier.

The Democratic Party also seemed to be picking up where Clinton left off. In 2000, it nominated Al Gore and Joe Lieberman, aggressive advocates of military action in the Balkans, and among the few Senate Democrats to have backed the Gulf War. In his first major foreign policy address of the campaign, Gore declared that "we are now in a global age . . . when our destinies and the destinies of billions of people around the globe are increasingly intertwined." His response was something he called "forward engagement," an effort to "address problems early in their development before they become crises, addressing them as close to the source of the problem as possible." The implications for international intervention were clear. And Gore argued that "to meet these challenges requires co-operation on a scale not seen before."

With a new liberal vision emerging, and conservatives confused and divided about their own post–cold war views, something intriguing began to happen: old, internecine rifts reappeared on the left. "Many in the Administration view the NATO war on Yugoslavia as the basis of . . . a new international military order," warned an editorial in *The Nation*. And they were right. Clinton had taken office assuming that U.S. interventions would go through the Security Council. But finding that too constraining, he had waged war in Kosovo with only NATO support, a model he clearly envisioned for the future. "The UN," lamented *The Nation*, "remains gravely, if not mortally, wounded."

For the Clintonites, conditioning U.S. intervention on Security Council approval had proved a recipe for inaction. But for their critics on the left, that was partly the point. Instead of a new era of military intervention, they hoped the post–cold war world would allow the United States to retreat from the global commitments it had amassed over the previous fifty years. The Clintonites prided themselves on their multilateralism. But as one *Nation* article put it, the *"real* debate about U.S. foreign policy . . . revolves not around how to administer the Pax Americana but whether there should be a Pax Americana at all." Michael Moore, now a famed documentary filmmaker, wrote during Kosovo that "Clinton and his disgusting, hypocritical fellow Democrats who support him in this war" had proved "there is little difference between the Democrats and the usually war-loving Republicans." From the perspective of the anti-imperialist left, Democrats didn't only resemble Republicans because they supported the use of force. They resembled Republicans because they wanted to preserve American primacy in the world.

With President Clinton being impeached, the public turned inward, and America on the verge of its strangest election in modern history, the post-Kosovo debate didn't attract widespread notice. But it mattered more than people at the time realized. The post-Vietnam liberal consensus had fractured, giving way to a new vision, and a new critique of that vision, each with roots in the cold war. Twenty-five years after the fall of Saigon, and fifty years after the meeting at the Willard Hotel, liberals were again divided over the purpose of American power. And although no one knew it, the purpose of American power was about to become the central issue of a new age.

4

Qutb's Children

HISTORY DOES NOT record whether Sayyid Qutb ever visited the Willard Hotel. But it's possible. In early 1949, the father of salafist totalitarianism lived just a few miles from the place antitotalitarian liberalism was born. To be sure, Qutb wasn't yet the father of anything in 1949. He was a lonely 42-year-old bureaucrat, on his first trip outside Egypt, visiting a country he couldn't stand.

Qutb's bosses in Egypt's Ministry of Education had sent him to the United States to cure his hatred of the West, a hatred at odds with Egypt's Western-oriented educational reforms. But instead, the trip merely deepened Qutb's loathing. Problems began on the transatlantic voyage, when a drunk, scantily clad woman showed up at Qutb's cabin, scandalizing the devout bachelor. Things got worse when the boat disembarked in New York, a city Qutb found "noisy," "clamorous," and spiritually empty. New Yorkers, he later wrote, were as aimless as their city's pigeons. By the time Qutb reached Washington, where he studied English at a teacher's college, he was filling his letters back home with grotesque descriptions of the people around him. From Washington he traveled to Colorado and California, where he grew even more certain that Americans suffered from a "deformity" of the soul. In August 1950, Qutb sailed back to Egypt, where his disgust helped spawn a political theory that would change the world.

Soon after his return, Qutb joined the Muslim Brotherhood, which for over two decades had been agitating for a government ruled by sharia, or Islamic law. The Brotherhood had criticized Egypt's King Farouk, whom it deemed a puppet of the country's former colonial masters, the British, who still garrisoned troops on Egyptian soil. And in 1952 it cheered the army coup that eventually brought Lieutenant Colonel Gamal Abdel Nasser to power.

But it soon became clear that while Nasser's secular government wanted to rid Egypt of the West's political influence, it was quite comfortable with its cultural influence. Disillusioned, Qutb and the Brotherhood became increasingly vocal critics of the new regime. Finally, in 1954, a Brotherhood member tried to assassinate Nasser. In retaliation, Nasser arrested some Brotherhood leaders, executed others, and burned the organization's headquarters to the ground. Qutb was sentenced to twenty-five years in Tura prison, south of Cairo, where he was brutally tortured. One day in June 1957, a group of Brotherhood inmates locked themselves in their cells, refusing to carry out their daily regiment of breaking rocks. Guards broke into the cells, and murdered twenty-one of them.

Qutb observed such events from the prison infirmary, where he battled consumption, and wrote. In late 1964, he was briefly released, before being rearrested several months later on charges of conspiracy. After a show trial marked by confessions elicited through torture, Qutb was sentenced to death. At dawn on August 29, 1966, he was hanged.

But Qutb's ideas lived on. From jail he authored two books, *Signposts* and *In the Shade of the Koran*, which became best sellers across the Muslim world. In them, he took the Brotherhood's ideology in an innovative, chilling direction. He began with the concept of *jahiliyya*, which denotes the ignorance, or barbarism, that reigned in Arabia before the Prophet Muhammad's birth. But he broadened the idea. "*Jahiliyya*," he wrote, "is not just a specific historical period . . . but a state of affairs." Qutb's experience in soulless America had convinced him that this state of affairs was alive and well in the non-Islamic world. But he went even further than that. Since *jahiliyya* signified "subservience to man rather than to Allah," he wrote, it described *any* society that ignored God's law—including Muslim societies ruled by principles other than sharia.

By God's law, Qutb meant something specific. The only true Islam, he argued, was the kind practiced by Muhammad and his companions, the *salafs*. They had swept away the barbarism of their time, but in the many centuries since, new forms of barbarism—masquerading as Islam—had taken root. Qutb's goal was purification—to strip away the layers of false Islam that encrusted the true faith.

That, in itself, was not a new idea. Since the nineteenth century, salafists had been calling for a return to the pure Islam of the Prophet. But they had done so through peaceful exhortation and missionary work—seeing Muslim leaders as stray sheep to be gently guided on the correct path. Even the Muslim Brotherhood had only sporadically opposed the Egyptian state. Qutb, however, sitting in his prison infirmary, did not see his jailors as benign or open to persuasion. "Those who have usurped the authority of God and are oppressing God's creatures are not going to give up their power merely through preaching," he insisted. He imagined a new kind of salafist, a warrior vanguard that would launch a holy war, or *jihad*, against "the kingdom of man to establish the kingdom of heaven on earth." It was for this future vanguard that Qutb wrote. "Brother," he instructed, "push ahead, for your path is soaked in blood. Do not turn your head right or left but look only up to heaven."

One such brother was a young Saudi named Osama bin Laden. In the mid-1950s, when Nasser outlawed the Muslim Brotherhood, many of its leaders escaped to Saudi Arabia. Oil was making the Saudis rich, but they badly needed teachers for their largely illiterate population. They also feared Nasser's secular Arab nationalism, which was capturing the imagination of many young Arabs and threatening Riyadh's influence in the Middle East. The erudite Egyptian refugees seemed like a perfect fit. After all, Saudi Arabia traced its roots to an eighteenth-century reformer named Muhammad ibn Abd al-Wahhab, who like Qutb had demanded a return to the Islam of Muhammad's time. The Saudi royals thought their kingdom embodied the moral and spiritual purity for which Qutb and his comrades yearned. That assumption, it would turn out, was deeply naïve.

By the time Bin Laden enrolled at Jidda's King Abdul Aziz University in 1975, Egyptian scholars were well ensconced in the Gulf. Among them was Sayyid Qutb's younger brother Muhammad, who used his perch at Abdul Aziz to publish, distribute, and explicate his brother's works. Bin Laden studied economics and public administration, a logical choice given that his family ran one of the great business empires of the Middle East. But he gravitated toward the salafists—both Muhammad Qutb, and a fiery, powerfully built Palestinian named Abdullah Azzam.

Born in Jenin, Azzam had received his doctorate in Egypt, where he befriended the Qutb family and a blind cleric named Omar Abdel Rahman, who would later inspire the first World Trade Center bombing. From Egypt, Azzam went to Jordan, where he taught Islamic law until his radical views cost him his job. In 1978, he moved to Abdul Aziz, where he taught Osama bin Laden.

Bin Laden's father had died when he was still a child, and one of his biographers describes his relationship with Azzam as "part mentor/disciple, part father/son." Like Sayyid Qutb, Azzam believed that only violent struggle would restore true Islam. And in December 1979, when the Soviet Union invaded Afghanistan, he saw the perfect opportunity to begin the fight.

If the Soviet invasion reignited the cold war—and helped bury Jimmy Carter—it also turned Qutb and Azzam's new jihadist salafism into an international movement. A European power had invaded a Muslim nation. Throughout the Middle East, public opinion was inflamed, governments were alarmed, and Azzam made his move. In 1980, he met with a group of Afghan pilgrims in Mecca. And soon afterward he moved to Islamabad, Pakistan, and then to Peshawar, near the Afghan border. At around the same time, his devoted student, Osama bin Laden, made the trip as well.

In 1984, Bin Laden and Azzam founded the Mekhtab al-Khadamat, or Bureau of Services, which organized Arabs to come and join the Afghan mujahedeen battling to expel the Soviets from their land. The Saudi and Pakistani governments enthusiastically aided the two men's work. (The United States, working through Pakistan's intelligence service, also sent money and weapons to the mujahedeen, but not to the far less militarily significant Arab volunteers.) Seeing the Afghan war as a way to spread their influence, the Saudi royals funded Bin Laden's efforts and offered cut-rate plane tickets to Muslims willing to join the jihad. Pakistan, fearing a hostile Communist government on its border, helped the effort as well, instructing its embassies to issue visas to anyone who wanted to come and fight.

But if Riyadh and Islamabad were playing power politics, the jihadist volunteers had something else in mind. Tens of thousands streamed in from across the Arab world. And in Peshawar's dusty guesthouses they got the same ideological education that Bin Laden had received at Abdul Aziz. The leading lights of salafist Islam moved to Peshawar to teach the young recruits, including the blind cleric Rahman and another Egyptian, Dr. Ayman al-Zawahiri, a Qutb disciple who had helped found a radical Muslim Brotherhood offshoot called the Jihad Group. For this emerging jihadist international, Afghanistan was only the first battle in a much larger war. "Jihad," wrote Azzam, "will remain an individual obligation until all other lands which formerly were Muslim come back to us and Islam reigns within them once again. Before us lie Palestine, Bukhara [central Uzbekistan], Lebanon, Chad, Eritrea, Somalia, the Philippines, Burma, South Yemen, Tashkent [eastern Uzbekistan], Andalusia [Spain and Portugal]." It was the beginning of something big.

THE AFGHAN WAR raged for nearly ten years, causing unspeakable horror. One million Afghans died. Five million—one-third of the country's population—went into exile. But in 1989, the Soviets finally withdrew in disgrace, and two years later, the USSR was no more. In reality, it was the Afghans themselves, not their far less numerous Arab helpers, who had defeated Moscow, and it was mostly internal factors that sparked the Soviet collapse. But the jihadists saw God's hand behind these momentous events. Their stunning victory left little doubt: true Islam was on the march.

In 1988, Bin Laden and Azzam created a new organization to continue the salafist jihad across the world: Al Qaeda. When the Afghan war began, Azzam had clearly been the senior partner. But by the war's end, Bin Laden's family wealth and his connections to the Saudi elite had made him an increasingly formidable figure. And the two men seem to have clashed over strategy and control. Nine months after the Soviets withdrew, a car bomb killed Azzam and both his sons.

In 1990, Bin Laden returned to Saudi Arabia to establish a welfare organization for Arab veterans of the Afghan campaign, now returning to their home countries. And that August, when Iraq invaded Kuwait, he offered to reassemble his troops to liberate the tiny Gulf kingdom. But Riyadh turned to the United States instead, and hundreds of thousands of American troops arrived on Saudi soil. For Bin Laden, the presence of armed infidels in such close proximity to Islam's holiest shrines was shocking evidence of *jahiliyya*'s intrusion into even a supposedly Islamic state like Saudi Arabia. He condemned the American presence, denouncing Interior Minister Prince Naif to his face. The Saudis responded by placing Bin Laden under virtual house arrest. But with the help of sympathetic members of the royal family, he escaped, traveling to Pakistan, Afghanistan, and finally to Sudan, where he would remain for the next five years.

In the early 1990s, Sudan was under salafist rule. Its leader, a debonair, Sorbonne-educated cleric named Hassan al-Turabi, welcomed Bin Laden to Khartoum. Bin Laden started several businesses in Sudan, helped Turabi's regime battle rebels in the country's south, and used his construction expertise to build a road from Khartoum to the Red Sea. In return,

Turabi allowed several thousand Afghan war veterans to train in secret Sudanese camps. From Sudan, Bin Laden assembled the Islamic Army Shura—an umbrella organization of salafist groups fighting to overthrow their home governments. But while Bin Laden supported these national efforts, his own focus was increasingly on the United States—"the head of the snake"—which buttressed un-Islamic regimes throughout the Middle East. In early 1992, Al Qaeda issued a fatwa against U.S. "occupation" of Muslim lands. And Bin Laden helped sponsor attacks on American soldiers in Saudi Arabia, and probably in Somalia as well.

Eventually, under pressure from the United States and its allies, Turabi told Bin Laden to leave. In May 1996, in a chartered jet packed with his three wives, thirteen children, and dozens of bodyguards and hangers-on, Bin Laden flew back to Afghanistan, now under very different rule.

FOR AFGHANS, THE fighting hadn't stopped when the Soviets pulled out. Instead, with the Russians and Arabs gone, the cold war over, and America no longer interested, the mujahedeen had turned viciously on each other. By the mid-1990s, civil war had reduced the country to rubble. And amid the brutality, destitution, and chaos, a group of religious students, or *talibs*—backed by Pakistan's intelligence services—began seizing territory. By 1996, they had taken Kabul. It was this government, the Taliban, that would come closest to implementing Qutb and Bin Laden's vision of a salafist state.

Most of the Taliban were Pashtuns, and some observers ascribed their harsh vision to the tribe's conservative social code. But in fact, the Taliban had not grown up in a Pashtun tribal milieu. And their policies represented, in the words of one scholar, a "radical departure . . . from established patterns of [Afghan] social authority," which had been largely tolerant of religious minorities and individual freedom. The real source of Taliban ideology was the religious schools, or madrasas, in which they had spent virtually their entire lives. When the Soviet invasion plunged Afghanistan into war, millions of refugees had fled across the border into Pakistan. With its educational system unable to cope, Islamabad had encouraged religious organizations to step into the breach. One that did—and educated much of the future Taliban leadership—was the Jamiat-e-Ulema Islam (JUI), a Pakistani religious party that grew out of an austere South Asian Islamic tradition called Deobandism. Starting in the 1920s, a radical Deobandist thinker named Maulana Maududi had urged an Islamic vanguard—

modeled on the seventh-century *salafs*—to rise up against man's authority and restore state sovereignty to God. Maududi's work deeply influenced Qutb, and decades later, the intellectual currents came full circle, as Saudi money poured into the JUI madrasas, helping bring salafism to a new generation. Asked in the late 1990s which regime best embodied the principles Al Qaeda hoped would govern the entire Muslim world, Bin Laden's London spokesman said the Taliban was "getting there."

Indeed, it is in the Taliban's policies that one can best see salafism's totalitarian character. The term *totalitarianism* originated in fascist Italy in the 1920s, and in the decade following World War II, a remarkable series of writers labored to explain it, including Schlesinger, George Orwell, Jacob Talmon, Carl Friedrich, Zbigniew Brzezinski, and most important, Hannah Arendt. Since totalitarianism was identified primarily with Nazi Germany and Stalinist Russia, few imagined that it would appear in the Muslim world. (According to some scholars, totalitarianism only emerges in the wake of failed popular revolutions, which Afghanistan never had. Arendt herself suggested that it requires countries so vast that governments can kill on a mass scale without risking depopulation.)

Totalitarianism, like democracy, is an ideal type. No movement or regime embodies it perfectly. But nonetheless, the concept fits today's salafists well. One of totalitarianism's contemporary interpreters, the political theorist Michael Walzer, has offered three distinguishing characteristics of a totalitarian state. The first concerns the relationship between "the totalitarian party" marked by "discipline, action and engagement" and the population at large. Since the party hoards all power, decision making is clandestine—in Schlesinger's words, "secret, sweaty and furtive." It is noteworthy, in this regard, that Qutb, Maududi, Azzam, and Bin Laden himself all speak of an Islamic vanguard, based on the original *salafs*, who withdraw from society in order to conquer and transform it. The Muslim Brotherhood included a "secret apparatus" that carried out attacks on the Egyptian state. Al Qaeda requires a secret loyalty oath for entry. The Taliban's governing structure, according to its foremost chronicler, the Pakistani journalist Ahmed Rashid, was "highly centralized, secretive, dictatorial and inaccessible." And a close observer dubbed Turabi's effort to govern Sudan through tightly knit party cadres, "Islamic bolshevism."

Since in a totalitarian state decisions are made in secret, public politics become, in Walzer's words, "ritual performance," in which the people are "present and accounted for, available for demonstrations and mass meetings," but utterly controlled. Given the technologically backward countries in which they took power, vanguards like the Taliban and Turabi's National Islamic Front had less capacity to mobilize the masses than did the Bolsheviks and Nazis. But they tried. Turabi's regime required all Sudanese students to join the Popular Defense Forces, where the emphasis was less on military training than on indoctrination and dramatic displays of ideological devotion. The Taliban sent trucks with loudspeakers into the streets to gather crowds for the government's Friday executions, held at Kabul's former soccer stadium. Just before victims were shot, stadium loudspeakers blared, "In revenge, there is life."

According to Walzer, totalitarianism's second defining feature is its "political messianism." Totalitarian regimes, in Arendt's words, claim "to have found a way to establish the rule of justice on earth." For salafists, that means God's rule, as they imagine it existed in Muhammad's time. Of course, many religious believers are messianic: they believe that one day God will establish His reign on earth. They may even believe their prayers and good works can hasten the process. But salafists seek to bring about God's rule *politically*—through the power of the state. The goal, according to Qutb, is to "abolish the dominion of man, to take away sovereignty from the usurper and return it to God." In his book *Holy War, Inc.*, the journalist Peter Bergen writes that the Taliban and another modern totalitarian movement, Cambodia's Khmer Rouge, "shared the same absolute certainty about how to create paradise on earth. The Khmer Rouge called this paradise the Year Zero. The Taliban called it the rule of sharia."

For totalitarian regimes, the challenge in creating paradise on earth is that a perfect society requires perfect individuals. And to make individuals perfectly virtuous, you must completely control them. This is what Walzer calls totalitarianism's "decisive" third characteristic: it "involves a systematic effort to control every aspect of social and intellectual life." All dictatorships outlaw behavior that threatens their hold on power—public protest, independent media, opposition parties, and the like. But a totalitarian regime goes further, banning any behavior, however apparently apolitical, that does not further its messianic project. Every institution in society must do its part to produce perfect human beings. As Arendt writes, "If totalitarianism takes its own claim seriously, it must come to the point where it has 'to finish once and for all with the neutrality of chess,' that is, with the autonomous existence of any activity whatsoever."

The Taliban banned chess. They also banned music, dancing, television, movies, card games, painting, photography, toothbrushes, statues representing the human form, makeup, high-heeled shoes, beauty salons, women's education, fashion magazines, kite flying, "British or American" hairstyles, Labor Day, and homing pigeons. Women were required to wear burkas that covered them head to toe. Men were required to wear *shalwars*, baggy trousers that stop above the ankle; to leave their beards untrimmed; and to pray five times a day. While the Taliban did little else to make government function, they enforced these regulations zealously. Religious police patrolled the streets in trucks, with mounted loudspeakers broadcasting the new rules. Thousands of informers reported infractions. In Kabul, there was an expression: "There's a Talib under every stone."

All this would have pleased the movement's ideological forefathers. As Maududi put it, an Islamic state's "sphere of activity is co-extensive with human life. . . . In such a state no one can regard any field of his affairs as personal and private." Qutb described Islam as enjoying "complete predominance over every human secular activity."

But for salafism, as for all species of totalitarianism, controlling behavior is just a means of controlling thought. To usher in God's rule, it is not merely people's actions that must change. They themselves must change. As Arendt notes, totalitarianism's ultimate goal is "the transformation of human nature itself." For the Taliban, this transformation meant not just acting Islamicly, but thinking Islamicly. Asked why the regime banned music, the Taliban education minister said, "It creates a strain in the mind and hampers study of Islam." Another Taliban official told Rashid, "Of course we realize that people need some entertainment, but they can go to the parks and see the flowers, and from this they will learn about Islam." Even Turabi's government, while less Orwellian than the Taliban, sought, in the words of one Sudanese critic, "to remold the Sudanese personality in an Islamic form." If you can purify people's actions, then you can purify their minds. And if you can purify their minds, then you can bring heaven on earth.

THIS OBSESSION WITH purity not only links salafism to European totalitarian movements from which it is culturally alien but also distinguishes it from contemporary Islamic movements to which it is culturally similar. In recent years, Egypt's Muslim Brotherhood—and many of the Islamist parties it helped inspire across the Muslim world—have begun seeking Islamic government through the ballot box, rather than through violent jihad. And while tentative and uneven, this shift marks a real break with Qutb's totalitarian vision. The non-salafist Islamists still demand a government based on sharia, but crucially, they don't see sharia's meaning as fixed and self-evident. Unlike Qutb and Bin Laden, who claim access to the pure Islam of the seventh century, more and more Sunni Islamists recognize that sharia requires human interpretation, and thus, no one person or faction can claim absolute truth. That doesn't mean they consider all interpretations equal, and it certainly doesn't mean that their favored interpretations are liberal. But it means that since no one can speak perfectly for God, the people should deliberate about how to best implement his teachings. This giant concession to relativism leads to an acceptance of democracy, since the people must choose representatives to deliberate. And just as importantly, since the government they choose is not God's direct agent, it cannot press the population into complete conformity with its vision of paradise. No wonder Zawahiri, Bin Laden's Egyptian-born deputy, has accused the Brotherhood of betrayal.

Salafists are also often lumped together with Shiite Islamists like the ayatollahs who rule Iran. In most of the Muslim world, Shiite totalitarianism faces a virtually insurmountable hurdle—because Shiites are a minority, they have no realistic hope of using the state to force the Sunni majority into conformity with their vision of perfect Islam. In Lebanon, for instance, Hezbollah has largely abandoned the goal of a Shiite Islamic state, recognizing that Lebanon's religious diversity simply makes it impossible. The Shiite Islamist parties running post–Saddam Hussein Iraq also recognize that while they can try to enforce their brand of Islamic law in the overwhelmingly Shiite south, they cannot do so nationally because of the country's large Sunni Arab and Kurdish communities.

Only in Iran, with its overwhelming Shiite majority, is a totalitarian regime possible. And even there, the system established by Ayatollah Khomeini falls short of Al Qaeda's dream or the Taliban's reality. To be sure, many of the Islamic revolutionaries who seized power in Tehran in 1979 envisioned a state ruled by the laws of God, not man. But the revolution represented a coalition of different forces, not all theocratic, and it did not entirely abolish long-standing republican institutions. The result, from the beginning, has been that while God supposedly rules, different factions are allowed—within limits—to publicly disagree about what His wishes might be. While unelected clerics wield far more power than Iran's elected president and parliament, the very fact of multicandidate elections creates unscripted political expression, something a totalitarian state cannot allow. And the state's inability to speak with one voice about what true Islam requires has undermined its efforts to impose Islamic virtue upon its citizens. Khomeini himself refused to ban non-Islamic music, art, and, yes, chess. And even hard-line president Mahmoud Ahmadinejad has remarked that young Iranians can "cut their hair the way they want. It's none of our business."

Tehran does dictate what Iranians can see on television and in movie theaters, and what women can wear on the street, but mostly because it deems these displays of Western influence a threat to its hold on power. Civil society organizations that shun politics, by contrast, are tolerated, and even welcomed, for the same reason they are welcomed in many authoritarian regimes: they divert public energy away from politics. By totalitarian standards, these independent groups make Iranian society highly impure, filled with cacaphonous voices and ideas ricocheting in different directions. But the corrupt clerics running the Iranian state are less interested in molding Iranian society than in protecting themselves from it. As Boston University's H. E. Chehabi has noted, if the totalitarian's motto is "those who are not for us are against us," Iran's is more like "those who are not against us are for us." Tehran's goal is not popular mobilization, but popular indifference.

A GOVERNMENT NEED not be totalitarian to be brutal, which Iran's certainly is. But the totalitarian quest for purity requires a more systematic use of domestic terror. In Arendt's words, "terror is the essence of totalitarian domination." The yoke is pressed most tightly on those groups that are deemed to have inherently impure tendencies. For salafists, women top the list, since by their very nature they tempt and corrupt. Even in Iran, where women suffer severe discrimination, they sit in parliament. A female Iranian human rights lawyer recently won the Nobel Peace Prize. Under the Taliban, by contrast, women's public presence was virtually eradicated. They could not wear white socks or noisy shoes under their burkas, since that might attract the attention of passing men, and those men might then think un-Islamic thoughts. Households were required to paint their windows black, so passersby could not see the women inside.

If female sexuality cannot exist publicly in the salafist vision, homosexuality cannot exist at all. "Our religious scholars are not agreed on the right kind of punishment for homosexuality," explained the Taliban's governor of Kandahar. "Some say we should take these sinners to a high roof and throw them down, while others say we should dig a hole beside a wall, bury them, then push the wall down on top of them."

People who practice religions other than Islam also threaten Muslim purity, and must therefore be kept rigidly apart. The Taliban ordered Hindus to wear yellow clothes and mark their houses with a yellow sash. Cohabitation with Muslims was prohibited. In Indian Kashmir in the early 1990s, salafists ethnically cleansed Hindus from large swaths of the state. In Egypt in the 1970s and 1980s, Omar Abdel Rahman's Islamic Group launched a campaign against "corrupt" elements in society, imposing a special tax on Coptic Christians who lived in areas where the group held sway and robbing and torching their stores if they refused to pay. And in the Iraqi city of Mosul, salafist insurgents have bombed numerous churches and Christian-owned businesses in an effort to render the city Christian-free.

Among those "non-Muslims" who impede the salafist effort to re-create the pure Islam of the seventh century are Muslim Sufis and Shiites. In keeping with salafists' deep hostility to many Sufi practices, which they see as foreign innovations grafted onto Islam, the Taliban banned pilgrimages to Sufi shrines. For a time, they banned Muharram, the Shiite month of mourning. And in 1997 and 1998, when the Taliban were battling for control of northern Afghanistan, Bin Laden ingratiated himself with his hosts by sending several hundred Al Qaeda fighters to help slaughter Shiites from the Hazara tribe. Graduates of Al Qaeda training camps have also massacred Shiites in Pakistan. And in Iraq, Bin Laden's ally, Abu Musab al-Zarqawi, has massacred vast numbers of Shiites, accusing them of having "declared a subtle war against Islam."

Then there are those Sunni Muslims who cease to be Muslim on account of their actions. In the early 1990s, Rahman's Islamic Group murdered one prominent Egyptian writer, Farag Foda, for advocating secularism and peace with Israel, and stabbed another, Naguib Mahfouz, for publishing indecent novels. When a professor at Cairo University applied modern literary techniques to the Koran, a salafist judge ruled that he was an apostate and therefore could not be married to his Muslim wife. Perhaps the most audacious declaration that Muslims were not Muslim came in Algeria, where in the 1990s salafists—some veterans of the Afghan war—slaughtered tens of thousands in their war against the military regime in Algiers. In 1997, one organization leading the Algerian jihad, the Armed Islamic Group, declared that "With the exception of those who are with us, all others are apostates and deserve to die." Sayyid Qutb had said Islamic societies were impure. His Algerian followers took the logic one step further: if people refused to purify themselves, they forfeited their right to live.

BUT PERHAPS THE most powerful contaminating force of all is the United States. Bin Laden has loathed America since at least the late 1980s, when he suggested boycotting U.S. goods in retaliation for its support of Israel. But he made the United States his primary target only after American troops entered Saudi Arabia in 1990. To underscore his displeasure, Bin Laden chose August 7, 1998, to blow up the U.S. embassies in Kenya and Tanzania, the eighth anniversary of the day U.S. troops arrived on Saudi soil.

Since Muhammad and his companions serve as the model for the pure Islam Bin Laden hopes to bring to the entire Muslim world, the purity of Arabia—where Muhammad lived—is vitally important. As he was dying, Muhammad said, "Let there be no two religions in Arabia." And so for thousands of infidel American soldiers to occupy Saudi Arabia—as they did from 1990 to 2003—represented *jahiliyyah*'s contamination of the Muslim world's inner sanctum. It signified a kind of ultimate violation, the deepest transgression yet against God's authority on earth.

But if America's military presence in Saudi Arabia constituted its greatest offense, it is hardly the only one. In recent years, the United States has withdrawn most of its troops from Saudi soil, but it occupies large bases elsewhere on the Arabian Peninsula, for instance, in Kuwait and Qatar. And, of course, it occupies Iraq. Beyond that, the United States supports Israel, Russia, India, and other non-Muslim governments that, in Al Qaeda's eyes, oppress Muslims. Finally, it supports Muslim governments in countries like Egypt, Jordan, and Pakistan, which flout sharia.

While different U.S. policies may be more or less important at different times, most experts agree that it is American actions ("what we do"), not American values ("who were are") that have made the United States the target of salafist jihad. While in his ideal world Bin Laden would certainly like to see the United States ditch its barbaric culture and convert to Islam, that is low on his list of concerns. As he himself has pointed out, if

Al Qaeda were offended primarily by the licentiousness Western societies practice at home, it would have attacked Sweden.

The problem is that while salafists might theoretically leave the United States alone if we left them alone, their concerns are vast and their hostility to liberal values is profound. Salafism is not a universalist ideology in the way that Communism was. (That is not to say its devotees do not dream of a world completely under God's rule—they do—only that the cultural barriers preventing, say, an Argentinean from adopting the religion of Qutb are far greater than the barriers preventing him from adopting the religion of Marx.) But neither is salafism easy to avoid. Bin Laden has said the United States can escape "this ordeal" of terrorism if "it leaves the Arabian Peninsula, and stops its involvement in Palestine, and in all the Islamic world." Unfortunately, Zawahiri, his second in command, has defined the Islamic world as stretching from "Eastern Turkestan [Xinjiang, in western China] to Andalusia [Spain and Portugal]." Azzam has gone further, including among the territory that must be "returned to us so that Islam will reign again" sub-Saharan African countries like Chad, Eritrea, and Somalia and Asian nations like Burma and the Philippines. Salafists want to restore the caliphate that once ruled much of the Islamic world. But even at its eighth-century peak, the caliphate only stretched from India to Spain. Under Al Qaeda's more expansive definition, it seems to include every country or region once under Muslim rule. To comply with those terms, the United States would have to retreat virtually to the Western Hemisphere.

Needless to say, for the United States to withdraw from a swath of territory stretching from West Africa to Southeast Asia would constitute a geostrategic revolution. American power is the guarantor of last resort for the government of Pakistan, which has nuclear weapons, a volatile border with nuclear-armed India, and salafist elements in its security services. It plays the same role in Jordan and Egypt, the lynchpins of peace between Israel and the Arab world. And, of course, America protects the Saudi monarchy, whose kingdom sits atop one quarter of the world's proven oil reserves. As the Bush administration has rightly recognized, these relationships are unsustainable in their current form, and America's long-term safety requires that its clients evolve in a democratic direction, even if it means they prove less compliant. But were the jihadist movement to force the United States to withdraw its military, political, or economic influence from these crucial areas—producing governments with dramatically different orientations—the consequences for American security, the world economy, and regional peace could be grave.

And a withdrawal from the Muslim world would not only imperil American interests, it would also imperil American values. Al Qaeda may not hate us for "who we are"—unless "who we are" obligates us to oppose what might be called "religious cleansing," the violent purification of large swaths of the globe. After all, if the United States withdrew from its war against salafism, salafism would still be at war. Al Qaeda's ultimate goal is not to expel the United States from Islamic lands; it is to establish a new caliphate that ushers in God's rule on earth. And the many enemies of that effort—non-Muslims, apostate Muslims, liberated female Muslims, gay and lesbian Muslims—would still blemish the Islamic world, representing *jahiliyyah* in its myriad sinful forms.

Where those enemies have no army to defend them, the result has been terror. Where they do, the result has been endless war. It is a virtual axiom of international politics that salafists will try to seize control of any local conflict—from the Philippines to Chechnya to Kashmir to Iraq—that pits Sunni Muslims against their neighbors. And the more they succeed, the less likely it is that such a conflict will end. Many Muslims, including many non-salafist Islamists, also support Muslim insurgencies around the world. In Iraq, they may support attacks on American troops. But since they see jihad as a means to some concrete goal, political compromise is possible. Salafists, however, who see jihad as a means to usher in a messianic age, will accept no outcome that leaves Muslims under non-Muslim rule, because such a compromise threatens the path to paradise.

In December 2004, when the CIA's National Intelligence Council tried to envision how the world might look in 2020, it suggested that "those states most susceptible to violence are in a great arc of instability from sub-Saharan Africa, through North Africa, into the Middle East, the Balkans, the Caucasus and South and Central Asia and through parts of Southeast Asia." One reason is that this arc includes virtually all the territory the salafist movement claims for its new caliphate. The more successful it is in the decades to come, the bleaker the fate of two great liberal values: liberty and peace.

THAT IS TRUE within American shores as well. As long as the United States remains an obstacle to salafism's goals in the Islamic world, its supporters will try to kill Americans. Fortunately, by the standards of the cold war, their capacity to do so is minuscule. Communists ran a superpower, which possessed thousands of nuclear warheads. With the overthrow of the Taliban, and Turabi's fall from power in Sudan, salafists no longer control even a single state.

But ironically, it is precisely this weakness that makes the new totalitarians dangerous. If control of a nuclear-armed superpower gave Communists an enormous capacity to harm the United States, it also gave them an enormous incentive not to. The Soviets had a regime to protect, and an attack on the United States would have produced a nuclear counterattack which put that regime in jeopardy. As the political scientist John Mearsheimer has argued, one of the primary reasons for "the peacefulness of the postwar era" was the "appearance of nuclear weapons, which vastly expanded the violence of war, making deterrence far more robust."

Jihadists, by contrast, cannot be deterred by the threat of death, since they welcome death. And they cannot be deterred by threats to their regimes, since they have no regimes to protect. All of which helps explain why the Soviet Union, although it fought proxy wars with the United States across the globe, proved extremely cautious about confronting the United States on its own soil. And why Al Qaeda, to put it mildly, has not.

If jihadists required state sponsors in order to kill, the United States might deter those sponsors. But increasingly, they don't. Since the Taliban's overthrow, jihadists have taken sanctuary in regions beyond any government's control—like northwest Pakistan and, most disastrously, Sunni Iraq. Even more important, they have replaced physical sanctuaries with virtual ones, using the Internet as what one expert calls "a virtual training camp." As Michael Scheuer, the former head of the CIA's Bin Laden unit, has written, the "Internet today allows militant Muslims from every country to meet, talk, and get to know each other electronically, a familiarization and bonding process that in the 1980s and early 1990s required a trip to Sudan, Yemen, Afghanistan, or Pakistan." Al Qaeda's thirteen-volume *Encyclopedia of Jihad*, which includes everything a terrorist needs to know to launch an attack, is available, in various languages, on the World Wide Web. According to some observers, the terrorists who blew up three Madrid trains in March 2004 may have been influenced by a document posted on an anonymous website that argued that Spain was the European country where an attack could have the greatest impact.

Since jihadists are not deterred by the threat of retaliation, it makes sense that they would pursue the most destructive attack possible. In particular, they have shown a keen interest in weapons of mass destruction. In May 2003, a young Saudi cleric named Nasir bin Hamid al-Fahd—perhaps on Al Qaeda's request, and certainly for its use—issued a twenty-five-page fatwa entitled "A Treatise on the Legal Status of Using Weapons of Mass Destruction Against Infidels." Fahd argued that such an attack would be permissible only in response to attacks upon Muslims, and only if it were proportional. But that is less comforting than it might seem, since he estimated the number of Muslims killed "directly or indirectly" by American weapons at almost 10 million.

The first type of unconventional weapon Al Qaeda has sought to acquire is the least deadly: a "dirty" bomb, which uses conventional explosives to spread radioactive material. In 2002, the United States accused Chicago gang-member-turned-jihadist José Padilla of trying to build one. More recently, British authorities arrested four people for trying to do so in London. It's unclear how far these efforts had progressed, but building a dirty bomb is far from impossible. The challenge is finding enough radioactive material. One source, cobalt-60, is used in hospital radiation therapy and food irradiation; another, cesium-17, is found in medical gauges; a third, americium, is used in smoke detectors and oil prospecting. But a terrorist would need vast quantities. As the *Washington Post*'s Dafna Linzer has reported, since each smoke detector contains only trace amounts of americium, it would take more than a million of them to build one bomb. If you could cobble together the radioactive material, however, the rest would be fairly simple. According to Charles Ferguson, coauthor of *The Four Faces of Nuclear Terrorism*, "Any person who could build a car bomb or suicide bomb, like the ones we've seen in Iraq or other places, could couple that to radioactive materials and that is it."

Chemical weapons are probably the next easiest for jihadists to construct. In fact, Al Qaeda has been experimenting with them for more than a decade. In the early 1990s, Bin Laden's men tried to learn how to manufacture chemical weapons from their Sudanese hosts. In Afghanistan in 1998, they tested cyanide on dogs and discussed putting it in the air vents of U.S. government buildings. In 2003, police in France, Britain, and Spain uncovered a jihadist plot to produce the toxin ricin using castor beans. And before becoming a household name, Mohamed Atta asked airport officials in the tiny Florida town of Belle Glade how far crop dusters could fly and how much poison they could disperse. He even inquired about securing a Department of Agriculture loan to purchase one.

Building a chemical weapon is harder than building a dirty bomb, which may explain why Al Qaeda has tried so many times and never managed a successful attack. But getting the materials is actually easier. There are thousands of tons of chemical weapons in the former Soviet Union, mostly in facilities where security is poor. And if terrorists can't steal a chemical weapon, they can always buy the precursor materials. In 2000, Defense Department officials told a Houston chemistry professor and Pentagon consultant named James Tour that it was impossible to purchase the elements for a chemical weapon. So Tour put in a request for the various ingredients necessary to make the nerve gas sarin. He ordered them from a single, reputable company, with all the ingredients listed on one form. They came by express mail the next day. A while later, a writer for *Scientific American* tried the same thing—with the same result.

If that's not worrisome enough, consider biological weapons. Right now, they're harder to get than chemical weapons—which may be why the CIA considers it less likely that jihadists have them. It's very difficult to buy anthrax. And obtaining smallpox, which is contagious and therefore far more dangerous, is almost impossible, since it exists at only two known sites, one in the United States and one in the former USSR. What's more, even if terrorists acquired biological agents, they'd find them hard to use. In the early 1990s, the cultists of Aum Shinrikyo tried to release anthrax near Tokyo's Imperial Palace. But the damp anthrax mixture congested the sprayers, and Aum's lunatics turned to something easier: releasing sarin into the Tokyo subway.

But biotechnology is today where computer technology was in the 1960s: about to take off. As Roger Brent, president of the Molecular Sciences Institute, told the *Washington Post*, "Novel DNA sequences are being designed and inserted into living cells by undergraduates." That raises the possibility that a group of rogue scientists, sitting in someone's kitchen, could create biological weapons that today don't exist and would therefore be extremely difficult to stop. As a panel convened by the National Academy of Sciences recently suggested, "advances in biotechnology, coupled with the difficulty in detecting nefarious biological activity, have the potential to create a much more dangerous biological warfare threat." In other words, chemical weapons and dirty bombs may be more dangerous today, but in the long run, biological weapons, especially highly contagious ones, scare experts far more.

Finally, there's the granddaddy of them all: nuclear weapons. In the movies, terrorists buy a bomb from a corrupt Russian colonel, or a fanatical Pakistani one. But in real life, that is extremely hard to do. For one thing, the Russians do a far better job of securing their nuclear weapons than their chemical ones. And even if terrorists obtained a nuclear weapon, they'd have trouble setting it off. Most off-the-shelf nukes contain plutonium, which is easy to trace. And all newer models, and even many older ones, require a complicated series of maneuvers—including changes in temperature, pressure, and environment—before they can be detonated. So Al Qaeda wouldn't just need a Russian or Pakistani bomb, they'd most likely need a Russian or Pakistani bomb maker as well.

For all these reasons, jihadists seem less intent on acquiring a finished nuclear weapon than on acquiring weapons-grade uranium and building the bomb themselves. In the early 1990s, Al Qaeda bought a 3-foot-long cylinder from a Sudanese military officer who said it contained South African highly enriched uranium. It turned out to be a hoax. Jihadists have reportedly made other failed attempts as well. Eventually, however, they could succeed. Moscow may adequately protect its nuclear weapons, but the National Academy of Sciences has warned that "large inventories of SNM [fissile material] are stored at many sites that apparently lack inventory controls." And the Russians reportedly experience one or two attempted thefts of that material a year—that they know of.

If Al Qaeda obtained 50 kilograms of weapons-grade uranium, the hardest part would be over. The simplest nuke to build is the kind the United States dropped on Hiroshima, a "gun-type," in which a mass of highly enriched uranium is fired down a large gun barrel into a second uranium mass. Instructions for how to make one are widely available. Just how widely available became clear to an elderly nuclear physicist named Theodore Taylor in 2002, when he looked up "atomic bomb" in the *World Book Encyclopedia* in his upstate New York nursing home, and found much of the information you'd need.

Even with directions, building a nuclear bomb would still be a monumental task. According to a *New York Times Magazine* article by Bill Keller, in 1986 five Los Alamos nuke builders wrote a paper called "Can Terrorists Build Nuclear Weapons?" They concluded that it would require people who understood "the physical, chemical and metallurgical proper ties of the various materials to be used, as well as characteristics affecting their fabrication; neutronic properties; radiation effects, both nuclear and biological; technology concerning high explosives and/or chemical propellants; some hydrodynamics; electrical circuitry." That sounds daunting. Yet, at the end of the paper, the scientists answered their question: "Yes, they can."

Finally, once terrorists built a nuclear weapon, they'd still have to smuggle it into the United States. The best way might be to put it in a shipping container, on one of the many supertankers that bring oil into American ports every day. The containers are huge, more than big enough to fit a gun-type nuke, which could be as small as 6 feet in length and 6 inches in diameter. Highly enriched uranium emits much less radiation than plutonium, and inside a supertanker's thick double-steel hull it would be hard for sensors to detect. What's more, a single ship can carry several thousand containers, most of which are never searched. On September 11, 2002, ABC News smuggled a 15-pound cylinder of depleted uranium in a cargo container past U.S. customs. On September 11, 2003, they performed the same exercise—and got the uranium past customs again.

SO THE IRONY of American national security after September 11 is that *in the world* we are far more secure than we were during the cold war. The United States has economic rivals but no serious military ones. Even China, which may one day challenge U.S. dominance in Asia, does not constitute the global, ideological threat that the Soviet Union did. "The likelihood of great power conflict escalating into total war in the next fifteen years," predicted the CIA in late 2004, "is lower than any time in the past century."

But at home, we are less secure—because of salafism. In 2004 and 2005, Senate Foreign Relations Committee Chairman Richard Lugar asked eighty-five nonproliferation and national security experts to assess the likelihood that the United States would be attacked with a weapon of mass destruction in the next ten years: the average answer was 70 percent. Then he asked them the same question about a nuclear attack: the average answer was 30 percent. And 80 percent of those polled predicted the attack would come not from a government, but from terrorists.

The effects of a weapon of mass destruction attack could vary dramatically. A 10-kiloton nuclear weapon, two-thirds the size of the one dropped on Hiroshima, if detonated at Grand Central Station, would kill half a million people instantly. But a chemical attack in the New York sub-way, like the one Aum Shinrikyo carried out in Tokyo, might only kill a few people. In fact, while nuclear weapons kill in vast numbers, and biological weapons may one day, chemical weapons are fairly poor killers, and dirty bombs are even worse.

But you don't need to kill a lot of Americans to change America. The Federation of American Scientists estimates that if a dirty bomb made of radioactive cobalt taken from a food irradiation plant were exploded on a calm day from the southern tip of Manhattan, roughly 1,000 square kilometers would be contaminated. The people living within 300 blocks of the blast would face a 1-in-10 risk of dying of cancer for the next forty years. And under current environmental standards, Manhattan would be-come uninhabitable. There would be far fewer dead than on 9/11. But the economic costs—which from 9/11 totaled roughly $80 billion—might be greater. And the full costs wouldn't be measurable in material terms.

All of which brings us back to salafism's threat to liberty—in this case, at home. In his recent book, *Surprise, Security and the American Experience,* John Lewis Gaddis cites a 1960 article by the great Southern historian C. Vann Woodward, in which Woodward argues that "free security"—the expec-tation that Americans were safe from foreign threats—helped define our national character. Among the attitudes that free security promoted was a skepticism toward government intrusion upon personal liberty. As Wood-ward wrote, America's "experience probably encouraged the tendency to regard power as bad in itself and any means of restraining or denying it as a positive good."

Woodward speculated that the development of nuclear missiles able to cross the oceans might change this predisposition. And compared to earlier periods in American history, perhaps it did. But although the cold war was terrifying, it brought no attack on American soil. Now Americans have experienced one, and experts predict there will be more. And the more our expectation of safety declines, the less free our society will be. Which is why American liberals—who sometimes show more passion for protecting civil liberties than for protecting American security—must rec-ognize that, ultimately, they are one and the same.

Partly, insecurity undermines freedom because of politics. As New York University law professor Stephen Schulhofer has argued, when Americans feel unsafe, they blame the government for failing to protect them. And government officials, wanting to avoid blame, respond that they lacked the power to do so. Thus, government power expands and individual liberty declines.

When September 11 hit, the Bush administration said it lacked the authority to stop terrorist plots. Six weeks later, Congress passed the Patriot Act, which gave the government broad new powers to search people's personal records—without informing them, without probable cause that they had committed a crime, and without permission from a judge. And much of that new authority extends to cases having nothing to do with terrorism, like drugs and white-collar crime. Barely anyone truly knows how the Bush administration has used these new powers, because the law itself permits so much secrecy. But the *Washington Post* has reported that "national security letters"—which allow the FBI to demand people's telephone, e-mail, and financial records in secret, and without any judicial or congressional review—have increased a hundredfold since the Patriot Act made them easier to issue. If the executive branch wanted to spy on its political opponents, as it did when the FBI tapped civil rights leaders' phones, or when Richard Nixon did the same to reporters, it could do so more easily today than at any point in the last three decades. A generation of civil liberties progress has been undone. And the single biggest reason is September 11.

But the Patriot Act is only the beginning. After 9/11, the government detained 1,200 foreign nationals, some for months, without charging them with crimes (almost none had committed any), without notifying their families, and without any independent judicial review. The National Security Agency has spied on thousands of Americans, in violation of a 1978 law that requires a court order to do so. In Guantánamo Bay, and in secret camps across the globe, the Bush administration has created a parallel prison system, where America holds suspected terrorists for months, or years, with no independent determination of their guilt. When the Supreme Court ruled that inmates at Guantánamo had due process rights—including the right to a habeas corpus review—the Bush administration responded with legalistic stonewalling intended to delay, or avoid, having to comply.

And if the Patriot Act's consequences are largely unknown, the consequences of America's shadow prison system have become hideously clear. Shielded from judicial review, ignored by a Congress petrified to challenge the executive, and operating in almost total darkness, virtually every one of these camps has produced credible allegations of torture. Before 9/11, such revelations would have been unthinkable. In the 2004 presidential campaign, by contrast, they barely even surfaced as an issue.

Indeed, while the Bush administration bears the blame for these horrors, White House officials exploited a shift in public values after 9/11. When asked by Princeton Survey Research Associates in 1997 whether stopping terrorism required citizens to cede some civil liberties, less than one-third of Americans said yes. By the spring of 2002, that had grown to almost three-quarters. Public support for the government's right to wiretap phones and read people's mail also grew exponentially. In fact, polling in the months after the attack showed Americans less concerned that the Bush administration was violating civil liberties than that it wasn't violating them *enough*.

What will happen the next time? It is, of course, impossible to predict the reaction to any particular attack. But in 2003, the Center for Public Integrity got a draft of something called the Domestic Security Enhancement Act, quickly dubbed Patriot II. According to the center's executive director, Charles Lewis, it expanded government power five or ten times as much as its predecessor. One provision permitted the government to strip native-born Americans of their citizenship, allowing them to be indefinitely imprisoned without legal recourse if they were deemed to have provided any support—even nonviolent support—to groups designated as terrorist. After an outcry, the bill was shelved. But it offers a hint of what this administration—or any administration—might do if the United States were hit again.

When the CIA recently tried to imagine how the world might look in 2020, it conjured four potential scenarios. One was called the "cycle of fear," and it drastically inverted the assumption of security that C. Vann Woodward called central to America's national character. The United States has been attacked again and the government has responded with "large-scale intrusive security measures." In this dystopian future, two arms dealers, one with jihadist ties, text-message about a potential nuclear deal. One notes that terrorist networks have "turned into mini-states." The other jokes about the global recession sparked by the latest attacks. And he muses about how terrorism has changed American life. "That new Patriot Act," he writes, "went way beyond anything imagined after 9/11."

"The fear cycle generated by an increasing spread of WMD and terrorist attacks," comments the CIA report, "once under way, would be one of the hardest to break." And the more entrenched that fear cycle grows, the less free America will become. Which is why a new generation of American liberals must make the fight against this new totalitarianism their own.

5

Reagan's Children

ON SEPTEMBER 11, 2001, Sayyid Qutb's children returned to Washington and New York in the cockpits of jetliners. Just a few months earlier, when the White House counterterrorism chief had mentioned Al Qaeda to the national security adviser, she had responded with a blank stare. Now the women and men of the Bush administration were in a terrifying struggle against a shadow foe. And in a world suddenly made unfamiliar, they fell back on what they knew: the cold war. In particular, they fell back on their memory of the cold war. And so conservative antitotalitarianism was reborn, to meet the challenge of a new age.

It took President Bush less than a day to declare the country at war. The implied contrast was law enforcement: America wouldn't send police to apprehend the terrorists; it would send soldiers to kill them. But it would be a "different kind of war." In the coming struggle there might be long stretches with no military engagements at all—yet even during those interregnums, the country would not be at peace. The echoes of the cold war, another "generational" struggle with long stretches between battles, were clear. For the Bush foreign policy team, which came of age in the 1970s and 1980s, "a different kind of war" was the kind they knew best.

What defined the cold war, even when the guns went silent, was ideological conflict. And nine days after 9/11, Bush defined the enemy in explicitly ideological terms. "We have seen their kind before," he told Congress on September 20. "They are the heirs of all the murderous ideologies of the 20th century . . . they follow in the path of fascism, and Nazism, and totalitarianism." The conservative press embraced the analogy. In *Commentary*, Norman Podhoretz called the new struggle "World War IV" (the cold war being number three). In *National Review Online*, Victor Davis Hanson declared that an "Iron Veil" had descended across the Muslim world.

But if America was fighting against Islamic totalitarianism, what was it fighting for? Islamic democracy was not the traditional conservative answer. In the early cold war, conservatives had repeatedly mocked liberals for suggesting the United States could help plant democracy in rocky, non-Western soil. While liberals like Kennedy urged a rapid end to colonial rule so the "lands of the rising people" could taste freedom, conservatives sourly predicted that these backward nations would instead descend into barbarism, or fall to Communism, or both. "Voters who cross themselves beneath the image of a rhinoceros, or of an elephant sitting on a triangle, do not necessarily institute governments as envisaged by Thomas Jefferson, Rousseau or Mazzini," declared an article in *National Review* in 1959. If granted independence, wrote William F. Buckley two years later, Africans "tend to revert to savagery against both whites and their own civilized minority." For most conservatives, thinking democracy could be successfully exported to alien, "primitive" societies was utopian and dangerous, which was to say, typically liberal.

The debate reemerged in the late 1970s, when Jimmy Carter began withdrawing support from pro-American autocrats—elevating democracy and human rights above anti-Communism and prompting a new group of conservatives to raise their voices in protest. Jeane Kirkpatrick, the cerebral daughter of an Oklahoma oil driller, had been a Scoop Jackson Democrat. But like other new, or "neo," conservatives, she had drifted right after the party nominated George McGovern. And in a 1979 *Commentary* article entitled "Dictatorships and Double Standards," she insisted that "decades, if not centuries, are normally required for people to acquire the necessary disciplines and habits" of democracy. The Carter administration's naïve belief "that one can easily locate and impose democratic alternatives to incumbent autocracies," she warned, was bringing anti-American movements to power across the third world.

Kirkpatrick's article took the right by storm. Ronald Reagan, on his way to the presidency, named Kirkpatrick his UN ambassador. And once in office, he quickly mended fences with anti-Communist strongmen like South Korea's Chun Doo Hwan, who had recently seized power in a coup. In 1982, Reagan invited Filipino dictator Ferdinand Marcos and his wife Imelda to the White House, where they were feted at a state dinner. For a time, it looked like he might even abolish the position of assistant secretary of state for human rights.

But over the course of Reagan's presidency, conservative antitotalitarianism took an unexpected turn. In 1980 and 1981, Poland's Solidarity movement rose up against Soviet domination—showing that a democracy movement could dramatically further the anti-Communist cause. Reagan responded, in a 1982 speech to the British Parliament, by pledging American support for "the democratic revolution . . . gathering new strength" across the globe. And once he had laid out the principle, it took on a life of its own. Reagan was fond of Marcos. But his ally's dictatorship, far from providing a bulwark against Communism, was fueling a Marxist insurgency. In January 1985, Reagan's assistant secretary of state for East Asian and Pacific Affairs went to Manila, and in a dramatic shift in administration policy, met with opponents of the Marcos regime. Thirteen months later, Marcos was on an American plane out of the country. Soon, the assistant secretary was helping pressure South Korea's Chun. And then he was named ambassador to Indonesia, where he called on that country's anti-Communist dictator to reform as well. In El Salvador—pressed by the New Democrats—other Reagan officials did the same thing. Conservatives had made a fundamental shift: they had accepted that totalitarianism can have root causes in repression. Democratization had become part of the right-wing creed. And an assistant secretary of state named Paul Wolfowitz had been at the center of it all.

When the cold war ended, the right lost its newfound enthusiasm for spreading democracy. Democratic evangelism had been fine when it helped fight Communism, but with the Soviets gone, Bill Clinton's efforts to spread democracy to bleak, strategically irrelevant countries like Haiti struck most conservatives as a colossal distraction from the national interest. In his 1994 book *Dead Right*, the conservative writer David Frum critiqued "the excessive rhetoric about Third World democracy in which many conservatives indulged in the 1980s." And running for president a few years later, George W. Bush seemed to agree. "It is sometimes important to admit that democratic development takes time," noted his chief tutor, Condoleezza Rice, in 1999. And in his second debate with Al Gore, Bush ventured that "I just don't think it's the role of the United States to walk into a country [and] say, 'We do it this way; so should you.' " The old conservative skepticism, it seemed, was back.

But one right-wing faction did not repudiate the "excessive rhetoric" of the 1980s, and strangely enough, they were called "neoconservatives." The new neocons were a generation younger than Kirkpatrick, and many had never been on the left. (In fact, some—like *Weekly Standard* editor William Kristol and the *New York Post*'s John Podhoretz—were the children of prominent first-generation neocons.) Reagan was their hero, and their template. And in the 1990s, they denounced the right's indifference toward democracy, an indifference they said betrayed Reagan's legacy. "The United States achieved its present position of strength not by practicing a foreign policy of live and let live," wrote Kristol and Robert Kagan in 1996. "During the Reagan years, the United States pressed for changes in right-wing and left-wing dictatorships alike, among both friends and foes." From the Balkans to North Korea to Iraq, the neocons proposed doing so again.

In the Clinton era, when conservatives were generally more interested in keeping the world from infecting America than in helping America reshape the world, the neocons were playing a weak hand. But that all changed on 9/11. Suddenly, the United States was fighting a new cold war, and conservatives wanted just what Kristol and Wolfowitz (now deputy secretary of defense) were peddling: neo-Reaganism. And while neo-Reaganism meant a lot of things, one of them was the spread of democracy. The analogy was clear. If the Reaganites had promoted democracy in the Philippines, where tyranny was breeding Communists who *might* threaten the United States, how could neo-Reaganites not promote it in Saudi Arabia and Egypt, where tyranny had produced the terrorists who murdered 3,000 people on American soil?

President Bush's campaign for Islamic democracy was not inevitable. It represents a large, and risky, expansion of Reagan's about-face. And it has been driven by strange, unforeseen events—above all, the failure to find weapons of mass destruction in Iraq. Bush's growing democratic zeal, coming just as his primary justification for overthrowing Saddam collapsed, has struck many liberals as suspiciously convenient. And his cosmic statements about America's democratic mission have often struck them as cloying and naïve—just as Reagan's once did. But the world is a better place because Reagan backed Solidarity and abandoned Marcos. And if liberals dislike Bush's happy democracy talk, they should consider the alternative: the pessimistic, sometimes racist, tradition that led early cold war conservatives to say America was fighting not for democracy but for Western civilization. That other, darker conservatism—which saw the cold war as a clash of civilizations and sees the war on terror the same way, with Islam as the new enemy—was everywhere in the months following 9/11. With a nod from the White House, it would have caught fire.

Whatever Bush's initial motivation for taking up democracy's ban-ner, his sincerity is now transparent. And although he has coddled his share of dictators, his rhetoric has pressured his actions, perhaps—as with Reagan—pushing him further than he initially expected to go. The Bush administration has sponsored free elections in post-Saddam Iraq, knowing full well that America's preferred candidates would not win. It has put more democratic pressure on Egypt's Hosni Mubarak than Bill Clinton ever dared. And it has backed a democratic revolution in Ukraine, a country whose dictator sent troops to fight alongside the United States in Iraq.

In America's new antitotalitarian fight, the Bush administration has gotten one big thing right: Tyranny does foster jihad. To be sure, de-mocracy is no quick fix. Terrorism can spike during chaotic transitions to freedom, as the police state crumbles and jihadists find it easier to do their deadly work. And as the United States has seen in Iraq and the Palestinian territories, free elections can bring Islamists to power. But democracy also offers the best hope of luring Islamists away from salafism's totalitarian vision, as it has in Turkey, where an Islamist prime minister presides over one of the most liberal governments in the Islamic world. In the long run, by giving people more control over their govern-ment, democracy can help drain the alienation on which totalitarianism feeds. Conservatives have traveled a tortured path to this realization. And if liberals deny it now, they forfeit their own heritage. Which would be the worst about-face of all.

UNFORTUNATELY, IF GEORGE W. Bush is heir to one admirable foreign policy tradition, he has inherited other, less admirable ones, each with its own roots in the conservative cold war. And together, these various strains have fashioned an ideology incapable of winning America's new antitotalitarian fight.

One such strain concerns the relationship between totalitarianism and economic despair. President Bush rightly believes that defeating jihadism requires promoting liberty. But he is much less sure that defeating jihadism requires promoting equality (or at least, equality of opportunity). And that is because while today's conservatives recognize totalitarianism's political root causes, they still largely deny its economic ones.

This denial has a long pedigree. If the early cold war right was gen-erally dubious that colonialism fostered Communism, it was even more loath to blame Communism on poverty. "The fact that some poor, illiterate people have 'gone Communist' does not prove that poverty caused them to do so," insisted Barry Goldwater. Burnham went further, suggesting that when liberals claimed the "only possibility of ending communism is by removing all the bad conditions, and creating a society with universal well-being and happiness," they were using an argument that "has been supplied to them by the communists themselves."

If America must give foreign aid, argued conservatives, the money should combat not poverty but Communism itself. Rather than send economic assistance to nonaligned countries in the vague and unlikely hope that it would bring prosperity, and thus undermine Communism's appeal, the United States should simply pay third-world governments to take the anti-Communist side. As Dulles had insisted, neutrality was unacceptable. "In return for any foreign aid in any form," declared *National Review*, "we should insist on a quid pro quo." And if Reagan altered the right's views about democratization, he upheld its principles on foreign aid. U.S. overseas military assistance almost doubled between 1980 and 1987. But development aid dropped by 15 percent.

When Communism collapsed, the left-right debates took different form. Over the course of his administration, Bill Clinton—in tandem with Tony Blair—grew increasingly concerned about the "dark side" of globalization. With technology making the world smaller, Clinton officials worried, the United States was increasingly imperiled by the weakness of other states— by their disfunctional financial systems, which produced global economic crises; by their inadequate health systems, which permitted global outbreaks of disease; and by their corrupt, crumbling militaries, which could not secure loose nuclear materials. Terrorism was a prime example of these new "nonterritorial" threats. Sometimes they might require military force, as part of a broader nation-building effort. Often they simply required stronger international institutions and greater foreign aid, to help other countries better govern themselves, and thus protect America.

To most conservatives, this new liberal rationale for development aid seemed as flimsy as the old ones. The 1996 Republican platform attacked the Clinton administration's "social welfare spending in the Third World." The 2000 platform attacked Al "Gore's new agenda for America as global social worker." And the Bush campaign left little doubt that in its view, the United States was threatened not by other countries' economic weakness, but by their military power—in particular, the power of large countries like China and Russia, and rogue regimes like Iraq, North Korea, and Iran. In January 2000, when she laid out Bush's foreign policy vision in a lengthy essay in *Foreign Affairs*, Rice never mentioned the word *globalization*.

Once in office, the Bush administration quickly relegated globalization to the back burner. In the Clinton years, treasury secretaries like Robert Rubin and Lawrence Summers had wielded as much foreign policy influence as secretaries of defense and state. By contrast, only one of the "Vulcans," the foreign policy team that mentored Bush in the 2000 campaign, Robert Zoellick, had any background in international economics. In fact, almost all of Bush's key advisers, as James Mann notes in his group biography, *Rise of the Vulcans*, cut their teeth in the Pentagon. Top Bush officials may have had competing views on military power. Colin Powell (a former chairman of the Joint Chiefs of Staff) and his State Department deputy, Richard Armitage (a former assistant secretary of defense), were more loathe to use it than Wolfowitz (a former undersecretary of defense), Rumsfeld (a former defense secretary), Cheney (ditto), and Rice. But for each of them, military power was what they knew best. (Even Rice, as Mann points out, got her first job in Washington working for the Joint Chiefs of Staff.) Aggravating the imbalance, Treasury Secretary Paul O'Neill had no foreign policy experience, and his powerlessness within the administration quickly became a Washington cliché.

This bias grew even stronger after 9/11. A president of almost any ideological stripe would have responded to the attacks with military action. But conservatives, in and out of government, went out of their way to deny that America's new war had an economic dimension. Podhoretz lauded Bush for making clear that "terrorism was no longer considered a product of economic factors." Paul Bremer, Bush's man in post-Saddam Iraq, was on record stating that "There's no point in addressing the so-called root causes of bin Laden's despair with us. We are the root cause of his terrorism. He doesn't like America." And Bush himself told Bob Woodward, "These aren't a bunch of poor people that are desperate in their attempt. These are cold, calculating killers."

But that's not quite right. Salafist terrorists may not all be poor, yet salafism feeds on economic despair. It takes deepest root where states cannot offer their citizens opportunity or hope. Consider Pakistan, where the Taliban were raised, and where many Al Qaeda leaders have made their home since 9/11. It spends less than 2 percent of its GDP on education (half as much as India, and one-tenth as much as it spends on defense). According to one study, "Government-run schools are generally considered horrendous. They often lack teachers, books, electricity, running water, and even roofs. A significant number are ghost schools, which exist only as a budget line item for corrupt bureaucrats to draw money from." Madrasas—which unlike government schools frequently offer free room, board, and even clothing—help fill the void. How many Pakistani children actually attend these religious schools is a topic of heated debate. And only a fraction of them, perhaps 10 to 15 percent, teach violent salafism. But that still provides an ample pool for jihad. One large Pakistani madrasa alone graduated much of the Taliban high command. Former Clinton administration counterterrorism officials Daniel Benjamin and Steven Simon estimate that two-thirds of the Pakistani jihadists in Indian-controlled Kashmir are madrasa graduates. And lest Americans think they are just India's problem, those jihadists have branched out into attacks on the West—including the 2002 beheading of *Wall Street Journal* reporter Daniel Pearl.

In other Muslim countries, madrasas play a smaller or more benign role. But salafism fills the vacuum left by failing states in other ways. In the early 1990s, Omar Abdel Rahman's Islamic Group virtually took over impoverished parts of Cairo, creating what Benjamin and Simon call "a parallel government that would provide . . . vital services, however crudely" to neighborhoods that received nothing from the Egyptian state. And as they provide services, salafists gain an audience. They offer explanations, and outlets, for the rage that many Muslims feel—not only about their own misery and oppression, but about the bloody images from the Palestinian territories, Chechnya, Kashmir, or Iraq, which fill their televisions and haunt their minds. As Bard College's Omar Encarnación has written, the Arab world in recent years has experienced a "general 'Islamization' and radicalization of society ensuing from the rigid religious and often intolerant character of the civil society organizations now performing functions previously in the hands of state authorities."

And even when salafists don't set up schools or hospitals, they find weak state institutions to be easy prey. By Pakistani standards, Saudi Arabia is not poor. But economic despair doesn't just stem from absolute deprivation; it stems from the gap between expectations and reality. And nowhere is that gap greater than in Saudi Arabia, where per capita income has dropped by more than half since the 1980s, thanks to plunging oil revenue and an escalating birthrate. No longer able to promise its citizens a better life, Riyadh has increasingly leaned on mullahs to bolster its legitimacy.

And salafist clerics have used their power to strip secular subjects from the kingdom's schools in favor of rote memorization of the Koran. It's true that many young Saudis attend university, but those universities are often little more than glorified madrasas themselves, pumping out thousands of Islamic studies degrees every year. Only 2 percent of Saudis entering the job market every year have college degrees in technical subjects like engineering. And many of the rest, lacking freedom, lacking opportunity, awash in downward mobility, and enraged by events in the world, do the one thing for which they have been trained: They dream of a purified Islam. As Saudi political scientist Turki Hamad puts it, "The problem in Saudi Arabia is that the middle class is shrinking . . . and the more poverty you have, the more fundamentalism you have."

It's no surprise that most of the 9/11 hijackers hailed from relatively prosperous Saudi Arabia, not the Karachi or Cairo slums. And it's no surprise that cells have sprung up in Europe, where young Muslims are far more privileged than their Middle Eastern counterparts, but experience a relative deprivation, and social rage, that resembles American inner cities in the 1960s. Terrorist groups, after all, are like any other employer: They accept the best candidates who apply. The University of Pennsylvania's Marc Sageman estimates that only 10 to 30 percent of the people who trained at Al Qaeda camps in the 1990s were invited to join the organization. And of those, an even smaller number were selected for spectacular attacks like 9/11, which require living undercover for years in the West. By design, these jihadist elites are more cosmopolitan, and better educated, than the movement they represent. After examining data on terrorists and would-be terrorists, Washington University's Ethan Bueno de Mesquita concluded that "individuals with low ability or little education are most likely to volunteer to join the terrorist organization. However, the terrorist organization screens the volunteers, only accepting the best recruits."

So what happens to the jihadist wannabes? Some become grunts, doing odd jobs or murdering closer to home—for instance, in salafist pogroms against Shiites in Pakistan or Iraq. Many more become mere sympathizers. But from Riyadh to Jakarta to the suburbs of Paris, they are the larger sea within which jihadist elites swim. They facilitate, encourage, and legitimize. And they protect against crackdowns by the state—in the same way alienated ghetto dwellers might protect drug dealers from the police. This broader community makes all the difference. The United States can produce Timothy McVeigh; Germany can produce the Baader-Meinhof gang. But without popular support, terrorists can't survive for long. With it, they can threaten the world.

WHY DOES THE right ignore this? Because for many conservatives today, like their cold war predecessors, discussing economic root causes is rationalizing. It shifts blame from the terrorists themselves, and thus threatens the quality conservatives cherish most: moral clarity. As conservative commentator William Bennett has written, the question "shouldn't we work on getting rid of the poverty and oppression that are the root causes of terrorism" bespeaks a "want of clarity about the difference between good and evil."

Unfortunately, this effort to preserve America's moral clarity about the enemy prevents America from fully fighting that enemy. In truth, salafism's political and economic root causes are intimately intertwined. Economic development isn't an absolute precondition for stable democracy, but it's an enormous help. And studies also show a strong correlation between democracy and increased primary education, especially for girls. On large swaths of the American right, however, suggesting that Pakistan's 70 percent female illiteracy rate might have something to do with the war on terror marks you as an apologist for evil.

Not surprisingly, given this view, the Bush administration has promoted Islamic democracy far more aggressively than Islamic development. For instance, in 2005, Bush proposed doubling the budget of the National Endowment for Democracy—a Reagan-era creation that promotes a free press, a free judiciary, and independent political parties overseas. But when it comes to economic development, Bush's efforts have been tepid and duplicitous. And even they have usually proved too much for the Republican Congress.

In 2002, the administration launched the Middle East Partnership Initiative (MEPI), which funds education, economic development, democratization, and women's rights—but not very much. In its first year, it received only $29 million. In 2003 and 2004, that rose to $90 million, then fell to $75 million in 2005, then grew to $99 million in 2006. That's for thirteen Arab countries, plus the Palestinian Authority. In 2004, the White House followed up with the Greater Middle East Initiative (which later evolved into the Broader Middle East and North Africa Initiative): a supposed grand bargain between the G-8 industrial powers and the Middle East, in which Muslim countries promised to reform politically and economically, and the West promised to give those reforms financial muscle. Neither has happened. In fact, the initiative has received barely any U.S. funding, leading conservative columnist Charles Krauthammer to describe it as "hopelessly watered down and understood by all to be a façade."

When it comes to development efforts that include both Islamic and non-Islamic countries, the same pattern plays itself out. First, the Bush administration exaggerates the money it plans to spend. Then, the GOP-controlled House and Senate cut it further. Then it turns out that much of the money is actually diverted from other programs that do the same thing. In March 2002, Bush announced the Millennium Challenge Account, pledging a 50 percent increase in core U.S. development assistance by 2006. But by 2005 that pledge had disappeared from administration websites. That's because in each of its first three years, the administration requested less money for the program than it had promised, and Congress allocated even less than that. In total, the program, which was supposed to receive $10 billion, has gotten just over half that. And other economic and food assistance programs have been sharply cut.

The striking thing about this game of bait-and-switch is that conservatives don't seem to mind. When the administration proposes insufficiently large tax cuts, conservatives howl in outrage. But Bush's repeated failure to fulfill his foreign aid promises has been met largely with silence, if not relief, on his side of the political aisle. In fact, after Hurricane Katrina, when the Congressional Republican Study Committee went looking for budget cuts to offset the money spent rebuilding the Gulf Coast, they proposed eliminating the Millennium Challenge Account altogether. Even when it comes to lifting U.S. barriers to Middle Eastern goods, an avowedly free market approach to Middle Eastern development, the right has been timid. The Bush administration has proposed a Middle East free trade zone by 2013, but while that is a worthy long-term goal, it has refused Pakistan's pleas to lift debilitating U.S. textile tariffs and opposed legislation to open American markets to the goods of all Muslim countries that support the war on terror. What's more, in 2002, Bush signed a $190 billion agriculture bill packed with subsidies that make it impossible for third-world farmers to export to the United States.

If the Bush administration thinks its development efforts have been sufficient, Arab commentators don't. When the administration announced the budget for MEPI, the Qatari newspaper *Al-Raya* scoffed that "$29 million is not even enough to launch an advertising campaign in the United

States for a local domestic product." *Al-Quds al-Arabi*, based in London, editorialized that "this sum is not only too little; it also reflects the extent to which the ruling elite in Washington despises the Arabs, and the degree to which it has no serious intention of resisting dictatorships in the region." Lebanon's *As-Sharq* noted that "The United States has allocated $29 million for [MEPI], while the supposed war against Iraq will be costing it $100 billion."

Notice what the Arab papers *didn't* say. They didn't reject the idea of American aid coupled with domestic reform. That's consistent with a 2005 study by the Council on Foreign Relations, based on focus groups in Morocco, Egypt, and Indonesia. Asked what they wanted from the United States, the people interviewed requested almost exactly what the Marshall Plan once provided: generosity without hubris, economic and educational development guided by local knowledge not American fiat. "Dear President Bush," said one Jakarta woman, whom the study said spoke for many: "Please help us with our economy, but let us manage our country!" Instead, the United States has offered the opposite: meager sums and an insistence that it knows best. Even Pakistani leader Pervez Musharraf has complained that while the Bush administration provides plenty of military aid, it has turned a deaf ear to his pleas for help with Pakistan's schools. It's the old conservative logic: payoffs to pro-American regimes are hard-headed; money to combat the conditions that threaten those regimes—and the United States—is social work.

Obviously, foreign aid alone does not produce economic development. It must be coupled with reforms that open Middle Eastern economies to the world. But as a massive 1997 World Bank study showed, without development aid, free market reforms don't do nearly as much good. This was the logic behind the 9/11 Commission's proposal for an International Youth Opportunity Fund to improve primary and secondary education in Muslim countries willing to commit their own money to the task. In the same spirit, the 2003 Arab Human Development Report—written by scholars from across the Middle East—called for universal basic education until at least grade 10, as part of the "long-term goal of draining the economic and political sources of terrorism." These are Marshall Plan–style proposals. Between 1948 and 1952, the United States spent between 2.5 and 5 percent of national income to combat the economic and social roots of totalitarianism in Western Europe: in today's terms, roughly $200 billion a year. Combine all the Bush administration's nonmilitary aid

to the Muslim world and you get a bit more than $1.5 billion a year. Add
in economic reconstruction for Afghanistan and Iraq, and you're a bit over
$8 billion, still only one-twentieth of the Marshall Plan. What kind of way
is that to fight World War IV?

IF TODAY'S CONSERVATIVES ignore the link between totalitarianism
and economic despair overseas, they display a parallel blindness to the link
between antitotalitarianism and economic strength at home. This blindness, too, has been a long time in coming. When the right abandoned
isolationism in the early 1950s and embraced the cold war, it suddenly
encountered a deep tension between its foreign policy principles and its
domestic ones. Conservatives wanted to fight Communism, and yet they
also wanted to starve the institution that fought Communism: the federal
government. McCarthyism offered some relief, since it located the Communist threat not overseas, where fighting it required expensive military
commitments, but at home, where the battle required only moral clarity
and an assault on free speech, both of which were cheap. But eventually,
the red scare faded, and the claim that the Communist threat stemmed
mostly from within became untenable. So most conservatives swallowed
hard and acknowledged that America must spend heavily on defense. "As
a conservative," wrote Goldwater in 1960, "I deplore the huge tax levy
that is needed to finance the world's number-one military establishment.
But even more do I deplore the prospect of a foreign conquest, which the
absence of that establishment would quickly accomplish."

Conservatives still insisted that a larger military and a smaller government could be reconciled—if the government slashed domestic spending. By the 1970s, however, the expanding welfare state was making that
hope a fantasy. In the real world, something had to give. And what gave,
when Reagan came to power, was intellectual honesty. For decades, conservatives had demanded low taxes and a balanced budget, a combina-
tion that required deep, and deeply unpopular, cuts in domestic spending.
Goldwater had even urged delaying tax cuts until after the grim work of
cutting spending was done, to ensure that deficits never reared their ugly
head. But Ronald Reagan—aided by the economically ludicrous Laffer
curve—insisted he could cut taxes, boost defense spending, maintain the
welfare state, and still balance the budget, since lower taxes would spur
epic economic growth, which would bring a cascade of new tax revenue,
which kept government in the black.

To the surprise of no one with a grasp on reality, the theory failed. The deficit exploded in the 1980s, forcing Reagan to *raise* taxes twice and leading his successors, George H. W. Bush and Bill Clinton, to raise them again. The government also slashed defense. As the cold war petered out, the military budget declined a whopping 12 percent in real terms between fiscal years 1985 and 1990.

For a time in the 1990s, the Soviet Union's demise offered the right some reprieve from the tension that had plagued it for four decades. Finally able to embrace defense cuts, conservatives could more easily pursue both lower taxes and a balanced budget. In 1995, the Gingrich Congress, in true Goldwater fashion, even tried to pass a constitutional amendment prohibiting the federal government from running a deficit.

But by the time George W. Bush took office, old strains were reappearing, with some on the right warning that the military had been cut too deep and demanding large infusions of cash to stop the bleeding. A month after taking office, Defense Secretary Donald Rumsfeld announced he would seek an immediate boost to the 2001 defense budget. The White House, however, shot him down. In June, Rumsfeld asked for a $35 billion increase in the military budget for 2002; the White House cut that in half. Defense-oriented conservatives were livid. "Here's some unsolicited advice for two old friends, Donald Rumsfeld and Paul Wolfowitz," editorialized the *Weekly Standard* in July: "Resign."

The reason Rumsfeld didn't get his defense buildup was simple: the Bush administration was still promising a balanced budget. And it was devoted, above all, to a big tax cut. That meant all discretionary spending—including defense—got squeezed. As Robert Kagan complained, "Tax rebate checks are on the way. Real help for the military is not."

THEN 9/11 HIT. With the country suddenly at war, Rumsfeld got everything he wanted, and more. The attack also gave Bush a ready-made excuse for abandoning a balanced budget. "I've told the American people," he said in April 2002, "we would have deficits only in the case of war, a recession, or a national emergency. In this case, we've got all three." The 1980s were back: conservatives were going to have it all.

In fact, Bush outdid Reagan. Reagan had at least pretended his policies would keep the budget in balance. And partly because of that, when his big 1981 tax cut sent deficits skyrocketing, he was forced to retrench—hiking taxes in 1982 and 1984. Bush, by contrast, followed his 2001 tax cut with another in 2002, and yet another in 2003. By 2006, America's ten-year fiscal outlook had deteriorated by more than $8 trillion, with 60 percent of the decline due to falling revenue.

And even this doesn't capture Bush's radicalism. For years, experts have been screaming that the government should be running a *surplus*. The reason is the baby boomers—that huge swath of humanity born after World War II who will begin retiring in 2008, driving the costs of Social Security and Medicare through the roof. In the Reagan years that crucible was several decades away. Today, it is several years away. Yet instead of piling up sandbags in preparation for the coming storm, Bush has spent his presidency jackhammering the country's fiscal foundation. Even his one proposal to supposedly address the entitlement crunch—the partial privatization of Social Security—would have actually made the problem far worse by potentially requiring the government to borrow additional trillions to replace the money diverted from Social Security for private retirement accounts.

If Bush's tax cuts are made permanent, as most conservatives demand, in the coming years the government will start hemorrhaging revenue just as its Social Security and Medicare costs explode—creating a deep fiscal crisis. Which may be just what some conservatives want. As Reagan's budget director, David Stockman, eventually admitted, he *knew* the Laffer curve wouldn't work—that it would produce not balanced budgets but massive, terrifying deficits. But he saw those deficits as an "opportunity," since they would force politicians to slash the size of government. It was exactly the gambit Goldwater had rejected: Congress "would have to dismantle its bloated, wasteful, and unjust spending enterprises—or risk national ruin."

Strangely enough, Stockman's strategy partly worked. America conquered the Reagan deficits through higher taxes and a booming economy, but also because government spending did, in fact, go down. Now Bush is following the Stockman strategy again, on a far grander scale, because America's deficit will be far worse. But there's a problem. Much of the Reagan-era spending cuts came in defense. As a share of GDP, the Pentagon budget fell by more than half between 1986 and 2000. And that was possible because of a fortunate, onetime, historical event: the Soviet Union disappeared.

No one expects the jihadist threat to disappear by the time George W. Bush starts drawing Social Security. Indeed, as the Bush administration likes to say, this is a "generational struggle." Yet unless conservatives abandon their old quest to defund the government, the United States won't have the money to wage it. Military spending has risen sharply since September 11, but as Congress's Government Accountability Office notes, this larger defense budget is "running head-on into the nation's unsustainable fiscal path."

In homeland security, the problem is even worse. Since 9/11, the Bush administration has boosted funding to protect the country from another attack—but not nearly enough. In 2003, the Council on Foreign Relations published a study entitled "Emergency Responders: Drastically Underfunded, Dangerously Unprepared." Noting that only 10 percent of American fire departments can adequately respond to a collapsed building, most public health laboratories can't analyze a WMD attack, and most police forces can't secure a site after one, it called for up to five times as much federal money for emergency responders. How did the Bush administration respond? A spokesman accused the study's authors of wanting "gold-plated telephones," and the White House proposed cutting emergency responder grants in 2006 by 25 percent. Similarly, the Coast Guard estimates it would cost more than $5 billion over ten years to make U.S. ports minimally secure—yet the Bush administration has provided just over one-seventh that amount. And it has spent one-twenty-fourth as much as the American Public Transportation Association recommends to protect against the kind of train bombing that hit Madrid in March 2004. As the Center for Strategic and Budgetary Assessments noted in its analysis of Bush's 2006 budget, "Given the enormous challenges related to homeland security that the United States faces, it is possible that substantially more funding may be needed than has been proposed by the administration." But given the Bush tax cuts, and the coming entitlement crunch, "substantially more funding" is impossible.

For the statesmen and thinkers who made U.S. foreign policy at the beginning of the cold war, nothing was more important than the long-term strength of the American home front. It was America's great advantage, to be guarded and nurtured as carefully as any asset deployed overseas. Yet in the years since September 11, our long-term economic strength has been imperiled with a recklessness that would have left them astonished, and sputtering with rage.

IF THERE IS one group of conservatives who should understand that— who should insist that fighting totalitarianism trumps defunding the government—it's the group that traces its lineage back to cold war liberalism:

neoconservatives. The first generation of neocons, like Kirkpatrick, were disillusioned liberals and radicals. The 1960s counterculture, they argued, had turned liberals against bourgeois morality. And Vietnam had turned them against anti-Communism. The neocons believed in both, and so they drifted into the arms of the right. "Come on in," beckoned *National Review* in 1971, "the water's fine."

But the water wasn't exactly fine. Unlike traditional conservatives, the neocons of the 1970s did not yearn to shrink government. They opposed some aspects of Lyndon Johnson's war on poverty, particularly the Community Action Program, which they felt promoted militancy among the poor. But most social spending in the 1960s—Medicare, Medicaid, food stamps, housing subsidies, the expansion of Social Security—fell within the tradition of the New Deal. And while the neocons sometimes critiqued these programs on practical grounds (considering them ill-designed or overly ambitious), they had no problem with them in principle. Perhaps the most famous neoconservative, William Kristol's father Irving, wrote that "it was *NR*'s [*National Review*'s] primordial (as we saw it) hostility to the New Deal that created a gulf between us and them . . . we felt a measure of loyalty to the spirit of the New Deal if not to all its programs and policies. . . . All of us had ideas on how to improve, even reconstruct, this welfare state. We were meliorists, not opponents, and only measured critics."

Partly, the "gulf" was about priorities. For traditional conservatives, rolling back government was almost as important as rolling back Soviet power. For neocons, by contrast, fighting Communism trumped everything. In the 1970s, many neocons supported the labor movement, which traditional conservatives had long considered a loathsome intrusion into the free market. As another famous first-generation neoconservative, Norman Podhoretz (John's father), explained, "the most important reason of all had nothing to do with personal sentiment or domestic affairs. It was the fact that the leadership of the labor movement was so staunchly anti-Communist."

Over time, however, neocon views evolved—not only on spreading democracy but on slashing government. Ronald Reagan brought many neocons into the Republican coalition, and as team players, they supported his small-government agenda. After all, the right's battle against taxes didn't threaten the neocons' battle against Communism. Reagan cut taxes *and* boosted defense, as the magical Laffer curve assured the right's various factions that they could have it all.

Had the cold war not ended, the neocons and their allies might have fallen out, as huge budget deficits forced the right to choose between raising taxes and cutting defense. But with Communism gone, big defense cuts weren't that divisive. Younger neocons like Wolfowitz and William Kristol pushed for a more interventionist, moralistic foreign policy. On domestic policy, however, the merger was largely complete. If neoconservatism "originally differed from the older varieties of conservatism in wishing to reform rather than abolish the welfare state," wrote Norman Podhoretz in 1996, "few traces of that difference remain visible today."

That's still true. And after 9/11, it's a big problem. Just like their forefathers in the 1970s, today's neoconservatives want to wield American power aggressively against a totalitarian foe. And once again, defeating that foe supposedly takes precedence over everything else. Except that it no longer does. Today's neocons are even more ensconced in the Republican coalition than the first generation. And they have dutifully applauded a conservative economic agenda that is steering the country toward fiscal crisis—a crisis that threatens America's ability to fight totalitarianism. The neocons still call themselves the true heirs of cold war liberalism, with its focus on strengthening America at home so it can defend freedom around the world. But by embracing the right's economic agenda, they have forfeited that claim. And the country is weaker as a result.

FINALLY, SEPTEMBER 11 has reawakened one last conservative foreign policy tradition. And it is the most dangerous tradition of all. Many of today's leading conservatives, like their predecessors, tell Americans they are inherently good.

In the early cold war, a great fear stalked conservative anti-Communism: the fear of moral relativism. Conservatives knew the United States was materially strong enough to defeat the Soviet Union. But they considered this a false comfort, since the true struggle was not material at all. Burnham mocked "those of our leaders who believe the answer to defeats in the Cold War to be one after another colossal weapons system heaped on the armament pile, or a compound growth rate for our economic plant." Material might, he insisted, was worthless without the will to use it. And that will was being sapped by moral relativism. Communists *knew* they were right—and this absolute faith made them an awesome foe. Americans, by contrast, possessed no such certainty. Liberalism, with its hidden sympathy for Communism, had undermined America's confidence that it embodied good and the USSR, evil. Maybe, the average American thought to himself, Communism was just a different point of view. Why not live and let live? It was this attitude, conservatives believed, that underlay America's reluctance to root out Communists at home, and its defeatist policy of containment abroad. Relativism was making Americans morally weak, subtly sapping them of the will to fight and, ultimately, in Burnham's words, of "the will to survive."

Cold war liberals also urged Americans to believe in the anti-Communist cause. In particular, they worried that "doughface" liberals like Henry Wallace—by requiring that American actions be morally pure— were making such belief practically impossible. But they were equally worried about uncritical belief, a moral hubris that blinded Americans to their capacity for injustice. "We must take, and must continue to take, morally hazardous actions to preserve our civilization," wrote Niebuhr. "We must exercise our power. But we ought neither to believe that a nation is capable of perfect disinterestedness in its exercise, nor become complacent about particular degrees of interest and passion which corrupt the justice by which the exercise of power is legitimized." For antitotalitarian liberals, the United States was capable of greatness, but only if it recognized its capacity for evil. And this humility underlay key aspects of Truman's foreign policy. It made his administration more tolerant of external restraints on American power. And it produced a reluctance to force countries into lockstep with the United States, as long as they remained independent of the USSR as well. Soviet Communism, George Kennan argued, constituted an empire, while the United States did not. And that was a hidden source of Moscow's weakness, and Washington's strength.

This was a far cry from the perspective of Burnham and Buckley and Dulles, who felt Americans were entirely too aware of their capacity for evil already. "Some think that peace can be assured if we see only the good that is in others and the evil that is in ourselves," wrote Dulles. "I believe that involves blurred vision rather than clear vision and that peace requires our seeing clearly what there is of righteousness in our institutions and defending that." The United States, in this view, didn't need to restrain its power; it needed to unleash it—so good could fight evil with all its force. In 1947, Burnham called for a global American empire—a "United States of the World"—with a monopoly over nuclear weapons. Other countries might chafe at first, he acknowledged. But eventually they would see that, although such an empire would be "set up at least in part through coercion (quite probably including war, but certainly the threat of war)," it would not devolve into "tyranny and despotism." Luckily for the rest of the world, the United States would not be corrupted, even by unlimited power.

For conservatives worried about America's lack of faith in itself, the reaction to Vietnam confirmed their worst fears. By the early 1970s, large chunks of the political elite seemed to have abandoned any conviction that American democracy was clearly superior to Communism. Indeed, it was this fury at the liberal establishment's apparent unwillingness to defend America—either from its New Left critics at home or from its leftist enemies abroad—that pushed so many neocons into the arms of the right. What the United States needed, as Jeane Kirkpatrick famously said after becoming Reagan's ambassador to the UN, was to remove the "kick me" sign pinned to its back.

There was some merit to the right's view: many Vietnam-era liberals *had* lost the confidence to defend American democracy against its critics. And Reagan forcefully shifted the pendulum back. Finally, an American president spoke the language conservatives had been yearning for since the 1950s: he called the Soviets an "evil empire." And in the 1983 speech where he uttered those famous words, Reagan reprised the old conservative theme: moral relativism. Invoking Whittaker Chambers, he told the crowd to resist the temptation "of blithely declaring yourselves above it all and label both sides equally at fault, to . . . remove yourself from the struggle between right and wrong and good and evil." After the speech, Buckley said Reagan would go down in history as a great man.

But even as Reagan replenished America's confidence, the legacy of Vietnam kept confidence from becoming hubris. Reagan could depict cold war battlefields like El Salvador and Afghanistan as showdowns between good and evil. He could even send weapons to help the anti-Communist side. But he never seriously contemplated deploying American troops. With the exception of his Potemkin invasion of Grenada, Reagan's behavior proved far more cautious than his rhetoric.

If Vietnam restrained American power, so did the cold war itself. The Reaganites generally distrusted international agreements and institutions, in 1982 scuttling the Law of the Sea Treaty, which the three preceding administrations had helped negotiate. But they never tried to liberate the United States from its core binding relationship: NATO. They didn't need to, since Western Europe had a deep interest in accommodating American power. Few prominent Europeans wanted the United States to vacate the Continent, leaving them at the mercy of the superpower on the other side of the Berlin Wall. So even as the European antinuclear movement howled, European governments deployed American Pershing and cruise missiles. And since the Reagan administration was as eager to keep Western Europe out of Moscow's clutches as were the Europeans themselves, it had its own interest in preserving consensus. All of which meant that while Reagan's America swelled with nationalist pride, it never degenerated into jingoism toward America's democratic allies.

WHEN THE COLD war ended, Reagan's successor, George H. W. Bush, briefly embraced international institutions, since with the Soviets gone, the United States could now bend them to its will. With a UN mandate, he gathered a large coalition to expel Saddam Hussein from Kuwait. And the 1992 Republican platform spoke of "new opportunities to build an international consensus on key issues."

But the right never fully trusted Bush, a man more comfortable with the cautious realism of Richard Nixon and Henry Kissinger than the Manichean Dulles-Reagan style. And as the 1990s wore on, conservatives began to remember why they had always feared giving other countries influence over American foreign policy. For the hawkish neocons, multilateralism kept the United States from intervening forcefully enough—for instance, in Iraq, where they blamed the UN coalition for preventing the United States from marching to Baghdad. For most conservatives, the problem was the reverse: as peacekeeping operations multiplied on Clinton's watch, international coalitions seemed to be dragging America into conflicts where it had no business. The 1994 Contract with America vowed to bar U.S. troops from serving under foreign command. And by 1996, Republican nominee Bob Dole was publicly taunting UN Secretary-General Boutros Boutros-Ghali, to the delight of conservative crowds. In Congress, the GOP aggressively pushed a missile defense shield, behind which the United States could safely retreat from a messy, corrupting world. Unlike Clinton, who argued that America must embrace the world's increased interdependence, conservatives were looking for ways to escape it.

Conservative foreign policy before 9/11 represented a partial reversion to the Taft-style isolationism of the late 1940s. America would oppose international restraints on its power, but since it had little desire to remake the world in its image, America would restrain itself. In its first eight months in office, the Bush administration repudiated the Kyoto Protocol on global warming, the Comprehensive Test Ban Treaty, the International

Criminal Court, the Anti-Ballistic Missile Treaty, an enforcement mechanism for the Biological Weapons Convention, and a treaty on the sale of small arms. For good measure, it forced out the heads of two UN agencies and ended high-level U.S. involvement in the Israeli-Palestinian dispute, the conflict in Northern Ireland, and disarmament talks with North Korea. These actions went over poorly abroad. But they were more churlish than menacing. Rather than projecting American power, President Bush seemed content to hoard it.

That all changed when the twin towers fell. On the right, there was virtual unanimity that the United States had been hit because Al Qaeda saw it as weak. Just as conservatives had blamed Soviet expansion in the 1970s on America's post-Vietnam crisis of confidence, they now accused the feckless Clintonites of allowing new enemies to think they could strike the United States and get away with it. American "weakness [and] vacillation," Cheney argued, had "encouraged people like Osama bin Laden . . . to launch repeated strikes against the United States and our people overseas and here at home, with the view that he could, in fact, do so with impunity."

Bernard Lewis, the eminent Arabist who became the Bush administration's leading guide to the Muslim world, explained that in the jihadists' view, "the United States had become morally corrupt, socially degenerate, and in consequence, politically and militarily enfeebled." And conservatives found that argument compelling because it matched their own deep fears about American society. They too saw the Clinton administration's foreign policy weakness as the product, ultimately, of its moral weakness—a weakness they feared had seeped into the marrow of American life. Beneath the superficial novelty of America's terror war lurked the same old conservative fears. Could America match the absolute confidence of its fanatical foes? Had liberalism produced a nation of relativists, unable to distinguish good from evil? The "religion of nonjudgementalism . . . has permeated our culture, encouraging a paralysis of the moral faculty," wrote William Bennett, in a book titled *Why We Fight: Moral Clarity and the War on Terrorism*. "We have been caught with our defenses down—our intellectual and moral defenses as much as our physical ones."

Dutifully, George W. Bush followed the Reagan script, applying the talismanic phrase "evil" to Iraq, Iran, and North Korea, America's supposed opponents in the terror war. Bush's deep evangelical faith was particularly reassuring to conservatives; ever since Whittaker Chambers, the right had suspected that secularism sapped America's ability to tell right from wrong. The Bush doctrine, Podhoretz wrote approvingly, is "built on a repudiation of moral relativism."

But there were great, gaping problems with applying the Reagan model after 9/11. Reagan had taken office in the wake of Vietnam, when American elites really had suffered a crisis of confidence, and American power was, to some extent, under siege. September 11, by contrast, had been preceded by no such cultural crisis—except in the mind of the right, which saw Clinton's popularity as a symptom of the nation's moral rot. And even with lower Manhattan in flames, American power was hardly in retreat. Whatever the frustrations of the 1990s, the core reality was that the United States had vanquished its chief ideological competitor and military rival, leaving it in a position of astonishing strength.

So in the Bush era, while the government needed to call Americans to action, it did not need to tell them they were infallible. To the contrary, it needed to remember they were not—since key external restraints on American power had melted away. Unlike Reagan, Bush was not limited by a second superpower. With the Soviet Union gone, America could wield military force almost anywhere, including—as Kosovo showed—the former Eastern bloc. What's more, the democratic revolutions of 1989 had left America far more confident of its creed than it had been when Reagan took office, and far more certain of democracy's universal reach. And finally, Vietnam's inhibiting memory had faded, obscured by more recent military victories in the Balkans and the Gulf. Even as lower Manhattan smoldered, the nation was feeling—and looking—extraordinarily strong. If conservatives fretted about American weakness, most of the planet agreed with France's foreign minister, Hubert Védrine, who called the United States a "hyperpower," a colossus that bestrode the world like no power since ancient Rome.

And there was one last restraint that had been lifted. The Kosovo intervention and Tony Blair, Bill Clinton, and Kofi Annan's statements in its wake had fostered an emerging ethic that justified infringements of national sovereignty in the name of human rights and other global goods. In the 1990s, the American right had viewed this new ethic with suspicion. Conservatives disliked Clinton's humanitarian interventions and feared that the United States would also be asked to surrender some of its sovereignty for the good of the world—a fear confirmed when other countries pressured it to alter its environmental practices in keeping with the Kyoto Protocol on global warming. In her 2000 article in *Foreign Affairs*, Rice expressed alarm that "the United States has decided to enforce notions of 'limited sovereignty' worldwide in the name of humanitarianism. This overly broad definition of America's national interest is bound to backfire as others arrogate the same authority to themselves."

But after 9/11, the Bush team dramatically reversed course and offered a sweeping new rationale for violating the sovereignty of other nations: terrorism. Any regime accused of supporting terror, especially if it was developing weapons of mass destruction, was now a possible candidate for American invasion. Preventive war (war against a potential threat)—which the Bush administration falsely labeled "preemption" (war against an imminent threat)—had long been rejected as too dangerous under international law. Yet it was now the explicit policy of the sole superpower on earth. The world, as Princeton's G. John Ikenberry put it, suddenly resembled a town where there was only one remaining policeman and the houses no longer had locks. To most foreign observers, in other words, the United States didn't need to prove it could wield power; it needed to prove it wouldn't become a predator. Niebuhr's old theme—the danger of unrestrained, unreflective power—had never been more relevant. And yet America's leaders believed American power was inherently, and self-evidently, good.

JOHN FOSTER DULLES, Arthur Schlesinger once noted, "had a complacent conviction of American moral infallibility—all other nations acted according to selfish motives, America was pure." And in this sense, as in others, men like Dick Cheney, Donald Rumsfeld, and Bush himself are Dulles's ideological heirs. "I'm amazed that there is such misunderstanding of what our country is about," Bush exclaimed in October 2001, never contemplating that foreign perceptions might stem from foreign experience. "Like most Americans, I just can't believe it. Because I know how good we are." Bush's aides boasted about his lack of self-doubt. After hearing Bush's second inaugural, former Reagan speechwriter Peggy Noonan, in a rare note of conservative criticism, commented on the Bush administration's disturbing "sense that there are few legitimate boundaries to the desires born in the goodness of their good hearts."

It was this assumption of automatic goodness that underlay the right's post-9/11 discussion of empire. Burnham had been able to float the idea in 1947 because the USSR did not yet have nuclear weapons. Now, in another single-superpower world, it was thinkable again. "People are now coming out of the closet on the word empire," declared Krauthammer in

2002. Usually, the new imperialists modified the word with an adjective like "liberal" or "benign." What these phrases really meant was that the United States would rid itself of external restraints on its power, but act in liberal or benign ways. The prospect that America might be corrupted by such unrestrained power—and thus act in a less than benign fashion—was breezily dismissed.

This imperial mentality was most obvious on questions of democracy and human rights, where the Bush administration replaced its pre-9/11 ethic, "Don't bother us, and we won't bother you," with a new one: "we set the rules, and you abide by them." In its treatment of terror suspects, the Bush administration informed the world, America would be bound by no international rules, only by its own, unfailing, moral sense. The White House refused to comply with the International Convention on Torture, which America had signed and ratified. Instead, the White House developed its own, strikingly narrow definition of torture, which banned only pain equivalent to "organ failure, impairment of bodily function, or even death." When the International Red Cross examined America's prisons in Iraq, the Bush administration hid "ghost detainees" whom the investigators were never allowed to see. And it hid entire prisons—CIA-run ghost facilities—whose locations remained a secret.

It was bad enough to take this position before 9/11, when the United States took an unsentimental view of other countries' domestic behavior. But it was far more audacious afterward, once President Bush had designated himself a kind of global missionary for human rights, declaring himself in solidarity with jailed political prisoners and suggesting that promoting freedom was America's destiny, as ordained by God. The Bush administration, critics argued, was missing a golden opportunity; it should use the detainee issue to prove that its human rights rhetoric was sincere. But conservatives responded with the same logic that had undergirded their support for Joseph McCarthy: America didn't need to prove anything; the righteousness of its cause was self-evident. Confronted by Amnesty International's charge that U.S. detention policies violated human rights, Bush responded, "It's an absurd allegation. The United States is a country that promotes freedom around the world."

IN FACT, FOR many conservatives, the criticism itself represented an attempt to shatter America's confidence and weaken it against its enemies. When the torture scandal began to unfold—as it became clear that Americans, freed from clear legal and moral restraints, could act just as bar-

barically as anyone else—few conservatives argued that the United States should comply with international law. Few even suggested greater oversight by Congress or the courts. Instead, they turned on the critics, especially foreign critics, accusing them of using human rights to mask their real agenda: anti-Americanism. Torture allegations, Podhoretz claimed, had become "another weapon in the war against the war."

The assumption—as Schlesinger said of Dulles—that "all other nations acted according to selfish motives" runs throughout post-9/11 conservative commentary. Just as the right insisted that European critics of U.S. torture policies weren't genuinely concerned about human rights, they also insisted that France and Germany's stated reasons for opposing the Iraq war concealed their real motive: preserving corrupt oil deals with Saddam (even as they dismissed as absurd the suggestion that oil played any role in U.S. decisions). And even in the days immediately following 9/11, with Europeans literally in the streets declaring their solidarity with the people of New York, the right began insisting that America's European allies could not be trusted. "Once the fighting starts," wrote Victor Davis Hanson one week after the attacks, "despite initial pledges of support, the Europeans will probably extend words of encouragement but lend no real material or military assistance." In their book *An End to Evil*, David Frum and Richard Perle wrote that after 9/11, "The United States asked its friends and allies to join in the fight against terror—and discovered that after the first emotional expressions of sympathy for the victims, those friends and allies were prepared to do little."

The irony is that far from spurning U.S. requests in the weeks and months following the attack, the Europeans were desperate to help. After 9/11, NATO for the first time invoked Article Five, which required member nations to aid an ally under attack. Gerhard Schroeder's insistence that Germany join the war on terror resulted in a parliamentary vote that nearly toppled his government. But the Bush administration interpreted these efforts as a subtle bid to reign in American power. And since it assumed that foreign constraints could only weaken the United States, never strengthen it, the Bush administration rejected NATO's help in Afghanistan. The more America trusted itself, it seemed, the less it could trust anyone else.

GIVEN THESE ASSUMPTIONS, it is not surprising that conservatives have generally greeted skyrocketing anti-Americanism with a shrug. "Resentment comes with the territory," explained the columnist Max Boot.

But if the "territory" is America's overwhelming power, it doesn't explain anti-Americanism's dramatic rise in the Bush era. In 1999 and 2000, the United States was viewed favorably by more than half of Turks and Brazilians, and roughly three-quarters of Germans, Moroccans, and Indonesians. When researchers checked again, between early 2003 and early 2004, U.S. popularity had dropped more than 20 points in Turkey and Brazil, 40 points in Germany, 50 points in Morocco, and a breathtaking 60 points in Indonesia. As the U.S. Advisory Group on Public Diplomacy in the Arab and Muslim World put it, "hostility toward America has reached shocking levels."

The reasons for this freefall vary. In Europe, where environmentalism is stronger than in the United States, Bush's rejection of the Kyoto Protocol—and his refusal to even offer a serious alternative—damaged his image from the very beginning. In the Middle East, U.S. support for Israeli policies toward the Palestinians plays a major role. Everywhere, there is anger over Iraq. But these specific objections are all symptoms of a larger phenomenon, and it is exactly the phenomenon that cold war liberals took such pains to forestall: fewer and fewer people around the world see American power as legitimate. Fewer and fewer think U.S. primacy benefits them. Partly this is because they feel unable to influence the United States. Surveys show that large majorities in country after country think Washington doesn't listen to their governments. And partly it is because they don't believe the United States really upholds the principles it claims to cherish. A 2005 Pew study concludes that "the rest of the world has become deeply suspicious of U.S. motives and openly skeptical of its word." America may say it is fighting terrorism or spreading democracy, but in Europe, the Middle East, and pretty much everywhere else, most people believe America's real goal is to control oil and dominate the world. The more fervently the Bush administration and its conservative allies insist upon America's essential virtue, the less people in foreign lands agree.

For the new struggle against totalitarianism, all this is a disaster. But it is a disaster that expresses itself differently in different places. In Europe, American illegitimacy means America can't get its allies to take risks in the fight against jihad. Conservatives sometimes say Europeans will cooperate against terrorism no matter how much they dislike the Bush administration because doing so is in their self-interest. But they also say Europeans don't see their self-interest the way Americans do. In fact, the United States needs European governments to do things they find difficult: pressure friendly dictatorships like Egypt and Pakistan to democratize; extradite terror suspects to the United States, even though we have the death penalty; pressure Russia to reach a political solution in Chechnya, which has become a salafist hotbed, and help with nation building in Afghanistan and Iraq.

European governments will always have an incentive to help America out; we're the most powerful country on earth. But in recent years they have gained a powerful incentive not to as well. It's called democracy. When most Europeans fear and resent American power, opposing American power is smart politics. In the fall of 2002, Gerhard Schroeder came from behind to win reelection by pandering to the German people's overwhelming opposition to the war in Iraq. In the spring of 2004, José Luis Rodríguez Zapatero's promise to pull Spain's troops out of Iraq won him his country's prime ministership. In May 2005, Prime Minister Tony Blair won reelection in Britain, but his support for Iraq and his close ties to President Bush cost him more than half his majority in Parliament. And even European leaders ideologically inclined to be pro-American, like Schroeder's successor, the right-leaning Angela Merkel, find themselves constrained by the hostility of their publics. The harsh truth is that there is barely a country in NATO whose population wants its leaders to aggressively back the war on terror, as George W. Bush defines it. The United States can still coerce, but it has largely lost its ability to persuade.

In the Islamic world, American illegitimacy is even more dangerous. As ex-CIA Bin Laden expert Michael Scheuer has argued, salafism is like a vast insurgency, seeking to overthrow governments across the Middle East. And in a counterinsurgency war, what matters most are the hearts and minds of the people with whom the insurgents live. In that battle, salafists have long had one big asset: Muslims hate their governments. But increasingly they have another: Muslims hate the United States. Studies show that Muslims who feel their religion is under attack from an outside power are more likely to support terrorism. And many now feel their religion is under attack from the United States. In the Arab world today, Al Qaeda is more popular than the United States, and it is popular largely *because* it opposes the United States. In the war on terror, the United States isn't providing the solution; it's fueling the problem.

The Bush administration thinks America can change that by championing democracy and human rights. But it's hard to effectively champion democracy when no one believes that's what you're really doing. When the

United States announced MEPI, a newspaper in the United Arab Emirates commented that America "allocates $29 million to defend democracy and freedom, while it opens Guantánamo camps."

The brave Middle Eastern liberals who are fighting for democracy and against salafism need us. They need our money, our expertise, and our example, just as anti-Communist liberals and socialists did in Western Europe more than a half-century ago. The United States should be—as George W. Bush says—the great ally of democratic revolutionaries around the world. But the more we're despised, the more we undermine the people we're trying to help. As Fareed Zakaria has noted, in the Arab world today, "the easiest way to sideline a reform is to claim that it is pro-American."

George W. Bush has faithfully carried out the great conservative project. He has stripped away the restraints on American power, in an effort to show the world that we are not weak. And in the process, he has made American power illegitimate, which has made us weak. He has denied America's capacity for evil, in an effort to bolster America's faith in itself. And in the process, America has committed terrible misdeeds, which have sapped the world's faith in us—and ultimately, our faith in ourselves.

6

Iraq

PLENTY OF LIBERALS backed the invasion of Iraq. I was one of them. But we were mostly spectators, cheering, and sometimes grimacing, from the sidelines. It was conservatives, of various stripes, who conceived, planned, and implemented the war. And the Bush administration's rationale for it drew on two of conservative antitotalitarianism's deepest traditions: the belief that only states wield real power in world affairs, and the belief that America's enemies cannot be contained.

In the first two decades of the cold war, one of the hidden assumptions of the American right was that what really mattered in the world were states. It remained hidden because liberals believed the same thing. (Only the far left dissented, clinging to the Marxist view that international capital and the international proletariat were the primary forces in international affairs.) With two nuclear-tipped behemoths arranging and rearranging the world seemingly at will, mainstream commentators took state power as self-evident. The issue barely came up.

But by the 1970s, states no longer looked so omnipotent. Multinational corporations were on the rise. So was international trade, which bound countries together and left governments less able to control their economic destinies. The military might that had made the superpowers so fearsome suddenly seemed less useful. After all, the United States hadn't been able to bludgeon a group of slipper-wearing Southeast Asian guerrillas into submission. Nor were nuclear weapons much help against OPEC, the oil-producing club whose members held the U.S. economy hostage in the mid-1970s. International relations scholars began musing about "interdependence"—a changed world in which no single government could achieve as much on its own. And for post-Vietnam liberals, increasingly concerned about problems like the environment, third-world poverty, and the threat of nuclear war, this seemed like good news. The United States, they suggested, should compete less, especially militarily, and cooperate more.

Conservatives, by contrast, suspected that all this talk of global problems and transnational cooperation was a fancy attempt to put anti-Communism out to pasture. Republican realists like Richard Nixon and Henry Kissinger had their own reasons for promoting cooperation with the Soviets. But traditional, *National Review*-style conservatives—along with the burgeoning neocons—didn't believe the Soviets were interested in cooperating on anything except taking over the world. And in their view, the more the United States tried to find common ground with the USSR—for instance, in the arms control talks that stretched throughout the 1970s—the more it got taken to the cleaners. So the right's invisible assumption became visible: what mattered in the world were states, especially large, heavily armed ones. And if American liberals had forgotten that, conservatives warned, the Soviets surely had not.

At decade's end, when the USSR invaded Afghanistan and détente collapsed, the cooperation talk died down. But it returned with a vengeance after the cold war, when interdependence gained a trendy new name: globalization. The Clinton administration didn't ignore traditional power politics, but it highlighted a new type of threat, which stemmed less from other governments than from forces other governments could not control: financial meltdowns, organized crime, loose nukes, environmental degradation, and disease. And once again, conservatives largely dismissed this as globaloney. Instead, they searched for the new military rivals that would succeed the USSR. The obvious candidate was China, a potential great power rapidly building up its arsenal. The others were "rogue states," like Iraq, North Korea, and Iran, seeking nuclear weapons. As early as 1991, Charles Krauthammer authored an influential essay arguing that "the rise of small aggressive states armed with weapons of mass destruction" posed the greatest challenge to post–cold war America. In 1998, when congressional Republicans appointed Donald Rumsfeld to head a commission on the danger ballistic missiles posed to U.S. security, he focused on these same "developing" threats. And when the Bush administration took office, it made missile defense its top foreign policy priority. The post–cold war right may have been split on how to deal with these new dangers—for neocons the answer was regime change; for others it was Fortress America—but at least they agreed that the new dangers, like the old one, came from states.

Not surprisingly, then, while the Clinton administration often described terrorism as a force beyond governments' control, post–cold war conservatives saw it as an instrument of state power. In her January 2000 *Foreign Affairs* essay outlining the Bush campaign's foreign policy principles, Condoleezza Rice argued that "the threat of rogue regimes and hostile powers . . . is increasingly taking the forms of the potential for terrorism and the development of weapons of mass destruction." In April 2001, when counterterrorism adviser Richard Clarke, a Clinton holdover, warned top Bush officials about the threat from Al Qaeda, Paul Wolfowitz challenged him. "You give bin Laden too much credit," Wolfowitz declared. "He could not do all these things like the 1993 attack on New York, not without a state sponsor." In fact, the CIA *did* believe jihadists had bombed the World Trade Center in 1993 without a state sponsor. But Wolfowitz—echoing the controversial conservative scholar Laurie Mylroie—insisted the attack had been masterminded by Iraq. On September 4, 2001, when Bush officials discussed terrorism again, Rumsfeld also tried to steer the conversation away from Al Qaeda and toward what he considered the greater terrorist threat: Saddam Hussein.

When 9/11 hit a week later, it was more of the same. Rumsfeld immediately asked Pentagon lawyers to investigate an Iraqi connection. The next morning, Wolfowitz suggested that such a massive attack could only have been carried out with state assistance. Cheney argued that "To the extent we define our task broadly . . . including those who support terrorism, then we get at states."

By September 15, Bush had decided to move against Afghanistan, not Iraq—perhaps because he was swayed by Colin Powell's argument that an attack on Iraq would lack international support and perhaps because there was no evidence Saddam was behind 9/11. But despite the lack of evidence—and the CIA's conclusion that, in fact, he was not—Bush remained unconvinced. "I believe Iraq was involved," the president told his aides two days later. And a state-centric view of terrorism became, as Undersecretary of Defense Douglas Feith later put it, the "principal strategic thought underlying our strategy in the war on terrorism. . . . Terrorist organizations cannot be effective in sustaining themselves over long periods of time to do large-scale operations if they don't have support from states."

This "strategic thought" was mostly wrong. By 2004, Bush's National Intelligence Council—echoing the Clinton view—would report that "in a globalized world, [terrorist] groups . . . are increasingly self-sufficient." Rumsfeld's own Defense Science Board insisted that "We must think in terms of global [terror] networks, both government and non-government. If we continue to concentrate primarily on states . . . we will fail." But in late 2001, as the Afghan war wound down, the Bush administration was describing salafist terrorism as a mere adjunct to rogue regimes.

In particular, Bush officials were preoccupied with weapons of mass destruction. It was an understandable fixation, fueled by the September and October anthrax attacks and terrifying intelligence reports that Pakistani nuclear scientists had traveled to Afghanistan to meet with Bin Laden. But when the administration described the potential for a terrorist attack using WMD, it rarely speculated that jihadists might buy, steal, or build an unconventional weapon without a government's knowledge. (Indeed, in its first budget, the Bush White House actually tried to cut funding for programs aimed at preventing the theft of nuclear stockpiles in the former Soviet Union.) Instead, it focused almost exclusively on the prospect of a rogue state *giving* terrorists WMD, even though experts considered that far less likely. In the Bush administration's view, jihadists were little different than missiles—just another weapon in the arsenal of state power.

In his January 2002 State of the Union address, Bush took this logic one remarkable step further. At first, he linked terrorists and rogue states, declaring famously that North Korea, Iran, and Iraq "and their terrorist allies, constitute an axis of evil." But two paragraphs later, as his discussion of the war on terror drew to a rousing conclusion, Bush dropped the reference to terrorism altogether, pledging that "I will not stand by, as peril draws closer and closer. The United States of America will not permit the world's most dangerous regimes to threaten us with the world's most destructive weapons." It was an astonishing sleight of hand. As William Kristol noted approvingly, in "the climactic paragraph" of Bush's most famous speech about terrorism, "the word 'terrorism' entirely disappeared."

BUT PRIORITIZING STATES is not the same as invading them. And here the Bush administration tapped into an equally venerable conservative tradition: rollback. In the 1950s and 1960s, hostility to containment was a defining feature of the cold war right. Barry Goldwater likened containment to a "boxer who refuses to throw a punch." If the United States tried merely to block the Soviet advance, he argued, it would grow inexorably weaker. Kennan had assumed the opposite—that as Washington parried Moscow's blows, it was the Soviets who would gradually tire and either modify their behavior or see their empire crack, as satellites broke away and their social system gave out. But conservatives, who harbored deep fears about America's strength of will, were more pessimistic. In the late 1940s, with the Soviets rushing to develop an atomic bomb, Burnham suggested preventive war—a first strike to preserve the American nuclear monopoly while there was still time.

Once Moscow got the bomb in 1949, forcibly liberating Eastern Europe became an even dicier proposition. Dulles loudly demanded it, even writing the denunciation of containment into the 1952 Republican platform. But as secretary of state he followed a more sober course. And when the 1956 Hungarian uprising created the perfect rollback moment, even the editors of *National Review* couldn't agree on a response, with Burnham surprising everyone and supporting the Eisenhower administration's refusal to intervene.

In the wake of Vietnam, with Republican presidents pursuing détente and liberals retreating from even containment, rollback was a distant dream. But if the policy seemed outlandish, the mentality behind it endured. For post-Vietnam conservatives, in fact, the fears of the 1950s—that the United States was growing inexorably weaker—were being fulfilled before their eyes. In the mid-1970s, a flamboyant RAND Corporation logician and nuclear strategist named Albert Wohlstetter published an influential series of articles arguing that the United States was seriously underestimating Soviet military strength. Wohlstetter had made his reputation pointing out America's hidden vulnerability to a Soviet nuclear strike. And his belief that the United States was more imperiled than policy makers knew—or cared to know—rubbed off on two of his star pupils, Paul Wolfowitz and Richard Perle. In 1976, Wolfowitz was appointed to serve on Team B, a commission partly prompted by Wohlstetter's articles, and tasked with reviewing the CIA's analysis of the Soviet threat. Not surprisingly, given its hawkish cast, Team B endorsed Wohlstetter's critique. Moscow, the commission concluded, was not seeking coexistence with the United States; it was seeking "global Soviet hegemony." The implicit message was the same one conservatives had been preaching for decades: unless America went on the offense, it would find itself in greater and greater peril.

When Reagan took office, that view finally became U.S. policy. Some key Reagan advisers had opposed containment from the beginning. CIA director William Casey, for instance, who served as a kind of shadow secretary of state, had helped found *National Review*, and denounced Eisenhower and Dulles's failure to liberate Eastern Europe. Others, like Kirkpatrick, Perle, Eugene Rostow, and Elliott Abrams, were cold war liberals who had drifted right. Together, they fashioned a foreign policy that fell somewhere between rollback and robust containment, depending on how one defines the terms. Reagan certainly sounded the old, anticontainment themes, asking in his 1982 speech to the British Parliament: "Must freedom wither in a quiet, deadening accommodation with totalitarian evil?" And many of his policies were clearly aimed at turning up the pressure on the Kremlin—from his massive military buildup to his demand that Moscow tear down the Berlin Wall to his support for counterrevolutionaries in the third world. Yet while Reagan sent weapons to combat Moscow's advance, he refused to send U.S. troops, even as the Sandinistas consolidated their leftist revolution in Nicaragua and tried to export it to El Salvador. In 1984, Norman Podhoretz bitterly attacked him for not taking more aggressive economic measures to undermine Communist control in Poland. Quoting a critic of John Foster Dulles, Podhoretz said Reagan "was always talking of 'calculated risks,' which in practice most often meant that he calculated a great deal and risked nothing."

Did Reagan pursue rollback? Ultimately, it doesn't matter. What matters is that once the Soviet Union fell, conservatives came to *believe* that he had. "It was the vision and will of Ronald Reagan," Dick Cheney would declare, "that gave hope to the oppressed, shamed the oppressors, and ended an evil empire." Rollback had become a myth and a template, waiting for a new conservative generation to make it their own.

TWO NEW REALITIES permitted George W. Bush to do what Dulles, and even Reagan, never could. For one thing, the world had become unipolar; there was no second superpower to limit America's reach. For another, 9/11 had introduced Americans to an enemy—jihadist terrorism—that truly could not be contained.

By conflating jihadists with Iraq, the Bush administration cited the attacks as powerful new evidence for the right's old anticontainment argument. "Containment is not possible when unbalanced dictators with weapons of mass destruction can deliver those weapons on missiles or secretly provide them to terrorist allies," declared Bush at West Point in

June 2002. "Old doctrines of security do not apply," added Cheney in August. What Cheney neglected to mention was that he and other top administration officials had never really believed in those "old doctrines" to begin with.

As during the cold war, the anticontainment argument rested on the assumption that America's enemies were more dangerous than they appeared. For Wolfowitz, that assumption had been honed first by Team B and then by his 1998 stint on Rumsfeld's ballistic missiles commission, which—to the surprise of no one—accused the intelligence agencies of underestimating the threat from rogue states. And on Iraq, Wolfowitz was particularly inclined to view the CIA as Pollyannaish. He had been worried about Saddam since the late 1970s, when he issued a report warning that Iraq could threaten the oil fields of the Persian Gulf. But the CIA had not shared his fears and, years later, had failed to foresee Saddam's invasion of Kuwait. The CIA, Wolfowitz wrote in 1994, allowed its analysts to "conceal ignorance of facts, policy bias or any number of things that may lie behind the personal opinions that are presented as sanctified intelligence judgments." So in late 2002, Wolfowitz created the Office of Special Plans, a kind of Team B within the Pentagon, to review intelligence on Iraq.

The problem was that by 2002, the right's assumption that foreign threats were greater than the CIA and the rest of the allegedly liberal foreign policy bureaucracy would acknowledge had become a theology. "Any intelligence estimate that would cause us to relax [about Saddam's nuclear program] would be about as useful as the ones that missed his nuclear program in the early 1990s, or failed to predict the Indian nuclear test in 1998 or to gain even a hint of the Sept. 11 attack," wrote Richard Perle, now chairman of Bush's Defense Policy Board. When informed by Richard Clarke that the intelligence agencies didn't believe Saddam had been involved in terrorism against the United States since 1993, Wolfowitz shot back, "Just because the FBI and CIA have failed to find the linkages does not mean they don't exist." "Intelligence estimates almost always underestimate capabilities," claimed Condoleezza Rice. All of which meant that for the Bush hawks, nothing the CIA found—or didn't find—could change their minds. The entire concept of preventive war (or "preemption, as the Bush administration falsely labeled it) put a premium on carefully sifting through empirical evidence. And yet Wolfowitz, Rice, and Perle were all but declaring empirical evidence beside the point.

Refracted through the conservative antitotalitarian prism—with its focus on states and its distrust of containment—9/11 had powerfully validated what Burnham called "the catastrophic point of view." Unless America struck first, he had argued in the 1940s, the Soviets would become unstoppable. Unless America began a rapid military buildup, argued Team B in the 1970s, the Soviets would gain strategic superiority. Unless America deployed a missile shield, argued the Rumsfeld Commission in the 1990s, rogue states would hold it hostage. The clock was always ticking; enemies were always growing stronger; time was never on our side. Containment strategies and CIA forecasts were comforting illusions peddled by liberals unwilling to stare evil in the face. "We have every reason to assume the worst," declared Bush. "Time is not on our side," added Cheney. For conservatives in the run-up to war with Iraq, America faced the same old question: Did it have the will to act before it was too late?

THERE WERE, OF COURSE, rationales for war that had nothing to do with whether the United States could contain Saddam. Iraq has huge reserves of oil, and establishing a friendly government there offered the prospect of reduced reliance on Saudi Arabia, whose instability 9/11 had laid bear. Saddam's military also looked weak, degraded by more than a decade of sanctions and allied bombing. For an administration yearning to make America's enemies fear it again after the supposedly feckless Clinton years, invading Iraq seemed to offer an easy, effective way. Finally, a liberal democracy in Iraq might provide a model for a Middle East caught between authoritarianism and jihad, and thus undermine the toxic forces that had produced 9/11.

All these arguments had their defenders. But President Bush never publicly made the first two, and only really made the third after his primary rationale—weapons of mass destruction and terrorist ties—had collapsed. It's not hard to understand why: they were too abstract to have won widespread support. To convince Americans to back the war, the Bush administration had to convince them that Saddam represented a direct, intolerable threat. And so the Iraq debate, at least the public one, hinged on whether containing Saddam was as impossible as the Bush hawks said it was. Was it such a pipe dream that America had no recourse but war?

The specific Iraqi threat that allegedly could not be contained was often left vague. But the Bush administration made essentially two arguments. The first was that Saddam would help jihadists carry out another 9/11, or worse. As Bush put it in his 2003 State of the Union address,

"Imagine those 19 hijackers with other weapons and other plans—this time armed by Saddam Hussein." The argument was always connected to weapons of mass destruction, with the implication that future hijackers might be armed with Iraqi WMD. In truth, however, weapons of mass destruction were superfluous to it. If Saddam had kept his supposed stockpiles to himself—but given the next Mohamed Atta $10 million instead—that would have been reason enough to invade. The specter of chemical, biological, or nuclear weapons gave this scenario its graphic punch, but it was really just an argument about Saddam's ties to terrorists who might strike the United States.

And that argument was terribly weak. "Saddam Hussein has long-standing, direct and continuing ties to terrorist networks," declared President Bush in a February 2003 radio address. But those networks were overwhelmingly directed against Israel, not the United States. Like many Arab leaders, Saddam had a long history of supporting anti-Israel terrorism. He backed the Palestine Liberation Organization in the early 1970s, then switched to the rival Abu Nidal organization, then took a hiatus, before paying the families of Palestinian suicide bombers once the second intifada broke out in 2000. He also sponsored terrorism against other regional rivals like Turkey and Iran.

All this was ugly. And it was all irrelevant to the Bush administration's case for war. Saddam hadn't attempted a terrorist attack *against the United States* since 1993, when his agents tried to assassinate former President Bush in Kuwait. And after 9/11, another attempt with Iraqi fingerprints would have been virtually suicidal, which was why the CIA predicted Saddam would try it only if his regime feared imminent U.S. attack.

Instead of striking the United States directly, Bush officials generally warned that Saddam would use Al Qaeda to obscure his role. And in the late 1990s, Al Qaeda *had* made contact with Iraqi intelligence, which isn't terribly surprising given that Al Qaeda had contacts, some far more extensive, with a range of Muslim regimes. But according to the 9/11 Commission, nothing came of these interactions: They never "developed into a collaborative operational relationship." The UN Monitoring Group on Al Qaeda came to the same conclusion. In the words of former Bush administration counterterrorism czar Richard Clarke, "Any Iraqi 'link' to al Qaeda is a minor footnote when compared to the links [that Al Qaeda had] with other regimes." And former Clinton administration Iraq expert Kenneth Pollack, a prominent supporter of the war, wrote that "terrorism is the least of the threats posed by Iraq to the interests of the United States . . . on the grand list of state sponsors of terrorism, Iraq is pretty far down." The Bush administration was right that if Iraq and Al Qaeda decided to jointly strike the United States, containment would be of little use. There just wasn't any evidence to suggest they would.

THE BUSH ADMINISTRATION'S second argument was intellectually stronger but politically weaker, since it was about neither terrorism nor attacks on American soil. It was that a rearmed Saddam might again menace his neighbors, but this time deter the United States from coming to their aid.

If the first argument required manipulating the word *terrorism*, the second required manipulating the acronym *WMD*. Weapons of mass destruction, of course, include chemical, biological, and nuclear arms. But for Saddam's quest to dominate the Middle East, the first two were largely irrelevant. Chemical and biological weapons have little offensive battlefield use, which may be why Saddam didn't use them when he invaded Kuwait. Defensively, chemical weapons can serve some function. Indeed, according to the Duelfer Report on Iraqi WMD, Saddam credited them with halting Tehran's ground offensives in the Iran-Iraq war. But while they may have helped against Iran, they offered little protection against the United States. This second argument for war envisioned Iraq again invading Kuwait, or another neighbor, and then using its WMD to deter the United States from expelling it. Yet Iraq *had* chemical weapons in 1990, and the United States *thought* it had them in 2003, and they didn't deter the United States at all. American troops just strapped on their gas masks and protective suits and destroyed Saddam's forces in battle.

Only an Iraqi nuclear weapon could conceivably have deterred the United States, and thus helped Saddam dominate the Gulf, with all that might have meant for the world's oil supply. In other words, the test of containment wasn't whether the United States could prevent Saddam from acquiring WMD. It was whether the United States could prevent him from joining the nuclear club.

Answering that question required determining how close Iraq was to obtaining a bomb. And on that crucial issue, the truth was shrouded in mystery. Saddam had fervently tried to develop a nuclear weapon in the run-up to the Gulf War. And after the war ended, inspectors from the International Atomic Energy Agency had spent years trying to verify that his nuclear program had been dismantled. By October 1997, the IAEA was reporting that "There are no indications that there remains in Iraq any physical capability for the production of amounts of weapons-usable nuclear material of any practical significance." But some Iraqi defectors disagreed, claiming that Saddam's nuclear program continued. Then, in 1998, with Saddam increasingly obstructing their work, the inspectors left, turning a hazy picture pitch black.

U.S. intelligence agencies responded to this new uncertainty with statements so vague they permitted virtually any possibility. In early 2001, the CIA claimed that Iraq "has probably continued at least low-level theoretical R&D associated with its nuclear program." But read carefully, that said almost nothing. "Low-level theoretical R&D" meant Saddam was reconstituting his nuclear program at the lowest possible level. "At least," therefore, meant that he might have a very slow moving nuclear program—or anything faster than that. And "probably" suggested that the CIA wasn't even sure he was reconstituting his program at all.

In 2002, as the Bush administration began its campaign for war, the intelligence assessments grew more confident and more alarming. In October, nine days before Congress voted on the war, an unclassified National Intelligence Estimate (NIE) stated that "most analysts assess Iraq is reconstituting its nuclear weapons program" and that Iraq "probably will have a nuclear weapon during this decade." In their public statements, top Bush officials went even further, with Dick Cheney insisting in September that "we do know, with absolute certainty, that he [Saddam] is using his procurement system to acquire the equipment he needs in order to enrich uranium to build a nuclear weapon." Bush repeatedly suggested that if Iraq bought weapons-grade uranium overseas, he could build a bomb within a year—while failing to note that the intelligence agencies considered such a purchase highly unlikely.

So in the fall of 2002, when members of Congress, and most Americans, were making up their minds about the war, they faced a strange situation. The intelligence agencies were saying Saddam was on his way to a nuclear bomb relatively soon, and some other governments seemed to agree. Yet a year earlier, U.S. intelligence had been far less certain.

And then, once inspectors returned to Iraq in late 2002, things began happening that should have set off alarm bells. In its claim that Saddam was rebuilding his nuclear program, the unclassified NIE had relied heavily on Iraq's supposed import of high-strength aluminum tubes. In fact, it was the only concrete evidence cited. But by February, the IAEA had rejected the claim, insisting the tubes were meant for conventional rockets. The IAEA also dismissed President Bush's statement in his 2003 State of the Union address that Iraq had tried to purchase weapons-grade uranium from Africa. And finally, on March 7—after several months of excellent access to Iraq's suspected nuclear sites—the agency declared that it had found "no indication of resumed nuclear activities" in the country whatsoever.

In mainstream political and journalistic circles, these revelations didn't receive the attention they deserved—because many people in Washington had already made up their minds on the war, because they contradicted the long-standing image of Saddam as obsessively pursuing nuclear weapons (an image that even most *opponents* of the war shared), and because the Bush administration derided the weapons inspectors as the international version of the CIA: naïve liberals deluded about the nature of evil. But in fact, the inspectors were far better informed than the United States. U.S. assertions about Iraqi WMD, as Colin Powell's February 5 presentation before the UN made clear, were based on satellite imagery and intercepted phone conversations. It was the IAEA inspectors who actually searched the buildings that the United States was photographing from thousands of miles away.

The IAEA's findings did not conclusively prove that Saddam had no nuclear program. (The inspectors said they still had more work to do.) But they raised it as a real possibility—enough of a possibility to justify continuing the inspections for weeks or months more. Given their near-theological certainty that Saddam was more dangerous than generally recognized, there was little chance that men like Cheney and Wolfowitz could have been convinced. Pro-war liberals, however, should have been more open-minded. It was reasonable to assume the worst about Saddam in the fall of 2002, given his frantic pursuit of a nuclear weapon before the Gulf War, his obstruction of the inspectors in the 1990s, and the recent statements of U.S. intelligence. But by spring of 2003, the picture was changing and worst-case analyses were no longer warranted.

September 11 had made worst-case logic seductive: the world had supposedly changed; the United States could no longer afford patience or tolerate risk; problems like Saddam needed to be solved once and for all. But in the case of Iraq, worst-case logic became a filter, preventing war supporters like myself from seeing the evidence mounting around us.

Apocalyptic thinking represented a break with the cold war liberal tradition, and a grave mistake.

IT IS IMPOSSIBLE to know for sure what would have happened if the inspections had continued into the spring and summer of 2003. But most likely, the inspectors would have grown increasingly certain that Saddam had no nuclear program, and then, at some point Saddam would have kicked them out. Sooner or later, in other words, the United States would have needed a new containment strategy.

The old one—which required Saddam to sell oil under UN supervision and tried to monitor everything he bought with it—had broken down even before the war, and been replaced with "smart sanctions," which sought to deny him a smaller list of purely military items. That deal essentially accepted that Saddam would continue to clandestinely export large quantities of oil across his borders. But that was a price worth paying if the United States and its allies could prevent him from *importing* the equipment required to rebuild his nuclear program. And the evidence from early 2003 suggested that was indeed possible. For one thing, by March the IAEA knew that Saddam was nowhere close to getting a nuclear bomb. "During the past four years," it reported, "at the majority of Iraqi [supposed nuclear] sites, industrial capacity has deteriorated substantially." For another, nuclear programs are far harder than other forms of WMD to hide. As the Carnegie Endowment has noted, in an exhaustive retrospective look at Saddam's weapons programs, "the weapon that poses by far the greatest danger—nuclear—is also the most detectable . . . and the most susceptible to nonproliferation techniques." (A point underscored by the fact that the United States had discovered the aluminum tube purchase that the Bush administration cited as a rationale for war.) Those techniques didn't have to be foolproof. They merely had to raise international alarms, which might have brought renewed sanctions or even American bombing. In fact, although Americans did not know it at the time, the Duelfer Report later showed that the *mere threat* of detection had a powerful impact on Saddam's behavior, convincing him not to reconstitute his nuclear program for fear of sparking tougher sanctions.

A new containment effort could certainly have failed. With more oil revenue at his disposal, Saddam might have gambled that he could reconstitute his nuclear program without the world finding out. Or he might simply have dared the world to do anything about it, in which case the

United States might one day have genuinely faced the choice the Bush administration falsely posed in 2003: an American invasion or an Iraqi nuke. Under the best of circumstances, a new containment effort would have been grueling and costly—just not as costly as a war rationalized on vanishing evidence and launched without international support. Given Saddam's genius for staying in power, the standoff could have lasted years or decades. But if America risked weariness, there was no guarantee that Saddam could go on forever either; brutal tyrannies often look indestructible before they self-destruct. Bush officials depicted the Iraq war as a great act of national will; inspiring evidence that a bloodied nation still had faith in itself. But containment required a different kind of faith, a confidence that America could persevere, adapt, and lead its allies in a long struggle that did not lend itself to knockout blows. It required affirming one of the key insights of the liberal antitotalitarian tradition: that restraint, too, can be a form of strength.

IF THE PREWAR debate was mostly about containment, the postwar debate has been mostly about democracy. Here, too, Iraq has put long-standing conservative assumptions to the test. And here, too, they have not fared well.

Before America invaded, democracy was a minor theme in President Bush's case for war, an optimistic flourish to round out speeches focused grimly on terrorist ties and WMD. And for some in the administration, the rhetoric may have been purely cosmetic. Even after 9/11, for instance, Donald Rumsfeld still peddled the realist line that had dominated conservative foreign policy in the 1990s. "I don't think," he said during the Afghan war, that deposing the Taliban "leaves us with a responsibility to try to figure out what kind of government that country ought to have."

For Bush, Wolfowitz, and even Cheney, however, the democracy rhetoric was secondary but sincere. Wolfowitz had been at the center of Reagan's democracy promotion efforts. And his belief in democratic transformation seems to have influenced the vice president, his boss at the Department of Defense in the first Bush administration. Though press reports at the time often depicted Cheney as a cautious realist in an administration full of them, by the early 1990s he was moving in a very different ideological direction from Kissinger disciples like Brent Scowcroft. While they supported Mikhail Gorbachev's efforts to preserve the USSR, Cheney urged an aggressive effort to dismember Ameria's old foe, in the

hopes of helping Boris Yeltsin midwife a democratic, pro-American Russia. "Intellectually," said Wolfowitz about Cheney in 1991, "we're very
much on similar wavelengths."

The problem is that while amoral realists like Rumsfeld and neo-
Reaganites like Wolfowitz and Cheney differed about ends, they agreed
on means: both camps disliked nation building. Rumsfeld didn't *want* the
United States to build democracy in Iraq, and Wolfowitz and Cheney
didn't think the United States *needed* to build democracy in Iraq, because it
would emerge virtually on its own.

Administration officials were explicit about this. "We had a theme
in our minds, a strategic idea, of liberation rather than occupation," explained undersecretary of defense, and Perle protégé, Douglas Feith. In
the Clinton years, the United States had done a lot of nation building:
from Somalia to Haiti to Bosnia to Kosovo. And in the run-up to the Iraq
war, veterans of those efforts—in the military, nongovernmental organizations, the State Department, and the CIA—urged the Bush administration to learn from their experience. They warned about the dangers of
postwar chaos, the necessity of careful planning, and the importance of
sufficient troops. But administration officials told them that since Iraq was
a liberation, not an occupation, those lessons didn't apply. "I would just
caution that Iraq is not East Timor or Kosovo or Afghanistan," declared
Rice, "Iraq is unique." "There's no relevant experience to draw on,"
added Perle. Bush officials did sometimes cite American nation-building
efforts in post–World War II Germany and Japan. In their descriptions,
however, those mammoth enterprises barely sounded like nation building
at all. "In the peace that followed a world war," declared President Bush,
"after defeating enemies, we did not leave behind occupying armies. We
left constitutions and parliaments." Yet the United States occupied postwar Japan for *seven years* and postwar Germany for four. And even as Bush
spoke, America had more than 110,000 troops stationed in the two countries, sixty years after the war's conclusion. By contrast, when the Bush
administration invaded Iraq in March 2003, staffers tasked with postwar
reconstruction were told to bring two suits. They would be home by the
end of summer, and U.S. troops would be mostly gone by fall.

There were political reasons for the administration's insistence that
democratizing Iraq would not require nation building: it let them downplay the occupation's potential cost. But it went deeper than that. Nation
building, after all, is armed development. Its cold war roots lie in such quin-

tessentially liberal efforts as the Marshall Plan, the Alliance for Progress, and Lyndon Johnson's call for a Tennessee Valley Authority in Vietnam's Mekong Delta. When conservatives embraced democracy promotion in the 1980s, they pursued a very different model. Reagan wasn't particularly interested in development aid, and he wasn't interested in sending U.S. troops to build democracy on foreign soil. (Even his 1982 dispatch of U.S. peacekeepers to help restore Lebanese sovereignty in the wake of Israeli and Syrian invasions didn't involve democracy building.) Instead, Reagan armed third-world counterrevolutionaries—"freedom fighters" in the conservative vernacular—to fight the Soviets. And he increased the political pressure on Moscow to free the captive nations of the Eastern bloc.

When Bush officials said they were pursuing liberation, not occupation, it was these Reagan efforts they had in mind. One of the ironies of the Iraq war is that the officials most intent on toppling Saddam were initially reluctant to back a full-fledged invasion. Throughout the 1990s, both Wolfowitz and Perle had advocated arming and funding Ahmed Chalabi and the Iraqi National Congress (INC), and, at most, offering them U.S. air support. The model was not Clinton's nation-building efforts, but Reagan's military aid to the Nicaraguan contras, the Afghan mujahedeen, Jonas Savimbi's UNITA in Angola, and anti-Communist rebels in Cambodia. As Wolfowitz wrote in 2000, one of the lessons "to be learned from the experience of the Cold War . . . [is] that it is far better to equip others to fight for their country than to send Americans to fight for them and that refusing to arm our friends, whether in Bosnia or Cambodia or Iraq, is a strategic as well as a moral mistake."

The model worked reasonably well in Afghanistan, where the Bush administration armed the Northern Alliance and provided American Special Forces and airpower. But while Wolfowitz, Feith, and Perle reluctantly conceded that overthrowing Saddam would require significant U.S. ground troops, they remained adamant that the United States was not bringing democracy to Iraq; it was merely assisting the democratic forces that were already there. They urged the creation of an Iraqi government in exile, presumably led by Chalabi, whose troops would accompany American soldiers as they overthrew Saddam. And along with Rumsfeld, they pushed for the smallest number of U.S. troops possible, as few as 40,000 by one estimate (one-tenth as many as the Army initially proposed). Rumsfeld had his own reasons for restricting the number of troops: it fit his vision of a lean, transformed American military. For Wolfowitz and Perle, however, fewer troops were an effort to make the invasion seem like the INC's victory, not America's. "The mold is set," explained a Pentagon official in 2003. "It's very much a return to Reaganite principles of adopting opposition movements."

But that alone doesn't explain why the neo-Reaganites were so sure the Iraqi opposition would usher in democracy. After all, for all his talk of "freedom fighters," Reagan had armed third-world counterrevolutionaries not because they were democrats (they mostly were not), but because they were anti-Communists. The confidence that Iraqi democracy would organically emerge has its roots in Reagan's other great cold war struggle: Eastern Europe. The revolutions of 1989 produced a new American certainty that democracy was every nation's desire and ultimate destiny. And after 9/11, no one was more certain than Bush. "The 20th century," he told the West Point cadets in June 2002, "ended with a single surviving model of human progress." Bush had essentially embraced Francis Fukuyama's famous argument that history—defined as "mankind's ideological evolution"—was over, and liberal democracy had won. Dictators were unnatural, and if the United States toppled them, as conservatives believed Reagan had in Eastern Europe, history would do the rest. No nation building was required. "'Export of democracy' isn't really a good phrase," said Wolfowitz about the Bush administration's foreign policy. "We're trying to remove the shackles on democracy."

The Bush administration's theory that democracy simply needed to be unshackled in Iraq—a country invented by colonial cartographers and held together by brute force—quickly collided with reality. In the days after Saddam fell, Iraq had no government, no law and order, and the Iraqis filling the political vacuum had more in common with the Ayatollah Khomeini than Václav Havel. But Rumsfeld surveyed the scene and declared that democracy was messily working its way to the surface. "Freedom's untidy," he explained, but Iraqis were "free to live their lives and do wonderful things, and that's what's going to happen here." Kanan Makiya, the influential Iraqi-born intellectual who had argued for war and a long-term nation-building effort, was astonished at the Bush administration's blithe reaction to the chaos. "There is a naïve belief stalking some corridors of power in Washington," he wrote, "that, since the United States has liberated Iraq, it can now stand aside and let 100 flowers bloom. This, supposedly, is democracy. Iraqis have no idea what to make of this bizarre conception."

To the Bush administration's credit, it soon shifted course, shelving its initial plans for a quick exit. But the damage was done. The United States had invaded with 150,000 troops (along with 45,000 from Britain and other countries)—between one-half and one-third as many as experts like Pollack, RAND's James Dobbins, and Army Chief of Staff Eric Shinseki had advised, after calculating troop-to-population ratios in Bosnia and Kosovo. And even the troops that did arrive had received little instruction on what to do once Saddam fell, even though numerous experts had warned that might prove the greatest challenge. According to the "After Action" report by the Third Infantry Division, the first Army unit to arrive in Baghdad, "Higher headquarters did not provide the Third Infantry Division (Mechanized) with a plan for Phase IV [postwar stabilization]. As a result, Third Infantry Division transitioned into Phase IV in the absence of guidance."

The result was $12 billion worth of looting, which razed virtually every government building in Baghdad. It also meant that for many Iraqis, their first taste of occupation was anarchy—which they generally ascribed to American malevolence, or weakness, or both. "The key to it all was the looting," American constitutional adviser Noah Feldman told *The New Yorker*'s George Packer. "That also told them they could fight against us—that we were not a serious force." By May, with the Coalition Provisional Authority (CPA) just barely formed, attacks on U.S. forces were already averaging thirteen a day. A study by the Center for Strategic and International Studies later concluded that the "fact that the United States failed to plan for meaningful stability operations and nation building was the most serious strategic mistake that led to the insurgency."

HAD THE BUSH administration realized before the war that Iraqi democracy had to be built, and not simply unleashed, the occupation would have gone better. But that does not mean it would have gone well. To some degree, America's problems occupying Iraq stemmed from the way America invaded it. From the very beginning, an occupation considered illegitimate by most of the world faced long odds in gaining legitimacy among the people of Iraq.

Partly, that was because an occupation considered illegitimate by most of the world was simply less able to improve Iraqis' daily lives. The Bush hawks had assumed virtually the opposite, arguing, in classic conservative fashion, that the key ingredient for postwar success was American freedom of action. They welcomed international support, but only if it in no way impeded America's ability to do whatever it wanted.

That view rested on an enormous faith in U.S. capacities and a deep disdain for those of America's allies and the UN. "The fact of the matter is for most of the others [countries] who are engaged in this debate," said Cheney in March 2003, "they don't have the capability to do anything about it anyway." Rumsfeld claimed that even Britain, America's staunchest ally, was dispensable. "To the extent they're not [in the war]," he mused, "there are workarounds." The conservative press heartily agreed. Charles Krauthammer mocked the Europeans, who "sit and pout. What else can they do? . . . The real problem is their irrelevance."

If overthrowing Saddam had been the only mission, these arguments would have been correct: the United States didn't need other countries to conquer Baghdad. In fact, had more participated, they would have made the invasion more complicated. But as quickly became clear, America's most difficult mission was not conquering Baghdad, it was governing it. And here the right's national chauvinism was wildly misplaced. When it came to nation building, the United States was not any more competent than the rest of the world. In fact, under the Bush administration, it was probably less so.

As James Dobbins has pointed out, the nation-building efforts of the 1990s produced a cadre of UN officials with extensive experience in postwar reconstruction. The U.S. government had built up a similar repository of knowledge, but it was concentrated at the State Department, which oversaw nation building in the Clinton years. And when Bush put the Defense Department in charge of postwar Iraq, Feith and other top Pentagon officials largely passed over these veterans, whom they deemed ideologically suspect. The result was that the Americans sent to run Iraq were vastly less qualified than their UN counterparts. Jay Garner, Rumsfeld's first choice to oversee postwar reconstruction, had done humanitarian work in Kurdistan, but was so ignorant of the rest of Iraq that, when advised to contact Grand Ayatollah Ali al-Sistani, the most powerful man in the country, he replied, "Who is this person?" His staff was little better: it not only included few Arabic speakers, it contained barely any Arabic *translators*. His successor, Paul Bremer, though a longtime diplomat, had no nation-building experience and no experience of any kind in the Middle East. By contrast, Kofi Annan's special envoy, Sergio Vieira de Mello, had worked in postwar Cambodia, Rwanda, East Timor, and Kosovo. And after de Mello's assassination, Annan sent Lakhdar Brahimi, a longtime Algerian diplomat, and native Arabic speaker, who had been the UN's special representative in Afghanistan, Haiti, and South Africa and led UN missions to Zaire, Yemen, Nigeria, and Sudan. Among conservatives, the UN's ineptness was a running joke. But Americans who had actually done nation building were often less haughty. In the run-up to war, Kenneth Pollack spoke to a group of U.S. Army civil affairs officers about to leave for Iraq. "Are we going to have the UN there?" they asked nervously, explaining that they were unaccustomed to doing nation building on their own.

Once Saddam fell, Tony Blair urged giving the UN responsibility for Iraq's political reconstruction. In a veiled criticism of the White House, he declared "let us start preferring a coalition and acting alone if we have to, not the other way around. True, winning wars is not easier that way, but winning the peace is." It wasn't just that Blair had more faith in the UN itself. He hoped that giving it political control would convince more countries to send troops. Iraq desperately needed military police units, for instance, and several European countries had special divisions trained for such work. In the first months after the war, both India and Russia suggested they might send peacekeepers if they could serve under a UN mandate. There's no telling whether foreign units could have made a significant difference. But given the dire shortage of U.S. troops—a shortage almost universally acknowledged by American commanders on the ground—any reinforcements would have helped.

The White House, however, refused. Bush said the UN would play a "vital" role in post-Saddam Iraq. But asked what that meant, he replied, "That means food. That means medicine. That means aid." What it didn't mean was influence over Iraq's attempted transition to democracy. As one UN aide put it, "The CPA had a plan and they were going to implement it, regardless of what the UN thought."

That plan quickly proved disastrous. Although prewar studies by the Army War College, the State Department, and the Center for Strategic and International Studies had all warned against disbanding the Iraqi military, Bremer did just that—and many of its former members promptly became insurgents. By the fall of 2003, with the insurgency dramatically retarding economic reconstruction, the Bush administration revised its view, offering the UN far more control and pleading with other countries to send troops. Its first instinct, however, had been that Americans, merely by virtue of being Americans, knew best. And by the time that view changed, it was too late.

BUT AMERICA DIDN'T only need international help to improve Iraqis' lives, it needed international help to win their trust. Many conservatives—considering American intentions pure and those of antiwar governments cynical and pecuniary—assumed exactly the opposite. Some worried that greater multinational participation might actually undermine the occupation's legitimacy, since the Iraqis would not feel Europe and the UN shared America's democratic idealism. "There's at least one group of people among whom the United Nations has no legitimacy," wrote the *Weekly Standard*'s Fred Barnes several weeks into the war. "That's the 24 million Iraqis." Also in the *Standard*, Reuel Marc Gerecht announced that "many Iraqis view the Europeans, especially the French and the Germans (and the United Nations), as sympathetic to Saddam Hussein's regime."

It was a remarkable display of self-delusion. In reality, Iraqis didn't believe the United States had invaded with only the purest of motives. Instead, after some initial gratitude, they quickly began worrying that America intended a long, colonial stay. This was entirely predictable. Historical studies suggest that one of the keys to the success of any foreign occupation is convincing the occupied population that they will get their country back. Iraqis did not love the French or the Germans, or Kofi Annan. But the great advantage of a UN-led multilateral occupation was that by its very nature, it looked less permanent. A study of Iraqi public opinion proposed handing over control to the UN "as there are less negative 'imperialist' impressions of this international body." And Grand Ayatollah Sistani met with both de Mello and Brahimi, while repeatedly snubbing Bremer.

As in the war on terror more generally, the Bush administration in Iraq exuded a complacent confidence in American virtue, a complacency that not only blinded it to Iraqi skepticism, but kept it from proving that skepticism wrong. The White House dismissed accusations of imperialism as absurd, but it never publicly stated that it would not seek permanent military bases in Iraq. Indeed, U.S. officials suggested they might do just that. And they never took clear steps to show Iraqis that the United States was not after their oil. Instead, during the looting that followed Saddam's fall, American troops guarded only the oil ministry. "When the Oil Ministry is the only thing you protect," exclaimed Feisal Istrabadi, an Iraqi American who had worked with the United States before the war, "what do you expect people to think?" And sure enough, by September 2003, polling showed that only 5 percent of Iraqis thought the United States was in their country "to assist the Iraqi people," while almost 50 percent said it was there "to rob Iraq's oil."

In fact, despite the right's insistence that only America believed in democracy, the Bush administration's plan for returning power to Iraqis was actually *less* democratic than the one favored by the UN. It was de Mello who, despite having little formal power over the occupation, in the summer of 2003 convinced Bremer to make the Iraqi council that advised the occupation more politically representative and less dominated by America's exile allies. And it was he who convinced Bremer to call it a "governing" rather than a "political" council, and to grant it the power to appoint cabinet ministers.

De Mello also urged Bremer to heed Sistani's call for direct elections to choose the assembly that would write Iraq's new constitution. The United States rejected the idea, proposing instead a complicated, quasi-democratic caucus system that few Iraqis trusted or even understood. It was only when that process collapsed and Sistani sent thousands of Shiites into the streets to denounce the occupation that the United States finally handed control over the transition to the UN. In February 2004, Brahimi convinced Sistani to postpone elections in return for scrapping Bremer's caucus plan. But by that time, the insurgency was already a self-perpetuating force.

The problem, in other words, wasn't merely that America failed to convince Iraqis it had their best interests at heart; it's that America did not always *have* Iraqis' best interests at heart. And because American officials didn't recognize that, they failed to quickly share power, which might have reduced the corrupting temptations of colonial rule. Larry Diamond, a former senior adviser to the Coalition Provisional Authority, saw this close up. And near the end of his depressing chronicle, *Squandered Victory*, he wrote that "American political leaders need to take a cold shower of humility: we do not always know what is best for other people, even when we think it is their interests we have in mind. And as I saw during my time in Iraq, it was frequently our interests that were driving decisions we were trying to impose." Niebuhr could not have put it better himself.

IRAQ WAS A war of hubris and impatience: impatience with containment and, to a lesser extent, impatience with tyranny. And while it has proved a fateful mistake, the latter instinct, at least, is admirable—as admirable as the right's yearning to liberate Eastern Europe decades ago. Only the most hardened partisan can resist feeling there is something profoundly right about seeing Saddam Hussein on trial, and seeing Iraqis trudge to the polls to choose his successors. Or feel anything but contempt toward the jihadists who wage war against democracy and seek to foment civil war.

It is even possible that the Iraq war may help the cause of Islamic democracy. Critics note that post-Saddam Iraq has not inspired the people of the Middle East; it has alarmed them. And that is true. But it is precisely that alarm which has helped spark anti-authoritarian tremors across the Arab world.

When the United States overthrew Saddam, commentary throughout the Middle East dwelled on one theme in particular: Arab weakness. As the Saudi writer Khaled Al-Dakhil put it in *Al-Hayat* in late December 2002, "The Arab world has never been so weak and the anticipated war on Iraq is part of the price." Or in the words of the Lebanese writer Ali Hamadeh in *An-Nahar*, "The fall of this regime by a foreign power . . . will show powerless Arabs how regimes are overthrown in the 21st century."

As the Brookings Institution's Tamara Cofman Wittes has pointed out, those regimes had been quietly weakening for years. The rise of Arabic satellite channels like Al Jazeera had made information harder for autocrats to control, and a regional baby boom, combined with economic decline, had left them with fewer resources to buy political quiescence. But if Arab regimes had been growing weaker, their years in power and the memory of their fierce crackdowns on dissent still gave them the illusion of strength. Saddam's overthrow shattered that illusion. As *Cairo Times* editor Hisham Kassem put it, "Today is a benchmark in Arab history. This is the fall of the first authoritarian regime. . . . I think it is going to have a domino effect throughout the Arab region." A cartoon in a Jordanian newspaper featured a statue of Saddam, its knees buckling, crashing into a statue of Syria's Bashar Assad, which was crashing into a statue of Egypt's Hosni Mubarak, which was crashing into another statue, whose face could not be seen.

It wasn't that Arabs hoped the United States would come and overthrow their autocrats as well. To the contrary, the lesson many drew from Iraq was that only by demanding greater participation could they build governments strong enough to resist the new colonialism that the U.S. invasion seemed to represent. As Mahdi Abdul-Hadi, head of the Palestinian Academic Society, put it, "There's not going to be obedience to rulers as before. . . . This has been a lesson to every Arab regime that they need to look to their people. If a storm comes from outside, the only way to stand is to have a constituency supporting you." In Egypt, the democracy movement Kifaya ("enough") actually organized mass protests against the Iraq war, which then morphed into protests against Hosni Mubarak's effort to extend his rule.

Of course, those protests failed. After titillating reformers by unexpectedly allowing multiparty presidential elections, Mubarak then disillusioned them by allowing his parliamentary henchmen to impose conditions that rendered the elections a farce. Still, the country's political dynamic has changed. If the Iraq war emboldened Egypt's opposition by making Mubarak's regime look weak, his political maneuvers have not restored his air of invincibility. When Egyptians went to the polls in late 2005, the ruling party used its old tactics of fraud and violence to ensure that it won most of the seats in parliament. But this time the tactics sparked an angry public response: independent monitors protested; the Egyptian judges club demanded that the interior minister resign; in some districts, voters battled government thugs. While Mubarak's hold on power remains firm, he is caught in a political pincer, between an increasingly restive public and a United States less willing to tolerate business as usual. As Kifaya spokesman Abdel-Halim Qandil told *Al-Ahram Weekly*, "The irony of history . . . might put us in the odd position of being in the protection of the enemy"—the United States. This new political reality may not force Mubarak from power. But it will make it far harder for him to pass on power to his son, or anyone else. And it owes a great deal to the war in Iraq.

In Lebanon, another country where a democracy movement has broken out after years of quiet, the symbiosis between an emboldened opposition and American pressure has been even clearer. In August 2004, Syria, which had occupied Lebanon since 1976, forced its parliament to extend the pro-Syrian prime minister's term. The United States and France, Lebanon's former colonial power, responded with a UN resolution demanding Syrian withdrawal. Then, on February 14, 2005, Lebanon's popular former prime minister, Rafik Hariri, was killed by a car bomb. Thousands streamed into Beirut's main square to accuse Syria of the crime. Meanwhile, the Bush administration loudly demanded that Damascus permit an independent investigation of the murder and leave Lebanon, both of which have now come to pass. Like Mubarak, Syria's Bashar Assad found himself caught between a growing protest movement and an international spotlight that made it harder to crack down. And that international spotlight would be much weaker had Iraq not made democratization a Bush administration obsession. As one Jordanian observer put it, referring to the city where Assad's father slaughtered 25,000 rebels with no international outcry, "The people in the streets of Beirut knew that no second Hama is possible."

Some commentators, trying to downplay Iraq's role in these events, note that reform movements existed before Saddam fell. But although they existed, they were not nearly as strong. As late as 2003, Freedom House was still writing that when it came to Arab democracy, "downward trends have outpaced gains post-9/11." Since then, in addition to events in Lebanon and Egypt, Saudi Arabia has held its first local elections in forty-two years, a move that one Democratic congressional staffer called "unmistakably connected to American actions." Six weeks before the Kuwaiti prime minister's 2005 trip to Washington, his government pushed through a constitutional amendment granting women the vote. To be sure, there is no guarantee this new openness will produce liberal democracy: in Saudi Arabia, religious conservatives won in most municipalities; in Egypt, the Muslim Brotherhood remains the most potent opposition force; and in Lebanon, sectarian squabbles have filled the post-Syrian vacuum. But at least competing political visions are being freely discussed. In the words of Egyptian political scientist Mohammed Kamal, "for the first time in many years, there is a serious debate going on in the Arab world about their own societies. The United States has triggered this debate."

TRAGICALLY, BY INVADING Iraq, the United States has triggered other forces as well. For people across the Middle East, the war has been a profound humiliation. And while that humiliation has emboldened some young Arabs to demand democracy, it has sent others (and some Arab Europeans as well) streaming into Iraq in service of jihad. If the jihadists emerge from Iraq victorious, or if they emerge at all, they will likely return emboldened to their native countries, like the Afghan Arabs who went home in the 1990s to terrorize Algeria and Egypt. In fact, the urban warfare techniques they are learning in Iraq may make them even more

dangerous than the Afghan alumni. And this new burst of jihadist terror could wreak havoc on the embryonic reform movements sprouting
in the Middle East. For autocratic regimes now on the defensive, such
violence would provide a powerful new pretext for repression—repression
the United States would be hard-pressed to oppose. And if those regimes
are no longer strong enough to carry out the Hama-style crackdowns that
in the 1990s smashed the Algerian and Egyptian jihads, the result could
be chaos, or even salafist revolution.

And if Iraq has strengthened our enemies, it has also weakened
us. More than 2,000 Americans have died, and over 15,000 have been
wounded. The Army, painstakingly rebuilt after the trauma of Vietnam,
has suffered enormous strain, the full consequences of which will not be
known for years to come. The war, which was supposed to reveal America's essential goodness, has instead bred international cynicism. Even
more disturbing, it has caused a deep weariness at home, a yearning to
turn inward and bind domestic wounds, which will make it harder to fight
salafist jihad in the years to come. After Vietnam, the United States took a
partial rest from the cold war, enjoying several years of détente before intense competition returned. But our new totalitarian enemy may not permit such a hiatus. And so the Bush administration may be creating exactly
the condition that conservatives have long feared: an America without the
will to fight.

Even more than Ronald Reagan, George W. Bush has fulfilled the
conservative dream: unrestrained American power married to unreflective American self-confidence, rushing into the breach to alter history's
course. He has torn the lid off the Arab world—weakening Arab tyranny,
weakening America, and leaving a great political void in which Islamic
democracy and Islamic totalitarianism vie for control.

It is against this unfamiliar backdrop that the embittered opponents
of conservative power—American liberals—have struggled to decide what
they believe.

7

Losing America

ONE DAY IN 1964, a New York investment banker named Howard Dean Jr. visited two of his sons at boarding school. They attended St. George's in Newport, Rhode Island, where Dean served as a trustee. The older boy would later attend Yale, like his father and grandfather. And from there he would go to Wall Street, like his father, grandfather, and great-grandfather.

The Deans, who had been prospering in America since the 1600s, valued tradition. So it came as something of a shock when one of the boys, 14-year-old Charlie, announced over dinner that he considered Lyndon Johnson a good president. The Deans, after all, were Republicans. And Howard Jr. was a particular fan of Johnson's Republican opponent, Barry Goldwater.

Annoyed, Howard Jr. glared at his son and declared, "I don't think you know what you are talking about." To which the teenager muttered, under his breath, "I don't think you know what you are talking about." Watching his younger brother upend the Dean universe, 16-year-old Howard Brush Dean III silently cheered.

Across millions of dinner tables that year, families like the Deans were having similar conversations. By nominating Goldwater, the conservative movement had captured the GOP. And by embracing civil rights, the Democrats had captured the imagination of the tolerant young. It was a time of political migrations. In the Democratic landslide of 1964, the scions of northern, affluent, Protestant families that had been voting Republican since the Civil War left the GOP. Many never returned, even four and eight years later, when working-class whites stampeded to Nixon and Wallace, ending the Democrats' hold on power.

Charlie Dean, the rebel, would chair the McGovern campaign at the University of North Carolina. Then he would travel to Southeast Asia, to see up close the war he loathed. And he would die there, in Laos, in circumstances never fully explained.

Howard Dean III would try to toe the family line. He went to Yale and then to Wall Street. But the cultural and political currents were too strong. His father, "Big Howard," belonged to an all-white country club, but at Yale, "Little Howard" requested black roommates. The father was a recreational anti-Semite, but the son left Wall Street for a historically Jewish medical school, where he met his Jewish wife.

The newlyweds moved to Vermont, a historic Republican bastion making its own journey across the political aisle. And it was there that Howard Dean launched a political career that would help define an era. He had become a liberal just in time to see cold war liberalism fall. And after September 11, he would see liberalism fall once again—only this time, he would have a front row seat.

BY THE TIME Bill Clinton left the White House, he had achieved historic goals and squandered historic opportunities. He had blunted race as a political weapon, finally defeating the Republican "Southern strategy" that helped doom Democratic presidential candidates from Hubert Humphrey to Michael Dukakis. He had convinced a skeptical country that government could work. And in his second term, he had fulfilled one of contemporary liberalism's great ambitions—ending the quarter-century-long stagnation in working-class standards of living.

But disastrous personal misconduct dominated his final years in office, exacerbating a new cultural gulf between liberals and many blue-collar whites, centered not on race, but on morality and religion. This new divide helped cost Al Gore the White House. And that loss cut short Clinton's final legacy: the new foreign policy vision emerging in the wake of the Kosovo war.

Instead, George W. Bush became president. And when September 11 hit, the debate Kosovo had unleashed among liberals continued against the backdrop of conservative power. Polling in the 1990s had shown grassroots Democrats increasingly supportive of the use of force, and their immediate reaction to 9/11 bore that out. Whether because of Clinton's legacy or the mere horror of the event, a *New York Times* poll in late September found that 60 percent of self-described liberals supported "military action against whoever is responsible for the attacks, even if it means that innocent people are killed"—more than three times the rate of liberals who opposed military action. In Washington, the enthusiasm for a military response was even greater. "The Democratic Party stands 100 percent with President Bush as he fights terrorism around the world," declared party chairman Terry McAuliffe in October. When Congress authorized military retaliation on September 14, every congressional Democrat except one voted yes.

But the critics of liberalism's post-Kosovo turn were hardly silent. If liberal hawks saw jihadism through the Balkan prism—as a fanatically illiberal foe that should be met with democratic ideals, international legitimacy, and military might—doves saw it through a Balkan prism of their own. For them, the fundamental issue, once again, was American imperialism. Al Qaeda might be despicable, but it was not autonomous. In fact, it was our Frankenstein, the bastard offspring of our evil deeds. For decades, America had abused, violated, and corrupted the third world—and now the bill was coming due.

Among anti-imperialists, the favored term was *blowback*. At its most literal, the charge was simple: Osama bin Laden had been our man. Michael Moore demanded that President Bush "tell us why your father and his partner Mr. Reagan trained Mr. bin Laden in how to be a terrorist!" An article in *The Nation* alleged that "Bin Laden has been attempting to bring the things the CIA taught him home to the teachers."

Then there was MoveOn Peace, a website founded after the attacks by a brainy, earnest recent college graduate named Eli Pariser. Pariser originally called his website 9-11peace.org, but renamed it after being absorbed by MoveOn.org, a liberal network organized to oppose Clinton's impeachment. "The US has become adept at creating monsters," declared a MoveOn Peace bulletin in May 2002. "Osama bin Laden is only the latest in a long line."

As it happened, the charge was false. The 9/11 Commission would find that "Bin Laden and his comrades . . . received little or no assistance from the United States." And Bin Laden's top aide, Ayman Al-Zawahiri, has called the allegation a slander, declaring that his men never took "one penny" from the hated Americans. But for anti-imperialists, the specific allegation was not the critical point. After all, America's reach is vast, and if it did not specifically train Bin Laden, it surely helped produce the injustice that motivated him to kill. In reality, blowback was less about explaining Al Qaeda—a task to which people like Michael Moore, and groups like MoveOn Peace, devoted little serious attention—than it was about explaining America. Liberal hawks saw the terrorists as the latest in an antiliberal, anti-American lineage that stretched through Milosevic back to the totalitarians of World War II and the cold war. But for the anti-imperialists, Bin Laden was not part of an anti-American tradition; he was part of a distinctly *American* tradition, a tradition of imperial chickens coming home to roost. A left-leaning Berkeley linguist named George Lakoff, on his way to becoming a Democratic Party guru, noted that "the United States has systematically promoted a terrorism of its own and has trained terrorists, from the contras to the mujahideen, the Honduran death squads, and the Indonesian military." MoveOn Peace traced the tradition back even further, noting that "while the US didn't 'create' Hitler, the ties between American business and the Nazi regime were so strong that in essence, Wall Street helped finance Hitler's rise to power."

A December 2001 article in *The Nation* imagined America on the couch, describing its powerful desire to kill the people responsible for 9/11. "You cannot face your real problem," explained the fictional therapist. "Your real problem is simply the way that millions and millions of people around the world feel about you" because "you kill people who are poor and desperate." In other words, America's "real problem" was America. Or more specifically, it was those forces inside America that perpetuated empire. Given that the United States had just been attacked by an enemy as ideologically, culturally, and geographically remote as could possibly be imagined, it was a strangely narcissistic diagnosis. But it was the same diagnosis that anti-imperialist liberals had offered a half-century earlier. In the late 1940s, of course, the American left boasted actual Communists, while there were no salafists infiltrating MoveOn.org. But most of Henry Wallace's supporters were not Communists; they simply considered Communism a distraction from the "real problem." When Communists pushed Czech foreign minister Jan Masaryk out of a window in March 1948, Wallace responded, "The Czechoslovakia story will repeat itself so long as our gun and dollar policies . . . are continued." Now America had been attacked, and Wallace's ideological progeny were blaming America's "gun and dollar policies" once again.

As at the start of the cold war, the essential divide was over whether liberals would define themselves in opposition to totalitarianism or only in opposition to the right. For the anti-imperialists, the answer was clear. "We have nothing to fear but George W. Bush," explained Moore. It's not that anti-imperialists didn't want to prevent terrorism; they did, just as

Wallace had wanted to prevent the Czech coup. But since salafist terrorism—like Communist oppression—was an American by-product rather
than an autonomous force, the *way* to prevent it was by fighting its real
authors: the imperialists inside the United States. As MoveOn's founders,
Wes Boyd and Joan Blades, put it: "Getting tough on terrorism means getting tough on some of the Bush administration's core constituencies and
old friends."

The premise that America could best fight terrorism by fighting its
own imperialist impulses made it difficult to endorse a military response
to 9/11. Anti-imperialist liberals wanted to apprehend, or even kill, the
people who planned the attacks, and they wanted to see the Taliban deposed. (*The Nation*, in particular, had been an eloquent, dogged critic of
the Taliban since the regime first took power.) But they had also wanted
to stop Milosevic's slaughter in Kosovo, and Wallace had wanted to stop
Turkey and Greece from falling to Communist rule. The problem was
how to do so without endorsing American military force, a cure that would
only inflame the disease.

The answer was that military action was acceptable only if it took no
innocent lives. "In bringing terrorists to justice," declared MoveOn, "the
U.S. must commit to protecting innocent civilians everywhere and ending the cycle of violence." But the two imperatives were incompatible. In
the real world, with jihadists taking cover among civilians, and Al Qaeda
virtually running the Taliban regime, there was simply no way the United
States could "bring the terrorists to justice" while "ending the cycle of
violence" and taking no innocent human life. It was what Schlesinger had
called doughface liberalism: America could only act against its enemies if
it remained morally pure.

Behind this recipe for self-righteous inaction lay another key doughface assumption: once America surrendered its moral purity, it became
no better than its enemies. It was an old argument. For some on the anti-
imperialist left, McCarthyism had proved America was no better than the
Soviet Union. For a later generation, Vietnam had proved the same thing.
And now, argued MoveOn, "If we retaliate by bombing Kabul and kill
people oppressed by the Taliban dictatorship who have no part in deciding
whether terrorists are harbored, we become like the terrorists we oppose."
Added George Lakoff, "Massive bombing of Afghanistan—with the killing of innocents—will show that we are no better than they." But the 9/11
terrorists had *aimed* to kill civilians (in the case of the World Trade Center,

only civilians). And they had done so in service of a totalitarian ideology. In bombing Kabul, the United States was *accidentally* killing civilians—in retaliation for an attack, and in the process of installing a vastly more humane government. The moral difference was about as stark as one could find in the real world of international affairs.

Yet that was precisely Schlesinger's point. At its core, doughface liberalism offers an escape from the choices the real world requires. A September 12 article in the liberal online magazine Salon.org argued that instead of military action, the United States should "bring the full force of domestic and international law to bear" against the terrorists. But a paragraph later, it warned against "expanding the FBI's surveillance powers." MoveOn Peace insisted that "war will not be an effective response to global terrorism," suggesting instead that the United States bring the terrorists "before some kind of ad hoc international court." But lest one assume that apprehending those terrorists might require an expanded intelligence-gathering effort, another MoveOn Peace bulletin suggested that "giving the C.I.A. more money and more free rein" was not the answer either.

Groups like MoveOn generally eschewed the word *liberal*—which the right had turned into an epithet—in favor of *progressive*, a term they used with little regard to its historical antecedents. But in at least one respect, the designation made perfect sense. The principles that guided the new progressives' response to September 11, and those that guided Henry Wallace's Progressives in the early cold war, were largely the same.

FOR THE FIRST year after the attacks, the anti-imperialists wielded little influence. Liberals overwhelmingly backed Bush's invasion of Afghanistan. Polls showed that Democrats were nearly as likely as Republicans to consider terrorism a "very serious" problem, and to consider the United States in a state of war. And in Congress, Democrats backed the Bush administration's military buildup and urged even greater spending on homeland security and foreign aid.

But Democrats were operating from a position of weakness. Although Clinton had shifted liberal views on the use of force, he had not erased the GOP's post-Vietnam advantage on national security. And when foreign policy retook center stage after 9/11, Americans picked up where the cold war had left off. They not only rallied around their Republican commander in chief, they told pollsters they trusted his party far more to keep them safe. Once Bush successfully overthrew the Taliban, his clout only grew.

In the fall of 2002, Bush took his considerable political capital and put it behind an invasion of Iraq. Liberals soon began telling pollsters they were uneasy. In Washington, however, two key groups of Democrats proved more sympathetic. The first was the party's foreign policy leadership, which was dominated by Clinton administration veterans. And crucially, they were not just any Clinton administration veterans. The former president's first-term foreign policy team—led by cautious men like former secretary of state Warren Christopher and former national security adviser Anthony Lake—was virtually invisible in the Washington of late 2002. Instead, it was their more hawkish second-term successors—Madeleine Albright, former UN ambassador Richard Holbrooke, and former national security adviser Sandy Berger—to whom congressional Democrats and aspiring Democratic presidential candidates turned for guidance. For these men and women, the administration's great victory had been Kosovo and its great frustration had been Iraq. They had gone to the brink with Saddam repeatedly in the late 1990s and watched with alarm as sanctions weakened and U.S. allies wearied of containment. "It was the frustration of knowing that what it would take to save containment under the current circumstances would never be adopted (and sustained) by the United States that led me, and many of my colleagues within government, to conclude that containment was no longer an option," wrote former Clinton official Kenneth Pollack in 2002. The Clintonites were deeply concerned that any U.S. military action enjoy international support, and their public comments were generally more muted than those of liberal hawks in the media who urged outright war. But on September 12, 2002, when Bush announced he would take Iraq to the Security Council and seek new resolutions requiring it to disarm, he temporarily allayed the Clintonites' concerns. So when Iraq came up for a vote in Congress a month later—and Bush said he needed congressional support to gain leverage at the UN—the Democratic foreign policy brain trust was broadly sympathetic. And since few congressional Democrats had much national security expertise of their own, the views of that brain trust loomed large.

The second group that tipped the balance was Democratic political consultants. Many remembered the aftermath of the Gulf War, when voting no had crippled Senator Sam Nunn's presidential prospects and voting yes helped elevate first Al Gore, and then Joe Lieberman, onto national

Democratic tickets. Moreover, the polls in late 2002 showed Democrats with an edge on domestic issues like health care and Social Security, and Republicans with a massive advantage on national security. With the mid-term elections looming, party strategists yearned to remove foreign policy from the campaign. And the only way to do that was to agree with President Bush on Iraq and then change the subject. As Democratic pollster Mark Mellman put it, "we'd rather have the newspapers filled with discussions of pensions."

So while Democrats with safe seats mostly voted against the war, the party's congressional leaders, its vulnerable incumbents, and its likely presidential candidates generally voted yes. And four days after they did, House minority leader Richard Gephardt gave a major campaign speech, in which he discussed a host of domestic issues and never once mentioned Iraq.

But the strategy failed. Disillusioned by their party's acquiescence, many liberal voters stayed home on election day. To make matters worse, Democrats didn't even successfully avoid a fight over national security. The Bush administration had suckered them into a dispute on homeland security—embracing a Democratic plan to create a new Department of Homeland Security but insisting on stripping its employees of many civil service protections. Unwilling to buck their powerful allies in the public-sector unions, the Democrats left themselves politically vulnerable.

And Republicans seized the opening, shamelessly attacking their Democratic opponents as weak on terror. In an echo of Richard Nixon's 1946 campaign against "the PAC," Republicans in New Hampshire, Arkansas, Colorado, and Minnesota assailed Democrats for taking money from the dovish Council for a Livable World. In Georgia, GOP ads attacking Democratic senator (and Vietnam War triple amputee) Max Cleland featured photos of Osama bin Laden and Saddam Hussein. Bush also took up the McCarthyite line, charging that Senate Democrats who opposed his version of the homeland security bill were "not interested in the security of the American people"—even though he himself had opposed a new cabinet department before switching positions. In the last five days of the campaign, he visited fifteen states, delivering a stump speech devoted almost exclusively to Iraq and the war on terror.

It worked masterfully. A poll taken just after the election gave Republicans an almost 40-point lead on "keeping America strong." Even a plurality of *Democratic* voters said the GOP was better on national defense. And for only the third time since the Civil War, the president's party gained seats in a midterm election.

Had Democrats run against the war, they would probably still have lost. Given Bush's popularity, the party's weak standing on national security, and the fact that most key Senate races were in conservative Southern and Midwestern states, a full-fledged partisan battle over Iraq would have been extremely difficult for Democrats to win. Yet the fact that party leaders ducked the fight and lost anyway would profoundly alter liberalism's course. For a year after 9/11, most American liberals had embraced the struggle against global jihad, the anti-imperialist left notwithstanding. But for many, the events of autumn 2002 bred not merely alienation from Democratic leaders in Washington, and not merely anger over the war in Iraq, but an emerging suspicion of the war on terror itself. Democratic politicians, experts, strategists, and pundits had failed to define a compelling liberal vision for the post-9/11 world, and many had fallen prey to the right's apocalyptic logic on Iraq. As a result, the balance of power in the liberal foreign policy feud began to shift beneath their feet.

INTO THIS VOLATILE landscape entered that child of New York Republicans turned liberal Vermont Democrat, Howard Brush Dean III. Dean's presidential campaign began in obscurity. His own mother called it "quixotic" and "preposterous." At a dinner in October 2002, Iowa senator Tom Harkin kept referring to him as John Dean, the figure from Watergate. The campaign also began as a domestic policy affair. A doctor turned governor with no foreign policy experience, Dean planned to campaign on the two issues he knew best: health care and early childhood development. "Pre-Iraq war," recounted his campaign manager, "that is all he ever talked about."

But that would change. The early Democratic frontrunners—John Kerry, John Edwards, Richard Gephardt, and Joe Lieberman—all shared two characteristics: they lived in Washington and they had voted for the Iraq war. In early 2003, with that war approaching and liberals bitterly angry at their leaders for supporting it, that left a gaping political vacuum. And on February 20, when the Democratic National Committee convened for its winter meeting, Dean stepped into it. One by one, the Washington Democrats took the stage and attacked George W. Bush. Then Dean took the stage and attacked the Washington Democrats.

"What I want to know," Dean thundered, "is why in the world the

Democratic Party leadership is supporting the President's unilateral attack on Iraq?" The room erupted in cheers. "What I want to know," he continued, "is, why are Democratic Party leaders supporting tax cuts?" More cheers. By the time Dean reached, "What I want to know is why our folks are voting for the President's No Child Left Behind bill," members of the audience were yelling "We want to know too!" That weekend before the DNC, Joe Lieberman's speech was interrupted by cheers three times; John Edwards's speech was interrupted four times. Dean's was interrupted by cheers *twenty-four times*. As a party official put it after Dean elicited a similar reaction from a Democratic crowd in California, "He was serving meat . . . and that was a hungry audience."

Dean, his pollster suggested, was "declaring war on the party and its establishment for their failure to oppose Bush strongly enough." And in that war, he began rapidly gaining ground. In the first quarter of 2003, Dean raised under $3 million, less than a third as much as John Kerry. In the second quarter, he raised $7.6 million, more than any of his competitors. In the third quarter, he raised almost $15 million, more than any Democratic presidential primary candidate in history. When Dean gave his February DNC speech, he was trailing Kerry in New Hampshire by 13 points. By August, he had a 21-point lead. And by January 2004, Harkin—who couldn't remember Dean's name a year earlier—had endorsed him. "It ain't over 'til it's over," declared the newspaper *Roll Call*, "but it's probably over."

Most of the people who powered the Dean crusade were like Dean himself: white, affluent, highly educated, and secular. They were the products of that great migration that began in the 1960s, which saw culturally liberal professionals moving into the Democratic Party and culturally conservative working-class whites moving out. Not surprisingly, their biggest issue was the Iraq war, which they vehemently opposed. And in general, they were more dovish than other Democrats, not to mention Americans as a whole. Remarkably, 70 percent said they sometimes visited MoveOn's website, far more than visited the website of the Democratic National Committee.

But that larger picture concealed intriguing divisions. While the press often portrayed Dean's supporters as disproportionately young, the largest cohort were actually baby boomers. And it was this group, perhaps because of its memory of Vietnam, whose views came closest to the anti-imperialist line. Dean activists under the age of 30, by contrast—perhaps because they had come of age during the Balkan debates or after 9/11—were more hawkish. A fall 2004 survey by the Pew Research Center found them more than twice as likely as their elders to say preemption was often or sometimes justified (the poll didn't define preemption or specify whether it was against terrorist groups or states), and almost twice as likely to support keeping U.S. troops in Iraq. In this regard, the younger Deaniacs were actually more like Dean himself, who had supported the Gulf War and the interventions in Bosnia and Kosovo. The overwhelming anger over Iraq, in other words, concealed hidden fault lines. The anti-imperialists may have been gaining influence. But three years after 9/11, a crucial segment of the liberal base still believed the United States had enemies worth fighting, even if Saddam Hussein wasn't one of them.

IF THE ACTIVIST boomers considered Howard Dean their hero, they saw John Kerry as a turncoat. In some ways, the senator from Massachusetts mirrored their political journey even better than the governor from Vermont. Like Dean, Kerry had attended an overwhelmingly Republican prep school, and then Yale. And like Dean and so many other liberal children of the 1960s, Kerry had used race to rebel. He befriended his prep school's lone African American teacher. And one day at Yale, according to his former brother-in-law, he even tried (and failed) to convince another scion of the New England elite, George W. Bush, of the virtues of interracial busing.

And like the Dean brothers, Kerry was deeply touched by Vietnam. First, he went there to fight, as did his best friend, who never came back. Then upon returning home, he became a renowned antiwar activist. In 1971, dressed in green fatigues, Kerry denounced the war before the Senate Foreign Relations Committee. Instantly, he became a generational icon, a symbol of how the nation's elite youth, the best and brightest, were turning against their parents' war.

Unlike Vermont, heavily Catholic Massachusetts had long been a Democratic-leaning state. But it was Kerry's generation, the baby boomers, who made it a dovish, culturally liberal state. In 1972, the 28-year-old Navy veteran ran for Congress in Massachusetts's fifth district, a region anchored by the struggling mill towns of Lawrence and Lowell. A celebrity because of his congressional testimony, Kerry crushed his primary opponents in the district's liberal, middle-class suburbs. But in its blue-collar, culturally conservative core, he was baited mercilessly over the war. When it came out that Kerry had helped write a book about veterans against the war, whose cover featured soldiers holding an upside-down American flag, the *Lowell Sun* called it "a gesture of contempt that has become synonymous with the attitude of youth groups protesting not only Vietnam but just about everything else there is to protest in the United States." It was an eerie foreshadowing of the attacks Kerry would face when he ran for president, thirty-two years later.

Kerry overcame a crowded primary field, but in the general election, he lost badly in Lawrence and Lowell, and a Republican claimed the seat. As one local reporter explained, "it was a class issue—class and resentment." Another observer, using Nixon's famous term for the people who fueled his victory that year over George McGovern, said Kerry was defeated by the "silent majority."

But Kerry would have his revenge. By the time he ran for office again ten years later, suburban, liberal reformers like Michael Dukakis, many with roots in the antiwar movement, had firmly wrested control of the party. And Kerry became one of their darlings. As a champion of the nuclear freeze, he was elected lieutenant governor in 1982, and two years later, he won a seat in the Senate, replacing Paul Tsongas. Three months after taking office, he flew to Nicaragua, and soon emerged as one of the chief congressional opponents of aid to the contras. "A central part of my [Senate] campaign," he would explain, "had been the notion that I would bring to the Senate the experience of the Vietnam period."

For baby boomers angry over Iraq, then, Kerry was an even more natural champion than Dean. He had been an articulate, passionate spokesman for the post-Vietnam liberal foreign policy consensus. He had criticized Reagan's invasion of Grenada, opposed the Gulf War, and opposed lifting the arms embargo against Bosnia. But in October 2002, with his eye firmly on a presidential run, Kerry voted to authorize the Iraq war. For alienated liberals, he became a symbol of Democrats' willingness to abandon their principles in order to win.

BUT IN A CRUEL twist of fate, the vote that was supposed to help Kerry defeat George W. Bush became an albatross in his campaign against Howard Dean. Unlike Richard Gephardt, with his close ties to labor, or John Edwards, with his son-of-a-millworker populism, Kerry's natural base was upscale liberals. But his convoluted efforts to defend his vote for a war they loathed soon became a quagmire. As the *New York Times* noted, "It dogs him at nearly every step on his presidential campaign: If Senator John Kerry is so critical of the Bush administration's handling of the war in Iraq and its aftermath, why did he vote to authorize the use of force in the first place?" By fall 2003, Dean looked unstoppable and Kerry's campaign was on the verge of collapse.

Events, however, offered Kerry a second chance. In October, Bush requested $87 billion in supplemental spending for the wars in Afghanistan and Iraq—a request that for many liberals symbolized the Iraq occupation's heavy cost, its indefinite duration, and the administration's lack of accountability over how it was waged. Kerry voted to pay for the $87 billion by partially repealing Bush's tax cuts. But when that failed, he voted not to spend the money at all. It was the opportunity he had been waiting for: He had finally shown he could stand up to the president.

The following month, Kerry fired his campaign manager and unveiled a new stump speech filled with blunt attacks on Bush's Iraq policy. Kerry, noted the *New York Times Magazine*'s James Traub, "began to sound more and more like an antiwar candidate." Yet even as he blurred differences on the war, he delivered another message: That unlike Dean, he could win a general election. "Yes, we can't beat him by being 'Bush light,' " he said at a debate in January, "but we can't beat him by being light on national security."

It was a careful balancing act. Kerry had to convince liberal primary voters that he agreed with them on Iraq while also convincing them that—unlike Dean—he was hawkish enough to beat Bush. And in this effort, Vietnam proved his ace card. In what many considered the most effective commercial of the primary campaign, one of Kerry's Vietnam boatmates testified that "the decisions that he made saved our lives." Three days before the Iowa caucuses, a soldier Kerry had rescued from drowning in 1969 made a surprise appearance at a campaign rally, stunning the crowd with a story that ended: "I figure I owe him my life."

Vietnam testified to Kerry's character. But even more important, it told primary voters that Republicans couldn't paint him as soft. Rank-and-file Democrats were furious over Iraq, but they were also desperate to reclaim the White House. And Kerry convinced them that he was the man who could do it. In the Iowa caucuses, among voters whose biggest concern was defeating Bush, Kerry beat Dean by 16 points. And fueled by his back-from-the-dead win there, he cruised to the nomination.

But if Kerry owed his victory to the Democrats' obsession with electability, that obsession had a strangely patronizing quality to it. For the most part, liberal voters weren't supporting Kerry because he had served in Vietnam. They were supporting him because they believed other, more hawkish, voters would support him because he had served in Vietnam. Democrats knew that the war on terror would be a central issue in the fall campaign, and that many Americans had anxieties about their party's strength on national security. But they chose to believe those anxieties were a matter not of ideology but of image. Americans, they decided, were looking for a tough guy—someone who had stared America's enemies in the face and shot them dead. And if Rambo was what Americans wanted, well, then, Rambo was who they would get.

So sure, in fact, were Democrats that the country's new national security debate was really about style that, beyond Iraq, they barely inquired about Kerry's actual foreign policy beliefs. Neither liberal activists nor Kerry's opponents drew attention to his antiwar rhetoric upon returning from Vietnam, or his views on Central America and the nuclear freeze, or his opposition to the Gulf War, or his claim that Bill Clinton's foreign policy rhetoric was arrogant. The reality was that while Democratic primary voters were intensely interested in whether John Kerry would have fought the war in Iraq, they were not particularly interested in how else he would have responded to 9/11. And they assumed other Americans were not, either. As it turned out, that was a serious mistake.

IN THE YEARS before 9/11, John Kerry had actually thought a great deal about terrorism, probably as much as any member of the Senate. And the roots of that thinking—like so much else about his political identity—can be found in the immediate aftermath of the Vietnam War.

If Dukakis was the quintessential domestic policy neoliberal, John Kerry applied the same sensibility to international affairs. As a young Catholic growing up in Massachusetts, he had idolized John F. Kennedy. But he had also watched firsthand as Kennedy's idealistic spirit was debased and defeated in Vietnam. The experience taught him that the world did not conform to grand visions. Instead, he saw it as a series of disparate, complex problems, to be managed by carefully studying the facts on the ground.

In the Senate, Kerry's defining issue became Central America, where the Reagan administration's messianic anti-Communism and tendency to stretch the truth reminded him of Vietnam. But as the cold war wound down, events in the region took him in a different direction. He began investigating Panamanian dictator Manuel Noriega's laundering of drug profits through the corrupt Bank of Credit and Commerce International (BCCI). And from there he grew interested in organized crime, a topic that would powerfully shape his view of the post–cold war world.

For Kerry, who had spent the years following his failed congressional bid as a prosecutor, transnational crime was a perfect fit, since it combined two of the things he understood best: foreign policy and law enforcement. But it was also a way of coming to terms with the phenomenon that was fixating Clinton and Blair: globalization. "If you don't mind my saying," Kerry remarked in 2004, "I think I was ahead of the curve on this entire dark side of globalization." And he was right. For Kerry, organized crime highlighted critical features of the post–cold war world: its economic interdependence, the way pathologies ricocheted across borders, and the need for international institutions that could handle problems too big for any one government.

In Kerry's view, however, globalization had one more defining feature: it made ideology less important. After all, crime syndicates were motivated by only one thing: money. In *The New War*, Kerry's 1997 book on global crime, he called terrorism its "fraternal twin." But because he saw terrorism as an adjunct to crime, Kerry downplayed its ideological dimension. "Our new enemies attack not by ideology or military might," he wrote, "but by the manipulation of human weakness, greed, and despair."

So while Blair and Clinton spoke of extending democracy's reach, Kerry described America's mission not as the spread of ideas, but the spread of methods. "Our greatest single task," he argued, "is to articulate and achieve a new international convention that totally overhauls our ability to jointly investigate, move evidence, secure witnesses, and most important, help build adequate legal institutions in other countries." In true neoliberal fashion, Kerry had defined the post–cold war world less as a clash of visions than as a set of problems—problems that could only be managed with America's help.

WHEN KERRY TALKED about the war on terror during the 2004 campaign, particularly off the cuff, the influence of his work on organized crime was plain to see. But his advisers weren't much interested in having Americans see it. Like the consultants who ran the Democratic campaigns of 2002, and those who had shepherded Kerry to victory in Iowa, the strategists who plotted Kerry's general election campaign were not particularly interested in offering a liberal vision for the war on terror. The polls, after all, showed that terrorism was Bush's greatest strength. The more people thought about it, assumed Kerry's advisers, the worse their candidate would do. So they developed a three-pronged strategy. Kerry would use Vietnam to show he was tough enough to protect the country. Having neutralized national security, he would focus on domestic issues, where the polls gave Democrats a clear edge. And all the while, the bad news streaming in from Iraq would turn the country against President Bush.

In early May, once the nomination was effectively locked up, the Kerry campaign took a massive bet on the power of Vietnam. They produced two 60-second biographical ads that dwelled heavily on Kerry's wartime heroism, spending more to air them than either side had spent on commercials to that point. Other than that, they concentrated on the economy and health care. According to one campaign aide, "the political consultants' view was that the war on terror was not our issue. . . . Whenever Bush was talking about the war on terror, the Kerry campaign would say he's changing the subject from the loss of 10 million jobs."

The Democratic Convention in July offered more of the same. Kerry arrived in Boston, the city where he was nominated, by boat—to evoke the swiftboat he had captained in Vietnam. His campaign plastered the Fleet Center with photos of his military service. And on the night he accepted the nomination, Kerry walked onto a stage filled with his Vietnam boat mates, saluted the audience, and declared, "I'm reporting for duty."

But the Vietnam storyline—which liberals had assumed would win over swing voters—when unveiled before actual swing voters, fell flat. The convention featured virtually no discussion of Kerry's Senate record, little about his view of the war on terror, and only gentle criticism of President Bush (because focus groups told Kerry's pollsters they didn't like negative campaigning). Instead of ideology, it offered biography. And biography didn't work: the convention boosted Kerry only a point or two in the polls.

To make matters worse, right after the convention ended, a group of conservative Vietnam veterans calling themselves Swift Boat Veterans for Truth began loudly attacking Kerry for having exaggerated his war injuries in Vietnam. It was a thuggish smear, and the GOP would likely have orchestrated it no matter how Kerry presented himself. But it was particularly devastating because virtually the only thing Americans knew about Kerry was that he was a war hero. His consultants' fear of discussing national security—and his own aversion to large, unifying themes—had left him dependent on a narrative of personal virtue. But for many Americans, the Swift Boat attacks threw that narrative into doubt. Kerry's favorability rating dropped 9 points in the month of August. It was as if Jimmy Carter, running on his small-town decency in the wake of Watergate, had been exposed as a liar.

Importantly, the Swift Boat attacks didn't only accuse Kerry of lying; they accused him of national betrayal. One ad opened with an image of an American flag rippling in the wind. "Symbols," declared the narrator, "they represent the best things about America." Then it showed Kerry as an antiwar protester, explaining that he had returned his medals. Finally, the narrator's voice returned: "How can the man who renounced his country's symbols now be trusted?" The ad was produced by the same agency that produced the famous 1988 commercial featuring Dukakis in a tank. And the message was the same: Democrats can't be trusted to defend America because they don't truly believe in America. "He dishonored his country," declared an anti-Kerry veteran in one Swift Boat ad. He "betrayed his country," announced the narrator in another. In the first presidential campaign of the post-9/11 era, the right's old cold war attack was back. And once again, liberals were vulnerable because they had no national greatness vision of their own.

THE THIRD ASPECT of Kerry's campaign strategy—to let the deteriorating situation in Iraq drag down President Bush's popularity—wasn't working either. Voters were certainly unhappy about Iraq; it was a prime reason so many of them told pollsters the country was on the "wrong track." But Kerry's own Iraq quagmire kept him from benefiting from Bush's woes. The Republicans used Kerry's shifting stance on the war, and particularly his vote against the $87 billion supplemental, to paint him as a spineless opportunist. The more Kerry tried to explain his views, the more entangled he became. And as the campaign entered the homestretch, Iraq seemed to be hurting Kerry more than it was hurting Bush.

Trailing by as much as 10 points on Labor Day, Kerry did the same thing he had done when he was losing to Howard Dean: he changed staff. In particular, he brought in a team of former Clinton aides who argued that until he cut the Gordian knot on Iraq, no one would listen to him on anything else. Finally, in late September, Kerry found his voice. At New York University, in perhaps his best speech of the campaign, he left little doubt that whatever his past views, he was now running against the war. "Iraq," he declared, "was a profound diversion from . . . the battle against our greatest enemy."

But if Iraq was a diversion from the real battle, that only highlighted the broader uncertainty about how Kerry would fight salafist terror. He had assembled a large, impressive, and generally hawkish foreign policy team—stocked with Clinton administration alumni—that produced reams of specific policies. But they didn't cohere into a worldview. Kerry and his longtime Senate aides resisted efforts to describe the war on terror as a struggle of ideas, sometimes stripping language about freedom and tyranny out of his prepared texts. Instead, in classic neoliberal fashion, Kerry promised competence. Again and again, he pledged to fight a "smarter, more effective war on terror." In two hours of interviews with the *New York Times Magazine*'s Matt Bai, he used the word *effective* eighteen times. Asked in the first question of the first presidential debate why he could prevent another 9/11 better than George W. Bush, Kerry cited his "better plan for homeland security," his "better plan to be able to fight the war on terror by strengthening our military," and vowed to do a "better job of training the Iraqi forces."

All in all during that first debate, which was devoted to foreign policy, Bush used variations of the words *freedom*, *democracy*, and *liberty* forty-five times; Kerry used them six times. Kerry came off as sharp, concise, and well informed, but he offered no larger message. As William Schneider had written years earlier, neoliberals "are efficient, effective, honest, intelligent, serious, and hardworking. They can solve problems, which is exactly what governors and members of Congress are supposed to do. But Presidents are supposed to do something else"—offer a vision.

Despite all this, exit polls on the afternoon of election day showed Kerry on his way to victory. Then, in the early evening, they began to turn—and as returns trickled in from the key battlegrounds, Ohio and Florida, Kerry fell further and further behind. Ultimately, Bush won with 286 electoral votes and 51 percent of the vote. "It became a vote," explained Kerry pollster Stanley Greenberg, in language eerily reminiscent of 1988, "on whether you agreed with [Bush's] worldview rather than his competence." And like Dukakis, Kerry had helped make it so by offering no worldview of his own. Several days after the election, Kerry made a surprise appearance at a party for campaign staffers. Speaking before the men and women who had run his campaign, he told them that contrary to conventional wisdom, they had indeed outlined a message for the country. "Everyone in that room was on edge," one staffer later remarked, "because everyone wanted to know: What was that message?"

INITIALLY, SOME COMMENTATORS said Bush had won because of gay marriage and abortion, a view fueled by exit polls showing that "moral values"—more than terrorism, the economy, or Iraq—was the public's single greatest concern. But this was misleading, since terrorism, the economy, and Iraq were discrete issues, while moral values was a vague catchall that could include everything from abortion to poverty to personal integrity. In fact, a close comparison to past elections showed no increase in the share of voters citing cultural concerns. And gay marriage initiatives, which the GOP placed on the ballot in eleven states partly to lure conservatives to the polls, had no statistically significant effect on turnout.

The real change was that after a post–cold war hiatus, national security had retaken center stage. In 2000, 12 percent of the electorate had cited "world affairs" as its paramount issue. In 2004, by contrast, 34 percent cited either "terrorism" or "Iraq." Kerry overwhelmingly won the "Iraq" voters, who were mostly antiwar. But he was swamped by the larger number who cited terrorism and favored Bush by an incredible 72 points. Crunching the numbers, University of Virginia political scientist Paul Freedman found that a 10-point rise in the percentage of voters citing "terrorism" as their primary concern raised Bush's vote in a given state by 3 percentage points. By contrast, a 10-point rise in the percentage of voters citing "moral values" made no difference at all.

But the deeper story of the 2004 election lay in *who* voted against John Kerry because of terrorism. Among upscale whites, who had been moving into the Democratic Party since the 1960s, Kerry performed well, better than Al Gore had four years earlier. He also did well among minorities. After the election, some activists suggested Kerry had failed to sufficiently rouse his liberal base. But in fact, they were at least as roused as their counterparts on the right. A study by Emory University political scientist Alan Abramowitz concluded: "Whatever success the Republican campaign had in mobilizing conservative evangelicals and other pro-Bush voters was apparently more than offset by the success of the Democratic campaign in mobilizing African-Americans, college students, and other anti-Bush voters."

Kerry lost the election among blue-collar whites. Clinton had won them by a single point in both 1992 and 1996. Gore had done far worse in 2000, losing them by 19 points. But if Kerry had simply held Gore's margin, he would have won the presidency. Instead, he dropped even further, losing them by a massive 24 points. The greatest drop occurred among working-class white women, who, polls showed, were the most worried about terrorism. In a grim historical footnote, it was working-class white women who had told pollsters they were most worried about the Soviet Union in 1988.

It was as if cold war liberalism had fallen all over again. Around the time Charlie Dean confronted Big Howard over dinner in 1964, highly educated whites had begun moving into the Democratic camp—just in time to see their blue-collar counterparts flee in the wake of civil rights and Vietnam. As the cold war ended, Bill Clinton had won them back. And now, as 9/11 cast a new shadow over American politics, they had left once again. In his first run for office in 1972, Kerry had won the upscale suburbs but lost working-class whites. Thirty-two years later, in the midst of another war, the same thing had happened again.

FOR DEMOCRATS, KERRY'S loss was a tragedy. But it was a temporary one. They took solace, as losing parties always do, in the deficiencies of their candidate and vowed to choose better the next time. The deeper and more enduring question concerns the kind of liberalism that has emerged in Kerry's wake. The core claim of the anti-imperialist left—that liberalism's only real enemies are on the right—found little support during the first year after 9/11. It was a minority view even among liberal opponents of the Iraq war, most of whom opposed overthrowing Saddam not because they rejected the concept of a war on terror, but because they feared (correctly) that invading Iraq would weaken America's ability to fight it. But the momentum started to shift after the elections of 2002. And by 2005, the anti-imperialist view was no longer marginal at all.

In May 2005, the Pew Research Center unveiled an in-depth study of the American electorate, something it has done every five years or so for the last two decades. In the 1990s, its studies had shown little difference between Democrats and Republicans on foreign policy. But by 2005, foreign policy did not merely divide members of the two parties; it divided them more than anything else. "Foreign affairs assertiveness now almost completely distinguishes Republican-oriented voters from Democratic-oriented voters," explained the Pew Report. "In contrast, attitudes relating to religion and social issues are not nearly as important in determining party affiliation." Commentators sometimes describe the United States as two countries: churched and unchurched. But in fact, Pew was saying, it is two countries: hawk and dove.

In fact, liberals and conservatives don't merely take different positions on international issues; they hold fundamentally different views about which international issues matter. More than four months after the 2004 election, the Center for American Progress and the Century Foundation asked self-described liberals and conservatives to rate their top two foreign policy goals. Conservatives were 29 points more likely to mention destroying Al Qaeda, 26 points more likely to mention denying nuclear weapons to hostile groups or nations, and 24 points more likely to mention capturing Osama bin Laden. In fact, while conservatives, and Americans in general, cited destroying Al Qaeda as their highest priority overall, for liberals, it tied for tenth.

It wasn't that liberals didn't have worthy goals. Their top priority was withdrawing troops from Iraq; number two was stopping the spread of AIDS; number three was working more closely with America's allies. But what the poll showed with startling clarity was that many liberals simply no longer see the war on terror as their fight. That conclusion was underscored by a November 2005 M.I.T. survey, which found that only 59 percent of Democrats—as opposed to 94 percent of Republicans—still approved of America's decision to invade Afghanistan. And only 57 percent of Democrats—as opposed to 95 percent of Republicans—supported using U.S. troops "to destroy a terrorist camp." George W. Bush, in other words, has used the war on terror to cover such a multitude of sins that for many liberals the whole idea of focusing the nation's energies on defeating global jihad (whether you call that effort the "war on terror" or something else) has fallen into disrepute. Just as Vietnam turned liberals against the cold war, Iraq has now turned them against the war on terror. America badly needs an alternative vision—rooted in the liberal tradition—for fighting global jihad. And yet the liberalism emerging today denies that fighting global jihad should even be a priority.

AS LIBERALS HAVE grown cynical about the struggle against jihad, growing numbers have accepted the implicit message of the anti-imperialist left: the United States can best protect itself by retreating from the world. When the Pew Research Center asked Americans in

October 2005 whether the "U.S. should mind its own business internationally," more than half of Democrats answered yes, compared to just over one-quarter among members of the GOP.

In the short term, these views may not hurt Democrats at the polls. In fact, with Americans wearying of the war in Iraq, liberalism's turn inward may fit the national mood. The elections of 2006 and 2008 could resemble the elections of 1974 and 1976, when foreign policy exhaustion, and Republican scandal, propelled Democrats to big gains. But that exhaustion is unlikely to last, or to be allowed to last. Most experts believe the United States will be living with the jihadist threat for years, if not decades, and that before it disappears, the United States will be hit again on its own soil. Liberals may regain power without an antitotalitarian vision of their own. But if the United States remains under threat, those victories will prove a false dawn, as they did during the Carter years. And eventually, the country will again lurch right, since whatever its failings, the right at least knows that America's enemies need to be fought.

The core issue, however, is not whether the struggle against totalitarianism helps liberals at the polls. It is whether that struggle helps define what liberalism is. Since John Kerry's defeat, the activists who propelled Howard Dean's campaign have begun taking over the Democratic Party, much as another generation of liberal activists did after 1968. MoveOn's membership has swelled to several million, and it has used its clout to help install Dean as chairman of the Democratic National Committee. Popular blogs like Daily Kos, some with roots in the Dean campaign, have become powerful players in the Democratic Party. These new forces have injected passion into Democratic politics. They are making liberalism a movement rather than merely a collection of interest groups. And they are building the grassroots infrastructure that the American left desperately needs. But their idealism, and their outrage, is directed almost exclusively against the right. Reading them, you could easily think liberals have no enemies more threatening, or more illiberal, than George W. Bush. Unlike the men and women who recreated liberalism at the dawn of the cold war, they have not put antitotalitarianism at the center of their hopes for a better country and a better world. And unless they do, the new liberalism being born in the shadow of 9/11 risks losing touch with America and with the best traditions of liberalism itself.

8

A New Liberalism

ULTIMATELY, DEBATES ABOUT American foreign policy are debates about America. Conservatives understand that. While the right has gone through many phases over the last half-century, a core vision has endured. It starts with a fear that Americans don't believe deeply enough in themselves. Corrupted by liberalism, and perhaps modernity itself, they doubt their superiority over America's enemies; they embrace relativism; they lose their nerve. Against fanatically self-confident foes, this makes them potentially weak. And so they must be convinced of their virtue, reminded again and again that they represent the struggle of good against evil. In conservative mythology, the last fifty years are a recurring story of America losing faith in itself, and finding it again. The New Deal, with its socialist principles, blurred the distinction between Soviet Communism and American freedom—until Joseph McCarthy insisted that Communism would no longer be tolerated. After Vietnam, Americans began to think they lived in a sick society with nothing to teach the world—until Ronald Reagan helped America stand tall. During the Clinton years, Americans lost their capacity for moral judgment—until George W. Bush called a new evil by its name. The lesson is always the same: When America is morally inhibited and institutionally restrained, it becomes weak. When it casts off those restraints, it grows strong.

This vision can be undermined by events. And it loses its salience when Americans do not feel under threat. But it tells a story about what makes America great. Liberals can churn out policy papers and nominate war heroes, but without their own narrative of American greatness, it will do them little good, either in gaining power or in wielding it.

The liberal story begins with a different fear. If conservatives worry that Americans do not see their own virtue, liberals worry that Americans see only their virtue. For liberals, the real danger is not doubt, but complacency. And the central paradox is that only when America recognizes that it is not inherently good can it become great. The awareness of moral fallibility creates the potential for moral progress. When liberals glance back at American history, they see not a country periodically rediscovering its pride, but a country periodically rediscovering its conscience.

From this different view of America, cold war liberals built a narrative of national greatness for their time. Because they recognized America's practical limits—its inability to guarantee prosperity and security on its own, either through isolation or empire—they built international institutions that stabilized capitalism and defended freedom. The goal was not merely greater liberty but greater equality as well, in the belief that the former required the latter to survive. And because they recognized America's *moral* limits, they used those institutions to genuinely share power. Statesmen like George Kennan and George Marshall knew that if America restrained itself, weaker countries would welcome its preeminence, and that preeminence would endure. And intellectuals like Reinhold Niebuhr knew that it was not just other countries that should fear the corruption of American power; we ourselves should fear it most of all. American exceptionalism—our superiority to the predatory powers of the past—rested on our willingness to accept the restraints that they eschewed. Ironically, if we assumed we were inherently different, we became no better than everybody else.

The belief that America strove for virtue—rather than embodying it—also shaped domestic policy. For men like Hubert Humphrey and Bayard Rustin, America was not a fixed model for a benighted world. Our own struggle for liberty and equality bound us in solidarity with people pursuing those same ideals around the world. And it was America's internal struggle—our willingness to address social problems rather than repressing them—that represented our great advantage over the Soviet Union, which held itself and its empire together through brute force. Containment relied on the confidence that, in a struggle lasting generations, America's alliances would not crack, and America itself would not crack. And that confidence was rooted in America's ability to restrain itself abroad and improve itself at home. From Truman to Kennedy, the liberal narrative of national greatness linked the world America hoped to build to the country America hoped to be.

A NEW LIBERAL narrative must again start with the recognition that we can guarantee neither prosperity nor security on our own—not through the right's Fortress America fantasies of the 1990s, nor through its neo-imperial fantasies of today. In fact, the world is far more interdependent than it was even a half-century ago. Globalization's economic and cultural benefits are profound. But disease, environmental degradation, loose nuclear materials, financial instability, and refugees all ride the same technologies of communication and transport that have shrunk the world in so many other ways. In 1997, hidden weaknesses in Thailand's banking system helped produce a financial stampede that nearly plunged the world into recession. Today, in rural China, environmental destruction forces migrating birds into contact with livestock and people, breeding potential pandemics. Greenhouse gas emissions from across the globe helped heat the water in the Gulf of Mexico, worsening Hurricane Katrina's fury.

And at the center of these mobile threats sits jihadist terrorism, the only one that consciously harnesses technological progress for mass murder. Unlike its totalitarian predecessors, salafist ideology directs no governments and no armies. As the stepchild to a particular religion, it doesn't even have Communism's universalist appeal. But globalization gives groups of individuals powers once reserved for states, and in that way, it makes the weak strong. As Walter Russell Mead has pointed out, a hundred years ago it would have taken the greatest navy in the world an entire morning to kill 3,000 New Yorkers. On September 11 it took a small band of men, trained in one of the most obscure countries on earth, motivated by an ideology few Americans knew anything about, pledging fealty to a man in a cave.

The Bush administration's answer to these new dangers is the spread of liberty. And there is no question that in the darkness of oppression, pathologies grow more easily. Thailand's lack of financial transparency made its economic meltdown far worse. In late 2002 and early 2003, with SARS quietly gathering force in the province of Guangdong, the Chinese government tried to suppress the news, squandering the chance to arrest the syndrome's growth before it spread across the globe. And in the Middle East, where autocrats have banished politics from the public square, dissent has taken refuge in the institution freest from state control: the mosque. And from Saudi-funded mosques, madrassas, and charities, salafists have built a totalitarian movement that stretches across the Arab world and beyond.

But liberty alone is not enough, because today's threats also have roots in underdevelopment and despair. It is China's pitiful public health system, as well as its governmental secrecy, that facilitates the spread of disease. And in the Islamic world, democracy is not the only thing states fail to provide their people. Exploding populations and stagnating economies have left governments from Algeria to Pakistan unable to provide decent schools, free medical clinics, even clean water. So salafists fill the economic void as well as the political one, providing services and gaining prestige. In one particularly nightmarish Cairo slum in the 1990s, the Islamic Group took such total control that residents began calling it the "Islamic Republic." When a reporter from *Le Monde diplomatique* recently ventured into the salafist stronghold of Lahraouyine, on the outskirts of Casablanca, she found a shantytown with "no schools, no dispensaries, no post office, no savings bank, no public transport" and coined a term to describe it: "state-forsaken."

In contrast to the antidemocratic left, the liberal tradition does not accept equality as a substitute for liberty. But from Roosevelt's Global New Deal to Truman's Point Four to Kennedy's Alliance for Progress, it sees their fates as intertwined. President Bush describes free elections as a finish line that nations cross and then live happily every after. Yet countries like Nigeria and Pakistan have been yo-yoing back and forth between democracy and dictatorship for decades, illustrating the insight that powered the Marshall Plan: when democracies do not improve their people's lives, they often fail. And even in the stable democracies of Western Europe, ghetto poverty and cultural alienation turns some young Muslims to jihad.

In *The Vital Center*, Arthur Schlesinger approvingly quoted Winston Churchill's "seven tests of freedom," including free speech, free elections, restraints on police power, and the rule of law. But "an adequate philosophy of free society," he argued, "would have to supplement the Churchill tests by such questions as these: Do the people have a relative security against the ravages of hunger, sickness and want? Do they freely unite in continuous and intimate association with like-minded people for common purposes? Do they as individuals have a feeling of initiative, function and fulfillment in the social order?"

In our time, Nobel Laureate economist Amartya Sen has called this broader concept "development as freedom"—the freedom to lead a productive, hopeful life, blighted by neither political repression nor economic and cultural despair. And when leading Middle Eastern scholars set out to evaluate their own societies in the now-famous Arab Human Development Reports, it was Sen's criteria they followed. Only by broadening the conception of freedom, argued Egyptian sociologist Nader Fergany, could they develop "genuinely valid yardsticks for measuring human development in this age of globalization." The results were shocking. Measured by these integrated criteria—which included women's empowerment, adult literacy, and environmental standards—the Arab world fell below even sub-Saharan Africa.

SO LIBERALISM'S FIRST response to totalitarianism in a globalized world is freedom broadly defined—freedom as both greater liberty and greater equality of opportunity. That requires a dramatic commitment to reducing the Middle East's female illiteracy rate, which is twice that of East Asia's, since countries that don't educate women are culturally oppressive and economically doomed. It requires a push for fundamental economic reform, so more of the world's fifty-seven Islamic countries—which today receive slightly more combined foreign investment than Sweden—can enter the global economy. And it requires helping develop an independent judiciary, a free press, multiple political parties, and, eventually, free elections, so Muslims can express their grievances without turning to violence.

All of this requires American generosity. During the Marshall Plan, the United States spent 15 percent of its budget on foreign aid; today it spends far less than 1 percent, near the bottom of the industrialized world. And even that money is undermined by the vast, immoral sums that the United States lavishes on agricultural subsidies, which help shut countries like Pakistan out of the most lucrative import market in the world. Many developing countries are also crippled by international debt, which they must service at the cost of spending on education and health. Yet European leaders like Tony Blair have pushed far more aggressively for debt relief than has the Bush administration. Overall, America's post-9/11 development efforts have been timid. As the 2003 Arab Human Development Report mournfully noted, the "long-term goal of draining the economic and political sources of terrorism has almost faded away."

It's no surprise that the Bush administration downplays the link be-

tween American generosity and American safety: that link threatens the
conservative narrative of national greatness. From James Burnham to William Bennett, conservative thinkers have rejected the connection between
totalitarianism and economic despair—calling it an apology for evil. In
this view, pointing out jihadism's material causes undermines moral clarity. And worse, in conservative eyes, it subtly shifts blame to the United
States—not only implying that America's enemies are not inherently evil,
but that America is not entirely good.

But in the liberal vision, there is no contradiction between recognizing that our enemies are not intrinsically evil, and recognizing that they
must be fought, just as there is no contradiction between recognizing that
although we are not intrinsically good, we must still fight them. America's
challenge lies not in recognizing our moral superiority, but in demonstrat-
ing it. The brilliance of the Marshall Plan was that by offering aid to
Soviet bloc governments if they accepted economic transparency, and
then watching the Kremlin refuse, the United States exposed the differences between East and West. Similarly, when liberals criticized the Bush
administration's initially meager response to the December 2004 Indian
Ocean tsunami, many conservative commentators dubbed the criticisms
anti-American. But when the administration reversed course and substantially increased U.S. assistance, that assistance transformed America's
image in Indonesia. Even more remarkably, it undermined support for
Osama bin Laden. In 2005, in fact, post-tsunami Indonesia became the
first major Muslim country to ever register plurality support for the U.S.
war on terror. Bush's tsunami about-face, in other words, represents one
of our greatest victories yet over jihad. By recognizing that American be-
nevolence needed to be proved—not asserted—the United States did not
undermine the moral distinction between us and our enemies, as conservatives feared; we strengthened it.

BUT IF AMERICA is more dependent than ever before on economic and
political development in other countries, it faces great dangers in trying to
dictate it. During the cold war, the structure of the international system
constrained U.S. power. The Soviet Union limited America's capacity to
intervene directly overseas, since in much of the world such intervention
would have risked nuclear war. Moscow also set the standard against which
America was judged. West Germans might not always have loved their
American occupiers, but they knew they had it better than their cousins

on the other side of the wall. No matter how unpopular Ronald Reagan became, Western European governments still wanted American missiles on their soil, because they feared the Soviet missiles pointed at them.

Today, however, there is no totalitarian superpower to put American actions in flattering context. And without the Soviet empire or the Communist model, U.S. military and economic influence knows few bounds. It is telling that in Latin America, the region where the United States has historically been least inhibited, it has been least popular. Now Latin America's fate has become virtually the entire world's.

As a result, American military, political, and economic intervention spawns more fear and resentment than ever before. The Muslim world needs fundamental reform. Yet if the United States draws up a blueprint, Muslims will most likely see it as serving our interests more than theirs. And they will not necessarily be wrong. After Saddam's fall, Paul Bremer, head of the Coalition Provisional Authority, unilaterally invalidated Iraqi laws that required foreign investors to reinvest part of their profits back in the country. He may have thought he was acting purely on Iraq's behalf, but that is only because he lacked the self-consciousness and humility to see that he was not.

The spirit underlying the Marshall Plan could not have been more different. The Truman administration did not draw up a plan for Europe's postwar recovery; it urged European governments to draw up such a plan, working together in a democratic process. And in contrast to the Bush administration in Iraq, it did not try to remake Europe's economy in America's image. Instead, it funded recovery efforts that, to American eyes, looked socialist. Truman's greatest concern was that the Marshall Plan enjoy legitimacy in Europe itself. As Assistant Secretary of State Willard Thorpe put it, "We should give support to political parties that offer Europeans a positive program suited to Europe's political needs and development . . . rather than looking for parties and individuals who seem to represent most exactly the political and economic ideology that has been successful in America."

In the Middle East today, the task is harder since many governments themselves lack legitimacy. But the Arab Human Development Reports offer a model. They paint a searing picture of the region's political, economic, and cultural failings and propose far-reaching reforms. But because their authors are respected, independent Middle Eastern scholars, their critique has prompted more serious debate and less defensiveness in the Arab world than George W. Bush's lectures about freedom. Using them as a template, the United States and its rich allies, along with international institutions like the UN, the World Bank, and the International Monetary Fund, should simply declare that we will generously fund an effort at Arab reform. The only conditions would be that Arab countries themselves develop a plan that enjoys clear popular support, conforms to broad democratic and market principles, and is completely transparent. If they comply, the United States should keep its promise, even if the plan deviates from American interests and preferences in a thousand specific ways. There is reason to hope some Middle Eastern governments would rise to the challenge—just as Turkey has embraced democracy and greater human rights in order to reap the economic windfall that comes with membership in the European Union. But if the region's autocratic regimes reject the bargain, as the Soviet bloc rejected the Marshall Plan, the effort would still have been worthwhile—since that rejection might spark widespread public discontent, and in the world's most repressive region, such discontent could itself further the cause of reform.

IT WOULD BE naïve, however, to think that freedom, even broadly defined, and pursued with generosity and humility, is enough to defeat jihadism. When governments lose control of their territory, unleashing threats that spill beyond their borders, no amount of investment or aid will help unless someone reestablishes order. Most of the time, that someone will be the government, bolstered by outside help. But some governments cannot reassert control and others are themselves the root of the problem. From the Middle East to Southeast Asia, from the Horn of Africa to the Sahel, the United States may need to enter stateless zones, capture or kill the jihadists taking refuge there, and stay long enough to begin rebuilding the state.

Such efforts may divide liberals. If America's political and economic mission overseas helps distinguish the liberal and conservative narratives of national greatness, its military mission often divides two different strains of liberalism. In his 1952 book, *The Irony of American History*, Niebuhr criticized the self-congratulatory right for its willingness to "cover every ambiguity of good and evil in our actions by the frantic insistence that any measure taken in a good cause must be unequivocally virtuous." But he also criticized the anti-imperialist left, which he said "would renounce the responsibilities of power for the sake of preserving the purity of our soul." In the liberal antitotalitarian tradition that Niebuhr helped create, America must recognize its capacity for evil and build the restraints that hold it in check. But it must still act to prevent greater evil. It cannot take refuge in the moral innocence that comes from no meaningful action at all. Throughout the decades, anti-imperialist liberals have been tempted by the hope that humanitarian methods could fully substitute for violent ones, so liberalism's enemies could be vanquished while America remained pure. But America could not have built schools for Afghan girls had it not bombed the Taliban first. And efforts to aid the people of Sarajevo were largely fruitless until NATO air strikes broke the Serbian siege. Democratic senator Joseph Biden recently described a meeting with liberal donors where he asked what they would recommend if the president learned he could capture or kill Osama bin Laden, but doing so would cost the lives of 500 to 5,000 U.S. troops. "The truth is," he recounted, "they put their heads down."

The central question dividing liberals today is whether they believe liberal values are as imperiled by the new totalitarianism rising from the Islamic world as they are by the American right. If they are—if the war on terror is our fight too—then liberals must support military as well as economic and political efforts to fight it, even if those efforts are morally imperfect. When elite college campuses ban the military from recruiting because it discriminates against gays, or when Michael Moore urges rallies against the CIA because of its flawed human rights record, or when liberals casually urge cutting the defense budget, although military spending made possible American interventions in the Balkans and Afghanistan, they are succumbing to the old siren song of purity and abdicating their responsibility to do what Niebuhr urged: make the tragic choices that defending freedom requires.

BUT DEFENDING FREEDOM does not justify every choice. War, after all, is the most corrupting form of intervention. And as a response to state breakdown, it mercilessly exposes the limits of American resources, knowledge, and good intentions. Men like Dick Cheney and Donald Rumsfeld favor military solutions because they believe that given America's unparalleled might, warfare—unlike diplomacy—does not require us to compromise with our allies. And if warfare's only purpose were toppling regimes, that would be true. But in today's world, where American security usually requires building something sustainable in those regimes' place, effective military action actually requires the greatest compromise of all.

As Iraq shows, unilateral nation building is impossible except under the best conditions. Yet nation building—defined as "the use of armed force in the aftermath of a crisis to promote a transition to democracy"—remains central to American security, and to liberalism's hopes for a better world. Had the United States and its allies not deployed large numbers of troops and large sums of money to Afghanistan and the Balkans after the bombing stopped, the Taliban might be back in power and Bosnia and Kosovo might no longer exist. And although Iraq has soured Americans on nation building, the historical record is far better than generally recognized. Without such efforts, according to an exhaustive RAND Corporation study, most countries emerging from conflict slip back into it. Of the eight countries or regions where the UN has led nation-building missions, by contrast, seven are today at peace and six are at least partial democracies.

Nation building, in other words—like development—can effectively combat state failure, as long America realizes the limits of what it can do alone. Before the Iraq war, conservatives derided the UN and America's Western European allies as less idealistic and less capable than the United States. But Germany and France proved more prescient than the Bush administration about the aftermath of Saddam's fall. British troops were often better trained than their U.S. counterparts for the civil-military missions that post-Saddam Iraq required. UN envoys were wiser about Iraq's political transition. And as the RAND study illustrates, the UN's overall nation-building record is actually better than America's.

The lesson is the same one Tony Blair and Bill Clinton had learned by the late 1990s: the more America wants to intervene militarily in other countries' affairs, the more it needs the legitimacy, and the capability, bestowed by strong international institutions. And were the Bush administration interested in strengthening those institutions—rather than bringing them to their knees—it would find willing partners. The UN is edging away from its traditional doctrine of noninterference in countries' internal affairs. After a landmark international report said that states have a "responsibility to protect," the abdication of which can justify international intervention, Kofi Annan called on the Security Council's permanent members not to veto interventions in cases of mass human rights abuse or genocide.

But the United Nations will never be enough. While America should support intervention in cases of genocide or humanitarian emergency, the stateless zones where jihadists take sanctuary may not be suffering either—which will make it harder to gain an international consensus. What's more, two members of the Security Council, China and Russia, are not American allies and do not share a broadly liberal vision of the world in which countries move toward greater democracy and human rights. Given that, to condition American military actions on UN approval—as *The Nation* urged on Kosovo—can be a form of doughfaceism, in which liberals urge action, knowing that no action will ever come.

As an alliance of twenty-six democracies, NATO has at least as much moral authority as the Security Council. Building on the Bosnia and Kosovo model, NATO is developing a 20,000-person rapid reaction force able to deploy anywhere in the world within five days, and stay for thirty. To avoid the taint of Western imperialism, NATO might partner with a regional organization, such as the African Union or the Association of Southeast Asian Nations, or even the G-20, a newly created body that brings industrial countries together with third-world heavyweights like India, Indonesia, and Brazil. Then, once the fighting is over, and the nation building has begun, it would be back to the UN to help oversee a long-term reconstruction effort, with NATO supplying extra-military muscle.

There is no point in romanticizing these efforts: winning wars and keeping the peace through international coalitions has costs. It took the United States years to convince its European allies to back the Bosnia intervention (though the Clinton administration's ambivalence contributed to the delay). And even in Kosovo, where NATO mustered the political will more quickly, the military process was labored and frustrating. But it was always thus: Victory in the cold war also required painstaking efforts at consensus among allies. It was America's willingness to persuade rather than simply coerce that distinguished it from the Soviet Union. America's recognition that it was neither all-powerful nor all-knowing was not a source of weakness; it was a deep source of strength. And liberals must make the case that it can be again.

TODAY'S CONSERVATIVES ARE not against persuasion. They simply reject the notion that America's ability to persuade relies on its willingness to be persuaded. And that is why they distrust international institutions, because while the UN and NATO do not ignore the realities of power—

the United States is first among equals in both bodies—they imply some level of reciprocity. For the Bush administration, by contrast, moral progress is a one-way conversation. The United States calls on other countries to embrace democracy; we even aid them in the task. But if they call back, proposing some higher standard that might require us to modify our actions, we trot out John Bolton. When other countries deny due process, it is barbaric, but when we do so, it is necessary. When other countries build nuclear weapons, they constitute a threat to international peace, but when we build a whole new class of nuclear weapons—not for deterrence, but for potential battlefield use—we are taking prudent steps in our defense. For the rest of the world, security and freedom require infringements upon national sovereignty. But for the United States, sovereignty trumps all.

To be sure, America will never be in perfect harmony with international opinion—we have our own interests and sometimes even our own values. But liberals reject the right's claim that American actions, simply by virtue of being American, are beyond moral judgment. In the fight against totalitarianism, the world needs independent organizations—dedicated to human rights and beholden to no nation—able to challenge governments in the name of freedom. And if they are doing their job, those organizations will sometimes challenge us. Rather than pretending our democratic credentials exempt us from scrutiny—as the Bush administration did when Amnesty International condemned its secret, indefinite detentions—we should see such criticism as an opportunity to invest those credentials with renewed meaning. And it is that internal effort—precisely because it is difficult, precisely because it requires us to confront our own capacity for injustice—that can build solidarity with the embattled democrats beyond our shores. The "most useful place to look for the inspirations that drive Arab democracy activists these days," writes the Lebanese journalist Rami Khouri, "is not the speeches of President George W. Bush, but rather the protest movements among American civil rights activists in the period 1956–1964." There may be no struggle in today's America with the capacity to so fully capture the imagination of the world. But in a global fishbowl, where non-Americans have vast exposure to what happens within our shores and our prisons, America's willingness to honor the principles that we evangelize for abroad can help invest our power with the legitimacy it badly needs.

In June 2005, in a statement in *Al-Ahram Weekly*, twenty-six Arab reformers answered George W. Bush's declarations on democracy with one of their own. "The West," they wrote, "from whose legacy of enlightenment and progress we hope to borrow, is itself in desperate need of a practical model of enlightenment and progress. The first and foremost prerequisite for this is to respect the law." And they are right. Conservatives rail against moral relativism. But, in fact, by denying there is a moral standard above and apart from American actions, it is they who have made morality situational. Since September 11, as America has sermonized about freedom to the rest of the world, we have begun labeling our own citizens "enemy combatants" and jailing them for years without due process. We have constructed detention centers across the globe, and tortured and murdered inside them. Yet the Bush administration expects people around the world to believe that because these actions have been committed by the United States, they cannot be offenses against freedom. Our infallibility should be as self-evident to them as it is to us.

It is the gap between the moral stringency we demand of others and the moral complacency we exhibit ourselves that has bred such bitterness among the very people who once took heart from America's example. As Hubert Humphrey declared in his call for civil rights at the 1948 Democratic Convention, "Our demands for democratic practice in other lands will be no more effective than the guarantee of those practices in our own." Both conservatives and liberals yearn for a return to the days when students carried a statue of liberty as they marched for democracy in the streets of Beijing. What liberals understand is that to bring about that day, we must begin carrying our own statues of liberty in the streets of Washington and New York.

IF RENEWING AMERICAN democracy can help restore American authority in the world, it is even more critical to American strength at home. During the cold war, the right's fear that Americans were weaker than their totalitarian foes fueled its fantasies of rollback and its apocalyptic style. Cold war liberals, by contrast, embraced containment because they believed that in a struggle lasting decades, American society could maintain its cohesion and its will. Today, there is no enemy superpower to contain. And state failure represents a greater threat than foreign foes. But America does face hostile dictatorships like North Korea and Iran, which either seek nuclear weapons or already have them. And it faces China, an authoritarian giant with dreams of regional dominance. In these confrontations, it is likely that conservatives will once again see time running out, with catastrophe looming unless America rushes to stay history's hand. The liberal tradition, by contrast, counsels patience. America must be prepared for defensive war, because armed vigilance is the best way to deter aggressive action. And it should pursue diplomacy in the hopes of convincing rogue states to limit their arsenals, and convincing China to avoid rash action. But it should not demand immediate transformations, or fear a long standoff. Deterrence and diplomacy are messy and imperfect, but they buy time to let the forces of change gnaw at dictatorship from within. As long as our society remains more cohesive than theirs, we can afford to wait. In the liberal narrative, America can be patient because time is on democracy's side.

But that is not a mandate for complacency. Time is only on democracy's side because democracy—unlike dictatorship—allows citizens to come together freely to meet common challenges. "The exercise of democracy," wrote Schlesinger, "can bring about a reconciliation between the individual and the community." And that "communion in action" can "produce a vigilance that never falters" and make freedom "a fighting faith."

Today, there is reason to fear that American democracy is no longer producing the "communion in action" necessary to meet the new threats of a globalized world. And this failure has its roots in deep transformations in American life. The era that produced cold war liberalism—the period between World War II and Vietnam—has been called "the golden age of civic engagement." Americans voted more, contacted their legislators more, volunteered for campaigns more, and believed in their government more than they had during the Gilded Age of the 1920s, and far more than they do now. And while Jim Crow cast a shadow over those glory days, by the era's end, the democratic spirit had spread even to the South, fully capturing Schlesinger's vision of a renewed democracy.

That era, not coincidentally, was also a golden age of economic equality. Between 1947 and 1973, overall family income roughly doubled. And remarkably, the poor and working class fared even better than the rich. With a high school degree or less, Americans found jobs that offered decent health care, guaranteed pensions, reasonable hours, rising wages, and the promise that it would all continue as far as the eye could see. In the 1950s and 1960s, working- and middle-class Americans enjoyed the kind of job security that only college professors have now.

Since then, the bottom has fallen out. The richest Americans have seen their family incomes continue to rise briskly. But for the poorest 40 percent of the population, income growth has slowed to a crawl. And the only reason poor and working-class Americans haven't seen their incomes *go down* is that they are working longer and longer hours. Largely as a result of women's increased entry into the workforce, the average two-parent family works a full twelve weeks more per year than it did in 1969.

In fact, as Yale University's Jacob Hacker shows in *The Great Risk Shift*, even solidly middle-class Americans, who on paper have their heads above water, don't enjoy anywhere near their parents' level of economic security. Compared to the 1970s, today's families experience roller-coaster swings in income, with little to fall back on if Mom loses her job or Dad gets seriously ill. Home foreclosures have tripled in less than twenty-five years. More families with children file for bankruptcy than file for divorce. And for every family that declares itself bankrupt, another seven are so deep in debt that they probably should.

What's going on? After World War II, a balance of power between labor and industry produced a balanced distribution of wealth. From 1947 to 1973, every dollar of productivity translated into a dollar of family income, as unions pressured companies to raise wages and benefits, and the mere threat of unionization led others to do the same. Government backed up the arrangement with social insurance programs like Social Security and Medicare, and with regular increases in the minimum wage. Since the 1970s, however, government has turned hostile to labor, labor has crumbled, and business has thrown the old compact out the window. The percentage of private-sector workers with defined-benefit pensions has dropped by more than half. The percentage with employer-based health care has dropped from two-thirds to just over one in two. And corporations have also found more subtle ways to shift the financial burden. Since most jobs no longer pay working-class men enough to support their families, women have flooded the workforce, creating huge child care costs—which, of course, companies don't cover.

Corporations haven't suddenly grown heartless; they're simply trying to survive in a harsher international environment. But instead of picking up the slack, government has retreated as well. Programs like unemployment insurance and food stamps have grown less generous since the 1970s. Taxes have become less progressive, with individuals now paying four times as much as corporations, as opposed to roughly the same amount in the late 1940s. And government hasn't taken responsibility for new costs like preschool and college tuition, which are increasingly essential in today's knowledge-based economy. As a result, as Elizabeth Warren and Amelia Warren Tyagi have noted, while the state used to cover 100 percent of a basic education, it now covers only two-thirds, with parents on the hook for the rest.

The result is inequality unseen since the 1920s. And excessive inequality threatens democracy at home, just as it does abroad. Since the 1960s, democratic participation has plummeted, particularly among the less well off. Unions once connected large numbers of working-class Americans to their government, giving them a voice and a stake. And labor provided much of the muscle to pass policies like Social Security and the GI bill, which sent messages of equal citizenship—and sparked greater political participation among beneficiaries. But in recent decades, unions and other organizations with working-class members have been in free fall. In today's Washington, lobbyists don't connect Americans to their government; they mostly connect corporations to their government. The result is a vicious circle in which average Americans receive less from Washington, feel less connected to Washington, and have less influence in Washington. Since the 1960s, voting rates among less educated Americans have nose-dived. The percentage of Americans saying government is run by a few big interests looking out for themselves has close to doubled. And as the exercise of democracy has frayed, it has produced less of the "communion in action" that Schlesinger envisioned. "The closing decades of the twentieth century," wrote the political scientist Robert Putnam, "found Americans growing ever less connected with one another and with collective life. We voted less, joined less, gave less, trusted less, invested less time in public affairs. . . . Our 'we' steadily shriveled."

AS AMERICANS HAVE disengaged from their democracy, government has grown increasingly subservient to powerful private interests, even when the country desperately requires enlightened public action. Three days after 9/11, at around midnight, with the House chamber nearly empty, the leaders of the House of Representatives asked for unanimous consent to pass legislation granting the ailing airline industry $15 billion in grants and loans. A lone congressman objected, noting that even the members of the Transportation Committee had not seen the bill. But eight days

later—aided by twenty-seven in-house lobbyists and forty-two outside lob-
bying firms—the airline industry pushed similar legislation through both
houses. Unlike the far smaller bailout of Chrysler in 1980, which provided
only loans and imposed tough conditions, the airlines got both loans and
cash. An effort to include retraining funds and extended unemployment
benefits for laid-off airline workers never even came up for a vote.

Such behavior has become typical for a House of Representatives
that, according to veteran Congress watchers Thomas Mann and Norman
Ornstein, is so dominated by lobbyists that it "more closely resembles the
House of the 19th century than that of the 20th, of the Gilded Age more
than the Cold War era." A month after the airline bailout, the House tried
to retroactively repeal the alternative minimum tax, giving corporations
such as IBM, General Motors, and General Electric an enormous windfall. Since then, Congress has passed a $190 billion farm bill that restores
the vast subsidies for large agricultural interests that were reduced during
the deficit-conscious 1990s. It has passed a prescription drug bill costing
over $1 trillion, 61 percent of which, according to one study, will end
up as drug company profit. It has passed an energy bill containing more
than $14 billion in corporate tax breaks. And for good measure, it has
passed two more rounds of upper-income tax cuts, in addition to the one
already passed in 2001. All this while massive structural deficits threaten
to bankrupt the government. Fifty years ago, Americans for Democratic
Action warned that a political system ruled by business would produce a
government too weak to defend freedom, and that warning is being borne
out today.

If Congress increasingly insulates itself from public influence, the
Bush administration has been just as brazen. George W. Bush has held
fewer press conferences than any president in a century. In what a *US News
and World Report* study calls "a reversal of a decades-long trend of openness
in government," his administration—even before 9/11—began putting
vast quantities of documents beyond public view. The White House initially opposed the very idea of a 9/11 Commission, then denied it access
to key documents and top administration officials. Even Congress has had
to repeatedly threaten subpoenas to get information once considered rou-
tine.

This too has undermined national security. NSC 68, the 1950 document that set out American strategy for the cold war, declared that "The
full power which resides within the American people will be evoked only

through the traditional democratic process: This process requires, firstly, that sufficient information regarding the basic political, economic, and military elements of the present situation be made publicly available so that an intelligent popular opinion may be formed. . . . Out of this common view will develop a determination of the national will and a solid resolute expression of that will." But as the public has grown less democratically engaged, it has grown easier to manipulate. The result, in the debate over Iraq, was that the Bush administration successfully prevented an "intelligent popular opinion" from being formed. It so relentlessly conflated 9/11 and Iraq that by the time the United States invaded, more than half of Americans believed Saddam was personally involved in the attacks and almost 90 percent believed he supported terrorist groups planning to strike the United States. Paul Wolfowitz declared that post-Saddam Iraq could "finance its own reconstruction, and relatively soon," even as the Bush administration kept secret a study showing that Iraq's oil sector was in extreme disrepair. And a subservient Republican-led Congress put little pressure on the Bush administration to justify its claims about Iraq's weapons of mass destruction, its terrorist ties, or America's postwar plans. Had the Bush administration been less insulated from democratic pressure, America would not have gone to war the way it did. And it might not have gone at all.

BUT THE GREATEST danger of this democratic disengagement is not its impact on American policy. It is its impact on the American people. In the weeks and months after September 11, Americans showed exactly the "solid resolute expression" of national will that NSC 68 envisioned. Trust in government and interest in public affairs shot up. Institutions stressing national service, like Teach for America, AmeriCorps, and even the CIA, were deluged with applications. Putnam said "a window of opportunity has opened for a sort of civil renewal that occurs only once or twice a century." America seemed to be undergoing a cultural revival based not on religion, as the right had long urged, but something more akin to what John F. Kennedy proposed after *Sputnik*: a cultural revival based on citizenship.

George W. Bush did not nurture this new spirit. He rarely asked Americans to serve their country. But the failure went far deeper than a lack of presidential exhortation. As Kennedy understood, a renewed national spirit requires the renewed exercise of democracy. Government cannot simply tell Americans that we are all in it together; it must show them. And from virtually the moment the twin towers fell, it has been doing the opposite.

Now, less than five years later, the surge in civic involvement is gone. Public hostility to government now exceeds pre-9/11 levels. Polls show the country even more bitterly divided than it was when Bill Clinton was being impeached. Isolationist sentiment is on the rise. Only a few years into this new struggle, Americans are exhausted and divided. Our army is close to broken; our public institutions are reviled; our culture war goes on and on. When global commentators use words like *dynamism* and *vigor*, they are far more likely to be discussing India or China than the United States. After Iraq, and Hurricane Katrina, observers are no longer particularly surprised or particularly disturbed when America fails.

And yet the struggle that began on September 11 goes on. For years and perhaps decades to come, Americans will live with the threat of attacks that could disfigure our society, in a conflict where technology's march slowly empowers our enemies. Today, even more urgently than when the struggle began, America faces the question Schlesinger posed in 1949: How to rally a splintered society to its own defense? How to make freedom a fighting faith?

Liberalism's answer is the same one it gave at the Willard Hotel: shared struggle based upon shared power and shared risk. Abroad, America shares power because we recognize our limits, both practical and moral. And we see that recognition not as a sign of weakness but of strength. At home, America shares power because only by reviving democracy—taking it back from the forces of private interest and concentrated wealth—can government call its citizens to great tasks. And America shares risk because Americans cannot accomplish great tasks abroad while at home they buckle in an economy that offers protection to only the rich and the old. National security relies on economic security. Generosity at home is the foundation for generosity overseas. Citizenship can be as powerful a force for moral revival as religion. And democracy is not America's gift to the world. It is the goal for which we struggle, against the injustice in our own society, in solidarity with those people struggling against the injustice in theirs.

In the liberal vision, national greatness is not inherited and it is not declared; it is earned. We cannot know whether we will defeat the totalitarianism of our time, just as past generations could not foresee the outcome of their struggles. But almost as important as the outcome is the way we conduct the fight. "In the years after the Second War," wrote Schlesinger, "Americans began to rediscover the great tradition of liberalism." May the same be said, one day, of us.

Notes

Introduction

ix *began with Franklin Roosevelt.* As Roosevelt put it, "The liberal party is a party which believes that, as new conditions and problems arise beyond the power of men and women to meet as individuals, it becomes the duty of Government itself to find new remedies with which to meet them. . . . The conservative party in government honestly and conscientiously believes the contrary. . . . It believes that, in the long run, individual initiative and private philanthropy can take care of all situations." James P. Young, *Reconsidering American Liberalism: The Troubled Odyssey of the Liberal Idea.* Boulder, Colo.: Westview Press, 1996, pp. 170–171. For a detailed discussion of Roosevelt's decision to adopt the term *liberal,* and the debate it provoked, see Ronald D. Rotunda, *The Politics of Language: Liberalism as Word and Symbol,* 1st ed. Iowa City: University of Iowa Press, 1986.

Chapter 1: A New Liberalism

1 *"How I wish you were at the helm."* Carl Solberg, *Hubert Humphrey: A Biography.* St. Paul, Minn.: Borealis Books, 2003, p. 112.

2 *Humphrey did.* Ibid., p. 113.

2 *"police governments" to the east.* Winston Churchill, "Sinews of Peace (*Iron Curtain Speech*) March 5, 1946." Viewed on September 9, 2005, at http://www.winstonchurchill.org/i4a/pages/index.cfm?pageid=429; Abbott Gleason, *Totalitarianism: The Inner History of the Cold War.* New York: Oxford University Press, 1997, p. 69.

2 *"peace based on mutual trust"* Alonzo L. Hamby, *Beyond the New Deal: Harry S. Truman and American Liberalism.* New York: Columbia University Press, 1976, p. 129. In fact, while Wallace's speech caused a crisis in the Truman administration because it was deemed too pro-Soviet, it was actually too *anti*-Soviet for his audience. When Wallace suggested that Russia might evolve toward greater personal freedom, the Madison Square Garden crowd, which included many Communists, loudly

booed. See Norman Markowitz, *The Rise and Fall of the People's Century: Henry A. Wallace and American Liberalism, 1941–1948*. New York: Free Press, 1973, p. 198.

3   *"assemblies of liberals ever brought together."* Hamby, *Beyond the New Deal*, p. 154.

3   *"millions upon millions of Americans."* Ibid., p. 155.

3   *"in the history of the country."* Markowitz, *The Rise and Fall of the People's Century*, p. 203.

3   *"is a delusion."* Hamby, *Beyond the New Deal*, p. 135; Stephen M. Gillon, *Politics and Vision: The ADA and American Liberalism, 1947–1985*. New York: Oxford University Press, 1987, p. 34.

3   *"on the Republican ticket in 1946."* Stephen E. Ambrose, *Nixon*, vol. 1: *The Education of a Politician, 1913–1962*. New York: Simon & Schuster, 1988, p. 117.

3   *"and its huge slush fund"* Ambrose, *Nixon*, vol. 1, p. 131.

3   *"Jerry Voorhis is a Communist?"* Ibid., p. 138.

3   *"between communism and Republicanism."* Richard M. Fried, "Electoral Politics and McCarthyism: The 1950 Campaign," in Robert Griffith and Athan Theoharis, eds., *The Specter: Original Essays on the Cold War and the Origins of McCarthyism*. New York: New Viewpoints, 1974, p. 193.

4   *a vehicle for Soviet subversion.* Richard Powers, *Not Without Honor: The History of American Anticommunism*. New Haven: Yale University Press, 1998, p. 197.

4   *a pitiful 32 percent by November* Markowitz, *The Rise and Fall of the People's Century*, p. 214.

4   *"most likely to gain victory."* Gillon, *Politics and Vision*, pp. 13, 248.

4   *"conservatism has hit America."* TRB, "Washington Wire: Forward in Reverse," *The New Republic*, November 11, 1946, p. 615.

4   *the Union for Democratic Action (UDA), did not.* The four largest liberal organizations were the National Citizens Political Action Committee; the CIO; the Independent Citizens Committee of the Arts, Sciences and Professions; and the National Farmers Union. Gillon, *Politics and Vision*, pp. 6–7.

4   *"the pariah of the liberal movement."* Ibid., p. 11.

4   *marked by barroom brawls and near-riots.* Damon Stetson, "Walter Reuther: Union Pioneer with Broad Influence Far Beyond the Field of Labor," *New York Times*, May 11, 1970, p. 38; Walter W. Ruch, "Reuther Elected President of UAW by Narrow Margin," *New York Times*, March 28, 1946, p. 1.

5   *the expansion of the New Deal.* Gillon, *Politics and Vision*, p. 21.

5   *lay claim to the American liberal tradition.* James Loeb, "Letter of the Week," *The New Republic*, January 27, 1947, p. 46.

5   *entered the American lexicon: totalitarianism.* Americans had become familiar with the term in the early years of World War II. See Gleason, *Totalitarianism*, p. 51.

5   *"obliteration of the individual."* Arthur M. Schlesinger Jr., *The Vital Center: The Politics of Freedom*, new ed. New Brunswick, N.J.: Transaction Publishers, 1998, p. 87.

5   *"the division in the liberal movement."* David M. Oshinsky, "Labor's Cold War: The CIO and the Communists," in Griffith and Theoharis, *The Specter*, p. 132.

5   *lauded Wallace in Chicago* Gillon, *Politics and Vision*, pp. 16, 24.

6   *"The Enemy Is Not Each Other."* Ibid., p. 24.

6   *"all its glory to the United States."* David Halberstam, *The Best and the Brightest*, 20th anniv. ed. New York: Ballantine, 1993, p. 333.

6   *vastly superior to "totalitarianism."* Walter LaFeber, *America, Russia, and the Cold War: 1945–2002*, 8th ed. New York: McGraw-Hill, 1997, p. 56.

7   *"subjugation by armed minorities"* "President Harry S. Truman's Address Before a Joint Session of Congress, March 12, 1947," *The Avalon Project at Yale Law School: Truman Doctrine.* Viewed on October 15, 2005, at http://www.yale.edu/lawweb/avalon/trudoc.htm.

7   *both stirring and dangerously broad.* In fact, Truman officials immediately began backtracking from the president's implication that the United States would prevent Communism's spread everywhere in the world. In September, Truman himself said, "Our resources are not unlimited. . . . We must apply them where they can serve the most effectively to bring production, freedom, and confidence back to the world." See John Lewis Gaddis, *Strategies of Containment: A Critical Appraisal of American National Security Policy During the Cold War.* New York: Oxford University Press, 1982, p. 59.

7   *called the aid proposal "American imperialism."* Markowitz, *The Rise and Fall of the People's Century,* p. 234.

7   *"democratic men with totalitarian principles."* Schlesinger, *The Vital Center,* p. 38.

7   *"accepting the consequences of the alternative."* Ibid., p. 43.

8   *"sinking while the doctors deliberate."* Stephen E. Ambrose and Douglas G. Brinkley, *Rise to Globalism: American Foreign Policy Since 1938*, 8th rev. ed. New York: Penguin Books, 1997, p. 83.

8   *"the political systems they embrace."* John Kenneth Galbraith, "Europe's Great Last Chance," *Harper's,* January 1949, p. 48.

8   *"to the benefit of Wall Street."* Gillon, *Politics and Vision,* p. 30.

8   *"the worse we are hated."* Hamby, *Beyond the New Deal,* p. 203.

9   *"a strong segment of the American public."* Robert A. Divine, "The Cold War and the Election of 1948," *Journal of American History* 59 (1) (June 1972), p. 92.

9   *his candidacy for president in 1948.* Henry A. Wallace, "I Shall Run in 1948," *Selected Works of Henry A. Wallace.* Viewed on June 13, 2005, at http://newdeal.feri.org/wallace/haw29.htm.

9   *likely Republican nominee Thomas Dewey.* Divine, "The Cold War and the Election of 1948," p. 94.

9   *out of reach for Truman as well.* Gillon, *Politics and Vision,* p. 34.

9   *and thirteen against.* Ibid., p. 43.

9   *"from a debacle in November."* "Little Accident," *Time,* March 15, 1948, quoted in Divine, "The Cold War and the Election of 1948," p. 95.

10   *"he knows the words"* Arthur Schlesinger Jr., "Political Culture in the United States," *The Nation,* March 13, 1948, p. 308. For a time, the ADA even considered trying to dump Truman as the Democratic nominee in 1948. But Dwight Eisenhower, who, liberals assumed on little evidence, shared their views, spurned their appeals. So did Supreme Court Justice William O. Douglas. Claude Pepper mounted a challenge, but found little support. Hamby, *Beyond the New Deal,* pp. 242–243.

10   *cut rates for low-wage workers* Hamby, *Beyond the New Deal,* p. 212.

10   *"in our practice of democracy."* Mary L. Dudziak, "Desegregation as a Cold War Imperative," *Stanford Law Review* 41 (1) (November 1988), p. 112.

11   *"health of our respective [political] systems"* Gaddis, *Strategies of Containment,* pp. 25, 50.

11   *"so hopelessly torn and divided."* "Fruit of the System," *Time*, July 19, 1948, quoted in Gillon, *Politics and Vision*, p. 47.

12   *"the bright sunshine of human rights."* Jeremy D. Sacks, "Sentiments of Responsibility: Union for Democratic Action and Americans for Democratic Action, 1941–1949," Honors Thesis, Wesleyan University, 1991, pp. 105–106.

12   *"the foreign policy of any nation."* Another resolution, which criticized both American business and military leaders *and* Moscow's "aggrandizement and power politics," did pass, however. Markowitz, *The Rise and Fall of the People's Century*, p. 288.

12   *an ADA house organ.* Sacks, "Sentiments of Responsibility," p. 120; Mary Sperling McAuliffe, *Crisis on the Left: Cold War Politics and American Liberals, 1947–1954.* Amherst: University of Massachusetts Press, 1978, p. 35.

13   *the Communist ties of prominent Wallace supporters.* Markowitz, *The Rise and Fall of the People's Century*, p. 277.

13   *"betrayal of free people throughout the world."* Ibid., p. 294.

13   *spur integration of the federal civil service.* Hamby, *Beyond the New Deal*, p. 247. Although Truman issued his executive order in mid-1948, he would have to battle the military, and in particular the Army, for several years before it was truly implemented. Ibid., pp. 342–344.

14   *labor rights, and progressive taxation.* Ibid., pp. 248–251; Gillon, *Politics and Vision*, p. 53.

14   *"serve you with everything I have."* Hamby, *Beyond the New Deal*, pp. 249, 251–253.

14   *the caption "The Next President"* Gillon, *Politics and Vision*, p. 54.

14   *"A miracle of electioneering"* Ibid.

14   *"authority for the country's liberals."* Ibid., p. 56.

15   *"deals with totalitarianism."* Schlesinger, *The Vital Center*, p. 165.

15   *"failure of nerve"* Ibid., p. 156.

15   *The first was containment:* Containment could also be defined more broadly, to include political and economic measures to stop Soviet expansion. Indeed, Kennan placed more emphasis on the former. But I am limiting it to military efforts, to distinguish it from "development."

15   *it would give up* Schlesinger, *The Vital Center*, p. 226.

15   *aggression would be difficult and costly.* Whether that meant all "doors," or only those in strategically important locations, was a topic on which Truman administration thinking evolved. In the first term, when Kennan enjoyed more influence, it was the former. But by 1950, the famed strategy document, NSC 68, authored by Paul Nitze, took a more global view. See Gaddis, *Strategies of Containment*, pp. 57–61, 91–95.

15   *"exertion of steady pressure"* Ibid., p. 49.

15   *the stamina for a long fight.* Indeed, in his famous February 1946 "long telegram" from Moscow, Kennan called the USSR "fragile and artificial in its psychological foundation, unable to stand comparison or contact with political systems of Western countries." Compared to the United States, he argued, Russia was "by far the weaker force." See Dana H. Allin, *Cold War Illusions: America, Europe and Soviet Power, 1969–1989.* New York: St. Martin's Press, 1994, p. 9; Sacks, "Sentiments of Responsibility," p. 58.

15   *what Schlesinger called "reconstruction."* Schlesinger, *The Vital Center*, p. 223.

16   *"growth of underdeveloped areas."* Gillon, *Politics and Vision*, p. 65.

16   *economic development was more important* For instance, in December 1947, Secretary of Defense James Forrestal noted that U.S. overseas priorities were "economic stability, political stability and military stability . . . in about that order. At the present time we are keeping our military expenditures below the levels which our military leaders must in good conscience estimate as the minimum which would in themselves ensure national security. By so doing we are able to increase our expenditures to assist in European recovery." See Gaddis, *Strategies of Containment*, p. 61.

16   *after the 1948 election.* Sacks, "Sentiments of Responsibility," pp. 41, 118.

16   *"to do always as we please."* Tony Judt, "The New World Order," *New York Review of Books* 52 (12) (July 14, 2005). Viewed on February 13, 2006, at http://www .nybooks.com/articles/18113.

16   *"both to the Soviet Union and the United States"* Gaddis, *Strategies of Containment*, p. 63. As Gaddis notes about U.S. policy in the early cold war, "It was not that the Americans lacked the capacity to force their allies into line. . . . What is surprising is how rarely this happened; how much effort the United States put into persuading— quite often even deferring to—its NATO partners. . . . The history of NATO, therefore, is largely one of compromise despite the predominant position of the United States." See John Lewis Gaddis, *Now We Know: Rethinking Cold War History*, rep. ed. New York: Oxford University Press, 1998, pp. 201–202.

17   *on the emerging cold war right.* James Burnham, *Suicide of the West.* New York: John Day, 1964, pp. 137–138; John B. Judis, *Grand Illusion: Critics and Champions of the American Century*, 1st ed. New York: Farrar Straus & Giroux, 1992, p. 154. As George Nash writes in his intellectual history of post–World War II conservatism, "James Burnham as much as anyone provided the theoretical formulation for the conservative critique of liberal foreign policies in the early cold war period. He as much as anyone made militant, global anti-Communism a characteristic of the postwar intellectual Right." See George H. Nash, *The Conservative Intellectual Movement in America*, 1st softcover ed. Wilmington, Del.: Intercollegiate Studies Institute, 1998, pp. 86–87. William F. Buckley himself called Burnham "beyond any question the dominant intellectual influence" at *National Review*. See Peter Coleman, review of *James Burnham and the Struggle for the World: A Life*, by Daniel Kelly, *Quadrant Magazine* 48 (10) (October 2004). Viewed on February 13, 2006, at http://www.quadrant.org.au/php/article_view.php?article_id=978.

17   *part of the money went to foreign aid.* Sam M. Jones, "From Washington Straight," *National Review*, May 30, 1956, p. 2.

17   *would not wholly commit to America's side.* In Dulles's words, the cold war pitted "the materialistic and atheistic philosophy of the Communist Party and the spiritual faith that animates the leaders and peoples of the non-communist states." See Mark G. Toulouse, *The Transformation of John Foster Dulles: From Prophet of Realism to Priest of Nationalism.* Macon, Ga.: Mercer University Press, 1986, p. 202.

17   *"principles of sovereignty and self-reliance"* Gaddis, *Strategies of Containment*, p. 182.

18   *"decisive world control."* Nash, *The Conservative Intellectual Movement in America*, pp. 82–83.

18   *"until we drop exhausted."* Townsend Hoopes, *The Devil and John Foster Dulles*, 1st ed.
      New York: Little, Brown and Co., 1973, p. 127.

18   *"can hope to survive for long."* Barry Goldwater, *The Conscience of a Conservative*. New
      York: MacFadden Books, 1961, p. 94.

18   *"and therefore more impregnable."* John Ehrman, *The Rise of Neoconservatism: Intellectuals
      and Foreign Affairs: 1945–1994*. New Haven: Yale University Press, 1996, p. 12.

18   *"our increasing abundance."* Gillon, *Politics and Vision*, p. 61.

19   *"the road to serfdom."* As Nash writes, "the belief in the fundamental continuity
      of liberalism and Communism—struck deep chords and became a fundamental
      part of the conservative 'case' in the 1950s and after." See Nash, *The Conservative
      Intellectual Movement in America*, p. 94.

19   *"he would be somehow wounding himself."* Burnham, *Suicide of the West*, pp. 289–290.

19   *"monstrosity of Bolshevik bureaucracy."* Stephen J. Whitfield, *The Culture of the Cold
      War*, Baltimore, Md.: Johns Hopkins University Press, 1991, p. 23. The AMA
      had called universal health care totalitarian before. In 1945, Dr. Morris Fishbein,
      editor of the *Journal of the American Medical Association*, said, "The movement for
      [the] placing of American medicine under the control of . . . federal compulsory
      sickness insurance is the first step toward a regimentation of utilities, of industries,
      of finance, and eventually of labor itself. This is the kind of regimentation that
      led to totalitarianism in Germany and the downfall of that nation." See Gleason,
      Totalitarianism, p. 67.

19   *"vehicle for totalitarianism."* Arthur M. Schlesinger, "The Politics of Nostalgia," in
      Arthur M. Schlesinger, *The Politics of Hope*, Cambridge, Mass.: Riverside Press, 1963,
      p. 77.

19   *crushed states' rights.* Dudziak, "Desegregation as a Cold War Imperative," p. 79.

19   *a vehicle for enhanced government power.* As Nash writes, "the dominant tone at *National
      Review* was one of criticism of the subsequent governmental drive—at Little
      Rock and elsewhere—toward integration." See Nash, *The Conservative Intellectual
      Movement in America*, p. 185.

19   *"Integration is communization."* Ibid., p. 389.

20   *"working and shaping policy in the State Department."* " 'Enemies from Within': Senator
      Joseph R. McCarthy and President Harry S. Truman Trade Accusations of
      Disloyalty," February 11, 1950. Viewed on May 8, 2005, at http://historymatters
      .gmu.edu/d/6456.html.

20   *"cease to exist."* Nash, *The Conservative Intellectual Movement in America*, p. 107. Liberals,
      Buckley and Bozell argued, would not defend U.S. institutions from Communist
      subversion because "they do not feel the faith they so often and so ardently
      express in democracy." See Ronald Lora, "A View from the Right: Conservative
      Intellectuals, the Cold War, and McCarthy," in Griffith and Theoharis, *The Specter*,
      p. 65.

20   *against their implacable Communist foe.* Judis, *Grand Illusion*, pp. 121, 128; Nash, *The
      Conservative Intellectual Movement in America*, pp. 92–93. Burnham, for instance, wrote
      that "Men become willing to endure, sacrifice and die for God, family, king, honor,
      country, from a sense of absolute duty or an exalted vision of the meaning of history.
      It is such traditional ideals and the institutions slowly built around them that are in

present fact the great bulwarks, spiritual as well as social, against the tidal advance of the world communist enterprise. And it is precisely these ideals and institutions that liberalism has criticized, attacked and in part overthrown as superstitious, archaic, reactionary and irrational." See Burnham, *Suicide of the West*, p. 291.

20 *"this sick society"* Whittaker Chambers, *Witness*, reissue ed. Washington, D.C.: Regnery Books, 1980, p. 4.

20 *"the losing world."* Judis, *Grand Illusion*, p. 128.

20 *"the ones who have been the most traitorous."* Griffith and Theoharis, *The Specter*, p. ix. Similarly, Chambers wrote in *Witness* that "No feature of the Hiss Case is more obvious, or more troubling as history, than the jagged fissure, which it did not so much open as reveal, between the plain men and women of the nation, and those who affected to act, think and speak for them." See Chambers, *Witness*, p. 793.

21 *"damage done to our prestige"* Reinhold Niebuhr, "Why They Dislike America," *The New Leader*, April 12, 1954, p. 5.

21 *"The free society does not fear,"* Powers, *Not Without Honor*, p. 213.

21 *"never for the opinions they have."* Hamby, *Beyond the New Deal*, p. 414.

21 *"an abject capitulation by liberalism to illiberalism."* McAuliffe, *Crisis on the Left*, p. 141.

22 *"worship of tax reductions and a balanced budget."* Gillon, *Politics and Vision*, p. 116.

22 *"vote against appropriations for military aid?"* Richard M. Fried, "Electoral Politics and McCarthyism: The 1950 Campaign," in Griffith and Theoharis, *The Specter*, pp. 203–204.

22 *liberals largely set the terms of national debate.* Liberals "run this country," wrote Buckley in the inaugural issue of *National Review*. Burnham acknowledged the same thing almost a decade later, writing that "liberalism rather broadly designated . . . is today, and from some time in the 1930's has been, the prevailing American public doctrine, or ideology. The predominant assumptions, ideas and beliefs about politics, economics, and social questions are liberal." See Nash, *The Conservative Intellectual Movement in America*, p. 136; Burnham, *Suicide of the West*, p. 31.

22 *The indefatigable Richard Nixon.* Whitfield, *The Culture of the Cold War*, p. 19.

23 *considered it a blow to national prestige.* Paul Dickson, *Sputnik: The Shock of the Century*. Berkeley: Berkeley Publishing Group, 2003, p. 23.

23 *"what freedom means to us"* Kevin Mattson, *When America Was Great: The Fighting Faith of Postwar Liberalism*. Oxford, England: Routledge, 2004, p. 147.

23 *"capacity to stir the minds and hearts of men."* Schlesinger, "The New Mood in Politics," in Schlesinger, *The Politics of Hope*, p. 83.

23 *"soft and effete."* Gillon, *Politics and Vision*, p. 121.

23 *"the reorganization of American values."* Schlesinger, "The New Mood in Politics," in Schlesinger, *The Politics of Hope*, p. 90.

24 *"where his heart ought to be."* Gillon, *Politics and Vision*, p. 133.

24 *McCarthy had employed his brother Robert.* Kennedy would later partially apologize for his abstention, citing his father and brother's ties to McCarthy, and the Wisconsin senator's popularity among Catholics in Massachusetts. See Robert Dallek, *An Unfinished Life: John F. Kennedy, 1917–1963*. New York: Little, Brown and Co., 2003, pp. 162, 189–192.

24 *Kennedy was ideologically acceptable.* Gillon, *Politics and Vision*, pp. 132–133.

24   *"embarked upon a program of world aggression."* Dallek, *An Unfinished Life*, p. 132.

25   *"dangerous to the cause of peace . . ."* Ibid., p. 290.

25   *"more than a childish bugaboo."* Powers, *Not Without Honor*, p. 304.

25   *"hand over a part of the Free World to the Communist World."* Christopher Matthews, *Kennedy and Nixon: The Rivalry that Shaped Postwar America*, rep. ed. New York: Free Press, 1997, p. 160.

25   *"ninety miles off the coast of the United States."* Ibid., p. 165.

25   *U.S. spy planes was trumped up* Robert Dallek suggests that the Eisenhower administration—and in particular CIA director Alan Dulles—would not show Kennedy proof that the missile gap was a hoax, which allowed him to believe it was true. But Kennedy may have merely been using this as an excuse to continue repeating a charge that he found politically useful. Dallek, *An Unfinished Life*, pp. 289–290.

25   *"tailored our strategy and military requirements"* Ibid., p. 289.

26   *"it depends upon what we do here."* Sidney Kraus, *The Great Debates: Kennedy vs. Nixon, 1960*. Bloomington: Indiana University Press, 1977, pp. 348–350.

26   *"because I promise them the easy, soft life."* Ibid., p. 384.

26   *"all those who desire to be free."* Theodore Harold White, *The Making of the President, 1960*, 1st Atheneum ed. New York: Atheneum, 1980, p. 340.

26   *"We set a very high standard for ourselves."* Kraus, *The Great Debates*, p. 374.

27   *"Candidate with a Heart, Senator Kennedy"* White, *The Making of the President*, pp. 321–323; Ambrose, *Nixon*, vol. 1, pp. 596–597.

28   *"the lands of the rising people."* Ambrose and Brinkley, *Rise to Globalism*, p. 173.

28   *"understanding of the desires of men to be free."* Dallek, *An Unfinished Life*, p. 167.

28   *"rewriting the geopolitical map of the world."* Ibid., p. 223.

28   *"the challenge of imperialism."* Ibid., p. 222; John F. Kennedy, "Imperialism: The Enemy of Freedom, July 2, 1957." Viewed on September 29, 2005, at http://www.jfklink.com/speeches/jfk/congress/jfk020757_imperialism.html.

28   *the threat of nuclear retaliation.* In fact, three key Truman advisers helped shape Kennedy's foreign policy: Dean Rusk, who had been Truman's assistant secretary of state for Far Eastern Affairs, served as Kennedy's secretary of state; Paul Nitze, the author of NSC 68, was Kennedy's assistant secretary of defense for International Security Affairs; and former secretary of state Dean Acheson regularly consulted with the young president, especially on the 1961 Berlin crisis. See Gaddis, *Strategies of Containment*, pp. 204–205, 214–216, 226–227.

28   *"the basic needs of the American people"* Dallek, *An Unfinished Life*, p. 341.

29   *"democracy versus totalitarianism."* Ronald Radosh, *American Labor and United States Foreign Policy*. New York: Vintage Books, 1970, pp. 415–434.

29   *"missionaries of democracy."* Hamby, *Beyond the New Deal*, p. 429.

29   *"inevitably invite the advance of totalitarianism."* John Cassidy, "Helping Hands: How Foreign Aid Could Benefit Everybody," *The New Yorker*, March 18, 2002.

29   *"the basis of our own"* Gaddis, *Strategies of Containment*, p. 225.

29   *"the system of Russian power."* Ibid., pp. 63–64.

30   *"bitter disappointment."* Gillon, *Politics and Vision*, p. 143.

30   *"the biggest single burden"* Thomas Borstelmann, *The Cold War and the Color Line: American Race Relations in the Global Arena.* Cambridge, Mass.: Harvard University Press, 2003, pp. 140–141. Borstelmann argues that the latter "was the key to unlocking the Kennedy administration's concern about racism." Ibid., p. 165.

31   *"we do not ask for whites only."* Ibid., p. 161.

31   *the biggest election victory in presidential history* Measured by the popular vote margin and the percentage of the vote, not the margin in the electoral college. See Gillon, *Politics and Vision*, p. 168.

31   *He began to cry.* Borstelmann, *The Cold War and the Color Line*, p. 190.

Chapter 2: Losing America

32   *the bogeymen of an earlier generation.* There were significant exceptions. A few of those present at Port Huron had parents who were Communists, and others, like Tom Kahn, were members of the Young People's Socialist League (YPSL), which was vehemently anti-Communist. See James Miller, *"Democracy Is in the Streets": From Port Huron to the Siege of Chicago.* Cambridge, Mass.: Harvard University Press, 1994, p. 117; Todd Gitlin, *The Sixties: Years of Hope, Days of Rage.* New York: Bantam, 1993, p. 112.

32   *"I've never seen one."* Miller, *"Democracy Is in the Streets,"* p. 117.

33   *"paranoid quest for [anti-Communist] decontamination."* Gitlin, *The Sixties*, p. 113.

33   *and cut off their funds.* Ibid., p. 118.

33   *scars from a brawl with communists in the 1930s.* Ibid., p. 120.

33   *a dedicated anti-Communist and a fierce partisan of labor.* Rachelle Horowitz, "Tom Kahn and the Fight for Democracy: A Political Portrait and Personal Recollection." Viewed on Oct. 5, 2005, at http://www.socialdemocrats.org/Kahn.html.

33   *the arrogant "Ivy League-type[s]" around him.* As Gitlin notes, the charge was unfair. Only two of the attendees at Port Huron hailed from the Ivy League. See Gitlin, *The Sixties*, p. 119.

33   *"You will try to destroy us."* Ibid.

34   *less than 6 percent of the state's black population was registered.* John D'Emilio, *Lost Prophet: The Life and Times of Bayard Rustin.* Chicago: University of Chicago Press, 2004, p. 379; Joseph A. Sinsheimer, "The Freedom Vote of 1963: New Strategies of Racial Protest in Mississippi," *Journal of Southern History* 55 (2) (May 1989), pp. 218–219.

34   *pariahs in the protest movements they once called home.* To be sure, Rustin's anti-Communism was not initially of the cold war liberal variety. Once a Communist himself, he had broken with the party in 1941 and spent the 1940s and 1950s as a Christian pacifist, even opposing the Korean War. But his anti-Communism was genuine, forged by a deep suspicion that the party was using the civil rights movement for its own purposes—so genuine, in fact, that he refused to associate himself with the supporters of Henry Wallace in 1948. In 1965, Rustin opposed allowing Communist groups to participate in the March on Washington to End the War in Vietnam, earning him the wrath of radicals like Staughton Lynd. And as the

1960s wore on, Rustin's anti-Communism began to subvert his pacifism, a trend that continued throughout the final decades of his life. "Bayard, like me, was a pacifist," wrote Ernest Lefever. "But as the reality of the larger world impinged on us in later years, we both moved away from our earlier utopian views, and embraced a morally concerned realist position. He became convinced, as I was, that the Soviet Union represented a serious threat to justice, freedom, and peace; and he was committed to an intelligent and thoughtful anti-communist posture." See Jervis Anderson, *Bayard Rustin: Troubles I've Seen*, rep. ed. Berkeley: University of California Press, 1998, p. 268, 292–295; D'Emilio, *Lost Prophet*, pp. 178–181, 480.

35   *the party's 1964 Convention in Atlantic City.* Originally, SNCC planned to challenge the legitimacy of the Mississippi congressional delegation in 1965. But when it saw that the state's convention delegates could be challenged on similar grounds, it turned its attention to that more immediate task. See William H. Chafe, *Never Stop Running: Allard Lowenstein and the Struggle to Save American Liberalism.* New York: Basic Books, 1995, pp. 196–197.

35   *"using people who don't really believe in freedom."* Ibid., p. 191.

35   *the day they were murdered.* Gitlin, *The Sixties*, p. 152.

36   *"I question America."* "Fannie Lou Hamer for the Mississippi Freedom Democratic Party: Democratic National Convention, 1964." Viewed on March 22, 2005, at http://www.public.iastate.edu/~aslagell/SpCm416/Fannie_Lou_Hamer_1964 .html; Gitlin, *The Sixties*, p. 153.

36   *"I left out of there full of tears."* Gitlin, *The Sixties*, pp. 154–155.

37   *and Moses refused to speak to him for 15 years.* Ibid., p. 162.

37   *"You're a traitor, Bayard, a traitor!"* Ibid., p. 160.

37   *"Next time no one can discriminate against Negroes."* D'Emilio, *Lost Prophet*, p. 391.

37   *"one of the high points of my lifetime."* Gitlin, *The Sixties*, pp. 159, 161.

37   *"the compromise on grounds of political expediency"* Ibid., p. 159; D'Emilio, *Lost Prophet*, p. 390.

38   *"the greatest opportunity for constructive liberalism in a generation."* Gillon, *Politics and Vision*, p. 169.

38   *residents spat on them.* D'Emilio, *Lost Prophet*, pp. 382–383.

38   *nonviolence was falling out of favor in SNCC as well.* Ibid., p. 384.

38   *"play our hand coolly and intelligently."* Ibid.

39   *"jobs in which Negroes are disproportionately concentrated."* Bayard Rustin, "From Protest to Politics: The Future of the Civil Rights Movement," in Devon Carbado and Donald Weise, eds., *Time on Two Crosses: The Collected Writings of Bayard Rustin*, 1st. ed. San Francisco: Cleis Press, 2003, p. 118.

39   *on exactly this insight.* See William Julius Wilson, *The Truly Disadvantaged: The Inner City, the Underclass, and Public Policy.* Chicago: University of Chicago Press, 1987.

39   *and received rave reviews.* D'Emilio, *Lost Prophet*, p. 393.

39   *"to choose one without the other,"* Ibid., p. 403.

39   *called nonviolence "a dying philosophy."* See http://www.core-online.org; D'Emilio, *Lost Prophet*, p. 427.

39   *"threatens to ravage the entire civil rights movement."* D'Emilio, *Lost Prophet*, p. 428.

39   *"Bayard's commitment is to labor,"* Ibid., p. 471.

39   *armed assaults rose 77 percent.* Arthur M. Schlesinger, *The Crisis of Confidence,* p. 19.

39   *almost doubled, to over 50 percent.* Thomas Edsall and Mary Byrne Edsall, *Chain Reaction: The Impact of Race, Rights, and Taxes on American Politics,* rep. ed. New York: Norton, 1992, p. 59.

40   *"product of a broken home?"* Ibid., p. 51.

40   *pronounced "the Great Society . . . except for token gestures, dead."* Johnson, sensing the political tides, also requested less antipoverty money. See Gillon, *Politics and Vision,* pp. 190, 205.

40   *relentless search for new markets.* Two other major revisionist works, Denna Fleming's *The Cold War and Its Origins* (1961), and Gar Alperovitz's *Atomic Diplomacy* (1965), were also written before the antiwar movement began in earnest. For a discussion of *The Tragedy of American Diplomacy,* and its impact, see Bradford Perkins, "The Tragedy of American Diplomacy: Twenty-Five Years After," *Reviews in American History* 12 (1) (March 1984), pp. 1–18.

40   *not indigenous Communist movements* See, for instance, John Lewis Gaddis, *Strategies of Containment,* pp. 41–44.

41   *"in powerful men's minds."* Halberstam, *The Best and the Brightest,* p. 148.

41   *more than $2 billion in aid* George C. Herring, *America's Longest War: The United States and Vietnam, 1950–1975,* 2nd ed. New York: McGraw-Hill, 1986, pp. 148–149; Thomas T. Hammond, *Witness to the Origins of the Cold War,* rep. ed. Seattle: University of Washington Press, 1986, pp. 98–122.

41   *"that part of the world."* Halberstam, *The Best and the Brightest,* p. xv.

42   *the true guardians of establishment power.* The prominent conservative academic Robert Nisbet has reflected that during the 1960s, "the Left never hassled me as they did the Kennedy liberals and the Old Socialists. . . . In later years, other conservatives . . . told me their experience had been the same as mine." See Alan Brinkley, "The Problem of American Conservatism," *American Historical Review,* April 1994, p. 413.

42   *"They are all liberals."* Robert J. Donovan, *Los Angeles Times,* November 28, 1965, p. H-1; Ronald Berman, *America in the Sixties: An Intellectual History.* New York: Free Press, 1968, p. 117.

42   *he received a raucous welcome.* Gitlin, *The Sixties,* p. 198.

42   *"no more sophisticated than rape."* "What Is a Liberal—Who Is a Conservative? A Symposium," *Commentary* 62 (3) (1967), pp. 78–79.

43   *"totalitarian tendencies of the one-dimensional society."* Herbert Marcuse, *One-Dimensional Man: Studies in the Ideology of Advanced Industrial Society,* with a new introduction by Douglas Kellner. Boston: Beacon Press, 1991, p. 256.

43   *"perspective for the coming period is fascism."* Berman, *America in the Sixties,* p. 114.

43   *"in the years before and during Nazi rule."* Ibid., pp. 112, 114; Gitlin, *The Sixties,* p. 130; Miller, *"Democracy Is in the Streets,"* p. 169; Young, *Reconsidering American Liberalism,* p. 197.

43   *"The Vietnamese revolutionaries"* Gitlin, *The Sixties,* p. 185.

43   *"arouse the sleeping dogs on the Right."* Ibid., p. 289. Putting this theory into practice, in 1968 Hayden endorsed George Wallace for president. See Irving Howe, *A Margin of Hope: An Intellectual Autobiography.* New York: Harcourt Brace Jovanovich, 1982, p. 312.

43   *"people in the affluent society"* E. J. Dionne Jr., *Why Americans Hate Politics*, rep. ed. New York: Simon & Schuster, 2004, p. 85.

43   *a new term to describe the police* Gitlin, *The Sixties*, p. 246.

43   *"millions of working people."* Tom Kahn, "The Problem of the New Left," *Commentary* (July 1966), p. 32.

44   *"the policeman on the beat."* Gillon, *Politics and Vision*, p. 220.

44   *"that'll be the last car he lays down in front of."* Gitlin, *The Sixties*, p. 304.

44   *"they have become the silent Americans."* Jonathan Rieder, "The Rise of the 'Silent Majority,' " in Steve Fraser and Gary Gerstle, eds., *The Rise and Fall of the New Deal Order, 1930–1980*. Princeton, N.J.: Princeton University Press, 1990, p. 260.

44   *the New Left's "politics of alienation."* Gitlin, *The Sixties*, p. 296.

45   *"American troops do the most difficult things with courage."* Chafe, *Never Stop Running*, p. 326.

45   *"led by an honor guard, and flanked by American flags."* Ibid., pp. 329–330.

45   *left-wing hecklers threw garbage on the stage.* Ibid., pp. 331, 335.

45   *battling Communist youth groups in the National Students Association.* Ibid., pp. 98–101; Gitlin, *The Sixties*, p. 296. It would later emerge that for much of the period Lowenstein was involved with the National Students Association, it was receiving funding from the CIA. Lowenstein's biographer, William Chafe, argues that he probably did not know about this connection, although it may have been willful ignorance. See Chafe, *Never Stop Running*, pp. 104–108.

45   *not "inherently sick."* Chafe, *Never Stop Running*, p. 337.

45   *yet always stays a liberal.* Ibid., p. 465.

45   *"entrance back into the political process."* Gillon, *Politics and Vision*, p. 207.

45   *more popular with intellectuals than ordinary voters.* McCarthy had given the nominating speech for Stevenson at the 1960 Democratic convention. See Dominic Sandbrook, *Eugene McCarthy: The Rise and Fall of Postwar American Liberalism*. New York: Knopf, 2004, pp. 102–105.

46   *"The better-educated people vote for us"* Ronald Steel, *In Love with Night: The American Romance with Robert Kennedy*. New York: Simon & Schuster, 2001, p. 173.

46   *at the Democratic National Convention in Chicago.* Theodore Harold White, *The Making of the President 1968*. New York: Atheneum Publishers, 1973, p. 38.

46   *support for a large defense budget.* Gillon, *Politics and Vision*, pp. 153–154.

46   *"old-hat, stale, and somewhat conservative."* Ibid., p. 152.

46   *"every liberal advance since the 1930s."* Ibid., p. 202.

46   *endorse McCarthy's presidential bid.* Ibid., p. 212.

46   *"The coalition," one labor leader declared, "is finished."* Ibid., pp. 212–213.

47   *"Don't you just wish that everyone was black?"* Evan Thomas, *Robert Kennedy: His Life*. New York: Simon & Schuster, 2000, p. 375.

47   *how much working-class white support he actually enjoyed.* For instance, Steel notes that Kennedy actually lost most of the white precincts in Gary, Indiana, where the myth of his "black and blue" coalition was born. Evan Thomas counters with evidence suggesting that Kennedy won the seven largest Indiana counties where George Wallace did best in 1964. See Steel, *In Love with Night*, pp. 175–176; Thomas, *Robert Kennedy*, pp. 375–376.

47 *powered by blue-collar Irish, Polish, and black votes* See Steel, *In Love with Night*, pp. 173–174; Thomas, *Robert Kennedy*, p. 375. In fact, in an intriguing sign of the two parties' shifting identities, while McCarthy struggled among working-class whites, he did well with upscale suburban independents—some of whom may have been former liberal Republicans. See Sandbrook, *Eugene McCarthy*, p. 210.

47 *"police the planet."* Chafe, *Never Stop Running*, p. 272.

47 *"judge the political systems of other nations."* Sandbrook, *Eugene McCarthy*, p. 195.

47 *"Kennedy has entirely renounced that misconception."* Ibid., p. 196.

48 *whether America had much to offer the world.* As McCarthy's biographer, Dominic Sandbrook, puts it, "McCarthy's attack was, in fact, the first criticism of Cold War orthodoxy by a major candidate in a presidential campaign since 1948." Kennedy biographer Ronald Steel agrees that on Vietnam, "McCarthy was by far the more radical candidate." See Sandbrook, *Eugene McCarthy*, p. 196; Steel, *In Love with Night*, p. 177.

48 *"our right to moral leadership of this planet."* Steel, *In Love with Night*, p. 146.

48 *Twenty-five hours later, he was dead.* Ibid., 187–189; Thomas, *Robert Kennedy*, pp. 390–391.

48 *without competing in a single primary.* Sandbrook, *Eugene McCarthy*, p. 193; Gillon, *Politics and Vision*, p. 218.

48 *"I've got his balls in my pocket."* Halberstam, *The Best and the Brightest*, p. 533.

48 *request such privileges from White House aides, in writing.* Ibid., p. 535.

49 *Schlesinger screamed at him.* Mattson, *When America Was Great*, p. 178.

49 *"no man can predict when that day will come."* Lewis Gould, *1968: The Election That Changed America*. Chicago: Ivan R. Dee, 1993, p. 143.

49 *"We have come to arrest you."* Jules Witcover, *Party of the People: A History of the Democrats*, 1st ed. New York: Random House, 2003, p. 565.

49 *"indulgence and permissiveness toward the lawless."* Ambrose, *Nixon*, vol. 1, p. 202.

49 *"If you mean it, we're with you."* Witcover, *Party of the People*, p. 566.

49 *hurt the workers they supposedly championed.* Gillon, *Politics and Vision*, p. 221; Horowitz, "Tom Kahn and the Fight for Democracy."

49 *defected to either Nixon or Wallace.* Kevin P. Phillips, *The Emerging Republican Majority*. New York: Anchor Books, 1970, p. 461.

50 *"ideological barriers can be expected gradually to erode away."* Powers, *Not Without Honor*, p. 320.

50 *"distinction between the Communist bloc and the Free World"* Graham T. Allison, "Cool It: The Foreign Policy of Young America," *Foreign Policy* (1) (Winter 1970–1971), p. 153.

50 *problem the superpowers needed to manage together.* Ehrman, *The Rise of Neoconservatism*, p. 25. See, for instance, the 1965 book *After 20 Years*, New York: Random House, 1965, authored by former Kennedy State Department official Richard J. Barnett and Marcus Raskin.

51 *"simple sense of individual morality"* Allison, "Cool It," p. 157.

51 *a "sick society."* Herring, *America's Longest War*, p. 175.

51 *"is undergoing a crisis of self-confidence."* Schlesinger, *The Crisis of Confidence*, p. ix.

51 *"into harsh critics."* Christopher Lasch, *The Agony of the American Left*. New York: Knopf, 1969, pp. 188–189.

51   *most Americans remained admirers.* A 1973 poll, for instance, showed that the military remained—even near the end of Vietnam—the most respected institution in American government. See Earl C. Ravenal, *Never Again: Learning from America's Foreign Policy Failures.* Philadelphia: Temple University Press, 1978, pp. 71–72.

52   *"we just won't solve it."* Robert G. Kaufman, *Henry M. Jackson: A Life in Politics.* Seattle: University of Washington Press, 2000, p. 230.

52   *disillusioned former SDSer Tom Kahn.* Horowitz, "Tom Kahn and the Fight for Democracy."

52   *saw Jackson as his greatest potential threat.* Kaufman, *Henry M. Jackson,* p. 228.

52   *"to consolidate the left-wing."* White, *The Making of the President, 1972.* New York: Scribner, 1985, pp. 44, 98, 169.

52   *foundation of the McGovern campaign was teachers.* Ibid., p. 99.

53   *"most decent man in the Senate."* Ibid., pp. 22–23.

53   *"compassionate views of [Henry] Wallace"* George S. McGovern, *Grassroots: The Autobiography of George McGovern.* New York: Random House, 1977, pp. 43, 45.

53   *"Hitler's effort to exterminate [the] Jews."* White, *The Making of the President, 1972,* p. 116.

53   *"we have to settle down and live with them."* Ibid.

53   *percentage of delegates under 30 quadrupled.* Witcover, *Party of the People,* p. 582.

53   *upper-middle-class reformers grew in number as well.* As Thomas Byrne Edsall notes, a 1956 survey of Democratic convention delegates on various political issues found an 11-percentage-point difference between them and a random sample of rank-and-file Democrats. By 1972, the gap had risen to almost 55 percentage points. See Thomas Byrne Edsall, *The New Politics of Inequality.* New York: Norton, 1985, pp. 55–56.

54   *"begin a diet by shooting himself in the stomach."* White, *The Making of the President, 1972,* p. 165.

54   *"forced into a compelled homogeneity."* Edsall and Byrne Edsall, *Chain Reaction,* pp. 94–95.

54   *policemen began wearing "Pigs is Beautiful" shirts.* Kaufman, *Henry M. Jackson,* p. 220.

54   *"If black is beautiful, olive is gorgeous."* Theodore Harold White, *America in Search of Itself: The Making of the President, 1956–1980,* reissue ed. New York: Warner Books, 1988, p. 218.

54   *"regional discrimination that took place in the Senate yesterday."* David Greenberg, "Clowns in Gowns," *Washington Monthly,* December 2001. Viewed on March 3, 2005, at http://www.washingtonmonthly.com/features/2001/0112.greenberg.html; Edsall and Byrne Edsall, *Chain Reaction,* p. 83.

54   *"differences between blacks and other racial and ethnic groups."* D'Emilio, *Lost Prophet,* p. 476; Rustin, "Affirmative Action in an Economy of Scarcity" in Carbado and Weise, eds., *Time on Two Crosses,* p. 260.

55   *"political dilemma for the labor union leaders and the civil rights groups."* Edsall and Byrne Edsall, *Chain Reaction,* p. 87.

55   *"I believe in the American system."* White, *The Making of the President, 1972,* p. 243.

55   *dubbed "neoliberals."* William Schneider, "JFK's Children: The Class of '74," *Atlantic Monthly* (March 1989), pp. 35, 39.

56   *"not a bunch of little Hubert Humphreys."* Ibid., p. 35.

56   *"oblivious to foreign problems and foreign issues."* Herring, *America's Longest War,* p. 274.

57 *"fails to project a vision larger than the problem"* James Fallows, "The Passionless Presidency: The Trouble with Jimmy Carter's Administration," *Washington Monthly* (May 1979), pp. 42–43.

57 *the "higher the office, the more ideology matters."* Schneider, "JFK's Children," p. 57.

58 *"the soul of our foreign policy."* Ambrose and Brinkley, *Rise to Globalism*, p. 281.

58 *taken power with the help of Cuban troops.* Ehrman, *The Rise of Neoconservatism*, p. 103; Major T. P. Sullivan, "Cuban Foreign Policy: Joint Objectives in Angola." April 6, 1984. Viewed on October 24, 2005, at http://www.globalsecurity.org/military/library/report/1984/STP.htm.

58 *began executing hundreds of political opponents.* White, *America in Search of Itself*, p. 223; "Iranian Civil Strife: Coming of the Revolution." Viewed on October 28, 2005, at http://www.globalsecurity.org/military/library/report/1984/STP.htm; Helen Chapin Metz, "Iran: A Country Study," Library of Congress Federal Research Division, 4th ed. Whitefish, Mont.: Kessinger Publishing, 2004, pp. 84–85.

58 *"advance the cause of human rights."* White, *America in Search of Itself*, p. 222.

59 *"paralyzed when they deal with powerful governments"* like the USSR. Arthur Schlesinger Jr., "Human Rights and the American Tradition," *Foreign Affairs: America and the World* 57 (3) (1978): 515–516.

59 *"firm application of power is a potential Vietnam."* Powers, *Not Without Honor*, p. 387.

59 *stood at 11 percent in 1973, rose to 56 percent by 1980.* Nelson W. Polsby, "The Carter-Kennedy Campaign," in Austin Ranney, ed., *The American Elections of 1980*. Washington, D.C.: American Enterprise Institute, 1981, p. 51.

59 *from 48 percent in 1975 to 70 percent five years later.* William Schneider, "Conservatism, Not Interventionism: Trends in Foreign Policy Opinion, 1974–1982," in Kenneth Oye et al., *Eagle Defiant: United States Foreign Policy in the 1980s*. New York: Scott Foresman, 1998, p. 36.

59 *more than two to one.* Witcover, *Party of the People*, p. 608.

60 *"decide whether we have war or peace."* Jack W. Germond and Jules Witcover, *Blue Smoke and Mirrors*. New York: Viking, 1981, p. 244.

60 *post-Vietnam liberal phrase "crisis of confidence."* White, *America in Search of Itself*, p. 268.

60 *"Pride in our country"* Rowland Evans and Robert Novak, *The Reagan Revolution: An Inside Look at the Transformation of the U.S. Government*. New York: Dutton, 1981, p. 159.

61 *"lost faith in their own country's past and tradition."* Ibid., pp. 159, 185.

61 *"When did it ever go away."* Gil Troy, *Morning in America: How Ronald Reagan Invented the 1980's*. Princeton, N.J.: Princeton University Press, 2005, p. 44.

61 *"the heritage and mission of Hubert Humphrey."* Germond and Witcover, *Blue Smoke and Mirrors*, p. 301.

61 *asking Democrats to "come home."* Ibid.

61 *Newsweek called it a "counter-revolution."* Troy, *Morning in America*, p. 49.

61 *"Our old enemy liberalism has died."* Gillon, *Politics and Vision*, p. 237.

61 *"leader of the Free World, proud of its greatness."* Kaufman, *Henry M. Jackson*, p. 404.

61 *"I still believe in the New Deal."* Ibid., p. 403.

61 *"Who cares about ADA? I don't."* Gillon, *Politics and Vision*, p. 237.

61 *urging the organization to disband.* Ibid., p. 243.

62   *halfway between JFK and RFK's graves.* Chafe, *Never Stop Running*, p. 463.

62   *"not even death can take from us."* Vernon Jordan, Bayard Rustin Memorial Service, Community Church of New York, October 1, 1997.

Chapter 3: After the Fall

63   *from the supporters of Henry Wallace.* Steven M. Gillon, *Democrats' Dilemma: Walter F. Mondale and the Liberal Legacy*. New York: Columbia University Press, 1992, pp. 17–24.

63   *Vietnam plank that won the support of both camps.* The compromise collapsed, however, when President Johnson objected. Ibid., pp. 114–115.

64   *"healed the breach of the Vietnam War."* Gillon, *Politics and Vision*, p. 240.

64   *number three on the* New York Times *best-seller list.* "Book Review Desk," *New York Times*, Sunday, September 5, 1982. Viewed on February 10, 2006, at http://select.nytimes .com/gst/abstract.html?res=FB0D14F83C5C0C768CDDA00894DA484D81.

64   *"sweeping the United States."* James Kelly, "Thinking About the Unthinkable: Rising Fears About the Dangers of Nuclear War," *Time*, March 29, 1982, p. 10.

64   *it was very much a movement of the left.* In fact, while large majorities of Americans told pollsters they backed a nuclear freeze, a more careful examination showed that their support rested on several conditions: that it could be verified, that it would lock the United States and the USSR in at rough nuclear parity, and that the Soviets would not cheat. When pollsters probed further, they found many supposed freeze supporters dubious that these conditions could, in fact, be met. See J. Michael Hogan and Ted J. Smith, "Polling on the Issue: Public Opinion and the Nuclear Freeze," *Public Opinion Quarterly* 55 (4) (Winter 1991), pp. 541–543.

65   *more than four-fifths of Democrats voted yes.* David Maraniss, "House Passes Nuclear Freeze Resolution; Opponents Win on Arms Amendment," *Washington Post*, May 5, 1983, A-1.

65   *endorsement of seven of the eight Democrats seeking the White House.* James A. Barnes, "From Sizzle to Fizzle," *National Journal* 35 (22) (May 31, 2003). Viewed on February 10, 2006, at http://nationaljournal.com/members/earlybird/archive/2003/ campaigninclude.030515.htm.

65   *dysfunctional social system could no longer compete.* As the historian John Lewis Gaddis wrote in 2005, in explaining Mikhail Gorbachev's revolutionary changes inside the Soviet Union, "internal developments were surely more important than external pressures and inducements, although in just what proportion may not be clear for decades. What one can say now is that Reagan saw Soviet weakness sooner than most of his contemporaries did; that he understood the extent to which détente was perpetuating the Cold War rather than hastening its end; that his hard line strained the Soviet system at the moment of its maximum weakness . . ." See Gaddis, *Strategies of Containment: A Critical Appraisal of American National Security Policy During the Cold War*, rev. and expanded ed. New York: Oxford University Press, 2005, p. 375.

66   *(far too responsive, in the eyes of much of the right).* See David S. Meyer, "Institutionalizing Dissent: The United States Structure of Political Opportunity and the End of the

Nuclear Freeze Movement," *Sociological Forum* 8 (2) (1993): pp. 173–174; Gaddis, *Strategies of Containment*, rev. and expanded ed., p. 375. As the columnist George Will wrote in June 1988, "For conservatives, Ronald Reagan's foreign policy has produced much surprise but little delight. His fourth, and one prays, final summit is a suitable occasion for conservatives to look back with bewilderment and ahead with trepidation. . . . Reagan's rhetoric has accelerated the nation's intellectual disarmament. In his seventh and eighth years, he has declared the Cold War over." See Sidney Blumenthal, *Pledging Allegiance: The Last Campaign of the Cold War*, rep. ed. New York: Perennial, 1991, pp. 240, 374.

66   *reconsideration was still several years away.* According to Mondale biographer Steven Gillon, his call for the passage of an equal rights amendment to the Constitution received roughly as much applause. See Gillon, *Democrats' Dilemma*, p. 319.

66   *Jackson's support until well after the Democratic convention.* Ibid., pp. 371–372. And even when Jackson pledged his support for Mondale in late August, he still refused to use the word *endorsement.* David S. Broder and Milton Coleman, "Jackson Promises Mondale 'Intense' Election Support," *Washington Post*, August 29, 1984, p. A-1.

66   *"are not a bunch of little Hubert Humphreys."* Schneider, "JFK's Children," p. 35.

67   *provide "free market incentives."* Gillon, *Democrats' Dilemma*, pp. 307–308.

67   *"locked up our party and this nation for too long."* George J. Church, "Bracing for a Marathon: The Race Between Hart and Mondale Heads Towards More Showdowns," *Time*, March 26, 1984, p. 12.

67   *"Where's the beef?"* Witcover, *Party of the People*, p. 623.

67   *"what this campaign was going to be all about."* Gillon, *Democrats' Dilemma*, p. 318.

68   *"The era of self-doubt,"* he proclaimed, *"is over."* Anatol Lieven, *America Right or Wrong: An Anatomy of American Nationalism.* New York: Oxford University Press, 2004, p. 16.

68   *"majority under normal circumstances simply does not exist."* Witcover, *Party of the People*, p. 632.

68   *his colleague Will Marshall, as its first staffers.* Ibid.; Kenneth S. Baer, *Reinventing Democrats.* Kansas City: University Press of Kansas, 2000, pp. 64, 66, 72–73.

68   *dubbed it the "Southern white boys' caucus."* Baer, *Reinventing Democrats*, p. 82.

68   *"won't stand up in the eighties."* Witcover, *Party of the People*, p. 633.

68   *"demeaning appeal to white Southern males."* Baer, *Reinventing Democrats*, p. 82.

70   *"armed aggression by Communist powers."* William M. LeoGrande, *Our Own Backyard: The United States in Central America, 1977–1992.* Chapel Hill: University of North Carolina Press, 1998, p. 86.

70   *"you will lose the support of the American people."* Cynthia J. Arnson, *Crossroads: Congress, the President, and Central America, 1976–1993*, 2nd ed. University Park: Pennsylvania State University Press, 1993, p. 136.

71   *"moral equal of our Founding Fathers."* Ambrose and Brinkley, *Rise to Globalism*, p. 327.

71   *"liberalism's only struggle was against the right."* Alexander Cockburn, "Michael meets Mr. Jones; Michael Moore fired from Mother Jones," *The Nation*, September 13, 1986, p. 198; Alex S. Jones. "Radical Magazine Removes Editor, Setting Off A Widening Political Debate," *New York Times*, September 27, 1986, p. A-7.

72   *prevent the Sandinistas from consolidating their dictatorship.* Robert Kagan, *A Twilight*

Struggle: American Power and Nicaragua, 1977–1990. New York: Free Press, 1996, pp. 370–371.

72   *became known as the El Salvador model.* Arnson, *Crossroads*, p. 186; Kagan, *A Twilight Struggle*, pp. 372, 378–379; Will Marshall interview, November 2005.

72   *Washington would cut the contras loose.* Democratic House Speaker Jim Wright also played an important role in facilitating Arias's negotiations. See Arnson, *Crossroads*, pp. 203–204.

73   *1,100-delegate bonanza for whichever Democrat could win over Dixie.* Six non-Southern states, accounting for roughly another 300 delegates, also held their primaries on Super Tuesday. See Paul Taylor, "Bush Rolls Over GOP Rivals in 'Super Tuesday' Contests As Dukakis, Jackson and Gore Split Democratic Ballot," *Washington Post*, March 9, 1988, p. A-1; Ron Harris, "Politics 88: Gore Seen as Needing Big Victory in South but Trails Jackson There," *Los Angeles Times*, Part 1, March 1, 1988, p. 16.

73   *"everyone being afraid of being outflanked on the left."* E. J. Dionne Jr., "Democratic Leaders in the South Say Gore Is Gaining in Presidential Race," *New York Times*, October 18, 1987, p. A-36.

73   *"neo-isolationism that has gripped some parts of the Democratic Party."* E. J. Dionne Jr., "Political Memo: Gore Fine-Tunes Hart Strategy of '84," *New York Times*, March 13, 1988, p. A-26; Richard Stengel, "Profiles in Caution: The Several Faces of Al Gore Are All Carefully Thought Out," *Time*, March 21, 1988, p. 28; Robert Shogan, "Politics '88: Gore Said Rivals' Dovish Views Jeopardize Democrats' Chances," *Los Angeles Times*, April 8, 1988, p. A-14.

73   *no longer remotely representative of the region as a whole.* A study by the DLC found that 35 percent of Super Tuesday voters described themselves as "liberal," while in 1984, only 21 percent of general election voters in those states had done so. By contrast, only 27 percent of Super Tuesday voters called themselves "conservative," versus 43 percent on election day 1984. See Jack W. Germond and Jules Witcover, *Whose Broad Stripes and Bright Stars: The Trivial Pursuit of the Presidency, 1988.* New York: Warner Books, 1989, p. 291.

74   *"population growth in the next century than . . . gut economic issues."* Thomas B. Edsall, "Gore Gambling on Primary Victories in March: Presidential Campaign Strategy Envisions Turnaround on 'Super Tuesday' in the South," *Washington Post*, October 18, 1987, p. A-4.

74   *ideology was suspect and quantification was king.* Between losing the governor's mansion in 1978 and winning it back in 1982, Dukakis had spent his exile at the Kennedy School's State and Local Government Program, a sojourn, according to journalist Sidney Blumenthal, that "had given him a renewed meaning." See Blumenthal, *Pledging Allegiance*, pp. 228, 230–231.

74   *favored rhetorical technique was the list.* Ibid., p. 243.

74   *"is not about ideology, it's about competence."* Witcover, *Party of the People*, p. 638.

74   *"the smartest clerk in the world."* Baer, *Reinventing Democrats*, pp. 122, 300.

74   *the comparison was instructive.* "Meet Michael Dukakis," *The Economist*, April 23, 1988, p. 11.

75   *Dukakis never delivered them.* Blumenthal, *Pledging Allegiance*, pp. 227–228.

75   *announced that the race was over.* Germond and Witcover, *Whose Broad Stripes and Bright Stars*, p. 446; Blumenthal, *Pledging Allegiance*, pp. 308–309; personal recollection from Michael Kelly.

75   *retained "a sort of veto power."* David C. Morrison, "Dogged by Defense," *National Journal* 20 (44) (October 29, 1988), p. 2722.

75   *Dukakis's wife had burned a flag.* Blumenthal, *Pledging Allegiance*, p. 292.

76   *no longer matched Old Glory.* Ibid., p. 270.

76   *"disdain for the simple and basic patriotism of most Americans."* Ibid., p. 295.

76   *"win their confidence in other key areas"* William Galston and Elaine Ciulla Kamarck, "The Politics of Evasion: Democrats and the Presidency," Progressive Policy Institute, September 1989. Viewed on February 13, 2006, at http://www .ppionline.org/ppi_ci.cfm?knlgAreaID=127&subsecID=171&contentID=2447.

77   *"a new politics of reciprocal responsibility."* Baer, *Reinventing Democrats*, p. 169; Witcover, *Party of the People*, p. 643.

78   *"in defense of vital American interests"* Stephen J. Solarz, "The Stakes in the Gulf," *The New Republic*, January 7–14, 1991, p. 25.

78   *Nunn came out in opposition.* Ambrose and Brinkley, *Rise to Globalism*, p. 390; Max Elbaum, "The Storm at Home." Viewed on November 20, 2005, at http:// www.revolutionintheair.com/histstrategy/gulf1.html; Will Marshall interview, November 2005.

78   *gave other Democrats hawkish cover for a dovish vote.* In the end, only ten Senate Democrats supported the resolution, with 45 against, a significantly lower percentage than in the House, where foreign policy specialists like Solarz and Armed Services chairman Les Aspin supported the war. See John B. Judis, "Jews and the Gulf: Fallout from the Six-Week War," *Tikkun* 16 (3) (May–June 1991), p. 13; John Zaller, "Strategic Politicians, Public Opinion, and the Gulf Crisis," Center for American Politics and Public Policy, February 4, 1993. Viewed on November, 19, 2005, at http://www.cappp.ucla.edu/papers/capp931.txt; Adam Wolfson, "Humanitarian Hawks?," *Policy Review*, December 1, 1999. Viewed on February 13, 2006, at http://www.policyreview.org/dec99/wolfson_print.html.

78   *the question of national security.* Jack W. Germond and Jules Witcover, *Mad as Hell: Revolt at the Ballot Box, 1992.* New York: Warner Books, 1993, p. 251.

79   *the percentage was almost zero.* Loren Griffith, "Where We Went Wrong: How the Public Lost Faith in Democrats' Ability to Protect Our National Security, and How to Stage a Comeback," *Truman National Security*, May 2005. Viewed on November 25, 2005, at http://www.trumanproject.org/trumanpaper3.html.

79   *"all aspiring national American politicians must pass."* Morrison, "Dogged by Defense," p. 2722.

79   *greatest foreign threat was illegal drugs.* William G. Hyland, *Clinton's World: Remaking American Foreign Policy.* New York: Praeger Trade, 1999, p. 140.

79   *Bruce Reed had helped author it.* Baer, *Reinventing Democrats*, p. 191.

79   *"something we have to apologize for."* Germond and Witcover, *Mad as Hell*, pp. 115–116; interview with Bruce Reed, December 2005.

79   *"I think government has a deadening impact."* Gillon, *Politics and Vision*, p. 239; Witcover, *Party of the People*, p. 653.

79   *"smack of trickle-down economics."* Germond and Witcover, *Mad as Hell*, p. 254.

80   *"fairness under the guise of promoting growth."* Ibid., p. 260.

80   *same message on both sides of the racial divide.* Clinton campaign officials invited the Kennedy comparison. As deputy campaign manager George Stephanopoulos put it, "[Clinton] believes it is impossible to win the White House without putting together the Bobby Kennedy coalition of working-class whites and blacks." See Michael K. Frisby, "Clinton Takes Bid to Blacks," *Boston Globe*, March 14, 1992, p. 8.

80   *"come together across racial lines."* Edsall and Byrne Edsall, *Chain Reaction*, pp. 182–183; Germond and Witcover, *Mad as Hell*, p. 264; John King, "Clinton Takes Unity Pitch to Reagan Democrat Country," *Associated Press*, March 13, 1992.

80   *"we want opportunity, but we accept responsibility."* Germond and Witcover, *Mad as Hell*, p. 264.

80   *Both audiences erupted in cheers.* Conversation with Bruce Reed, December 2005; King, "Clinton Takes Unity Pitch to Reagan Democrat Country."

80   *"hooted down not too many years ago."* Baer, *Reinventing Democrats*, p. 202.

81   *"rejected the old tax-and-spend politics."* Germond and Witcover, *Mad as Hell*, p. 442.

81   *"we must be a military superpower."* Ibid., p. 443.

81   *"who do you trust?"* Ibid., p. 444.

81   *"it's a question of avoiding the truth."* Ibid., p. 445.

81   *he even won veterans.* Witcover, *Party of the People*, p. 665; John B. Judis and Ruy Teixeira, *The Emerging Democratic Majority*. New York: Scibner, 2002, pp. 63–64; Germond and Witcover, *Mad as Hell*, p. 512.

81   *"couldn't make it as salient as the economy"* Germond and Witcover, *Mad as Hell*, p. 513.

81   *"Foreign policy is not what I came here to do"* Ambrose and Brinkley, *Rise to Globalism*, p. 399.

82   *"Don't take too much of his time"* Tom Mathews, "Clinton's Growing Pains," *Newsweek*, May 3, 1993, p. 34.

82   *"democratic enlargement."* Hyland, *Clinton's World*, p. 24.

82   *powered by economic integration and technological change.* As National Security Advisor Anthony Lake put it, "Information, ideas and money now pulse across the planet at light speed. This borderless global economy has generated an entrepreneurial boom and a demand for political openness." See Ambrose and Brinkley, *Rise to Globalism*, p. 408.

82   *the second coming of Jimmy Carter.* Maureen Dowd, "The Gap: Guess Who's Coming to Diplomacy?" *New York Times*, September 25, 1994, p. D-1.

83   *the air strikes that Clinton had promised three years earlier.* Michel Feher, *Powerless by Design: The Age of the International Community*. Durham, N.C.: Duke University Press, 2000, p. 2. Another factor that pushed Clinton toward air strikes was his realization that even if the United States wanted to wash its hands of the Bosnia mess, it would *still* have to intervene militarily, to rescue the UN peacekeepers stationed there. In other words, the real choice was not over intervention; it was over intervention to save Bosnia, or intervention to let it die. See transcript of Clinton's speech on Bosnia, November 1995. Viewed on December 14, 2005, at http://www.cnn

.com/US/9511/bosnia_speech/speech.html; Piers Robinson, "Misperception in Foreign Policy Making: Operation 'Deliberate Force' and the Ending of War in Bosnia," *Civil Wars* 4 (4) (Winter 2001), pp. 119–126.

84 *"intervention (because we are democrats)."* Destroying Kosovo: NATO Attacks Seem to Be Failing," *The Nation*, April 19, 1999, p. 3.

84 *"a new doctrine of international community."* Tony Blair, "Doctrine of the International Community: Speech by UK Prime Minister Tony Blair," Foreign and Commonwealth Office, April 22, 1999. Viewed on November 26, 2005, at http:// www.globalpolicy.org/globaliz/politics/blair.htm.

84 *"threats to international peace and security."* Ibid.

85 *"reformed international institutions with which to apply them."* Ibid.

85 *"deal with problems before they harm our national interests."* "Remarks by The President on Foreign Policy," The White House, February 26, 1999. Viewed on July 19, 2005, at http://mtholyoke.edu/acad/intrel/clintfps.htm.

85 *"play by the same rules we hold others to."* Will Marshall, "Democratic Realism: The Third Way," DLC, *Blueprint*, January 1, 2000. Viewed on November 19, 2005, at http://www.dlc.org/print.cfm?contentid=1123.

86 *UN Security Council to reform itself to make such action easier.* John Sloboda and Chris Abbot, "The 'Blair Doctrine' and After: Five Years of Humanitarian Intervention," *Open Democracy*, April 22, 2004, p. 2. Viewed on February 13, 2006, at http://www .oxfordresearchgroup.org.uk/publications/briefings/blairdoctrine.pdf.

86 *"as close to the source of the problem as possible."* Al Gore, "Questions from the Floor," International Press Institute, Opening Ceremony, Sunday, April 30, 2000. Viewed on November 26, 2005, at http://www.freemedia.at/Boston_Congress_Report/ boston3.htm.

86 *"requires co-operation on a scale not seen before."* Ibid.

86 *"war on Yugoslavia as the basis of . . . a new international military order."* "Destroying Kosovo," p. 3.

86 *"remains gravely, if not mortally, wounded."* "Dark Victory: The Kosovo Conflict, a Destructive and Useless War," *The Nation*, June 28, 1999, p. 3.

87 *"whether there should be a Pax Americana at all."* Benjamin Schwarz, "Left-Right Bedfellows," *The Nation*, June 28, 1999, p. 5.

87 *"the usually war-loving Republicans."* "Mike's Letter: The Bombing of Kosovo," April 15, 1999. Viewed on July 22, 2005, at www.michaelmoore.com/words/message/ index.php?messageDate=1999-04-15.

Chapter 4: Qutb's Children

88 *Qutb ever visited the Willard Hotel.* My transliterations of Arabic names follow the *New York Times*.

88 *at odds with Egypt's Western-oriented educational reforms.* Others suggest the real motive was to silence Qutb's increasingly harsh criticism of the Egyptian regime. See John Calvert, "The World Is an Undutiful Boy! Sayyid Qutb's American Experience," *Islam and Christian-Muslim Relations* 11 (1) (2000), p. 92.

88 *scandalizing the devout bachelor.* Ibid., p. 93.

88 *"noisy," "clamorous" and spiritually empty.* Ibid.

88 *grotesque descriptions of the people around him.* Ibid., p. 94.

88 *a "deformity" of the soul.* Ibid., pp. 95–98.

89 *murdered twenty-one of them.* Gilles Kepel, *Muslim Extremism in Egypt: The Prophet and the Pharoah.* Berkeley: University of California Press, 2003, p. 28.

89 *he was hanged.* Ibid., pp. 28, 42.

89 *he authored two books* Sometimes translated as *Milestones* or *Signposts on the Road,* and *In the Shade of the Koran.*

89 *reigned in Arabia before the Prophet Muhammad's birth.* "Understanding Islamism," International Crisis Group, Middle East/North Africa Report #37 (March 2, 2005), p. 7.

89 *"not just a specific historical period . . . but a state of affairs."* Quintan Wiktorowicz, "A Genealogy of Radical Islam," *Studies in Conflict and Terrorism* 28 (March/April 2005), p. 79.

89 *Muslim societies ruled by principles other than sharia.* Ibid.

90 *sheep to be gently guided on the correct path.* "Understanding Islamism," pp. 9–10.

90 *"give up their power merely through preaching"* Anthony Shadid, *Legacy of the Prophet: Despots, Democrats, and the New Politics of Islam.* Boulder, Colo.: Westview Press, 2002, p. 60.

90 *launch a holy war, or* jihad. Jihad's meaning is broader than holy war. It can refer to any struggle on Islam's behalf, including efforts to change oneself or to peacefully change the behavior of others. In this book, however, I use the term to mean only violent jihad. See Rudolph Peters, *Jihad in Classical and Modern Islam.* Princeton, N.J.: Markus Weiner, 1996; Quintan Wiktorowicz, "The New Global Threat: Transnational Salafis and Jihad," *Middle East Policy* 8 (4) (December 1, 2001). Viewed on February 10, 2006, at http://groups.colgate.edu/aarislam/wiktorow.htm.

90 *"establish the kingdom of heaven on earth."* Daniel Benjamin and Steven Simon, *The Age of Sacred Terror.* New York: Random House, 2002, p. 65.

90 *"but look only up to heaven."* "Extracts from Al-Jihadi Leader Al-Zawahiri's New Book." Viewed on April 5, 2005, at http://www.fas.org/irp/world/para/ayman_bk.html.

90 *demanded a return to the Islam of Muhammad's time.* Malise Ruthven, *A Fury for God: The Islamist Attack on America.* London: Granta, 2002, pp. 134–135; Robert Wuthnow, ed., *The Encyclopedia of Politics and Religion,* 2 vols. Washington, D.C.: Congressional Quarterly, 1998, pp. 670–672. Given Wahhab's enormous influence on Saudi Islam, commentators sometimes use the term *Wahhabism* to describe what I call salafism. But there are two problems with this approach. First, it implies that the ideology traces its roots only to the Arabian Peninsula. Second, the term is rejected by many so-called Wahhabis themselves as idolatrous, since it suggests they follow a person, rather than God. See Wiktorowicz, "A Genealogy of Radical Islam," p. 94.

90 *Egyptian scholars were well ensconced in the Gulf.* Robert McFadden, "Bin Laden's Journey from Rich, Pious Boy to the Mask of Evil," *New York Times,* September 30, 2001, p. A-5. Steve Coll of *The New Yorker* has reported that Bin Laden was influenced in high school by a Syrian refugee whose ideas resembled Qutb's. This early exposure

may explain why Bin Laden later gravitated to the salafists at university. See Steve Coll, "Young Osama," *The New Yorker*, December 5, 2005. Viewed on February 13, 2006, at http://www.newyorker.com/printables/fact/051212fa_fact.

91   *"part mentor/disciple, part father/son."* Peter L. Bergen, *Holy War, Inc.: Inside the Secret World of Osama bin Laden*. New York: Free Press, 2002, p. 52; Ruthven, *A Fury for God*, pp. 208, 306.

91   *into an international movement.* It is important to note that there are other salafist strains that support incumbent Muslim regimes and oppose unprovoked violence. In fact, their adherents likely outnumber the so-called jihadist salafists inspired by Qutb. But in the interest of clarity, I use the term *salafism* to denote only the jihadist variety. It is also worth noting that people like Abu Musab al-Zarqawi, self-proclaimed leader of Al Qaeda in Iraq, call themselves salafist or salafi. See "Indonesia Backgrounder: Why Salafism and Terrorism Mostly Don't Mix," *International Crisis Group*, Asia Report 83, Southeast Asia/Brussels (September 13, 2004), pp. 2–4; "Understanding Islamism," pp. 9–14.

91   *then to Peshawar, near the Afghan border.* Another account suggests Azzam was sent to teach in Islamabad by the Muslim World League, a salafist missionary organization funded by the Saudi government, and that he moved from there to Peshawar in 1984. See Gilles Kepel, *Jihad: The Trail of Political Islam*, 2nd printing, trans. Anthony F. Roberts. New York: Belknap Press, 2003, pp. 72, 145.

91   *the far less militarily significant Arab volunteers.* National Commission on Terrorist Attacks, *The 9/11 Commission Report: Final Report of the National Commission on Terrorist Attacks upon the United States of America.* New York: Norton, 2004, pp. 56, 467; Bergen, *Holy War, Inc.*, pp. 56, 63–75.

91   *streamed in from across the Arab world.* According to Kepel, estimates range from 8,000 to 25,000. See Kepel, *Jihad*, p. 147.

91   *and another Egyptian, Dr. Ayman al-Zawahiri, a Qutb disciple* In his 2001 manifesto, *Knights Under the Prophet's Banner*, Zawahiri calls Qutb "the most prominent theoretician of the fundamentalist movements." See Wiktorowicz, "A Genealogy of Radical Islam," p. 80.

92   *"Tashkent [eastern Uzbekistan], Andalusia [Spain and Portugal]"* Kepel, *Jihad*, pp. 146–147; "Fig 13. Uzbekistan: Administrative Divisions, 1996." Viewed on April 19, 2005, at http://www.lib.utexas.edu/maps/commonwealth/uzbekistan_admin96.jpg.

92   *one-third of the country's population—went into exile.* Bergen, *Holy War, Inc*, p. 49.

93   *buttressed un-Islamic regimes throughout the Middle East.* National Commission on Terrorist Attacks, *The 9/11 Commission Report*, pp. 58–59; Bergen, *Holy War, Inc*, pp. 85–86.

93   *U.S. "occupation" of Muslim lands.* National Commission on Terrorist Attacks, *The 9/11 Commission Report*, p. 59.

93   *in Saudi Arabia, and probably in Somalia as well.* Bergen, *Holy War, Inc.*, pp. 82–83, 87.

93   *back to Afghanistan, now under very different rule.* Ahmed Rashid, *Taliban: Militant Islam, Oil, and Fundamentalism in Central Asia.* New Haven: Yale University Press, 2001, p. 133.

93   *harsh vision to the tribe's conservative social code.* William Maley, "On Fundamentalism, Traditionalism, and Totalitarianism," in William Maley, ed., *Fundamentalism Reborn?:*

Afghanistan and the Taliban. Lahore, Pakistan: Vanguard Books, 1998, p. 19; Rashid, *Taliban*, p. 90.

93   *tolerant of religious minorities and individual freedom.* Maley, "On Fundamentalism, Traditionalism, and Totalitarianism," in Maley, ed., *Fundamentalism Reborn?*, p. 20; Rashid, *Taliban*, pp. 82–85.

93   *austere South Asian Islamic tradition called Deobandism.* Rashid, *Taliban*, pp. 88–92.

94   *restore state sovereignty to God.* Although Maududi's ultimate vision of society greatly resembled Qutb's, he had not advocated violence to achieve it. See Charles J. Adams, *"Mawdudi and the Islamic State,"* in John L. Esposito, ed., *Voices of Resurgent Islam.* Oxford, U.K.: Oxford University Press, 1983, p. 113; Kepel, *Jihad*, pp. 34, 36; Benjamin and Simon, *The Age of Sacred Terror*, p. 59.

94   *Maududi's work deeply influenced Qutb* Ruthven, *A Fury for God*, p. 71.

94   *the Taliban was "getting there."* Bergen, *Holy War, Inc.*, p. 13.

94   *kill on a mass scale without risking depopulation.* Michael Walzer, "On 'Failed Totalitarianism,'" in Irving Howe, ed., *1984 Revisited: Totalitarianism in Our Century.* New York: HarperCollins, 1983, p. 107; Hannah Arendt, *The Origins of Totalitarianism*, 2nd enlarged ed. New York: Meridian Books, 1958, pp. 310–311.

94   *"discipline, action and engagement"* Walzer, "On 'Failed Totalitarianism,'" in Howe, *1984 Revisited*, p. 105.

94   *"secret, sweaty and furtive."* Schlesinger, *The Vital Center*, p. 151.

94   *society in order to conquer and transform it.* Kepel, *Jihad*, p. 34; Ruthven, *A Fury for God*, pp. 87, 205, 211.

94   *"highly centralized, secretive, dictatorial and inaccessible."* Rashid, *Taliban*, p. 95.

94   *"Islamic bolshevism."* Shadid, *Legacy of the Prophet*, pp. 61–62; Anthony Shadid, "Sudan's Bold Experiment in Orthodoxy Risks War, Alienation," *Associated Press*, December 2, 1996.

94   *"available for demonstrations and mass meetings"* Walzer, "On 'Failed Totalitarianism,'" in Howe, *1984 Revisted*, p. 105.

95   *"In revenge, there is life."* Erik Eckholm, "A Nation Challenged: Penalties; Taliban Justice: Stadium Was Scene of Gory Punishment," *New York Times*, December 26, 2001, p. B-1; Dexter Filkins, "Afghans Pay Dearly for Peace," *Los Angeles Times*, October 22, 1998, p. A-1.

95   *"establish the rule of justice on earth."* Arendt, *The Origins of Totalitarianism*, pp. 461–462.

95   *through the power of the state.* Islam, of course, is hardly the only religion that has produced politically messianic movements. A minority Zionist tradition, for instance, associated with religious settler groups like Gush Emunim, sees Israel's dominion over all the biblical land of Israel as a way to usher in the messianic age. In the United States, the Christian Identity Movement, which influenced Oklahoma City bomber Timothy McVeigh, envisions a violent struggle with a Jewish-dominated conspiracy, followed by the establishment of the Kingdom of God. See Gideon Aran, "Jewish Zionist Fundamentalism: The Bloc of the Faithful in Israel (Gush Emunim)," in Martin E. Marty and R. Scott Appleby, eds., *Fundamentalisms Observed.* Chicago: University of Chicago Press, 1994, pp. 265–344; Benjamin and Simon, *The Age of Sacred Terror*, pp. 439–445.

95   *"from the usurper and return it to God."* Shadid, *Legacy of the Prophet*, p. 60.

95   *"the rule of sharia"* Bergen, *Holy War, Inc*, p. 156.

95   *"every aspect of social and intellectual life."* Walzer, "On 'Failed Totalitarianism,' " in Howe, *1984 Revisted*, p. 106.

95   *"autonomous existence of any activity whatsoever."* Arendt, *The Origins of Totalitarianism*, p. 322.

96   *"There's a Talib under every stone."* Carla Power, "City of Secrets," *Newsweek*, July 13, 1998, p. 10.

96   *"his affairs as personal and private."* Adams, "Mawdudi and the Islamic State," in Esposito, *Voices of Resurgent Islam*, p. 119.

96   *"predominance over every human secular activity."* Paul Berman, *Terror and Liberalism*. New York: Norton, 2003, p. 91.

96   *"transformation of human nature itself."* Arendt, *The Origins of Totalitarianism*, p. 458.

96   *"hampers study of Islam."* Rashid, *Taliban*, p. 115.

96   *"they will learn about Islam."* Ibid.

96   *"Sudanese personality in an Islamic form."* Shadid, *Legacy of the Prophet*, p. 165.

96   *helped inspire across the Muslim world* For instance, Jordan's Islamic Action Front and Algeria's Movement for National Reform. See "Understanding Islamism," p. 6.

97   *conformity with its vision of paradise.* Ibid., pp. 6–8. In 2004, the Brotherhood pledged that "Comprehensive reform [in Egypt] cannot be achieved except by implementing democracy, which we believe in, and whose fundamentals we commit ourselves to . . . while fully accepting that the people are the source of all authorities." This marks a striking contrast from earlier statements, which echoed Qutb's view that democracy represents the usurpation of God's authority. For instance, in 1981, Brotherhood leader Mustafa Mashhour wrote, "Democracy contradicts and wages war on Islam. Whoever calls for democracy means they are raising banners contradicting God's plan and fighting Islam." See Dr. Sayed Mahmoud Al-Qumni, "The Muslim Brotherhood's Initiative as a Reform Program: A Critical Review," The Conference on Islamic Reform, Saban Center for Middle East Policy, Brookings Institution, October 5–6, 2004. Viewed on February 10, 2006, at http://www.brookings.edu/fp/research/projects/islam/cairopaper1.pdf.

97   *Lebanon's religious diversity simply makes it impossible.* "Understanding Islamism," p. 23. As a Hezbollah representative in Parliament recently put it, "Nobody can force a political system on a society that doesn't have the characteristics proper for that system. Lebanon is a country with freedoms and a variety of ways of living. We respect that variety and we live with it. The Lebanese political system will reflect that variety." See "Meet Hizbollah," Reason Online, March 11, 2004. Viewed on October 12, 2005, at http://www.reason.com/interviews/hizbollah.shtml.

98   *refused to ban non-Islamic music, art, and yes, chess.* Ervand Abrahamian, *Khomeinism: Essays on the Islamic Republic*. Berkeley: University of California Press, 1993, p. 16.

98   *"It's none of our business."* "Iran: What Does Ahmadi-Nejad's Victory Mean?" *International Crisis Group*, August 4, 2005, p. 7.

98   *"those who are not against us are for us."* H. E. Chehabi, "The Political Regime of the

Islamic Republic of Iran in Comparative Perspective," *Government and Opposition* 36 (1) (Winter 2001), p. 69.

98   *"terror is the essence of totalitarian domination."* Arendt, *The Origins of Totalitarianism*, p. 464.

99   *"push the wall down on top of them."* Rashid, *Taliban*, pp. 6, 115.

99   *"declared a subtle war against Islam."* "Text from Abu Mes'ab al-Zarqawi Letter," GlobalSecurity.org. Viewed on October 16, 2005, at http://www.globalsecurity .org/wmd/library/news/iraq/2004/02/040212—al-zarqawi.htm. In fact, Zarqawi has been so bloodthirsty and indiscriminate in his attacks on Shiites that the circle around Bin Ladin has grown concerned. In a letter to Zarqawi discovered in October 2005, Zawahiri—while acknowledging that the Shiites are treacherous— suggested that the campaign against them "be put off until the force of the mujahed movement in Iraq gets stronger." One motivation for his plea may be the salafists being held captive in Iran. "Do the brothers forget," asked Zawahiri, "that we have more than one hundred prisoners—many of whom are from the leadership who are wanted in their countries—in the custody of the Iranians?" See "Letter from al-Zawahiri to al-Zarqawi," Office of the Director of National Intelligence, October 11, 2005. Viewed on January 31, 2006, at http://www.dni .gov/release_letter_101105.html.

100 *"others are apostates and deserve to die."* Wiktorowicz, "A Genealogy of Radical Islam," p. 88; Wiktorowicz, "The New Global Threat"; "Armed Islamic Group: Algeria, Islamists," Terrorism: Q & A, Council on Foreign Relations. Viewed on April 18, 2005, at http://www.terrorismanswers.org/groups/gia_print.html; James Bruce, "The Azzam Brigades," *Jane's Intelligence Review* 7 (4) (April 1, 1995), p. 175. Viewed on April 22, 2005, at http://www.habluetzel.com/terrorist-gropups.htm.

100 *"no two religions in Arabia."* Bergen, *Holy War, Inc.*, p. 77.

100 *against God's authority on earth.* As Bin Laden wrote in a February 23, 1998, fatwa against the United States and Jews across the world, "The Arabian peninsula has never—since God made it flat, created the desert, and encircled it with seas— been stormed by any forces like the Crusader armies spreading in it like locusts." See Magnus Ranstorp, "Interpreting the Broader Context and Meaning of Bin Laden's *Fatwa*," *Studies in Conflict and Terrorism* 21 (4) (June 1998), p. 328.

100 *ditch its barbaric culture and convert to Islam* Bin Laden has repeatedly urged Americans to convert to Islam, offering himself as their spiritual guide. See Michael Scheuer, *Imperial Hubris: Why The West Is Losing the War on Terror.* Dulles, Va.: Brassey's, 2004, pp. 153–154.

101 *it would have attacked Sweden.* "Bin Laden: 'Your security is in your own hands,' " CNN.com, October 29, 2004. Viewed on October 16, 2005, at htpp://cnn. worldnews.printthis.clickability.com/pt/cpt?action=cpt&title=cnn.com+-+Bin.

101 *preventing him from adopting the religion of Marx.* On December 9, 2001, for instance, Bin Laden called on his supporters to "continue jihad till all the anti-Islamic forces are wiped off the face of this earth and Islam takes over the whole world." See Bruce Hoffman, "Al Qaeda, Trends in Terrorism and Future Potentialities: An Assessment," Rand Corporation, 2003. Viewed on February 10, 2006, at http:// www.rand.org/pubs/papers/P8078/P8078.pdf.

101   *"in all the Islamic world."* Scheuer, *Imperial Hubris*, p. 153.

101   *"to Andalusia [Spain and Portugal]."* Ibid.; "East Turkistan," Unrepresented Nations and Peoples Organisation. Viewed on April, 19, 2005, at http://www.unpo.org/member.php?arg=21.

101   *nations like Burma and the Philippines.* Bergen, *Holy War, Inc.*, p. 53.

102   *compromise threatens the path to paradise.* In one typical example, the salafist leader in Dagestan, in southern Russia, announced that the region would eschew independence only if Russia—all of Russia!—became an Islamic state. See Wiktorowicz, "The New Global Threat."

102   *"through parts of Southeast Asia."* "Mapping the Global Future: Report of the National Intelligence Council's 2020 Project," National Intelligence Council, December 2004, p. 97.

103   *supporters will try to kill Americans.* In 2004, CIA director George Tenet testified that "a spectacular attack on the US homeland is the 'brass ring' that many [jihadists] strive for." See "The Worldwide Threat 2004: Challenges in a Changing Global Context," *DCI's Worldwide Threat Briefing*, February 24, 2004, p. 7.

103   *salafists no longer control even a single state.* Of course, salafists may have influence in various governments, for instance, Pakistan and Saudi Arabia, but they clearly do not control them.

103   *"expanded the violence of war, making deterrence far more robust."* John J. Mearsheimer, "Back to the Future," *International Security* 15 (1) (Summer 1990), p. 11.

103   *"a virtual training camp."* Lawrence Wright, "The Terror Web," *The New Yorker*, July 26, 2004. Viewed on April, 11, 2005, at http://www.newyorker.com/printables/fact/040802fa_fact.

103   *"a trip to Sudan, Yemen, Afghanistan, or Pakistan."* Scheuer, *Imperial Hubris*, p. 81.

103   *where an attack could have the greatest impact.* Wright, "The Terror Web"; Tracy Wilkinson, "Terror in Madrid," *Los Angeles Times*, March 12, 2004, p A-1; Daniel Benjamin and Steven Simon, *The Next Attack: The Failure of the War on Terror and a Strategy for Getting It Right.* New York: Henry Holt and Company, 2005, pp. 3–18, 51–79.

104   *American weapons at almost 10 million.* Scheuer, *Imperial Hubris*, pp. 154–156.

104   *used in smoke detectors and oil prospecting.* Bill Keller, "Nuclear Nightmare," *New York Times Magazine*, May 26, 2002. Viewed on April 12, 2005, at http://www.mtholyoke.edu/acad/intrel/bush/keller.htm.

104   *a million of them to build one bomb.* Dafna Linzer, "Attack with Dirty Bomb More Likely, Officials Say," *Washington Post*, December 29, 2004, p. A-6.

104   *"couple that to radioactive materials and that is it."* Ibid.

105   *securing a Department of Agriculture loan to purchase one.* Bergen, *Holy War, Inc.*, p. 36.

105   *tried the same thing—with the same result.* Joby Warrick, "An Easier, but Less Deadly Recipe for Terror," *Washington Post*, December 31, 2004, p. A-1.

105   *less likely that jihadists have them.* Jonathan S. Landay, "U.S. Now Believes Al-Qaida Has Ominous Arsenal, Official: Terrorists Have Chemical Weapons, Maybe Biological Agents," *Charlotte Observer*, October 13, 2001, p. 10-A.

105   *"inserted into living cells by undergraduates."* John Mintz, "Technical Hurdles Separate Terrorists From Biowarfare," *Washington Post*, December 30, 2004, p. A-1.

105   *"dangerous biological warfare threat."* "The Darker Bioweapons Future," Central
       Intelligence Agency, November 3, 2003. Viewed on January 31, 2006, at http://
       www.fas.org/irp/cia/product/bw1103.pdf.

106   *"apparently lack inventory controls"* Jonathan Medalia, "Nuclear Terrorism: A Brief
       Review of Threats and Responses," *CRS Report for Congress*, February 10, 2005, p. 7.

106   *found much of the information you'd need.* Keller, "Nuclear Nightmares."

107   *"Yes, they can."* Ibid.

107   *got the uranium past customs again.* Medalia, "Nuclear Terrorism," p. 5.

107   *average answer was 30 percent.* Richard G. Lugar, "The Lugar Survey on Proliferation
       Threats and Responses," June 2005. Viewed on January 31, 2006, at http://lugar
       .senate.gov/reports/NPSurvey.pdf.

107   *not from a government, but from terrorists.* Ibid.

107   *would kill half a million people instantly.* Medalia, "Nuclear Terrorism," p. 3.

108   *Manhattan would become uninhabitable.* "Testimony of Dr. Henry Kelly, President,
       Federation of American Scientists Before the Senate Committee on Foreign
       Relations," March 6, 2002. Viewed on April 12, 2005, at http://www.fas.org/
       ssp/docs/030602—kellytestimony.htm.

108   *"restraining or denying it as a positive good."* Woodward, "The Age of Reinterpretation,"
       p. 7.

109   *government power expands and individual liberty declines.* Interestingly, while September
       11 clearly had this effect, Hurricane Katrina—perhaps because it had no direct
       human cause—did not. See the September 22, 2005, survey by the Pew Research
       Center for the People and the Press: "Katrina Has Only Modest Impact on
       Basic Public Values." Viewed on January 31, 2006, at http://people-press.org/
       commentary/display.php3?AnalysisID=117.

109   *without permission from a judge.* Section 215 of the Patriot Act allows law enforcement
       to search personal records in secret without a warrant or probable cause. Law
       enforcement officials must merely certify to a judge that the effort is part of "an
       investigation to protect against international terrorism." (There is reason to doubt
       such certifications: a 2003 study by the Government Accountability Office found
       that 75 percent of the Justice Department's "international terrorism" convictions
       had little to do with terrorism.) Section 505 allows the government to obtain such
       records without any judicial oversight at all; authorities are allowed to rely on
       "national security" letters that they themselves write.

109   *since the Patriot Act made them easier to issue.* Barton Gelman, "The FBI's Secret Scrutiny:
       In Hunt for Terrorists, Bureau Examines Records of Ordinary Americans,"
       Washington Post, November 6, 2005, p. A-1.

109   *single biggest reason is September 11.* September 11 is the single biggest reason, but not
       the only one. Congress began weakening checks on government power—although
       less dramatically—after another terrorist attack, the April 1995 bombing in
       Oklahoma City.

110   *read people's mail also grew exponentially.* "2001 Polling on Civil Rights," nationaljournal
       .com. Viewed on April 11, 2005, at http://nationaljournal.com; Greg M. Shaw
       et al., "The Polls: Trends; Crime, the Police, and Civil Liberties," *Public Opinion
       Quarterly* 62 (1998): pp. 422–423.

110   *wasn't violating them* enough. A CNN/Gallup/*USA Today* poll in late November 2001 found that 60 percent of Americans believed the Bush administration had been "about right" in "restricting people's civil liberties in order to fight terrorism," while 26 percent said it had "not gone far enough" and only 10 percent said it had "gone too far." See "2001 Polling on Civil Rights."

110   *five or ten times as much as its predecessor.* Charles Lewis and Adam Mayle, "Justice Dept. Drafts Sweeping Expansion of Anti-Terrorism Act," Center for Public Integrity, February 7, 2003. Viewed on April 11, 2005, at http://www.publicintegrity.org/printer-friendly.aspx.aid=94; "Transcript: Bill Moyers Interviews Chuck Lewis," WETA NOW. Viewed on April 11, 2005, at http://www.pbs.org/now/printable/transcript_lewis2_print.html.

110   *to groups designated as terrorist.* Timothy H. Edgar, "Interested Person's Memo: Section-by-Section Analysis of Justice Department Draft 'Domestic Security Enhancement Act of 2003,' Also Known as 'Patriot Act,'" American Civil Liberties Union, February 14, 2003. Viewed on December 15, 2005, at http://www.aclu.org/safefree/general/172031eg20030214.html.

110   *might do if the United States were hit again.* In fact, Lewis said, "I'm afraid they're waiting for a war or something and then they're gonna pop this baby out and then try to jam it through." See "Transcript: Bill Moyers Interviews Chuck Lewis."

110   *"large-scale intrusive security measures."* "Mapping the Global Future," p. 104.

110   *recession sparked by the latest attacks.* Ibid., p. 104B.

110   *"went way beyond anything imagined after 9/11."* Ibid., p. 104A.

111   *"once under way, would be one of the hardest to break."* Ibid., p. 104C.

Chapter 5: Reagan's Children

112   *responded with a blank stare.* Richard A. Clarke, *Against All Enemies: Inside America's War on Terror.* New York: Free Press, 2004, p. 229.

112   *declare the country at war.* He used the word in a statement to reporters on the morning of September 12. See Bob Woodward, *Bush at War.* New York: Simon & Schuster, 2002, p. 45.

112   *"different kind of war."* Bush used the phrase in his October 11, 2001, press conference. See "President Holds Prime Time News Conference," October 11, 2001. Viewed on May 23, 2005, at http://www.whitehouse.gov/news/releases/2001/10/20011011-7.html.

112   *was the kind they knew best.* As Defense Secretary Donald Rumsfeld put it, the war on terrorism "undoubtedly will prove to be a lot more like a cold war than a hot war. . . . If you think about it, in the Cold War, it took fifty years, plus or minus. It did not involve major battles. It involved continuous pressure. . . . It strikes me that that might be a more appropriate way to think about what we are up against here." See "Secretary Rumsfeld Media Availability with Traveling Press," United States Department of Defense, October 4, 2001. Viewed on December 19, 2005, at http://www.dod.mil/transcripts/2001/t10042001_t1004sd2.html.

112   *"fascism, and Nazism, and totalitarianism."* "Address to a Joint Session of Congress

and the American People," September 20, 2001. Viewed on April 28, 2005, at http://www.whitehouse.gov/news/releases/2001/09/print/20010920-8.html.

112   *(the cold war being number three).* Norman Podhoretz, "World War IV: How It Started, What It Means, and Why We Have to Win," *Commentary* 118 (2) (September 1, 2004). Viewed on February 10, 2006, at http://www.commentarymagazine .com/A11802017_1.pdf. In fact, there was a conservative tradition of calling the cold war "World War III." James Burnham's column in *National Review* was called "Third World War." See Nash, *The Conservative Intellectual Movement in America,* p. 239.

113   *an "Iron Veil" had descended across the Muslim world.* Victor Davis Hanson, "The Iron Veil," in Victor Davis Hanson, *An Autumn of War: What American Learned from September 11 and the War on Terrorism,* 1st ed. New York: Anchor Books, 2002, p. 200.

113   *"Jefferson, Rousseau or Mazzini"* Martin Staniland, *American Intellectuals and African Nationalists, 1955–1970.* New Haven: Yale University Press, 1991, p. 249.

113   *"both whites and their own civilized minority."* Staniland, *American Intellectuals and African Nationalists, 1955–1970,* p. 248.

113   *utopian and dangerous, which was to say, typically liberal.* In fact, many conservatives saw rapid decolonization as yet more evidence that the West, under liberalism's corrupting influence, had lost the moral confidence that once fueled its civilizing mission. Decolonization, wrote founding *National Review* editor Frank Meyer, was a "tragedy of impatience" resulting from the West's "decay of belief [and] failure of nerve and confidence." James Burnham blamed decolonization in Asia on the West's "moral funk and mental stupor. See Staniland, *American Intellectuals and African Nationalists, 1955–1970,* p. 225; Nash, *The Conservative Intellectual Movement in America,* p. 135.

113   *"disciplines and habits" of democracy.* Jeane Kirkpatrick, "Dictatorships and Double Standards," *Commentary* 68 (5) (November 1979), p. 37. As ex-liberals who felt that they—not the post-Vietnam Democrats—were the Truman administration's true heirs, some neoconservatives might have denied there was anything particularly conservative about Kirkpatrick's thesis. But John Ehrman, a highly sympathetic chronicler of neoconservative thought, acknowledges that "Kirkpatrick's developing emphasis on letting democracy evolve rather than be planned [represented]—a hands-off approach closer to that of Friedrich Hayek and Milton Friedman than to the Americans for Democratic Action of the 1940s and 1950s." See Ehrman, *The Rise of Neoconservatism,* p. 122.

113   *anti-American movements to power across the third world.* Jeane Kirkpatrick, "Dictatorships and Double Standards," p. 38. As *Weekly Standard* editor William Kristol has conceded about the early 1980s, "I don't think that neoconservatives at that time were particularly strong supporters of democracy [overseas]." See James Mann, *Rise of the Vulcans: The History of Bush's War Cabinet.* New York: Viking, 2004, p. 130.

113   *abolish the position of assistant secretary of state for human rights.* Paul Wolfowitz, "Remembering the Future," *The National Interest.* Viewed on February 10, 2006, at http://www.findarticles.com/p/articles/mi_m2751/is_2000_spring/ai.

114   *"gathering new strength" across the globe.* Ronald Reagan, "Address to Members of the

British Parliament," June 8, 1982. Viewed on October 31, 2005, at http://usa
.usembassy.de/etexts/speeches/empire.htm.

114 *helping pressure South Korea's Chun.* Harry Anderson and Tracy Dahlby, "South
Korea: The Return of Kim Dae Jung," *Newsweek*, February 11, 1985, p. 48.

114 *Paul Wolfowitz had been at the center of it all.* Mann, *Rise of the Vulcans*, pp. 130–134;
Sam Tanenhaus, "Bush's Brain Trust: So Right, They're Wrong? The NeoCons
Who Pull George W. Bush's Strings," *Vanity Fair* (515) (July 2003), p. 117; David
Adesnik, "Reagan's 'Democratic Crusade': Presidential Rhetoric and the
Remaking of American Foreign Policy." D. Phil diss., Oxford University, 2006,
pp. 263–314.

114 *"conservatives indulged in the 1980s."* David Frum, *Dead Right*, rep. ed. New York:
HarperCollins, 1995, p. 152.

114 *"democratic development takes time"* Jacob Heilbrunn, "Condoleezza Rice: George
W.'s Realist," *World Policy Journal* 16 (4) (Winter 1999/2000), p. 50.

114 *"We do it this way; so should you."* Mann, *Rise of the Vulcans*, p. 257.

115 *betrayed Reagan's legacy.* "Is this the party of Reagan?" asked Kristol and Robert
Kagan in 1999, while excoriating Republicans for opposing the war in Kosovo.
"Right now, it's hard to tell." See William Kristol and Robert Kagan, "Kosovo and
the Republican Future," *Weekly Standard*, April 5–12, 1999. Viewed on October
24, 2005, at http://www.ceip.org/people/kagstan10.htm.

115 *"among both friends and foes."* William Kristol and Robert Kagan, "Toward a Neo-
Reaganite Foreign Policy," *Foreign Affairs*, July/August 1996. Viewed on February
14, 2006, at http://www.foreignaffairs.org/19960701faessay4210/william-
kristol-robert-kagan/toward-a-neo-reaganite-foreign-policy.html.

115 *but for Western civilization.* Conservatives often described the cold war as a struggle for
"Western civilization." For instance, in 1947, John Foster Dulles wrote: "There is a
world-wide struggle primarily ideological between Western (Christian) civilization
and Communism." Burnham named his 1964 cold war polemic "The Suicide of
the West." See Toulouse, *The Transformation of John Foster Dulles*, p. 189.

115 *in the months following 9/11.* In October 2001, for instance, evangelist Franklin
Graham—who delivered the invocation at Bush's first inaugural—called Islam
"a very evil and wicked religion." Four months later, Pat Robertson said, "I have
taken issue with our esteemed president in regard to his stand in saying Islam is
a peaceful religion. It's just not." Later in 2002, influential conservative activist
Paul Weyrich declared that "Islam is at war with us." For his part, prominent
conservative commentator William Bennett wrote, "To a greater extent than we
have permitted ourselves to say, this war has to do with religion." See Ken Garfield,
"Graham Stands by Comments on Islam: But 'Evil and Wicked' Quote Doesn't
Cancel Christian Love, He Says," *Charlotte Observer*, November 19, 2001, p. 9-A;
"Bill Press: Minister's Preach War on Islam," CNN.com/Inside Politics, February
28, 2002. Viewed on February 14, 2006, at http://archives.cnn.com/2002/
ALLPOLITICS/02/28/column.billpress; Dana Milbank, "Hawks Chide Bush
over Islam," *Washington Post*, December 2, 2002. Viewed on June 14, 2005, at
http://www.globalpolicy.org/wtc/fundamentalism/2002/1202hawks.htm;

William J. Bennett, *Why We Fight: Moral Clarity and the War on Terrorism*, updated ed. Washington, D.C.: Regnery Publishing, 2003, p. 90.

116   *find it easier to do their deadly work.* At least three empirical studies show a correlation between more freedom and less terrorism. The first, and most famous, is the study by Princeton University's Alan B. Krueger and Charles University's Jitka Maleckova, which found that "at a given level of income, countries with greater civil liberties . . . are less likely to be a wellspring of international terrorists." A second study, by Krueger and Stanford's David D. Laitin, again found that "Countries with a high degree of civil liberties are unlikely to be origin countries for terrorist acts." And an October 2004 working paper by Alberto Abadie of Harvard's Kennedy School of Government found that "Political freedom is shown to explain terrorism." It is important to note, however, that while these studies show that countries with the greatest political freedom produce the fewest terrorists, countries in the middle range spawn more terrorists than the most repressive regimes, which suggests that while successful transitions from authoritarianism to democracy can reduce terrorism, incomplete transitions can have the opposite effect. See Alan B. Krueger and Jitka Maleckova, "Education, Poverty and Terrorism: Is There a Causal Connection," *Journal of Economic Perspectives* 17 (4) (Fall 2003), pp. 139–140; Alan B. Krueger and David D. Laitin, "Kto Kogo?: A Cross-Country Study of the Origins and Targets of Terrorism" (unpublished paper), November 23, 2004, p. 21. Viewed on January 31, 2006, at http://www.krueger.princeton.edu/terrorism3.pdf; Alberto Abadie, "Poverty, Political Freedom, and the Roots of Terrorism," NBER Working Paper No. 1085, October 2004, pp. 1, 3. Viewed on February 10, 2006, at http://www.nber.org/papers/w10859.

117   *loath to blame Communism on poverty.* As the University of Toledo's Ronald Lora notes, in an essay about the early cold war right, its "apocalyptic vision precluded any analysis of the ways in which poverty, political oppression, and economic exploitation drove men and governments to solutions inhospitable to those prescribed by the American ethos." See Lora, "A View from the Right," in Griffith and Theoharis, *The Specter*, p. 69–70.

117   *"does not prove that poverty caused them to do so"* Goldwater, *The Conscience of a Conservative*, p. 97. Although published under Goldwater's name, the book's real author was William F. Buckley's brother-in-law, L. Brent Bozell. See Godfrey Hodgson, *The World Turned Right Side Up: A History of the Conservative Ascendancy in America*. New York: Mariner Books, 1997, p. 97.

117   *"supplied to them by the communists themselves."* Daniel Kelley, *James Burnham and the Struggle for the World: A Life.* Wilmington, Del.: ISI Books, May 2002, p. 209.

117   *"insist on a quid pro quo."* "Foreign Aid: Principles," *National Review*, May 23, 1956, p. 5. Goldwater made the same point, arguing that the United States should "confine foreign aid to military and technical assistance to those nations that need it and that are committed to a common goal of defeating world Communism." One biographer writes that "as secretary of state, [John Foster] Dulles betrayed a lack of enthusiasm for providing foreign aid to nations that refused to choose sides in the Cold War." See Goldwater, *The Conscience of a Conservative*, p. 99; Toulouse, *The Transformation of John Foster Dulles*, p. 222.

117   *development aid dropped by 15 percent.* John W. Sewell and Christine E. Contee, "Foreign Aid and Gramm-Rudman," *Foreign Affairs*, Summer 1987, p. 1015.

117   *new "nonterritorial" threats.* For one use of the phrase, see "New World, New Deal: A Democratic Approach to Globalization," published in *Foreign Affairs* by former Clinton officials W. Bowman Cutter, Joan Spero, and Laura D'Andrea Tyson, which offered a Democratic foreign policy vision for the 2000 campaign. "Traditional security threats," argued the authors, were giving way to "nonterritorial" problems "like international terrorism, organized crime, drug trafficking, and environmental degradation." As another former Clinton foreign policy official, Jonathan Winer, has suggested, "The Clinton administration started out with a very traditional Democratic or even mainstream approach to foreign policy: big-power politics, Russia being in the most important role; a critical relationship with China; European cooperation; and some multilateralism . . . [But] they moved much more to a failed-state, global-affairs kind of approach, recognizing that the trends established by globalization required you to think about foreign policy in a more synthetic and integrated fashion than nation-state to nation-state." See W. Bowman Cutter, Joan Spero, and Laura D'Andrea Tyson, "Campaign 2000: New World, New Deal: A Democratic Approach to Globalization," *Foreign Affairs*, March/April 2000. Viewed on February 14, 2006, at http://www.foreignaffairs .org/20000301faessay29/w-bowman-cutter-joan-spero-laura-d-andrea-tyson/ campaign-2000-new-world-new-deal-a-democratic-approach-to-globalization. html.; see Joshua Micah Marshall, "Kerry Faces the World: What Would a John Kerry Foreign Policy Look Like? In Some Ways a Lot Like One the Current President's Father Could Endorse," *The Atlantic Monthly*, July 1, 2004. Viewed on February 14, 2006, at http://www.theatlantic.com/doc/prem/200407/marshall.

117   *"welfare spending in the Third World."* "1992 Republican Party Platform." Viewed on February 3, 2006, at http://www.cnn.com/ELECTION/2000/conventions/ republican/features/platform.92.

117   *"agenda for America as global social worker."* Ibid.

118   *never mentioned the word* globalization. Condoleezza Rice, "Campaign 2000: Promoting the National Interest," *Foreign Affairs*, January/February 2000. Viewed on February 10, 2006, at http://www.foreignaffairs.org/200001faessay5/condoleeza-rice/.

118   *working for the Joint Chiefs of Staff.* Mann, *Rise of the Vulcans*, pp. xiii, 274.

118   *"a product of economic factors."* Podhoretz, "World War IV," p. 19.

118   *"We are the root cause of his terrorism."* Ruthven, *A Fury for God*, p. 30; Paul R. Pillar, *Terrorism and U.S. Foreign Policy*. Washington, D.C.: Brookings Institution Press, 2001, pp. 32–33.

118   *"cold, calculating killers."* Bob Woodward, *Bush at War*, p. 117.

118   *one-tenth as much as it spends on defense.* "Human Development Report," United Nations Development Programme, 2004. Viewed on February 3, 2006, at http:// hdr.undp.org/reports/global/2004/?CFID=862570&CFTOKEN=25093558.

119   *"corrupt bureaucrats to draw money from."* P. W. Singer, "Pakistan's Madrassahs: Ensuring a System of Education, Not Jihad," The Brookings Institution, Analysis Paper 14, November 2001. Viewed on February 14, 2006, at http://www .brookings.edu/views/papers/singer/20020103.pdf.

119   *teach violent salafism.* Jessica Stern, "Pakistan's Jihad Culture," *Foreign Affairs*, November/
      December 2000. Viewed on February 14, 2006, at http://www.foreignaffairs.org/
      20001101faessay940/jessica-stern/pakistan-s-jihad-culture.html.

119   *beheading of* Wall Street Journal *reporter Daniel Pearl.* "Kashmir Militant Extremists:
      Kashmir, Islamists," Terrorism: Q & A, Council on Foreign Relations. Viewed on
      October 17, 2005, at http://cfrterrorism.org/groups/harakat_print.html.

119   *received nothing from the Egyptian state.* Benjamin and Simon, *The Age of Sacred Terror*, p.
      180; "Islamism in North Africa II: Egypt's Opportunity, *Middle East and North Africa
      Briefing*, International Crisis Group, April 20, 2004, p. 7; Kepel, *Jihad*, p. 282.

119   *"functions previously in the hands of state authorities."* Omar Encarnación, "The Globalization
      of Democracy: Myths, Realities, and Lessons," *The Bard Journal of Global Affairs* 4
      (Fall 2003), p. 18. Viewed on February 14, 2006, at http://www.bard.edu/bgia/
      journal/vol4/5-19.pdf. Graham Fuller, former vice chairman of the CIA's National
      Intelligence Council, cites Turkey, Egypt, Algeria, Pakistan, and Morocco as countries
      where the "social programs of many Islamist organizations . . . provide vital social
      services that the state can no longer supply." Of course, not all these Islamist groups
      are salafist. And in heavily Shiite slums, like the suburbs of Beirut, Hezbollah plays
      a similar role. See Omer Taspinar, "Terrorism and Education." Presented at the
      Academy of Educational Development 2004. Unpublished, p. 29; Daniel Byman,
      "Should Hezbollah Be Next?" *Foreign Affairs*, November/December 2003. Viewed
      on February 14, 2006, at http://www.foreignaffairs.org/20031101faessay82606/
      daniel-byman/should-hezbollah-be-next.html.

119   *plunging oil revenue and an escalating birthrate.* Ian Bremmer, "The Saudi Paradox,"
      World Policy Journal 3 (21) (September 22, 2004), p. 3.

120   *"the more poverty you have, the more fundamentalism you have."* Ibid., p. 5.

120   *resembles American inner cities in the 1960s.* In a strange parallel to rust-belt American
      cities like Detroit, where one generation of African American migrants found
      work in heavy industry, while deindustrialization then left their children without
      access to decent jobs, the deindustrialization of industrial cities in northern
      England, where many Indian, Pakistani, and Bangladeshi immigrants came to
      work in the 1950s and 1960s, has produced high Muslim unemployment rates
      in neighborhoods like Beeston, in Leeds, which spawned three of the July 2005
      London subway bombers. Almost a third of the community is on welfare, and
      nationally, unemployment for British men of Pakistani origin is almost 30 percent.
      Similarly, in France, salafism has taken greatest hold in the ghettos that ring major
      cities, where many young Muslim men experience a toxic brew of economic
      despair, political marginalization, anti-American fury, and cultural confusion. In
      the words of Mamoun Abdelali, an imam in the city of Mantes La Jolie, "This
      is an ideal breeding ground—unemployment, ignorance, academic failures,
      professional failures, a feeling of rejection by French society because there is no
      work or housing, and for the most part, a very low education level, and thus very
      little knowledge of Islam. And added to that is an enormous level of frustration
      and a huge identity complex." See Amy Waldman, "Seething Unease Shaped
      British Bombers' Newfound Zeal," *New York Times*, July 31, 2005, p. A-1; Nina

Bernstein, "In America's Mill Towns, No Mirror Image of the Muslims of Leeds," *New York Times*, July 21, 2005, p. B-1; Olivier Roy, *Globalized Islam: The Search for the Ummah*. New York: Columbia University Press, 2004, pp. 303, 315; Marc Sageman, *Understanding Terror Networks*. Philadelphia: University of Pennsylvania Press, 2004, pp. 95–97; "How Restive Are Europe's Muslims?" *The Economist*, October 20, 2001. Viewed on February 23, 2006, at http://www.economist.com/printededition/displayStory.cfm?Story_ID=824394; Neil Docherty and Lowell Bergmann, "Al Qaeda's New Front," PBS, January 25, 2005. Viewed on February 3, 2006, at http://www.pbs.org/wgbh/pages/frontline/shows/front/.

120   *people who trained at Al Qaeda camps in the 1990s were invited to join* Sageman, *Understanding Terror Networks*, p. 92.

120   *"only accepting the best recruits."* This helps explain Bueno de Mesquita's overall finding that "actual terrorist operatives are not poor or lacking in education. And yet lack of economic opportunity and recessionary economies are positively correlated with terrorism." See Ethan Bueno de Mesquita, "The Quality of Terror," unpublished paper, Department of Political Science, Washington University. Viewed on February 14, 2006, at http://www.nyu.edu/gsas/dept/politics/seminars/ebdm.pdf.

120   *Germany can produce the Baader-Meinhof gang.* I am indebted to the Brookings Institution's P. W. Singer for this point. Interview, May 13, 2005.

121   *"the difference between good and evil."* Bennett, *Why We Fight*, pp. 15–16.

121   *the war on terror marks you as an apologist for evil.* "Pakistan: Adult Illiteracy, Females," *Globalis: Pakistan*. Viewed on December 19, 2005, at http://www.globalis.gvu.unu .edu/indicator_detail.cfm?IndicatorID=126&C.

121   *thirteen Arab countries, plus the Palestinian Authority.* U.S. Department of State, Middle Eastern Partnership Initiative. Viewed on March 20, 2006, at http://mepi.state .gov/mepi/c10128.htm; Jeremy Sharp, "US Foreign Assistance to the Middle East: Historical Background, Recent Trends, and the FY2006 Request," Congressional Research Report for Congress, June 13, 2005. Viewed on February 14, 2006, at http://www.fas.org/sgp/crs/mideast/RL32260.pdf; Nawja Saad, "US Earmarks $5 Billion in Foreign Aid to the Mideast in FY05, Middle East Partnership Initiative to Receive $75 Million," State Department, Washington File. Viewed on February 14, 2006, at http://usinfo.state.gov/mena/Archive/2004/Dec/14—506545.html.

122   *"watered down and understood by all to be a façade."* Jeremy Sharp, "US Foreign Assistance to the Middle East"; Charles Krauthammer, "In Defense of Democratic Realism," *The National Interest*, Fall 2004. Viewed on February 14, 2006, at http:// www.findarticles.com/p/articles/mi_m2751/is_77/ai_n6353159; Al Kamen, "In the Loop," *Washington Post*, June 7, 2004. Viewed on February 14, 2006, at http://www.washingtonpost.com/wp-dyn/articles/A20686-2004Jun6.html.

122   *that pledge had disappeared from administration websites.* Michael M. Phillips, "Bush Falls Behind on Promises for Antipoverty, AIDS Funding," *Wall Street Journal*, January 27, 2005, p. A-4.

122   *assistance programs have been sharply cut.* Elizabeth Becker and David E. Sanger, "Some Aid Is Cut to Pay for Increases Elsewhere," *New York Times*, February 8, 2005, p. A-23.

122   *of all Muslim countries that support the war on terror.* Paul Blustein, "U.S. Free-Trade
       Deals Include Few Muslim Countries," *Washington Post*, December 3, 2004, p.
       E-1. To its credit, the Bush administration has concluded free trade deals with
       Morocco and Bahrain, countries with industries small enough that their exports
       don't threaten American manufacturers. But it has refused to take such steps with
       larger countries like Pakistan, Egypt, and Turkey. See Al Kamen, "In the Loop";
       Evelyn Iritani, "Mideast Building Trade Ties with U.S.," *Los Angeles Times*, March
       28, 2005, p. C-1.

122   *"in the United States for a local domestic product."* Marina Ottaway, "Promoting
       Democracy in the Middle East: The Problem of U.S. Credibility," Working Paper,
       Democracy and Rule of Law Project, Carnegie Endowment for International Peace,
       March 2003, p. 12.

123   *"intention of resisting dictatorships in the region."* Ibid.

123   *"war against Iraq will be costing it $100 billion."* Ibid.

123   *"let us manage our country!"* Craig Charney and Nicole Yakatan, "A New Beginning:
       Strategies for a More Fruitful Dialogue with the Muslim World," Council on
       Foreign Relations: Council Special Report 7 (May 2005), pp. 6, 20–21.

123   *free market reforms don't do nearly as much good.* The World Bank studied fifty-six
       countries over two decades. It found no correlation between foreign aid and
       economic growth. Among those countries that pursued sound economic policies,
       however, it found that foreign aid mattered a lot. That aid boosted their growth
       rates far above the level of countries that pursued sound policies alone. See
       Cassidy, "Helping Hands," pp. 60–66; Craig Burnside and David Dollar, "Aid,
       the Incentive Regime, and Poverty Reduction," Macroeconomics and Growth
       Group, The World Bank (Draft), April 1998, p. 3.

123   *commit their own money to the task.* National Commission on Terrorist Attacks, *The
       9/11 Commission Report*, p. 378.

123   *"draining the economic and political sources of terrorism."* The Arab Human Development
       Report 2002: Creating Opportunities for Future Generations. New York: United Nations
       Development Programme, Regional Bureau for Arab States, 2002, pp. 22, 167.

123   *roughly $200 billion a year.* Rachel Bronson, "Talk Is Cheap, a Marshall Plan Isn't,"
       Los Angeles Times, August 4, 2003, p. 11.

124   *still only one-twentieth of the Marshall Plan.* These rough estimates are based on
       the economic support funds allocated to each country in the yearly foreign
       operations appropriations legislation. Excluded are funds for military assistance
       and expenditures by U.S. government programs that support regional projects
       with their own budgets. The numbers for Iraq reconstruction are artificially lower
       because the war has been funded through supplemental requests that do not
       follow the annual budgetary cycle. See Kenneth Katzman, "Afghanistan: Post-
       War Governance, Security, and U.S. Policy," CRS Report for Congress, updated
       June 15, 2005. Viewed on February 15, 2006, at http://www.fas.org/sgp/crs/
       row/RL30588.pdf; Curt Tarnoff, "Iraq: Recent Developments in Reconstruction
       Assistance," CRS Report for Congress, updated August 12, 2005. Viewed on
       February 15, 2006, at http://digital.library.unt.edu/govdocs/crs/data/2005/

upl-meta-crs-7419/RL31833_2005Aug12.pdf; Jeremy M. Sharp, "U.S. Foreign Assistance to the Middle East."

124   *Communist threat stemmed mostly from within became untenable.* Joseph McCarthy remained popular among conservatives even after he was censured by the Senate in 1954. But by the early 1960s, even *National Review* had tired of conspiracy-mongering about Communist infiltration and denounced the lunatic, but popular, John Birch Society, whose leader, Robert Welch, claimed Eisenhower was a Communist. See Nash, *The Conservative Intellectual Movement in America*, pp. 275–276; "Censure of Senator Joseph McCarthy (1954)." Viewed on October 25, 2005, at http://usinfo .state.gov/usa/infousa/facts/democrac/60.htm.

124   *"absence of that establishment would quickly accomplish."* Goldwater, *The Conscience of a Conservative*, p. 111.

124   *deficits never reared their ugly head.* "As a practical matter," Goldwater wrote, "spending cuts must come before tax cuts. If we reduce taxes before firm, principled decisions are made about expenditures, we will court deficit spending and the inflationary effects that invariably follow." See ibid, pp. 62–63.

125   *leading his successors, George H. W. Bush and Bill Clinton, to raise them again.* Reagan essentially raised taxes a third time, closing corporate tax loopholes in 1986, and bringing in more corporate revenue overall. But that tax reform also lowered individual and corporate rates. See Anne Swardson, "Hill Conferees Approve Tax-Code Overhaul; Top Individual Rate Would be 28%," *Washington Post*, August 17, 1986, p. A-1. William G. Gale and Peter R. Orszag, "Bush Administration Tax Policy: Revenue and Budget Effects." *Tax Notes*, October 4, 2004, p. 114.

125   *in real terms between fiscal years 1985 and 1990.* Ibid.

125   *"Resign."* Robert Kagan and William Kristol, "No Defense," *Weekly Standard*, July 23, 2001. Viewed on February 3, 2006, at http://www.newamericancentury.org/ defense-20010723.pdf.

125   *still promising a balanced budget.* "You hear a lot of them talking in Washington about, 'Oh, the tax cut might cause a deficit.' No. What causes a deficit is too much spending. . . . They try to over-spend. . . . You'll have a president who will veto those budget-busting bills," vowed Bush in August 2001. See Glenn Kessler, "Administration Implements Accounting Change; Move Allocates $4 Billion for Additional Spending Without Dipping into Social Security Fund," *Washington Post*, August 16, 2001, p. A-10.

125   *"Real help for the military is not."* "Indefensible Defense Budget Policy," *Washington Post*, June 20, 2001, p. A-31.

125   *"only in the case of war, a recession, or a national emergency."* "President Bush Discusses New Economic Numbers and Middle East," April 26, 2002. Viewed on May 26, 2005, at http://www.whitehouse.gov/news/releases/2002/04/20020426.html.

126   *60 percent of the decline due to falling revenue.* In fact, while conservatives often blame excessive spending for the Bush administration's budget deficits, spending as a share of GDP is not particularly high compared to its average level between 1960 and 2000. Revenue as a share of GDP, on the other hand, *is* particularly low. See Alan J. Auerbach, William G. Gale, and Peter R. Orszag, "New Estimates of the

Budget Outlook," The Brookings Institution, February 2006, pp. 1–2. Viewed on March 20, 2006, at http://www.brookings.edu/views/papers/200602_iiep_galeorszag.pdf.

126   *"unjust spending enterprises—or risk national ruin."* Daniel Patrick Moynihan, *Came the Revolution: Argument in the Reagan Era*. New York: Harcourt Brace Jovanovich, 1988, p. 281.

126   *government spending did, in fact, go down.* Federal spending was 23.5 percent of GDP in 1983, at the deficit's height, but only 19.2 percent by 1998, the year the government turned a surplus.

126   *budget fell by more than half between 1986 and 2000.* Interview with the Brookings Institution's Peter Orszag, July 2005.

127   *"the nation's unsustainable fiscal path."* Leslie Wayne, "White House Tries to Trim Military Cost," *New York Times*, December 6, 2005, p. C-1.

127   *federal money for emergency responders.* Richard A. Clarke, Warren B. Rudman, and Jamie F. Metzel, "Emergency Responders: Drastically Underfunded, Dangerously Unprepared," Council on Foreign Relations, June 2003. Viewed on February 15, 2006, at http://www.cfr.org/content/publications/attachments/Responders_TF.pdf.

127   *wanting "gold-plated telephones."* Clarke, *Against All Enemies*, p. 260.

127   *emergency responder grants in 2006 by 25 percent.* "A Budget Plan with More Losers Than Winners," *Congressional Quarterly Weekly*, February 12, 2005.

127   *has provided just over one-seventh that amount.* "U.S. Port Grants Announced," *Lloyd's List*, September 20, 2005, p. 14.

127   *bombing that hit Madrid in March 2004.* "Testimony of the American Public Transport Association before the Subcommittee on Homeland Security of the House Committee on Appropriations," Public Transportation and Homeland Security, April 14, 2003. Viewed on December 19, 2005, at http://www.apta.com/government_affairs/apatest/testimony030414.cfm.

127   *"proposed by the administration"* Steven M. Kosiak, "Overview of the Administration's FY2006 Request for Homeland Security," Center for Strategic and Budgetary Assessments, May 3, 2005. Viewed on February 3, 2006, at http://www.csbaonline.org/4Publications/Archive/U.20050503.FY06HomelandSecBudget/U.20050503.FY06HomelandSecBudget.pdf.

128   *"the water's fine."* Peter Steinfels, *The Neoconservatives: The Men Who Are Changing America's Politics*. Carmichael, Calif.: Touchstone, 1980, p. 48.

128   *"not opponents, and only measured critics."* Irving Kristol, "American Conservatism, 1945–1995," *The Public Interest* (Fall 1995). Viewed on February 3, 2006, at http://www.thepublicinterest.com/notable/article2.html.

128   *"the labor movement was so staunchly anti-Communist."* Norman Podhoretz, "Neoconservatism: A Eulogy," *Commentary* 101 (3) (March 1996). Viewed on February 15, 2006, at http://www.questia.com/PM.qst?a=o&d=5000332127.

129   *"few traces of that difference remain visible today."* Ibid.

129   *"compound growth rate for our economic plant."* James Burnham, *Suicide of the West*, p. 23.

130   *"the will to survive."* Ibid., p. 24.

130 *"the exercise of power is legitimized."* David Brooks, "A Man on a Gray Horse," *The Atlantic Monthly*, September 2002. Viewed on February 15, 2006, at http://www.theatlantic.com/doc/200209/brooks.

130 *they remained independent of the USSR as well.* As John Lewis Gaddis writes, the Truman administration believed "that American interests—and global equilibrium generally—could best be served by the emergence of independent and self-confident centers of power overseas rather than spheres of influence subservient to Washington." See Gaddis, *Strategies of Containment*, pp. 63–64.

130 *hidden source of Moscow's weakness, and Washington's strength.* As Gaddis puts it, Kennan was fond of "what one might call an 'imperial analogue'—the idea that international communism, whatever its surface manifestations, in fact differed little from and was subject to many of the same self-destructive tendencies of classical imperialism." See Ibid., p. 47.

130 *"righteousness in our institutions and defending that."* Toulouse, *The Transformation of John Foster Dulles*, p. 191.

130 *a monopoly over nuclear weapons.* Daniel Kelley, *James Burnham and the Struggle for the World*, pp. 53–54. Burnham was not the only early cold war conservative to propose American empire. The British-born former Communist Freda Utley, in her 1947 book, *Last Chance in China*, called for a "new kind of world hegemony"—"a Pax Americana as the only alternative to a Communist totalitarian world or the destruction of civilized life through an atomic war." See Lora, "A View from the Right," in Griffith and Theoharis, *The Specter*, p. 51.

131 *even by unlimited power.* Daniel Kelley, *James Burnham and the Struggle for the World*, p. 54; Lora, "A View from the Right," in Griffith and Theoharis, *The Specter*, p. 53. Dulles made that assumption explicit, arguing that the United States' behavior at the United Nations had shown that it "had no lust for more power, but only a desire to safeguard institutions that respected human liberty." See Toulouse, *The Transformation of John Foster Dulles*, pp. 221–222.

131 *remove the "kick me" sign pinned to its back.* Ronald Reagan, "Remarks at the Conference Luncheon of the Women Business Owners of New York," April 5, 1984. Viewed on October 22, 2005, at http://www.reagan.utexas.edu/archives/soeeches/1984/40584a.htm.

131 *"struggle between right and wrong and good and evil."* Powers, *Not Without Honor*, pp. 408–409. In the speech, Reagan did say that "Our nation, too, has a legacy of evil with which it must deal. . . . We must never go back" to "racism, anti-Semitism, or other forms of ethnic and racial hatred." But Reagan was casting the nation's evil in the past, something we had left behind and must not return too. In the here and now, the United States was the "right" in right and wrong, and the "good" in good and evil. See John J. Pitney Jr., "The Man Who Called Out Evil," *National Review*. Viewed on October 10, 2005, at http://www.nationalreview.com/script/printpage.p?ref=/comment/pitney2004060809.asp.

131 *would go down in history as a great man.* Powers, *Not Without Honor*, p. 409. The speech had actually been written by a Buckley protégé, Tony Dolan. Interview with John B. Judis, August, 2005.

131   *seriously contemplated deploying American troops.* As Reagan put it in a 1986 speech, "For our own security, the United States must deny the Soviet Union a beach-head in North America. But let me make one thing plain: I'm not talking about American troops. They are not needed; they have not been requested." See "Address to the Nation on the Situation in Nicaragua," March 16, 1986. Viewed on December 19, 2005, at http://www.presidency.uscb.edu/ws/index .php?pid=36999.

132   *"build an international consensus on key issues."* "1992 Republican Party Platform."

132   *serving under foreign command.* "Republican Contract with America." Viewed on May 2, 2005, at http://www.house.gov/Contract/CONTRACT.html.

133   *could strike the United States and get away with it.* In fact, parallels between Carter's foreign policy and Clinton's had been a theme of neoconservative writing in the 1990s. In the summer of 1996, William Kristol and Robert Kagan wrote: "In a way, the current situation is reminiscent of the mid-1970s." On May 25, 1998, the *Weekly Standard* editorialized: "From where we sit, the present moment looks a lot like the late 1970s. . . . Bill Clinton's foreign policy has become the post–Cold War equivalent of Jimmy Carter's. . . . Where are the new 'Scoop' Jacksons and John Towers? And above all, who will be this era's Ronald Reagan?" See Kristol and Kagan, "Toward a Neo-Reaganite Foreign Policy"; "Clinton's Feckless Foreign Policy," *Weekly Standard*, May 25, 1998, p. 11.

133   *"he could, in fact, do so with impunity."* Ivo H. Daalder and James M. Lindsay, *America Unbound: The Bush Revolution in Foreign Policy*. Washington, D.C.: Brookings Institution Press, 2003, p. 84.

133   *guide to the Muslim world* In the months after 9/11, Lewis had a private dinner with Cheney, a private meeting with Rice, and at Karl Rove's request, addressed the National Security Council and White House staff. Journalist Ron Suskind noticed a copy of Lewis's *What Went Wrong?* on Karen Hughes's coffee table, and then-White House speechwriter David Frum saw Bush carrying a marked up copy of a Bernard Lewis article. See Peter Waldman, "Power and Peril: America's Supremacy and Its Limits," *Wall Street Journal*, February 3, 2004, p. A-1; Ron Suskind, "Mrs. Hughes Takes Her Leave," *Esquire Magazine*, July 2002. Viewed on February 3, 2006, at http://www.ronsuskind.com/newsitw/srticles/archives/000005.html; David Frum, *The Right Man: The Surprise Presidency of George W. Bush*. New York: Random House, 2003, p. 175.

133   *"in consequence, politically and militarily enfeebled."* Bernard Lewis, *The Crisis of Islam: Holy War and Unholy Terror*. New York: Modern Library, 2003, p. 63.

133   *"encouraging a paralysis of the moral faculty"* Bennett, *Why We Fight*, p. 62.

133   *"intellectual and moral defenses as much as our physical ones."* Ibid., p. 22.

133   *America's supposed opponents in the terror war.* David Frum, the Bush speechwriter who helped conceive the words *axis of evil*, later wrote: "With his 'axis of evil' speech, President Bush served notice to the world: He felt no guilt and no self-doubt." See Frum, *The Right Man*, pp. 238, 244.

134   *"a repudiation of moral relativism."* Podhoretz, "World War IV."

135   *"arrogate the same authority to themselves."* Rice, "Promoting the National Interest."

135   *the houses no longer had locks.* John Ikenberry, "A Liberal Leviathan," *Prospect*, October
       23, 2004. Viewed on February 3, 2006, at http://ftp.cc.utexas.edu/lbj/news/
       fall2004/Ikenberry_article.pdf.
135   *"America was pure."* Schlesinger, *The Crisis of Confidence*, p. 149.
135   *"I know how good we are."* Daalder and Lindsay, *America Unbound*, p. 194.
135   *"the goodness of their good hearts."* Peggy Noonan, "Way Too Much God," *Wall Street
       Journal*, January 21, 2005, p. A-8.
135   *"out of the closet on the word empire"* Emily Eakin, "All Roads Lead to DC," *New York
       Times*, March 31, 2002, p. D-4.
136   *adjective like "liberal" or "benign."* See, for instance, Max Boot's articles, "The Case for
       American Empire," *Weekly Standard*, October 15, 2001. Viewed on February 3, 2006,
       at http://www.weeklystandard.com/Utilities/printer_previewasp?idArticle
       =318. And "Neither New nor Nefarious: The Liberal Empire Strikes Back,"
       Current History 12 (667) (November 2003). Viewed on February 3, 2006, at
       http://www.mtholyoke.edu/acad/intrel/bush/boot.htm.
136   *"impairment of bodily function, or even death."* Noah Feldman, "The Laws of a War
       Against Evil: Ugly Americans," *The New Republic*, May 30, 2005. Viewed on May 5,
       2005, at http://www/tnr.com/docprint.mhtml?i=20050530&s=feldman053005.
136   *"ghost detainees"* Josh White, "Army Documents Shed Light on the CIA 'Ghosting':
       Systematic Concealment of Detainees Is Found," *Washington Post*, March 24, 2005,
       p. A-15. Conservatives sometimes argued that they opposed only international
       constraints, that U.S. policies should be regulated internally, through the
       democratic process. But in fact, Justice Department lawyers argued that President
       Bush's authority as commander in chief in a time of war exempted him from
       even *American* antitorture laws. And in its conduct of the war on terror, the Bush
       administration has resisted oversight from Congress and the press as fiercely as
       it has resisted oversight from abroad. See Feldman, "Ugly Americans"; David
       Cole, "What Bush Wants to Hear," *New York Review of Books* 52 (18) (November
       17, 2005). Viewed on December 13, 2005, at http://www.nybooks.com/articles/
       18431.
136   *as ordained by God.* In fact, as Gerard P. Fogarty has noted, the military tribunals the
       Bush administration instituted for Guantánamo Bay detainees "are the exact types
       of trials that the United States openly condemns in the international community."
       See Gerard P. Fogerty, "Is Guantanamo Bay Undermining the Global War on
       Terror?" *Parameters*, Autumn 2005. Viewed on October 21, 2005, at http://www
       .carlisle.army.mil/usawc/Paramenters/05autumn/fogarty.htm.
136   *"promotes freedom around the world."* "Bush: Amnesty Report 'absurd,' " CNN.
       com, May 31, 2005. Viewed on May 31, 2005, at http://www.cnn.com/2005/
       POLITICS/05/31/bush.newsconference.ap.
137   *"the war against the war."* Matt Welch, "Who's Tortured? What Prominent
       Conservative Commentators Have Said About Prisoner Abuse," *Reason*, Decem-
       ber 27, 2004. Viewed on May 20, 2005, at http://www.rppi.org/phprint.php.
137   *preserving corrupt oil deals with Saddam.* In their book, *Allies at War*, Philip H.
       Gordon and Jeremy Shapiro debunk that argument, noting that, in reality,

French and German trade with Iraq was minuscule. See Gordon and Shapiro, *Allies at War: America, Europe, and the Crisis over Iraq*. New York: McGraw-Hill, 2004, pp. 77–78.

137   *"no real material or military assistance."* Hanson, "War Myths," in Hanson, *An Autumn of War*, p. 17.

137   *"friends and allies were prepared to do little."* David Frum and Richard Perle, *An End to Evil*. New York: Random House, 2003, p. 235.

137   *"Resentment comes with the territory"* Gordon and Shapiro, *Allies at War*, p. 51.

138   *the United States was viewed favorably* "Global Opinion: The Spread of Anti-Americanism," The Pew Research Center for the People and the Press, January 24, 2005. Viewed on February 10, 2006, at http://people-press.org/commentary/display.php3?AnalysisID=104.

138   *a breathtaking 60 points in Indonesia* Ibid.

138   *"hostility toward America has reached shocking levels."* Thomas Carothers, "Democracy: Terrorism's Uncertain Antidote," *Current History*, December 2003, p. 404.

138   *Washington doesn't listen to their governments.* "A Year After Iraq War: Mistrust of America in Europe Even Higher, Muslim Anger Persists," Pew Research Center for the People and the Press, March 16, 2004. Viewed on February 3, 2006, at http://people-press.org/reports/print.php3?PageID=796.

138   *"openly skeptical of its word."* "Global Opinion," p. 106.

139   *constrained by the hostility of their publics.* As the German newspaper *Der Spiegel* noted when Secretary of State Condoleezza Rice arrived for a December 2005 meeting with Merkel, in the midst of reports that the United States had abducted suspected terrorists from European soil and sent them abroad for torture, "Washington has long since lost the battle for hearts and minds of many Europeans. In Germany and elsewhere, America is simply no longer given the benefit of the doubt." See Marc Young, "Losing European Hearts and Minds," Spiegel Online, December 6, 2005. Viewed on December 17, 2005, at http://service.spiegel.de/cache/international/0,1518,druck-388917,00.html.

139   *largely lost its ability to persuade.* In fact, in a September 2004 report, the Bush administration itself admitted that "America's power to persuade is in a state of crisis." See "Defense Science Board Task Force on Strategic Communication," Office of the Under Secretary of Defense, September 2004, p. 14.

139   *overthrow governments across the Middle East.* Scheuer, *Imperial Hubris*, pp. 198–199.

139   *outside power are more likely to support terrorism.* C. Christine Fair and Bryan Shepherd, "Who Supports Terrorism? Evidence from Fourteen Muslim Countries," *Studies in Conflict and Terrorism* 29 (2006). Viewed on February 15, 2006, at http://www.foreignpolicy.com/story/cms.php?story_id=3359&fpsrc=ealert060130.

139   *religion is under attack from the United States* "Global Opinion," p. 110.

139   *popular largely* because *it opposes the United States* Shibley Telhami and James Steinberg, "Fighting Binladenism," Saban Center for Middle East Policy, Brookings Institution, March 25, 2003. Viewed on February 3, 2006, at http://www.brookings.edu/fp/saban/analysis/20050325roadahead.pdf.

140 *"while it opens Guantánamo camps."* Marina Ottaway, "Promoting Democracy in the Middle East," Carnegie Endowment for International Peace, pp. 12–13.

140 *"reform is to claim that it is pro-American."* Fareed Zakaria, "The Good, the Bad, the Ugly," *Newsweek* (May 31, 2004), p. 33.

Chapter 6: Iraq

141 *planned and implemented the war.* The Iraq war is often associated not with conservatism in general, but with neoconservatism. But that, as *National Review*'s Ramesh Ponnuru has noted, is "an odd assertion. If it were true, it would mean that the conquest of Iraq was a distinctively neoconservative rather than a conservative project. Thus unhyphenated conservatives who supported it—and almost everyone who considers himself a conservative did support it—had either absorbed the neocon premises or had, as the cabal-mongers say, been hoodwinked. It's worth remembering that right-wing opponents of the first Gulf War in 1990–91 said that it, too, was a neocon war. Support for the war on the right was much more uniform this time. Yet for some reason the claim that the war reflected the priorities of a small faction within the Right has gotten more credence than it did a decade ago." See Ramesh Ponnuru, "Getting to the Bottom of this 'Neo' Nonsense: Before You Talk About Conservatives, Know What You're Doing," *National Review* June 16, 2003. Viewed on February 15, 2006, at http://www .findarticles.com/p/articles/mi_m1282/is_11_55/ai_102540273.

141 *superpowers so fearsome suddenly seemed less useful.* The influential liberal international relations theorist Stanley Hoffmann commented on "the increasingly obvious irrelevance of military power to most of the goals pursued by states." Similarly, Paul Warnke, soon to become George McGovern's chief foreign policy adviser, and Les Gelb, then a visiting professor at Georgetown, argued that "Perhaps the principal lesson of the past decade is that military force is a singularly inept instrument of foreign policy." See Joshua Muravchik, "The Strange Debate Over Bosnia," *Commentary* 14 (5) (November 1992), p. 33.

141 *government could achieve as much on its own.* See, for instance, Robert Keohane and Joseph Nye, eds., *Transnational Relations and World Politics*. Cambridge, Mass.: Harvard University Press, 1972; Robert O. Keohane and Joseph Nye, *Power and Interdependence*. Boston: Little, Brown and Co, 1977, as well as Stanley Hoffmann, *Primacy or World Order*. New York: McGraw-Hill, 1978. The theory has also been called "complex interdependence" or "global society." See Ole R. Holsti, "Models of International Relations and Foreign Policy," in G. John Ikenberry, ed., *American Foreign Policy: Theoretical Essays*, 4th ed. London: Longman, 2004, p. 19.

142 *potential great power rapidly building up its arsenal.* For an example of this concern, see Ross Munro and Richard Bernstein, *The Coming Conflict with China*. New York: Knopf, 1997.

142 *the greatest challenge to post–cold war America.* Charles Krauthammer, "The Unipolar

Moment," *Foreign Affairs: America and the World* 70 (5) (1990/1991). Viewed on February 15, 2006, at http://www.foreignaffairs.org/19910201faessay6067/charles-krauthammer/the-unipolar-moment.html.

143   *"development of weapons of mass destruction."* Rice, "Promoting the National Interest."

143   *"the 1993 attack on New York, not without a state sponsor."* Clarke, *Against All Enemies*, pp. 231–232.

143   *bombed the World Trade Center in 1993 without a state sponsor.* The 9/11 Commission would later agree that Iraq was not involved. See National Commission on Terrorist Attacks, *The 9/11 Commission Report*, p. 559.

143   *the greater terrorist threat: Saddam Hussein.* Clarke, *Against All Enemies*, pp. 237–238.

143   *investigate an Iraqi connection.* Woodward, *Plan of Attack*, p. 25.

143   *carried out with state assistance.* Clarke, *Against All Enemies*, p. 30.

143   *"those who support terrorism, then we get at states."* Bob Woodward, *Bush at War*, p. 43.

143   *no evidence Saddam was behind 9/11.* Bob Woodward, *Bush at War*, pp. 84–85; Gordon and Shapiro, *Allies at War*, p. 95; National Commission on Terrorist Attacks, *The 9/11 Commission Report*, p. 335.

143   *"I believe Iraq was involved"* Clarke, *Against All Enemies*, pp. 30, 33; Woodward, *Bush at War*, p. 99.

143   *"periods of time to do large-scale operations"* Daalder and Lindsay, *America Unbound*, p. 85.

144   *"increasingly self-sufficient."* "Mapping the Global Future," p. 94.

144   *"we will fail."* "Defense Science Board Task Force on Strategic Communication," September 2004. Viewed on February 6, 2006, at http://www.acq.osd.mil/dsb/reports/2004-09-Strategic_Communication.pdf.

144   *the prospect of a rogue state giving terrorists WMD* In late 2004, when Senate Foreign Relations Committee chairman Richard Lugar asked eighty-five national security and nonproliferation experts how terrorists were most likely to acquire a nuclear weapon, far more predicted a black market purchase than predicted a transfer or sale by a state. See Lugar, "The Lugar Survey on Proliferation Threats and Responses," p. 16.

144   *"the world's most destructive weapons."* "President Delivers State of the Union Address," January 29, 2002. Viewed on February 15, 2006, at http://www.whitehouse.gov/news/releases/2002/01/20020129-11.html.

144   *"the word 'terrorism' entirely disappeared."* William Kristol, "Taking the War Beyond Terrorism," *Washington Post*, January 31, 2002, p. A-25. Over the following year, Bush went further, saying explicitly that Iraq was a greater danger than Al Qaeda. "We are hunting down Al Qaeda one-by-one," he informed members of Congress in a September 2002 meeting, according to Bob Woodward. "The biggest threat, however, is Saddam Hussein and his weapons of mass destruction." In his 2003 State of the Union address, Bush declared that "the gravest danger in the war on terror, the gravest danger facing America and the world, is outlaw regimes that seek and possess nuclear, chemical and biological weapons." And on February 26, 2003, he told the American Enterprise Institute that, "we are opposing the greatest danger in the war on terror, outlaw regimes arming with weapons of mass destruction." See Woodward, *Plan of Attack*, p. 186; Joseph Cirincione

et al., "WMD in Iraq: Evidence and Implications," Carnegie Endowment for International Peace (January 2004). Viewed on February 15, 2006, at http://www.carnegieendowment.org/files/Iraq3FullText.pdf; "President Bush Discusses the Future of Iraq," February 26, 2003. Viewed on June 21, 2005, at http://www.whitehouse.gov/news/releases/2003/02/print/20030226-11.

145 *"boxer who refuses to throw a punch."* Goldwater, *The Conscience of a Conservative*, p. 94.

145 *while there was still time.* Lora, "A View from the Right," in Griffith and Theoharis, *The Specter*, p. 58; Scott A. Silverman, "Can Democracies Initiate Preventive War? America's Confrontation with the Soviet Union and Iraq." Paper presented at the International Studies Association Annual Convention, February 2003, p. 17.

145 *the Eisenhower administration's refusal to intervene.* Judis, *Grand Illusion*, p. 156.

145 *seriously underestimating Soviet military strength.* Albert Wohlstetter, "Is There a Strategic Arms Race?" *Foreign Policy* 15 (Summer 1974); "Rivals but No 'Race,' " *Foreign Policy* 16 (Fall 1974); "Spreading the Bomb Without Quite Breaking the Rules," *Foreign Policy* 25 (Winter 1976/1977); "How to Confuse Ourselves," *Foreign Policy* 20 (Fall 1975); Fred Kaplan, *The Wizards of Armageddon*. New York: Simon & Schuster, 1983, p. 95.

145 *seeking "global Soviet hegemony."* Mann, *Rise of the Vulcans*, pp. 73–74; Hodgson, *The World Turned Right Side Up*, p. 234.

146 *"deadening accommodation with totalitarian evil?"* Ronald Reagan, "Address to Members of the British Parliament," June 8, 1982. Viewed on October 31, 2005, at http://usa.embassy.de/etexts/speeches/empire.htm.

146 *undermine Communist control in Poland.* Norman Podhoretz, "The First Term: The Reagan Road to Détente," *Foreign Affairs, America and the World* (1984). Viewed on February 23, 2006, at http://www.foreignaffairs.org/19850201faessay8415/norman-podhoretz/the-first-term-the-reagan-road-to-detente.html.

146 *"calculated a great deal and risked nothing."* Ibid.

146 *"shamed the oppressors, and ended an evil empire."* "Remarks by the Vice President at the Ronald Reagan Library and Museum," March 17, 2004. Viewed on November 4, 2005, at http://www.whitehouse.gov/news/releases/2004/03/20040317-3.html.

146 *"weapons on missiles or secretly provide them to terrorist allies."* "President Bush Delivers Graduation Speech at West Point," June 1, 2002. Viewed on November 5, 2005, at http://www.whitehouse.gov/news/releases/2002/06/print/20020601-3.html. As the *Wall Street Journal*'s Robert Bartley commented after Bush's West Point speech, "No talk of this ilk has been heard from American leaders since John Foster Dulles talked of rolling back the Iron Curtain." See Robert L. Bartley, "At Dawn in a New Diplomatic Era," *Wall Street Journal*, June 17, 2002. Viewed on November 9, 2005, at http://www.opinionjournal.com/forms/printthis.html?id=1100018554.

147 *"Old doctrines of security do not apply."* Gordon and Shapiro, *Allies at War*, p. 99.

147 *"presented as sanctified intelligence judgments."* Spencer Ackerman and Franklin Foer, "The Radical," *The New Republic*, December 1–8, 2003. Viewed on February 23, 2006, at http://www.tnr.com/doc.mhtml?pt=xGmMghBV8jodL8t7x2Vig2%3D%3D.

147 *"gain even a hint of the Sept. 11 attack"* Richard Perle, "The U.S. Must Strike at Saddam Hussein," *New York Times*, December 28, 2001, p. A-19.

147 *"linkages does not mean they don't exist."* Clarke, *Against All Enemies*, p. 232.

147   *"almost always underestimate capabilities," claimed Condoleezza Rice.* Nicholas Lemann,
      "Without a Doubt," *The New Yorker,* October 14, 2002. Viewed on February 20,
      2006, at http://newyorker.com/fact/content/articles/021014fa_fact3.

148   *"the catastrophic point of view."* James Burnham, *The Coming Defeat of Communism.*
      Princeton, N.J.: John Day Company, 1950, p. 12.

148   *"reason to assume the worst"* "Q: Does Saddam Hussein and His Regime Pose a
      Threat to the United States and Its Allies." Viewed on June 17, 2005, at http://
      www.usiraqprocon.org/bin/procon/procon.cgi?database=5-A.

148   *"Time is not on our side"* "Vice President Speaks at VFW 103rd National Convention,"
      August 26, 2002. Viewed on June 21, 2005, at http://www.whitehouse.gov/news/
      releases/2002/08/print/20020826.html.

148   *weapons of mass destruction—had collapsed.* As the Carnegie Endowment's Joseph
      Cirincione, Jessica T. Mathews, George Perkovich, and Alexis Orton note in
      WMD in Iraq: Evidence and Implications, "the definitive voice of U.S. policy—the
      president's—was unequivocal that the reason for going to war was the present
      threat to U.S. security posed by Iraq's WMD. From Mr. Bush's first detailed case
      for the war on October 7, 2002, to the declaration of war on March 17, 2003,
      the purpose is always clear: 'Saddam must disarm himself—or for the sake of
      peace, we will lead a coalition to disarm him.' Other than warnings addressed to
      the Iraqi military and reassurances to the American people regarding homeland
      security, the declaration of war address was *only* about WMD until the closing
      paragraphs, which touched on human liberty and a better future for the Iraqi
      people." See Cirincione et al., "WMD in Iraq."

149   *"this time armed by Saddam Hussein."* Ibid.

149   *"continuing ties to terrorist networks"* Ibid.

149   *"a collaborative operational relationship."* National Commission on Terrorist Attacks,
      The 9/11 Commission Report, p. 66.

149   *"links [that Al Qaeda had] with other regimes."* Clarke, *Against All Enemies,* p. 270.

150   *"list of state sponsors of terrorism, Iraq is pretty far down."* Kenneth M. Pollack, *The
      Threatening Storm: The Case for Invading Iraq,* 1st ed. New York: Random House,
      2002, p. 153.

150   *Tehran's ground offensives in the Iran-Iraq war.* Comprehensive Report of the Special
      Advisor to the DCI on Iraq's WMD, September 30, 2004. Viewed on February 6,
      2006, at http://www.cia.gov/cia/reports/iraq_wmd_2004/.

151   *"weapons-usable nuclear material of any practical significance."* Cirincione et al., "WMD
      in Iraq."

151   *the inspectors left* Pollack, *The Threatening Storm,* p. 174. U.S. intelligence had relied
      heavily on the inspectors for information about Iraq's nuclear and other weapons
      programs, and when they were expelled, the impact was dramatic. As Kenneth
      Pollack puts it, "The end of the inspections eliminated the single best means of
      vetting what information intelligence agencies could gather independently about
      Iraq. . . . When the inspectors suddenly left, the various intelligence agencies were
      caught psychologically and organizationally off balance." In the words of David
      Kay, who led the initial U.S. investigation into Saddam's WMD programs after the

war, "UNSCOM was like crack cocaine for the CIA. . . . They could see something from a satellite or other technical intelligence, and then direct the inspectors to go look at it." See Kenneth M. Pollack, "Spies, Lies, and Weapons: What Went Wrong," *Atlantic Monthly,* January/February 2004. Viewed on October 31, 2005, at http://www.theatlantic.com/doc/print/200401/pollack; James Risen, "Ex-Inspector Says C.I.A. Missed Disarray in Iraqi Arms Program," *New York Times,* January 26, 2004, p. A-1.

151 *"associated with its nuclear program."* Cirincione et al. "WMD in Iraq."

151 *"will have a nuclear weapon during this decade."* "Iraq's Weapons of Mass Destruction Programs," National Intelligence Estimate, October 2002. Viewed on February 6, 2006, at http://www.cia.gov/cia/reports/iraq_wmd/Iraq_Oct_2002.htm; Cirincione et al., "WMD in Iraq." The Senate Select Committee on Intelligence received the NIE at 10 p.m. on October 1; the House voted on October 10, and the Senate voted the next morning.

151 *intelligence agencies considered such a purchase highly unlikely.* Cirincione et al., "WMD in Iraq"; Pollack, "Spies, Lies, and Weapons."

151 *some other governments seemed to agree.* In particular, press reports in 2001 suggested that German intelligence believed Saddam was three to six years away from a nuclear weapon. See Pollack, *The Threatening Storm,* p. 175.

152 *the only concrete evidence cited.* The only other evidence that the unclassified NIE presented for its claim that Saddam had reconstituted his nuclear program was meetings he had held with nuclear scientists, and his failure to fully comply with past inspections. The NIE also obliquely acknowledged that not all agencies agreed that the tubes were meant for a nuclear program. In fact, the Department of Energy—which had the greatest expertise on the issue—believed they were designed for conventional rockets. See "Iraq's Weapons of Mass Destruction Programs," NIE, October 2002, pp. 1, 5–6; Cirincione et al., "WMD in Iraq"; "Q: Did Saddam Hussein Try to Acquire Aluminum Tubes for the Purpose of Uranium Enrichment?" Viewed on June 17, 2005, at http://www.usiraqprocon .org/bin/procon/procon.cgi?database=5-B.

152 *insisting the tubes were meant for conventional rockets.* "Q: Did Saddam Hussein Try to Acquire Aluminum Tubes."

152 *purchase weapons-grade uranium from Africa.* Cirincione et al., "WMD in Iraq."

152 *"no indication of resumed nuclear activities"* On January 27, 2003, IAEA Chief Mohamed ElBaradei reported to the UN that "In support of the International Atomic Energy Agency inspections to date, the Iraqi authorities have provided access to all facilities visited, including presidential compounds and private residents, without conditions and without delay. The Iraqi authorities also have been cooperative in making available additional original documentations in response to requests by IAEA inspectors." On March 7, 2003, ElBaradei told the UN, "I should note that in the past three weeks, possibly as a result of ever-increasing pressure by the international community, Iraq has been forthcoming in its cooperation, particularly with regard to the conduct of private interviews and in making available evidence that could contribute to the resolution of matters of

IAEA concern." See "Mohamed ElBaradei Report to the U.N. January 27, 2003. Viewed on February 6, 2006, at http://www.pbs.org/newshour/bb/middle_east/iraq/elbaradei_report.html; "Transcript of ElBaradei's U.N. presentation," March 7, 2003. Viewed on February 6, 2006, at http://www.cnn.com/2003/US/03/07/sprj.irq.un.transcript.elbaradei/.

153   *"industrial capacity has deteriorated substantially."* Cirincione et al., "WMD in Iraq."

153   *"most susceptible to nonproliferation techniques."* Ibid.

154   *tyrannies often look indestructible before they self-destruct.* In fact, Kenneth Pollack would later speculate that one reason Saddam never acknowledged his lack of WMD was that he feared doing so might threaten his hold on power. And although it would have been hard to know at the time, it is possible continued inspections could have done just that. After leading the postwar investigation into Saddam's WMD, David Kay commented in 2004 that the regime had been weaker than commonly recognized. "The regime was no longer in control," he told the *New York Times.* "It was like a death spiral." See Pollack, "Spies, Lies, and Weapons"; Peter Grier, "From Iraq to Libya, U.S. Knew Little on Weapons," *Christian Science Monitor,* January 27, 2004. Viewed on December 21, 2005, at http://www.csmonitor.com/2004/0127/p01s01-usfp.htm.

154   *"figure out what kind of government that country ought to have."* Woodward, *Bush at War,* p. 220.

155   *"we're very much on similar wavelengths."* Ackerman and Foer, "The Radical."

155   *"strategic idea, of liberation rather than occupation."* Warren Strobel and John Walcott, "Post War Planning Non-Existent," Knight Ridder, October 17, 2004. Viewed on February 23, 2006, at http://www.realcities.com/mld/krwashington/9927782.htm?template=; George Packer, *The Assassin's Gate: America in Iraq.* New York: Farrar, Straus, and Giroux, 2005, pp. 29–30.

155   *"Iraq is unique."* Fred Barnes, "The UN's Iraq Power Grab," *Weekly Standard,* April 6, 2003. Viewed on February 6, 2006, at http://www.weeklystandard.com/Content/Public/Articles/000/000/002/507kznvg.asp.

155   *"no relevant experience to draw on"* Sam Tanenhaus, "Bush's Brain Trust," p. 114.

155   *sixty years after the war's conclusion.* Jonathan Weisman and Mike Allen, "Officials Argue for Fast U.S. Exit From Iraq," *Washington Post,* April 21, 2003, p. A-1.

155   *postwar reconstruction were told to bring two suits.* Daalder and Lindsey, *America Unbound,* p. 152.

155   *U.S. troops would be mostly gone by fall.* Douglas Porch, "Occupational Hazards: Myths of 1945 and U.S. Iraq Policy," *The National Interest,* Summer 2003. Viewed on February 15, 2006, at http://www.findarticles.com/p/articles/mi_m2751/is_72/ai_105369894; George Packer, "War After the War: What Washington Doesn't See in Iraq," *The New Yorker,* November 24, 2003. Viewed on February 16, 2006, at http://www.newyorker.com/fact/content/?031124fa_fact1.

156   *didn't involve democracy building.* John H. Kelly, "Lebanon: 1982–1984." Viewed on November 7, 2005, at http://www.rand.org/publications/CF/CF129/CF-129.chapter6.html; Reagan did send troops to overthrow a leftist government in Grenada, but they stayed for only two months. See "Operation Urgent Fury,"

globalsecurity.org. Viewed on November 7, 2005, at http://www.globalsecurity
.org/military/ops/urgent_fury.htm.

156 *at most, offering them U.S. air support.* Richard N. Perle, "Iraq: Saddam Unbound,"
in Robert Kagan and William Kristol, eds., *Present Dangers: Crisis and Opportunity
in American Foreign and Defense Policy.* New York: Encounter Books, 2000, p. 109.
"I changed my view after 9/11," said Paul Wolfowitz in 2005. "Contrary to the
myth that I have been waiting all along for an excuse to invade Iraq, before then I
really didn't want to even think about sending in U.S. ground forces. I had always
thought the idea of occupying Baghdad was both unnecessary and a mistake.
What was needed was to arm and train the Iraqis to do the job themselves—
the way, in effect, the Afghans did." See Mark Bowden, "Wolfowitz: The Exit
Interviews," *Atlantic Monthly*, July/August 2005. Viewed on June 21, 2005, at
http://www.theatlantic.com/doc/print/200507/bowden.

156 *"a strategic as well as a moral mistake."* Paul Wolfowitz, "Statesmanship in the
New Century," in Kagan and Kristol, *Present Dangers*, p. 323. In the same essay,
Wolfowitz wrote that "it is no surprise that the use of the American military to
build a democracy there [in Haiti] has been an expensive failure. Oddly, we seem
to have forgotten what Vietnam should have taught us about the limitations of
the military as an instrument of 'nation building.' " Another neoconservative, the
American Enterprise Institute's Joshua Muravchik, put it even more explicitly, in
a November 3, 1999, *Wall Street Journal* op-ed entitled "Apply the Reagan Doctrine
to Iraq." See Wolfowitz, "Statesmanship in the New Century," in Kagan and
Kristol, *Present Dangers*, p. 320; Joshua Muravchik, "Apply the Reagan Doctrine
to Iraq," American Enterprise Institute for Public Policy Research, January 1,
2000. Viewed on November 4, 2005, at http://www.aei.org/include/pub_print
.sap?pubID=11044.

156 *accompany American soldiers as they overthrew Saddam.* Jeffrey Goldberg, "A Little
Learning: What Douglas Feith Knew, and When He Knew It," *The New Yorker*,
May 9, 2005. Viewed on February 16, 2006, at http://www.newyorker.com/fact/
content/articles/050509fa_fact; Seymour M. Hersh, "The Iraq Hawks: Can
Their War Plan Work?" *The New Yorker*, December 24, 2001, p. 58. George Packer
quotes a Defense Department official saying, "Rummy and Wolfowitz and Feith
did not believe the US would need to run post-conflict Iraq. Their plan was to
turn it over to these exiles very quickly and let them deal with the messes that
came up." See Packer, "War After the War."

156 *(one-tenth as many as the Army initially proposed).* Strobel and Walcott, "Post War
Planning Non-Existent."

157 *"return to Reaganite principles of adopting opposition movements."* Robert Kagan,
"The Bush Doctrine Unfolds," *Weekly Standard*, March 4, 2002. Viewed on
November 4, 2005, at http://www.carnegieendowment.org/publications/index
.cfm?fa=print&is=930.

157 *"single surviving model of human progress."* "President Bush Delivers Graduation
Speech at West Point."

157 *and liberal democracy had won.* Francis Fukuyama, "The End of History," *The National*

Interest, Summer 1989. Viewed on November 8, 2005, at http://www.marion
.ohiostate.edu/fac/vsteffel/web597/Fukuyama_history.pdf.

157 *"trying to remove the shackles on democracy."* Bowden, "Wolfowitz," p. 2.

157 *"free to live their lives and do wonderful things."* James Fallows, "Blind into Baghdad,"
Atlantic Monthly, January/February 2004. Viewed on June 5, 2005, at http://www
.theatlantic.com/doc/print/200401/fallows.

157 *"to make of this bizarre conception."* Kanan Makiya, "The Wasteland," *The New
Republic*, May 5, 2003. Viewed on February 6, 2006, at http://www.tnr.com/doc
.mhtml?i=20030505&s=makiya050503.

158 *might prove the greatest challenge.* "There has been major looting in every important
post-conflict situation of the past decade," noted former State Department official
Robert Perito. "It was entirely predictable that in the absence of any authority
in Baghdad that you'd have chaos and lawlessness," concurred Feisal Istrabadi,
an exile who worked on the Future of Iraq Project, a prewar State Department
planning effort that the Bush administration largely ignored. "The looting was not
a surprise," added Sandra Mitchell, vice president of the International Rescue
Committee, who met with Bush officials in the run-up to war. "Anyone who has
witnessed the fall of a regime while another force is coming in on a temporary
basis knows that looting is standard procedure." See David Rieff, "Blueprint for
a Mess," *New York Times*, November 2, 2003. Viewed on February 24, 2006, at
http://select.nytimes.com/search/restricted/article?res=F7071FF83A550C718
CDDA80994DB404482

158 *"into Phase IV in the absence of guidance."* Rieff, "Blueprint for a Mess"; Tony Perry and
Geoffrey Mohan, "US Invades 'Heart of Baghdad'; Army and Marine Columns
Meeting Little Resistance in Rapid Advance," *Los Angeles Times*, April 5, 2003, p. 1.

158 *"we were not a serious force."* Packer, "War After the War."

158 *U.S. forces were already averaging thirteen a day.* Daalder and Lindsay, *America Unbound*,
p. 155.

158 *"strategic mistake that led to the insurgency."* Anthony H. Cordesman, "Iraq's Evolving
Insurgency." Working draft, Center for Strategic and International Studies, May
16, 2005, p. 3.

159 *"capability to do anything about it anyway."* Daalder and Lindsay, *America Unbound*,
p. 136.

159 *"there are workarounds"* Mann, *Rise of the Vulcans*, pp. 354–355.

159 *"The real problem is their irrelevance."* Charles Krauthammer, "The Axis of Petulance,"
Washington Post, March 1, 2002, p. A-25.

159 *deemed ideologically suspect.* Larry Diamond, *Squandered Victory: The American Occupation
and the Bungled Effort to Bring Democracy to Iraq*. New York: Times Books, 2005, pp.
35, 30; Packer, "War After the War." As a Center for Strategic and International
Studies report put it, Coalition Provisional Authority staffers were "often chosen
on the basis of political and ideological vetting, rather than experience and
competence." The *Washington Post*'s Anthony Shadid writes that the CPA's "staff
had been chosen more for their partisan loyalty than for diplomatic skills suited to
the management of an occupation of one of the Middle East's most strategically
important countries. . . . Their political trustworthiness was unquestionable—most

were enthusiastic Republicans—but their experience was woefully lacking." See Cordesman, "Iraq's Evolving Insurgency," p. 4; Anthony Shadid, *Night Draws Near: Iraq's People in the Shadow of America's War*. New York: Henry Holt, 2005, p. 260.

159 *"Who is this person?"* Diamond, *Squandered Victory*, p. 35.

160 *unaccustomed to doing nation building on their own.* Interview with Kenneth Pollack, December 2005.

160 *"winning wars is not easier that way, but winning the peace is."* "Tony Blair's Speech to the U.S. Congress," July 18, 2003. Viewed on June 25, 2005, at http://www.guardian .co.uk/print/0,3858,4714986—103550,00.html.

160 *any reinforcements would have helped.* In an April 2004 memo to Condoleezza Rice, for instance, Larry Diamond, a senior adviser to the Coalition Provisional Authority, wrote: "In my weeks in Iraq, I did not meet a single military officer who felt, privately, that we had enough troops. Many felt we needed (and need) tens of thousands more soldiers." See Diamond, *Squandered Victory*, pp. 241–242.

160 *"That means medicine. That means aid."* Richard W. Stevenson, "A Nation at War: The President; Bush Sees Aid Role of UN as Limited in Rebuilding Iraq," *New York Times*, April 9, 2003, p. A-1.

160 *"going to implement it, regardless of what the UN thought."* Diamond, *Squandered Victory*, p. 56.

160 *former members promptly became insurgents.* Fallows, "Blind into Baghdad"; Diamond, *Squandered Victory*, p. 39. As the Army War College Study put it, "To tear apart the [Iraqi] Army in the war's aftermath could lead to the destruction of one of the only forces for unity within the society. Breaking up large elements of the army also raises the possibility that demobilized soldiers could affiliate with ethnic or tribal militias." See Conrad C. Crane and W. Andrew Terrill, "Reconstructing Iraq: Insights, Challenges, and Missions for Military Forces in a Post-Conflict Scenario," Army War College Study, February 2003, p. 32.

161 *"That's the 24 million Iraqis."* Reuel Marc Gerecht, "Help Not Wanted," *Weekly Standard*, August 18, 2003. Viewed on February 6, 2006, at http://www .weeklystandard.com/Content/Public/Articles/000/000/002/973dbqks.asp.

161 *"sympathetic to Saddam Hussein's regime."* Ibid.

161 *"impressions of this international body."* Ibrahim Al-Marashi and Katherine Durlacker, "Iraqi Perceptions of UK and American Policy in Post-Saddam Iraq," Nathan Hale Foreign Policy Society Policy Background and Options Paper. Viewed on February 6, 2006, at http://www.foreignpolicysociety.org/iraq.pdf. This comports with an August 2003 poll by Zogby International, which found that 50 percent of Iraqis predicted the United States would "hurt" their country over the next five years, while only 36 percent said it would "help." For the UN, however, 50 percent said "help," while only 18 percent said "hurt." See "Zogby International Survey of Iraq August 2003." Viewed on February 6, 2006, at http://www.taemag.com/ docLib/20030905_IraqpollFrequencies.pdf.

161 *"what do you expect people to think?"* Rieff, "Blueprint for a Mess"; Packer, *The Assassin's Gate*, pp. 78–79.

162 *"to rob Iraq's oil."* Diamond, *Squandered Victory*, p. 26.

162 *"driving decisions we were trying to impose."* Ibid., p. 333.

163   *"anticipated war on Iraq is part of the price."* "Weekly Arab Press Review," ArabiaLink,
       January 6–12, 2003. Viewed on February 16, 2006, at http://www.arabialink
       .com/Archive/GWVoices/GWV2003/GWV_WAPR_2003_01_06.htm.

163   *"how regimes are overthrown in the 21st century."* Ibid. For other examples, see Ahmed
       Bahjat in *Al Ahram*, January 1, 2003, and Ali Said Al-Ghamedi in *Al-Watan*,
       January 1, 2003. See ibid.

163   *with fewer resources to buy political quiescence.* Tamara Cofman Wittes interview, June 2005.

163   *"domino effect throughout the Arab region."* "Doubt and Fear in the Arab World,"
       CNN.com, April 10, 2003. Viewed on June 17, 2005, at http://cnn.com/
       worldnews.printthis.clickability.com/pt/cpt?action=cpt&title=CNN.

163   *whose face could not be seen.* Youssef M. Ibrahim, "Will the Mideast Bloom?"
       Washington Post, March 13, 2005, p. B-1.

164   *"to stand is to have a constituency supporting you."* Hassan Fattah, "Unkindest Cut,"
       The New Republic, April 16, 2003. Viewed on June 17, 2005, at http://www
       .aijac.org.au/updates/Apr-03/220403.html. For other examples of this view, see
       Erfan Nizameddin in *Al-Hayat*, "The Fall of What Is Already Fallen," April 21,
       2003, and Khaled Abdel-Aziz Al-Saad in *Al-Siyasa*, April 20, 2003. See Amina
       Elbendary, "The Day After," *Al-Ahram Weekly*, April 24–30, 2003. Viewed on
       June 17, 2005, at http://weekly.ahram.org.eg/print/2003/635/sc9.htm.

164   *voters battled government thugs.* As *The Economist* noted in its report on the Egyptian
       election, "Such [government] crudeness . . . is not new to Egyptian politics. But
       this time it prompted something that is: broad and vocal outrage." See "Not
       Yet a Democracy: Egypt's General Election," *The Economist*, December 10,
       2005. Viewed on February 17, 2006, at http://www.economist.com/agenda/
       displayStory.cfm?story_id=5277459.

164   *"position of being in the protection of the enemy."* Amira Howeidy, "The American
       Factor: How does the US Fit Within the Highly Complicated Domestic Political
       Puzzle?" *Al-Ahram Weekly*. Viewed on January 30, 2006, at http://weekly.ahram
       .org.eg/print/2005/746/eg2.htm.

165   *"knew that no second Hama is possible."* Fouad Ajami, "Bush Country," *Wall Street
       Journal*, May 16, 2005, p. A-16.

165   *"have outpaced gains post-9/11."* Adrian Karatnycky, "Gains for Freedom amid Terror
       and Uncertainty," Freedom in the World 2004. Viewed on February 7, 2006, at
       http://www.ecoi.net/detail.php?id=21021&linkid=25439&cache=1&iflang=en&
       country=all.

165   *"connected to American actions."* Reuel Marc Gerecht, *The Islamic Paradox: Shiite Clerics,
       Sunni Fundamentalists, and the Coming of Arab Democracy*. Jackson, Tenn.: The AEI
       Press, 2004, p. 6.

165   *"United States has triggered this debate."* Jackson Diehl, "Listen to the Arab Reformers,"
       Washington Post, March 29, 2004, p. A-23.

166   *fight salafist jihad in the years to come.* A November 2005 Pew Research Center poll shows
       isolationist sentiment at its highest level since the mid-1990s. "Opinion Leaders
       Turn Cautious, Public Looks Homeward," Pew Research Center for the People
       and the Press. November 17, 2005. Viewed on December 18, 2005, at http://

people-press.org/reports/print.php3?PageID=1016. And at least one student of public opinion has begun talking of an "Iraq syndrome." See John Mueller, "The Iraq Syndrome," *Foreign Affairs*, November/December 2005. Viewed on December 18, 2005, at http://www.foreignaffairs.org/20051101faessay84605/john-mueller/the-iraq-syndrome.html.

Chapter 7: Losing America

167   *Howard Brush Dean III silently cheered.* Tatsha Robertson and Sarah Schweitzer, "Born to Privilege, Searching for a Purpose," *Boston Globe*, September 21, 2003, p. A-1.

168   *journey across the political aisle.* When Vermont backed Lyndon Johnson in 1964, it was the first time it had ever voted Democratic for president. In 1962, it elected its first Democratic governor in 108 years. And in 1974, it elected its first-ever Democratic senator. It has now voted Democratic in the last four presidential elections.

168   *stagnation in working-class standards of living.* Between 1985 and 1992, for instance, average real earnings among workers with a high school degree but no college degree fell 0.7 percent, while between 1993 and 2000 they rose 12.6 percent. Average real earnings among workers without even a high school degree fell 8.5 percent between 1985 and 1992, but rose 17.9 percent between 1993 and 2000. "Fact Sheet on Higher Education," American Council on Education, May 2004. Viewed on March 21, 2006, at http://www.acenet.edu/Arn/Template.cfm?Section=Home&TEMPLATE=lcrn/ContentDisplay.cfm&CONTENTID=10492.

168   *centered not on race, but on morality and religion.* For a discussion of Clinton's mixed political legacy, see William A. Galston and Elaine C. Kamarck, "The Politics of Polarization," published by the Democratic organization Third Way in October 2005. Viewed on February 17, 2006, at http://www.third-way.com/press/release/9.

168   *Democrats increasingly supportive of the use of force.* A 1994 poll by the Pew Research Center, for instance, found Democrats as likely as Republicans to support the use of military force in North Korea, and even more supportive of using force in Haiti. See "The People, The Press and Politics: The New Political Landscape," The Pew Research Center for the People and the Press, September 21, 1994, p. 82.

169   *rate of liberals who opposed military action.* CBS News/*New York Times* Poll, September 20–23, 2001. Viewed on February 8, 2006, at http://www.pollingreport.com/terror9.htm.

169   *"stands 100 percent with President Bush as he fights terrorism"* Mark Z. Barabak, "Democrats Juggle Party Loyalty and Support for Bush's Agenda," *Los Angeles Times*, October 28, 2001, p. A-32.

169   *"trained Mr. bin Laden in how to be a terrorist!"* Michael Moore, "Across America Tonight," September 14, 2001. Viewed on January 12, 2006, at http://www.michaelmoore.com/words/message/index.php?messageDate=2001-09-14.

169   *"things the CIA taught him"* Chalmers Johnson, "Blowback: US Actions Abroad Have Repeatedly Led to Unintended, Indefensible Consequences," *The Nation*, October 15, 2001, p. 13.

169   *"bin Laden is only the latest in a long line."* Susan V. Thompson, ed., "MoveOn Peace: The Frankenstein Syndrome," May 29, 2002. Viewed on July 14, 2005, at http:// web.archive.org/web/20030428072833/at http://peace.moveon.org/bulletin31 .php3.

169   *"received little or no assistance from the United States."* National Commission on Terrorist Attacks, *The 9/11 Commission Report*, p. 56. In addition, Milt Bearden, the CIA's chief Afghanistan operative in the late 1980s, has stated that "the CIA never recruited, trained or otherwise used Arab volunteers." Marc Sageman, one of Bearden's Afghan case officers from 1987 to 1989, affirms that "No U.S. official ever came in contact with the foreign volunteers." And Vincent Cannistraro, head of the Reagan administration's Afghan Working Group between 1985 and 1987, says he never even heard Bin Laden's name. The reasons are fairly simple: the CIA had barely any presence on the ground in Afghanistan during the war between the Soviets and the mujahedeen—it merely funneled money through Pakistan, which distributed it to favored Afghan commanders. Bin Laden's Arab volunteers were also peripheral to the war and few in number. And even if the United States *had* tried to fund them, it is unlikely they would have taken the money, since, as Peter Bergen has noted, they "demonstrated a pathological dislike of Westerners," and as early as 1982, Bin Laden was already publicly denouncing the United States. See Milton Bearden and James Risen, *The Main Enemy: The Inside Story of the CIA's Final Showdown with the KGB*. New York: Random House, 2003, p. 243, cited in "Did the U.S. 'Create' Osama bin Laden?" January 14, 2005. Viewed on July 20, 2005, at http://usinfo.state.gov/media/Archive/2005/Jan/24-318760.html. Sageman, *Understanding Terror Networks*, pp. 57–58, cited in "Did the U.S. 'Create' Osama bin Laden?" Bergen, *Holy War, Inc.*, pp. 51, 64–66; Peter Beinart, "Back to Front," *The New Republic*, October 8, 2001, p. 8.

169   *"one penny" from the hated Americans.* National Commission on Terrorist Attacks, *The 9/11 Commission Report*, p. 467

170   *"United States has systematically promoted a terrorism of its own"* According to Lakoff's book, this quote comes from an essay written on September 16, 2001, and then edited in August 2004. See George Lakoff, *Don't Think of an Elephant: Know Your Values and Frame the Debate—The Essential Guide for Progressives*. White River Junction, Vt.: Chelsea Green, 2004, p. 66.

170   *"finance Hitler's rise to power."* Thompson, "MoveOn Peace: The Frankenstein Syndrome."

170   *"kill people who are poor and desperate."* Wallace Shawn, "The Foreign Policy Therapist," *The Nation*, December 3, 2001, p. 23.

170   *"story will repeat itself so long as our gun and dollar policies"* Divine, "The Cold War and the Election of 1948," p. 96.

170   *"but George W. Bush"* Michael Moore, *Dude, Where's My Country?* New York: Warner Books, 2003, p. 103.

171   *"Getting tough on terrorism"* Wes Boyd and Joan Blades, "Us and Them," *The New Republic*, December 27, 2004–January 10, 2005, p. 16.

171   *"ending the cycle of violence."* MoveOn.org, "Justice, not Terror." Viewed on

July 12, 2005, at http://web.archive.org/web/20010925191755/www.moveon
.org/justice/index.html.

171 *"we become like the terrorists we oppose."* Ibid.

171 *"we are no better than they."* Lakoff, *Don't Think of an Elephant,* p. 58.

172 *"expanding the FBI's surveillance powers."* Bruce Shapiro, "Terrorists are made, not
born," Salon.com, September 12, 2001. Viewed on January 12, 2006, at http://
www.salon.com/news/feature/2001/09/12/blowback/.

172 *"some kind of ad hoc international court."* Eli Pariser and David Pickering, "500,000
Worldwide Call for Justice, Stability, Cooperation," MoveOn Peace, October 9, 2001.
Viewed on July 13, 2005, at http://web.archive.org/web/20030219182530/www
.peace.moveon.org/10-9-01petition.php3; Susan V. Thompson, ed., "Toward an
International Criminal Court," MoveOn Peace. Viewed on July 15, 2005, at http://
web.archive.org/web/20030219194452/www.peace.moveon.org/bulletin15
.php.

172 *"more money and more free rein"* "The C.I.A. and Afghanistan," MoveOn Peace.
Viewed on July 15, 2005, at http://web.archive.org/web/20021127071123/
www.peace.moveon.org/bulletin5.php3. In an act of what might be called
retroactive doughfaceism, MoveOn Peace in May 2002 detailed the 1995
slaughter of Bosnians in Srebrenica, but also linked approvingly to an article that
condemned the "Iran-Contra style operation—in flagrant violation of the UN
security council arms embargo" that produced "a vast secret conduit of weapons
smuggling through Croatia." MoveOn Peace scolded the U.S. government for
being "unwilling to address American complicity in the issue." Yet it never
mentioned that it was precisely this arms smuggling that helped preserve Bosnia's
existence, preventing other cities from suffering Srebrenica's fate. See Susan V.
Thompson, ed. "Coups and Dirty Wars," MoveOn Peace, May 8, 2002. Viewed
on July 14, 2005, at http://web.archive.org/web/20030118004658/www.peace
.moveon.org/bulletin28.php.

172 *in a state of war.* When asked "How serious a problem is terrorism in the United
States today—very serious, only somewhat serious, or hardly serious at all?"
87 percent of Democratic respondents said very serious, versus 88 percent of
Republican respondents. When asked, "In your opinion, is the United States now
in a state of war, or not?" 70 percent of Democratic respondents said yes, while 23
percent said no. Seventy-four percent of Republican respondents said yes, while
24 percent said no. See *Los Angeles Times* poll, "Study 462: Nation, Terrorism in
America, September 2001," September 13–14, 2001, pp. 2–3.

173 *began telling pollsters they were uneasy.* A December 10 and 11, 2002, poll by the *Chicago
Tribune* and WGN-TV, for instance, found that only 35 percent of Democrats
favored military action against Iraq, with 45 percent opposed. Among Republicans,
by contrast, 74 percent were in favor and only 15 percent opposed. See *Chicago
Tribune*/WGN-TV Poll, December 10–11, 2002. Viewed on January 12, 2006, at
http://www.pollingreport.com/iraq9.htm.

173 *"containment was no longer an option"* Pollack, *The Threatening Storm,* p. 242.

174 *massive advantage on national security.* One October 2002 poll, for instance, showed

Americans favoring Republicans over Democrats on the issue of terrorism by 55 points. See Judis and Teixeira, *The Emerging Democratic Majority*, p. 183.

174   *"filled with discussions of pensions."* Dana Milbank, "Democrats Question Iraq Timing," *Washington Post*, September 16, 2002, p. A-1.

174   *presidential candidates generally voted yes.* In the Senate, 29 Democrats voted yes and 21 voted no. In the House it was the reverse, with 126 voting no and only 81 voting yes. But House Minority Leader Richard Gephardt and Senate Majority Leader Tom Daschle voted yes, as did presidential hopefuls John Kerry, John Edwards, and Joe Lieberman. So did Georgia's Max Cleland, Louisiana's Mary Landrieu, South Dakota's Tim Johnson, Montana's Max Baucus, Iowa's Tom Harkin, and Missouri's Jean Carnahan, six of the seven most vulnerable Democratic senators seeking reelection. See U.S. House of Representatives, "Final Vote Results for Roll Call 455," October 10, 2002. Viewed on November 11, 2005, at http://clerk .house.gov/evs/2002/roll455.xml; U.S. Senate, "On the Joint Resolution (H.J.Res. 114)," October 11, 2002. Viewed on November 11, 2005, at http://www.senate .gov/legislative/LIS/roll_call_lists/roll_call_vote_cfm.cfm?congress=107&session= 2&vote=00237.

174   *opposed a new cabinet department before switching positions.* Carl Hulse and Todd S. Purdum, "Daschle Defends Democrats' Stand on Security of U.S.," *New York Times*, September 26, 2002, p. A-1.

174   *devoted almost exclusively to Iraq and the war on terror.* Jim Puzzanghera, "Campaigning to Capitalize; Invoking War on Terrorism Was Core of GOP's Strategy," *San Jose Mercury News*, November 10, 2002, p. 1; Judis and Teixeira, *The Emerging Democratic Majority*, p. 186.

174   *40-point lead on "keeping America strong."* Stan Greenberg, James Carville, and Bob Shrum, "The Price of Silence," Democracy Corps, November 5–6 2002, Questionnaire, p. 14.

174   *the GOP was better on national defense.* Gary C. Jacobson, "Terror, Terrain, and Turnout: Explaining the 2002 Midterm Elections," *Political Science Quarterly* 118 (1) (2003), p. 14

175   *"quixotic" and "preposterous."* Joe Trippi, *The Revolution Will Not Be Televised: Democracy, the Internet, and the Overthrow of Everything.* New York: Regan Books, 2005, p. 75.

175   *John Dean, the figure from Watergate.* Walter Shapiro, *One-Car Caravan: The Amazing True Saga of the 2004 Democratic Race from Its Humble Beginnings to the Boston Convention.* New York: PublicAffairs, 2004, p. 109.

175   *"that is all he ever talked about."* Roger Simon, "Is He the One?" *U.S. News & World Report*, January 19, 2004, p. 20.

176   *"We want to know too!"* "Remarks by Gov. Howard Dean, Democratic National Committee Winter Meeting," February 21, 2003. Viewed on January 12, 2006, at http://www.gwu.edu/~action/2004/dnc0203/dean022103spt.html.

176   *John Edwards's speech was interrupted four times.* "Remarks of Senator Joe Lieberman, Democratic National Committee Winter Meeting," February 21, 2003. Viewed on January 12, 2006, at http://www.gwu.edu/~action/2004/dnc0203/ lieb022103spt.html; "Senator John Edwards, Democratic National Committee

Winter Meeting," February 22, 2003. Viewed on January 12, 2006, at http://www.gwu.edu/~action/2004/dnc0203/edw022203spt.html.

176 *interrupted by cheers* twenty-four times. "Remarks by Gov. Howard Dean, Democratic National Committee Winter Meeting."

176 *"that was a hungry audience."* Evelyn Nieves, "Short-Fused Populist, Breathing Fire at Bush," *Washington Post*, July 6, 2003, p. A-1.

176 *"failure to oppose Bush strongly enough."* Paul Maslin, "The Front-Runner's Fall," *Atlantic Monthly*, May 2004, p. 96

176 *"but it's probably over."* Mark Singer, "Running on Instinct," *The New Yorker*, January 12, 2004, p. 43.

176 *white, affluent, highly educated, and secular.* According to a Pew Research Center survey conducted in late 2004, 92 percent of Dean activists were white, compared to 68 percent of Democrats as a whole; 54 percent had attended graduate school, compared to 11 percent of Democrats as a whole; 65 percent earned over $50,000 a year, compared to 31 percent of Democrats overall; and 59 percent attended religious services "seldom" or "never," compared to 25 percent of Democrats overall. See Pew Research Center for the People and the Press, "The Dean Activists: Their Profile and Prospects," April 6, 2005, pp. 34–35.

176 *their biggest issue was the Iraq war* Ibid., pp. 2, 4, T-2.

176 *they were more dovish than other Democrats* For instance, 96 percent of Dean activists said "good diplomacy" rather than "military strength" was the best way to ensure peace, compared to 76 percent of Democrats overall and 55 percent of Americans. Nineteen percent said "pre-emptive" force was often or sometimes justified, compared to 44 percent of Democrats as a whole and 60 percent of Americans. See "The Dean Activists," pp. 4, 27, T-18, T-19.

176 *70 percent said they sometimes visited MoveOn's website* Ibid., p. T-35.

176 *the largest cohort were actually baby boomers.* Ibid., pp. 1–2.

177 *twice as likely to support keeping U.S. troops in Iraq.* Thirty-one percent of Dean activists aged 15 to 29 said preemption was often or sometimes necessary, compared to 13 percent of activists over fifty. Sixty-one percent of those aged 15 to 29 said the United States should keep troops in Iraq, versus 34 percent of activists over fifty. The survey was conducted from September through December 2004 and published in April 2005. See ibid., pp. 1, 4, 31.

177 *the virtues of interracial busing.* Michael Kranish, Brian C. Mooney, and Nina J. Easton, *John F. Kerry: The Complete Biography by the Boston Globe Reporters Who Know Him Best.* New York: PublicAffairs, 2004, p. 40.

177 *Massachusetts had long been a Democratic-leaning state.* Massachusetts voted Democratic for president in every election from 1928 to 1952, and then again from 1960 to 1980.

178 *"to protest in the United States."* Todd Purdum, "Echoes of a 1972 Loss Haunt a 2004 Campaign," *New York Times*, September 24, 2004, p. A-1; Kranish et al., *John F. Kerry*, pp. 154–155.

178 *"a class issue—class and resentment."* Ibid., p. 162.

178   *defeated by the "silent majority."* Ibid., p. 159.

178   *"the experience of the Vietnam period."* Ibid., p. 226.

178   *opposed lifting the arms embargo against Bosnia.* He did, however, support the Kosovo war.

179   *"authorize the use of force in the first place?"* David M. Halbfinger, "Kerry Still Nagged by Questions on Vote to Authorize Iraq War," *New York Times*, October 24, 2003, p. A-1.

179   *shown he could stand up to the president.* According to Senator Joseph Biden, a Kerry confidant, Kerry's vote against the $87 billion was an effort "to prove to Dean's guys I'm not a warmonger." See Philip Gourevitch, "Damage Control," *The New Yorker*, July 26, 2004, p. 50.

179   *"sound more and more like an antiwar candidate."* James Traub, "The Things They Carry," *New York Times Magazine*, January 4, 2004, p. 28.

179   *"can't beat him by being light on national security."* Democratic Presidential Candidates' Debate Sponsored by National Public Radio, January 6, 2004. Viewed on February 17, 2006, at http://www.npr.org/programs/specials/debate2004/.

179   *"decisions that he made saved our lives."* Shapiro, *One-Car Caravan*, p. 236.

179   *"I owe him my life."* Kranish et al., *John F. Kerry*, p. 377.

179   *beat Dean by 16 points.* CNN, "Entrance Polls: Iowa," January 19, 2004. Viewed on November 14, 2005, at http://www.cnn.com/ELECTION/2004/primaries/pages/epolls/IA/.

180   *Bill Clinton's foreign policy rhetoric was arrogant.* Kranish et al., *John F. Kerry*, pp. 196–197. In 1997, when Clinton called the United States the "indispensable nation" in his second inaugural address, Kerry derided the phrase as "arrogant" and "obnoxious." See Spencer Ackerman, "Idea Man," *The New Republic*, October 25, 2004, p. 15.

181   *"entire dark side of globalization."* Matt Bai, "Kerry's Undeclared War," *New York Times Magazine*, October 10, 2004. Viewed on February 8, 2006, at http;//select.nytimes.com/gst/abstract.html?res=FA0810FD35C0C738DDDA90994DC404482.

181   *called terrorism its "fraternal twin."* John Kerry, *The New War: The Web of Crime That Threatens America's Security.* New York: Simon & Schuster, 1997, p. 26.

181   *"manipulation of human weakness, greed, and despair."* Ibid., p. 32.

181   *"build adequate legal institutions in other countries."* Ibid., p. 172.

182   *"subject from the loss of 10 million jobs."* Interview with Kerry campaign aide, July 2005.

182   *exaggerated his war injuries in Vietnam.* The Swift Boat Veterans began attacking Kerry in May, but their assault became much more intense after the convention.

183   *dropped 9 points in the month of August.* Nina J. Easton, Michael Kranish, Patrick Healy, Glen Johnson, Anne E. Kornblut, and Brian Mooney, "On the Trail of Kerry's Failed Dream," *Boston Globe*, November 14, 2004, p. 24.

183   *"renounced his country's symbols"* Jennifer Koons, "Veterans Group Condemns Kerry for Renouncing Medals," NationalJournal.com, September 1, 2004. Viewed on December 19, 2005, at http://nationaljournal.com/members/adspotlight/2004/09/0901sbvft1.htm.

183   *"He dishonored his country"* Jennifer Koons, "Veterans Question Kerry's War Record," NationalJournal.com, August 5, 2004. Viewed on December 19, 2005, at http://nationaljournal.com/members/adspotlight/2004/08/0805sbvft1.htm.

183   *"betrayed his country"* Jennifer Koons, "Swift Vets: Kerry Held Secret Meeting with 'Enemy,' " NationalJournal.com, September 22, 2004. Viewed on December 19, 2005, at http://nationaljournal.com/members/adspotlight/2004/09/0922sbvft1.htm.

184   *"battle against our greatest enemy."* "Kerry Lays Out Iraq Plan," *Washington Post*, September 20, 2004. Viewed on July 15, 2005, at http://www.washingtonpost .com/ac2/wp-dyn/A35515-2004Sep20.

184   *freedom and tyranny out of his prepared texts.* Interview with Kerry campaign aide, July 2005.

184   *"smarter, more effective war on terror."* "John Kerry's Remarks at the Democratic Convention," *USA Today*, July 29, 2004. Viewed on February 17, 2006, at http://www.usatoday.com/news/politicselections/nation/president/2004-07-29-kerry-speech-text_x.htm. Indeed, one of the epithets Kerry often used to describe Bush's foreign policy was "ideological." In December 2003, for instance, he said "the Bush administration has pursued the most arrogant, inept, reckless, and ideological foreign policy in modern history." In the summer of 2004, he told *The New Yorker*'s Philip Gourevitch, "You have to be careful of ideology clouding your decision-making process, which I think this Administration has been exceedingly guilty of." See "Democratic Presidential Debate in Durham, NH," December 9, 2003. Transcript. Viewed on February 24, 2006, at http://www.washingtonpost.com/ac2/wpdyn/A50859-2003Dec9?language=printer; Phillip Gourevitch, "Damage Control," *The New Yorker* July 26, 2004. Viewed on February 17, 2006, at http://www.newyorker.com/fact/content/?040726fa_fact.

184   *used the word* effective *eighteen times.* Matt Bai, "Kerry's Undeclared War."

184   *"better job of training the Iraqi forces."* "Debate Transcript: The First Bush-Kerry Presidential Debate," September 30, 2004. Viewed on July 14, 2005, at http://www.debates.org/pages/trans2004a_p.html.

184   *offered no larger message.* The *New York Times Magazine*'s Matt Bai commented that during the debate, "while Kerry bore in on ground-level details, Bush, in defending his policies, seemed, characteristically, to be looking at the world from a much higher altitude, repeating in his brief and sometimes agitated statements a single unifying worldview. . . . Kerry seemed to offer no grand thematic equivalent." Matt Bai, "Kerry's Undeclared War."

184   *"Presidents are supposed to do something else."* Schneider, "JFK's Children," p. 21.

184   *"worldview rather than his competence."* Ryan Lizza, "Bad Message," *The New Republic*, November 22, 2004. Viewed on February 8, 2006, at http://www.tnr.com/doc .mhtml?i=20041122&s=lizza112204.

185   *"What was that message?"* Ibid.

185   *increase in the share of voters citing cultural concerns.* In 2004, 22 percent of voters cited "moral values" as their primary concern. But in 1992, when the exit poll categories were divided differently, a combined 27 percent of voters mentioned either "family values" or "abortion." In 1996 and 2000, when voters could offer their two most important issues, those two categories totaled 49 percent. See Andrew Sullivan, "Gay Marriage Isn't Political Death," *The New Republic*, November 22, 2004. Viewed on February 8, 2006, at http://www.tnr.com/doc .mhtml?i=20041122&s=sullivan112204.

185   *no statistically significant effect on turnout.* Alan Abramowitz, "Terrorism, Gay Marriage, and Incumbency: Explaining the Republican Victory in the 2004 Presidential Election," *The Forum* 2 (4) (2004), art. 3. Viewed on February 24, 2006, at http:// www.bepress.com/forum/vol2/iss4/art3/.

185   *34 percent cited either "terrorism" or "Iraq."* Peter Beinart, "A Fighting Faith," *The New Republic*, December 13, 2004. Viewed on February 8, 2006, at http://www.tnr .com/doc.mhtml?i=20041213&s=beinart121304.

185   *mostly anti-war.* Since one of the defining differences between supporters and opponents of the Iraq war was whether they believed it was part of the war on terrorism, it is not surprising that antiwar voters cited "Iraq" as their concern, while prowar voters cited "terrorism."

185   *favored Bush by an incredible 72 points.* Among the 15 percent of voters who said Iraq was their biggest concern, Kerry defeated Bush 73–26. But among the 19 percent who cited terrorism, he lost 86–14. See "CNN.com Election Results," November 17, 2004. Viewed on February 8, 2006, at http://www.cnn.com/ ELECTION/2004/pages/results/states/US/P/00/epolls.0.html.

185   *"moral values" made no difference at all.* Paul Friedman, "The Gay Marriage Myth," Slate, November 5, 2004. Viewed on February 8, 2006, at http://www.slate.com/ toolbar.aspx?action=print&id=2109275.

185   *better than Al Gore had four years earlier.* Kerry won voters who had attended graduate school by 11 points, 3 points better than Gore's total in 2000. He won college-educated women by 9 points, 8 points worse than Gore had done. And while he lost college-educated men by 8 points, he gained 6 points over Gore's margin. See John Judis and Ruy Teixeira, "Movement Interruptus," *The American Prospect*, January 2005. Viewed on February 20, 2006, at http://www.prospect.org/ web/view-print.ww?id=8955; Anna Greenberg, "Mind the Gender Gap: Why Democrats are Losing Women at an Alarming Rate," *The American Prospect*, December 6, 2004. Viewed on February 24, 2006, at http://www.prospect.org/ web/page.ww?section=root&name=ViewPrint&articleId=8884.

185   *also did well among minorities.* Kerry's share of the African American and Hispanic votes dipped slightly compared to 2000, but he still won both groups by huge margins, and they turned out in record numbers. Kerry won 89 percent of the black vote, down 1 point from 2000. He won roughly 60 percent of the Hispanic vote, down 4 or 5 points from 2000. (Initial surveys, which suggested a greater Hispanic drop, seem to have been overstated. For a discussion, see Ruy Teixeira, "Did Bush Really Get 44 Percent of the Hispanic Vote?," *The Emerging Democratic Majority*, November 18, 2004. Viewed on February 24, 2006, at http://www .emergingdemocraticmajorityweblog.com/donkeyrising/archives/000951.php). And minority turnout went up. After constituting 19 percent of the electorate in 2000, minorities represented 23 percent in 2004. In Cleveland and Columbus, for instance, the cities with the largest African American populations in Ohio, Kerry got 52,000 more votes than Gore. See Stanley Greenberg, *The Two Americas: Our Current Political Deadlock and How to Break It*, revised and expanded ed. New York: St. Martin's Press, 2005, p. 319; Don Hazen, "Making Sense of 2004," in Don

Hazen and Lakshmi Chaudhry, eds., *Start Making Sense*. White River Junction, Vt.: Chelsea Green, 2005, p. 13.

185   *failed to sufficiently rouse his liberal base.* For instance, Markos Moulitsas Zúniga, founder of the influential blog Daily Kos, noted, "We won the center and it wasn't enough. . . . So, clearly, we have to reach out more to our base." The left-populist author Thomas Frank suggested that 2004 was "what Karl Rove called a 'mobilization election' in which victory would go to the party that best rallied its faithful." See Ronald Brownstein, "The Internet and Democrats," *National Journal*, July 2, 2005. Viewed on February 8, 2006, at http://www.dailykos.com/storyonly/2005/8/5/15134/56717; Thomas Frank, "What's the Matter with Liberals," *New York Review of Books* 52 (8) (May 12, 2005). Viewed on July 4, 2005, at http://www.nybooks.com/articles/17982.

185   *"mobilizing African-Americans, college students, and other anti-Bush voters."* Abramowitz, "Terrorism, Gay Marriage, and Incumbency."

186   *losing them by a massive 24 points.* Judis and Teixeira, "Movement Interruptus"; Ruy Teixeira, "Old Democrats and the Shock of the New," in Peter Berkowitz, ed, *Varieties of Progressivism in America*. Palo Alto, Calif.: Hoover Institution Press, 2004, p. 28.

186   *the most worried about terrorism.* Judis and Teixeira, "Movement Interruptus." Among working-class white women, Kerry dropped 7 points over Gore's total in 2000. See Stan Greenberg, "The Tale of Two Gaps: The Role of Gender and Education in the 2004 Elections," *Democracy Corps*, October 27, 2004. Viewed on February 24, 2006, at http://www.democracycorps.com/reports/analyses/The_Tale_of_Two_Gaps.pdf; "Women's Vote, 2004," Greenberg, Quinlan & Rosner. Viewed on December 21, 2005, at http://www.usavotenet.com/Greenberg,%20Quinlan%20&%20Rosner.htm.

186   *most worried about the Soviet Union in 1988.* Blumenthal, *Pledging Allegiance*, p. 299.

186   *little difference between Democrats and Republicans on foreign policy.* "The People, the Press and Politics: The New Political Landscape," Pew Center for the People and the Press, September 21, 1994, p. 82.

187   *"not nearly as important in determining party affiliation."* "Beyond Red vs. Blue: Republicans Divided About Role of Government—Democrats by Social and Personal Values," Pew Research Center for the People and the Press, May 10, 2005. Viewed on January 13, 2006, at http://people-press.org/reports/display.php3?ReportID=242.

187   *more likely to mention capturing Osama bin Laden.* "American Attitudes Toward National Security, Foreign Policy and The War on Terror," Top Lines, A National Telephone Survey Conducted January 23–27, 2005. Security and Peace Institute, January 23–27, 2005, pp. 14–15. Viewed on March 21, 2006, at http://www.securitypeace.org/pdf/AmAttitudes.TopLines.pdf.

187   *for liberals, it tied for tenth.* Ibid., p. 24.

187   *working more closely with America's allies.* Ibid.

187   *supported using US troops "to destroy a terrorist camp."* The M.I.T. Public Opinion Research Training Lab Survey results were published in *The Boston Review*,

January/February 2006, p. 6. Viewed on March 21, 2006, at http://bostonreview .net/BR31.1/stateofthenation.pdf.

188   *just over one-quarter among members of the GOP.* "Opinion Leaders Turn Cautious, Public Looks Homeward," Pew Research Center for the People and the Press, November 2005. Viewed on February 8, 2006, at http://peoplepress.org/reports/ display.php3?ReportID=263.

Chapter 8: A New Liberalism

191   *pledging fealty to a man in a cave.* Walter Russell Mead, "Edited Transcript of Remarks," Carnegie Council on Ethics and International Affairs, May 27, 2004. Viewed on February 20, 2006, at www.carnegiecouncil.org/viewMedia.php/ prmTemplateID/8/prmID/4988; National Commission on Terrorist Attacks, "Overview of the Enemy, Staff Statement," *The 9/11 Commission Report*, p. 15.

192   *provide decent schools, free medical clinics, even clean water. The Arab Human Development Report 2002*, p. 127; "The Millennium Development Goals in Arab Countries," United Nations Development Programme, December 2003. Viewed on February 20, 2006, at http://www.undp.org/mdg/Arab_RegionalReport_english.pdf.

192   *the "Islamic Republic."* Benjamin and Simon, *The Age of Sacred Terror*, p. 180; National Commission on Terrorist Attacks, *The 9/11 Commission Report*, pp. 56– 57; "Islamism in North Africa II: Egypt's Opportunity," *International Crisis Group*, Middle East/North Africa Briefing 13 (April 20, 2004), p. 7.

192   *"No post office, no savings bank, no public transport"* Selma Belaala, "Morocco: Slums Breed Jihad," *Le Monde Diplomatique*, November 2004. Viewed on June 24, 2005, at http://mondediplo.com/2004/11/04moroccoislamists.

192   *"function and fulfillment in the social order?"* Schlesinger, *The Vital Center*, pp. 8, 249.

193   *nor economic and cultural despair.* As Sen writes, "Development consists of the removal of various types of unfreedoms that leave people with little choice and little opportunity of exercising their reasoned agency. The removal of substantial unfreedoms, it is argued here, is *constitutive* of development." Amartya Sen, *Development as Freedom.* New York: Anchor Books, 2000, p. xii.

193   *"measuring human development in this age of globalization."* Omer Taspinar, "Fighting Radicalism with Human Development," draft copy. The Brookings Institution: Project on U.S. Policy Towards the Islamic World, p. 14.

193   *fell below even sub-Saharan Africa.* Ibid.

193   *are culturally oppressive and economically doomed.* Ibid., pp. 19, 40.

193   *can enter the global economy.* "Progressive Internationalism: A Democratic National Security Strategy," Progressive Policy Institute, October 30, 2003, p. 18. Viewed on February 24, 2006, at http://www.ppionline.org/documents/Progressive_ Internationalism_1003.pdf.

193   *near the bottom of the industrialized world.* Gregg Easterbrook, "Safe: The Case for Foreign Aid," *The New Republic*, July 29, 2002. Viewed on February 24, 2006, at http://www.tnr.com/doc.mhtml?i=20020729&s=easterbrook072902.

193 *"political sources of terrorism"* Arab Human Development Report 2003, United Nations Development Programme. Viewed on February 20, 2006, at http://www .undp.org.sa/Reports/AHDR%202003%20-%20English.pdf.

194 *commentators dubbed the criticisms anti-American.* Conservative columnist Mona Charen, for instance, called liberal criticism of the U.S. response to the tsunami an example of "the anti-American spirit." See Kathryn Jean Lopez, "The Road to Hell," National Review Online, January 4, 2005. Viewed on February 20, 2006, at http://www.townhall.com/clumnists/monacharen/archive.shtml.

194 *distinction between us and our enemies* A 2005 poll released by the group Terror Free Tomorrow found that compared to 2003, the percentage of Indonesians with unfavorable opinions of the United States had dropped from 83 percent to 54 percent. The percentage that opposed American counterterrorism efforts dropped from 72 percent to 36 percent, with 40 percent now supportive. Confidence in Osama Bin Laden dropped from 58 percent to 23 percent. And 65 percent of Indonesians said they felt more favorably toward the United States because of its response to the tsunami. See "A Major Change of Public Opinion in the Muslim World," *Terror Free Tomorrow.* Viewed on January 13, 2006, at http://www .terrorfreetomorrow.org/articlenav.php?id=40.

195 *"political and economic ideology that has been successful in America."* Gaddis, *Strategies of Containment,* p. 64.

196 *George W. Bush's lectures about freedom.* As the Brookings Institution's Omer Taspinar notes, the Arab Human Development Reports "do not represent a Western perspective or agenda for the Arab world, but instead try to frame the challenge of development with a well-balanced mix of universal and local terms. As such, these reports have already achieved an unprecedented level of legitimacy and recognition in the eyes of diverse Arab communities, and across the Islamic world." See Taspinar, "Fighting Radicalism with Human Development," p. 13.

196 *that comes with membership in the European Union.* Benjamin and Simon, *The Next Attack,* p. 225.

197 *"preserving the purity of our soul."* Reinhold Niebuhr, *The Irony of American History*, rev. ed. New York: Scribner, 1985, p. 5.

197 *"they put their heads down."* Jeffrey Goldberg, "The Unbranding: Can the Democrats Make Themselves Look Tough?" *The New Yorker*, March 21, 2005. Viewed on February 9, 2006, at http://www.newyorker.com/fact/content/index.ssf?050321fa_fact.

197 *tragic choices that defending freedom requires.* "Student Protest Prevents CIA Recruiting Event at New York University: Antiwar Students Hope to Hold Unique CIA College Marketing Effort at NYU," MichaelMoore.com, April 4, 2005. Viewed on February 20, 2006, at http://www.michaelmoore.com/words/print.php?id=2086; Columbia, Harvard, Yale, and Brown all ban ROTC. In addition, a coalition of thirty-six law schools, including Georgetown, Stanford, and New York University, went to the Supreme Court to defend their right to exclude military recruiters because the military discriminates against gays and lesbians. In March 2006, they lost their case. See Will Marshall, "Valuing Patriotism," *Blueprint,* July 23, 2005. Viewed on July 26, 2005, at http://www.dlc.org/print.cfm?contentid=253472; David G.

Savage, "Ruling Lets the Military Recruit on Campuses," *Los Angeles Times*, March 7, 2006. Viewed on March 21, 2006, at http://www.latimes.com/news/nationworld/nation/&la-na-scotus7mar07,0,697174.story?coll=&la-home-headlines.

198 *"to promote a transition to democracy"* James Dobbins et al., "The UN's Role in Nation Building from the Congo to Iraq," Rand Corporation 2005. Viewed on January 13, 2006, at http://www.rand.org/pubs/monographs/MG304.

198 *seven are today at peace, and six are at least partial democracies.* Those eight countries or regions, according to the Rand Corporation, are Namibia, El Salvador, Cambodia, Mozambique, eastern Slavonia, Sierra Leone, and Congo. Of these, only Congo remains at war; only Congo and Cambodia are "not free" according to 2006 rankings by Freedom House. Freedom House ranks countries on a scale of 1 to 7 in two categories: political rights and civil rights. One is the best ranking and 7 is the worst. Based on these rankings, Freedom House labels a country as "free," "partly free," or "not free." See Ibid, pp. 234, 237, 238; http://www.freedomhouse.org/uploads/pdf/Charts2006.pdf.

198 *nation-building record is actually better* Of the eight countries or regions where the United States has conducted nation-building exercises—Japan, Germany, Kosovo, Bosnia, Haiti, Somalia, Afghanistan, and Iraq—four are currently at peace (Japan, Germany, Kosovo, and Bosnia). Freedom House ranks five as "free" or "partly free" (Japan, Germany, Afghanistan, Bosnia, and Serbia and Montenegro, of which Kosovo is a part). See Dobbins et al., "The UN's Role in Nation Building," pp. 234, 237–238; Freedom House Rankings, http://www.freedomhouse.org/uploads/pdf/Charts2006.pdf.

198 *cases of mass human rights abuse or genocide.* "A More Secure World: Our Shared Responsibility," United Nations General Assembly, December 2, 2004. Viewed on February 9, 2006, at http://www.un.org/secureworld/report.pdf.

199 *liberals urge action, knowing that no action will ever come.* "Dark Victory," p. 3.

199 *third-world heavyweights like India, Indonesia, and Brazil.* The idea of using the G-20 comes from Anne-Marie Slaughter, dean of Princeton's Woodrow Wilson School of Public and International Affairs, who proposed it as part of a report entitled *Restoring American Leadership: 13 Cooperative Steps to Advance Global Progress*, sponsored by the Open Society Institute and the Security and Peace Institute. See Anne-Marie Slaughter, "Help Develop Institutions and Instruments for Military Intervention on Humanitarian Grounds," *Restoring American Leadership* 2005. Viewed on February 9, 2006, at http://www.securitypeace.org/pdf/Chapter5.RAL.HumanitarianIntervention.pdf.

200 *"American civil rights activists in the period 1956–1964."* Rami G. Khouri, "Egypt Could Inspire Wider Arab Reforms," *Agence Global*, May 10, 2005. Viewed on June 13, 2005, at http://www.agenceglobal.com/Article.asp?Id=498.

201 *"prerequisite for this is to respect the law."* "Document: The Liberalism We Espouse," *Al-Ahram Weekly*, June 9–15, 2005. Viewed on March 21, 2006, at http://weekly.ahram.org.eg/2005/746/op19.htm.

201 *"more effective than the guarantee of those practices in our own."* Gitlin, *The Sixties*, p. 62.

202   *make freedom "a fighting faith."* Schlesinger, *The Vital Center*, pp. 250–251.

202   *"golden age of civic engagement."* Jacob S. Hacker, Suzanne Mettler, and Dianne Pinderhughes, "Inequality and Public Policy," in Lawrence R. Jacobs and Theda Skocpol, eds., *Inequality and American Democracy: What We Know and What We Need to Learn*. New York: Russell Sage Foundation, 2005, p. 196.

202   *overall family income roughly doubled.* Lawrence R. Jacobs and Theda Skocpol, "American Democracy in an Era of Rising Inequality," in Jacobs and Skocpol, *Inequality and American Democracy*, p. 4.

202   *working class fared even better than the rich.* The poorest fifth of Americans saw their family income grow by 115 percent, while the wealthiest fifth saw theirs rise by only 84 percent. See Ibid., p. 4.

202   *job security that only college professors have now.* Walter Russell Mead, "Edited Transcript of Remarks."

203   *income growth has slowed to a crawl.* Between 1973 and 2000, the wealthiest fifth of Americans saw their family income grow by 61 percent, while the poorest fifth saw theirs grow by 10 percent and the second poorest fifth saw theirs grow by 15 percent. See Jacobs and Skocpol, "American Democracy in an Era of Rising Inequality," in Jacobs and Skocpol, *Inequality and American Democracy*, p. 4.

203   *works a full twelve weeks more per year than it did in 1969.* Jared Bernstein and Karen Kornbluh, "Running Faster to Stay in Place: The Growth of Family Work Hours and Incomes," research paper, New America Foundation, June 2005. Viewed on February 9, 2006, at http://www.newamerica.net/Download_Docs/pdfs/Doc_File_2437_1.pdf.

203   *anywhere near their parents' level of economic security.* Jacob Hacker, *The Great Risk Shift*, in press.

203   *Mom loses her job or Dad gets seriously ill.* Depending on what dates you use, income instability is between two and five times higher than it was in the early 1970s. See Jacob S. Hacker, "False Positive," *The New Republic*, August 16, 2004. Viewed on August 5, 2005, at http://www.tnr.com/docprint.mhtml?i=20040816&s=hacker081604.

203   *so deep in debt that they probably should.* Elizabeth Warren and Amelia Warren Tyagi, "Middle Class and Broke," *The American Prospect*, May 2004. Viewed on February 21, 2006, at http://www.prospect.org/web/page.ww?section=root&name=ViewPrint&articleId=7635.

203   *unionization led others to do the same.* Harley Shaiken, "The High Road to a Competitive Economy: A Labor Law Strategy," Center for American Progress, July 25, 2004, p. 4. Viewed on February 9, 2006, at http://www.americanprogress.org/atf/cf/%7BE9245FE4-9A2B-43C7-A521-5D6FF2E06E03%7D/unionpaper.pdf; Jared Bernstein and Karen Kornbluh, "Running Faster to Stay in Place: The Growth of Family Work Hours and Incomes."

203   *defined-benefit pensions has dropped by more than half.* Jonathan Weisman, "Pension Promise No Guarantee of Security; Bankruptcies Can Mean Sharply Reduced Payouts," *Washington Post*, October 12, 2004, p. A-6.

203   *dropped from two-thirds to just over one in two.* John Sommers, "Employer-Sponsored Health Insurance Characteristics, by Average Payroll for the Private Sector, 2002," Medical Expenditure Panel Survey, June 2004. Viewed on January 13, 2006, at http://www.meps.ahrq.gov/papers/st48/stat48.pdf; Jack A. Meyer and Elliot K. Wicks, "Covering America: Real Remedies for the Uninsured, Volume III," Economic and Social Research Institute, December 2003, p. 226.

203   *Taxes have become less progressive* Charles M. Sennott, "The $150 Billion 'Welfare' Recipients: U.S. Corporations," Boston Globe Online, July 7, 1996. Viewed on August 17, 2005, at http://www.corporations.org/welfare/globe2.html.

204   *covers only two-thirds, with parents on the hook for the rest.* Warren and Tyagi, "Middle Class and Broke"; Lynn A. Karoly and James H. Bigelow, "The Economics of Investing in Universal Preschool Education in California," Rand Corporation, 2005. Viewed on February 9, 2006, at http://www.rand.org/pubs/monographs/2005/RAND_MG349.pdf.

204   *inequality unseen since the 1920s.* Hacker, Mettler, and Pinderhughes, "Inequality and Public Policy," in Jacobs and Skocpol, *Inequality and American Democracy*, p. 156.

204   *a voice and a stake.* According to one study, if unionization rates had held steady since 1954, 17 million more, mostly blue-collar, Americans would have voted in 2000. Shaiken, "The High Road to a Competitive Economy," p. 9.

204   *greater political participation among beneficiaries.* Policies like Social Security and the GI Bill, based upon "universalism, generosity, and [a] message of equal citizenship—made beneficiaries much more inclined toward civic involvement." See Hacker, Mettler, and Pinderhughes, "Inequality and Public Policy," in Jacobs and Skocpol, *Inequality and American Democracy*, pp. 185, 189.

204   *voting rates among less educated Americans have nose-dived.* Richard B. Freeman, "What, Me Vote?," National Bureau of Economic Research (Working Paper 9896), August 2003. Viewed on February 9, 2006, at http://www.nber.org/papers/w9896.

204   *has close to doubled.* "American Democracy in an Age of Rising Inequality," Task Force on Inequality and American Democracy, American Political Science Association, 2004. Viewed on February 9, 2006, at http://www.apsanet.org/imgtest/taskforcereport.pdf. In a CBS/*New York Times* poll conducted from July 11–15, 2004, when asked, "Would you say the government is pretty much run by a few big interests looking out for themselves or that it is run for the benefit of all people?" 64 percent of respondents said government was run by a few big interests. See http://www.pollingreport.com/institut.htm.

204   *"Our 'we' steadily shriveled."* Robert D. Putnam, "Bowling Together," in E. J. Dionne, Kayla Meltzer Drogosz, and Robert E. Litan, *United We Serve: National Service and the Future of Citizenship.* Washington, D.C.: Brookings Institution Press, 2003, p. 13.

205   *"more closely resembles the House of the 19th century"* Norman Ornstein and Thomas Mann, *The Broken Branch,* in press.

205   *an enormous windfall.* The repeal was stripped from the legislation that ultimately became law. See David E. Rosenbaum, "A Nation Challenged: The Interests; Since Sept. 11, Lobbyists Put Old Pleas in New Packages," *New York Times*, December 3,

2001, p. B-1; Greg Goldin, "Bailout: Another Free Lunch for Fat Cats," *Los Angeles Times*, November 4, 2001, p. M-4; Richard W. Stevenson, "Senate Approves Economic Stimulus Bill," *New York Times*, March 9, 2002, p. A-13.

205   *end up as drug company profit.* M. Asif Ismail, "Drug Lobby Second to None: How the Pharmaceutical Industry Gets Its Way in Washington," Center for Public Integrity, July 7, 2005. Viewed on August 11, 2005, at http://www.publicintegrity.org/rx/printer-friendly.aspx?aid=723; Ceci Connolly and Mike Allen, "Medicare Drug Benefit May Cost $1.2 Trillion. Estimate Dwarfs Bush's Original Price Tag," *Washington Post*, February 9, 2005, p. A-1.

205   *passed two more rounds of upper-income tax cuts* William G. Gale and Peter Orszag, "Bush Administration Tax Policy: Revenue and Budget Effects," *Tax Notes*, October 4, 2004, p. 106.

205   *fewer press conferences than any president in a century.* David Shaw, "Is Bush Really Implementing a Full-Court Press on Media," *Los Angeles Times*, March 13, 2005, p. E-14.

205   *vast quantities of documents beyond public view.* Christopher H. Schmitt and Edward T. Pound, "Keeping Secrets," *U.S. News and World Report*, December 22, 2003. Viewed on February 21, 2006, at http://www.usnews.com/usnews/news/articles/031222/22secrecy.htm.

206   *"a solid resolute expression of that will."* "NSC 68: United States Objectives and Programs for National Security," April 7, 1950. Viewed on March 21, 2006, at http://www.seattleu.edu/artsci/history/us1945/docs/nsc68-1.htm.

206   *it has grown easier to manipulate.* Polling shows that from the 1940s through the 1990s public knowledge about government remained roughly steady. But far from being cause for reassurance, that is actually quite damning, given that education levels rose dramatically over the same period. See Michael Delli Carpini and Scott Keeter, *What Americans Know About Politics and Why It Matters.* New Haven: Yale University Press, 1997, pp. 105–134.

206   *supported terrorist groups planning to strike the United States.* "Iraq," PollingReport.com, March 2003. Viewed on December 5, 2005, at http://www.pollingreport.com/iraq8.htm.

206   *Iraq's oil sector was in extreme disrepair.* Jonathan Chait, "The Case Against George W. Bush: Part II," *The New Republic*, July 26, 2004. Viewed on February 21, 2006, at http://www.tnr.com/doc.mhtml?i=20040726&s=chait072604; Fallows, "Blind into Baghdad."

206   *would not have gone to war the way it did.* As Thomas Mann and Norman Ornstein write, "We can't help wondering whether some of the disastrous consequences in Iraq after Saddam's regime fell might have been avoided if Congress had done its job." See Ornstein and Mann, *The Broken Branch*, in press.

206   *"civil renewal that occurs only once or twice a century."* Putnam, "Bowling Together," in Dionne, Drogosz, and Litan, *United We Serve*, p. 17.

207   *hostility to government now exceeds pre-9/11 levels.* "Opinion Leaders Turn Cautious, Public Looks Homeward," The Pew Research Center for the People and the Press, p. 83.

207   *more bitterly divided than it was when Bill Clinton was being impeached.* John Mueller, "The Iraq Syndrome," *Foreign Affairs*, November/December 2005. Viewed on February 9, 2006, at http://www.foreignaffairs.org/20051101faessay84605/john-mueller/the-iraq-syndrome.html.

207   *Isolationist sentiment is on the rise.* "Opinion Leaders Turn Cautious, Public Looks Homeward," The Pew Research Center for the People and the Press, p. 106.

208   *"began to rediscover"* Schlesinger, *The Vital Center*, 165.

Acknowledgments

I used to think authors acknowledged people just to be nice. Then I set out to write a book, and quickly realized how utterly incapable I was of doing so on my own. That this book exists at all, let alone contributes usefully to the public debate, is largely due to the kindness of colleagues, friends, and family. Having spent roughly a year profiting from their generosity, I will be gratefully repaying it for many more.

My debts to *The New Republic* are wide and deep, and they start at the top. In 1995, Martin Peretz saved me from an unpromising academic career, and gave me the opportunity to write and edit in the iconoclastic, exuberant journalistic environment that he has overseen for more than three decades. I will never stop being grateful. More recently, Roger and Susan Hertog have become both mentors and friends, who by their example have taught enduring lessons about how to live a life. When I asked for almost a year off from my job to write this book, *The New Republic*'s owners responded with generosity and encouragement. And in conversations throughout the writing process, they enriched the final product in many ways.

Equally profound is my debt to the editors who put out the magazine in my absence: Adam Kushner, Jeremy Kahn, Kate Marsh, and especially Peter Scoblic, who took on a difficult task with extraordinary skill and grace. Over the years, I have also benefited from innumerable conversations with TNR's writers, many of whom I am privileged to call friends, in particular Jonathan Chait, Jonathan Cohn, Franklin Foer, Noam Scheiber, Jeffrey Rosen, Andrew Sullivan, Spencer Ackerman, Lawrence Kaplan, Michelle Cottle, Michael Crowley, and Ryan Lizza. Jason Zengerle read the entire manuscript, and helped its structure a great deal. So did Christopher Orr, who reminded me why he is one of the most talented editors in America today. Leon Wieseltier had characteristically brilliant comments on virtually ever chapter. Steven Groopman cheerfully put in long hours in the manuscript's latter stages. And John Judis spent so many hours correcting my historical and analytical mistakes that I sometimes felt I had dragooned him into a yearlong, one-student tutorial. I came away from it not merely awed by his knowledge, but moved by his kindness.

This book also exists thanks to the Brookings Institution, which for close to a year gave me an office and full access to its resources and staff. I am particularly grateful to William Antholis, Strobe Talbott, and above all, Pietro Nivola, for giving me the opportunity to return to Brookings after more than a decade's absence. E. J. Dionne, Tom Mann, Jonathan Rauch, Gregg Easterbrook, Katherine Moore, and Stephen Hess were delightful floor mates. Phillip Gordon, Peter Orszag, Kenneth Pollack, P. W. Singer, Omer Taspinar, Michael O'Hanlon, and Tamara Cofman Wittes patiently answered questions and read chapters. Gladys Arrisueno and Bethany Hase helped me adjust to think-tank life in ways big and small.

My agent, the remarkable Tina Bennett, shepherded me through the book-proposing and book-writing process with wisdom, toughness, and warmth. And I am grateful to her for introducing me to Tim Duggan at HarperCollins, who proved a supportive, insightful, sweet-tempered collaborator at every stage. I'm also grateful to Kate Pruss for so diligently and creatively publicizing the book.

Space does not permit me to adequately thank the many other people who helped in writing this book. But I am grateful to Fouad Ajami, Bernard Aronson, Kenneth Baer, Gary Bass, Warren Bass, Alexander Belenky, Daniel Benjamin, Peter Bergen, Paul Berman, Laura Blumenfeld, Stacey Bosshardt, Joseph Braude, David Brooks, Daniel Byman, Soner Cagaptay, Thomas Carothers, Joshua Cherniss, Andrei Cherny, Joseph Cirincione, Derek Chollet, Eric Columbus, Jared Curhan, Jacquelyn Davis, Christine Fair, Eve Fairbanks, Dan Feldman, David Frum, John Lewis Gaddis, Robert Geilfuss, Seth Gitell, Nathan Glazer, Jonah Goldberg, Robert Gordon, David Greenberg, Steven Gillon, Jacob Hacker, Amr Hamzawy, Ian Halpern, Jeffrey Herf, Hendrik Hertzberg, Bruce Hoffman, Deneen Howell, Serena Hoy, Mike Hurley, Nancy Jacobson, Robert Kagan, Erez Kalir, Juliette Kayyem, Will Marshall, Dmitri Mehlhorn, Siddhartha Mukherjee, Carrie Nixon, Davide Panagia, Robert Pape, Mark Penn, Ramesh Ponnuru, Bruce Reed, Jim Reilly, Adam Rothman, Joshua Safran, Stephen

Schulhofer, Jeff Shesol, Stephen Solarz, Amy Sullivan, Gene Sperling, Paul Starr, Jessica Stern, Ray Takeyh, Ruy Teixeira, Baruch Weiss, Sarah Wildman, Quintan Wiktorowicz, and Sacha Zimmerman. Certainly, none of those listed above is responsible for this book's flaws, and some of them would disagree fundamentally with its argument. Yet I benefited enormously from their help.

For more than a year, Alexander Dryer was a gifted researcher, intellectual partner, and simple pleasure to be around. I was lucky to have him as a colleague, am even luckier to consider him a friend, and know that his formidable journalistic talents will bring him great success in the years to come.

My parents-in-law, Arthur and Marlene Hartstein, were endless sources of support and good cheer as I was writing this book, as they have been since I first entered their family. Robert Brustein read the entire manuscript, and strengthened it with his insights and encouragement. From far away, my grandmother Adele Pienaar fortified me in our weekly talks. My sister, Jean Stern, was an inspiration, as she has been my entire life.

To thank my mother, Doreen Beinart, and my father, Julian Beinart, is beyond my capacity. It is their ideals—the ideals that brought them to this country—that suffuse this book. As I grow older, I revere and love them more and more.

Finally, this book coincided with two of the greatest blessings that life can bestow. The first was the birth of our son, Ezra, who looks up from his crib in wonder, as we look down in wonder at him. The second blessing is being married to Diana Hartstein Beinart, a true woman of valor. More than me, she bore the burden of this book. And even more than usual, I relied on her strength and guidance during the sometimes trying days during which it was written. Throughout the process, I was sustained by the knowledge that when it was over, I could return fully to her. Being able to do so is the greatest gift of all.

Index